Democracy in Aotearoa New Zealand

A Survival Guide

Democracy in Aotearoa New Zealand

A Survival Guide

Geoffrey Palmer
Gwen Palmer Steeds

TE HERENGA WAKA
UNIVERSITY PRESS
VICTORIA UNIVERSITY OF WELLINGTON

Te Herenga Waka University Press
PO Box 600, Wellington
New Zealand
teherengawakapress.co.nz

A catalogue record is available from the
National Library of New Zealand.

ISBN9781776920167

Printed in Aotearoa New Zealand by Blue Star

Contents

Part Three: Public engagement

Media

Engagement

The future

Part One

History and politics

1 You're the *demos*

Living in a democratic society means that everyone should get a say: that the governed should play a part in how they are governed. The root word of 'democracy' comes from the Greek word *demos,* which means 'the people' – that means you! What this means is that politics should be conducted in the interests of all people. Despite this, the curious world of politics can often seem daunting, uninviting, and unrepresentative to many of us.

What you hold in your hands right now is a survival guide to democracy in Aotearoa New Zealand. This book aims to unravel the mysteries of our political system and provide an account for how you, as a member of this democracy, can navigate the political world and influence decisions made by government in Aotearoa New Zealand.

Politics is the process of making decisions about how the country should be governed. These decisions impact almost every part of our lives. Politics affect what rights you have and how they are protected, who you are able to marry, what opportunities are available to you, the price of housing and secure accommodation, who can drive, how your rubbish and recycling is collected in the morning, the quality of the water that comes out of your taps, and how much freedom you are able to enjoy. Politics also determines how much tax you pay, how that money is spent, what laws are passed, how the health system works, what education is available, what rules you must follow to conduct a business, and much, much more.

Around the world, democracy is in peril. The number of democracies in the world has decreased and democracy is seen to be in retreat. A recent and rigorous 2020 report produced by the Centre of the Future of Democracy at the University of Cambridge concluded: *'We found that dissatisfaction with democracy has risen over time, and is reaching an all-time global high, in particular in developed democracies.'*

The report states there has been an especially acute crisis of democratic faith in the Anglo-Saxon democracies. Dissatisfaction has increased. Aotearoa New Zealand, however, has avoided the *'trajectory of soaring public discontent'* and the report suggests this may be because it is the only country in the group to have adopted a proportional representation electoral system in which the vote of every voter has equal value. Despite this, undemocratic tendencies that have arisen elsewhere could easily travel here unless New Zealanders take care to understand and protect their good fortune to live in a functioning democracy. Decay and rot can easily set in for any form of government.

Avoidance of decay provides a vital reason to educate people in the skills of citizenship and political literacy. When apathy reigns and people do not see politics and government as central to their lives decay comes closer. The government has great power to restrict individual liberty and the freedom of people to serve the wider public interest. How this works in any given instance is complicated. Restrictions due to the Covid-19 pandemic are a potent example. Freedom of movement was greatly curtailed in these circumstances. Since many people do not know and have not been taught how the government works, they are at risk of making bad decisions. Hazards lurk for the ignorant.

One element of our sense of community in Aotearoa New Zealand lies in the diversity of the ethnic identities of the people who live here. Māori were the first people here and are the tangata whenua of this land. Following sporadic whalers and sealers, European settlers arrived in greater numbers after 1840. By 1860, Pākehā had replaced Māori as the largest ethnic group. The first Chinese immigrants came to Aotearoa New Zealand during the 1860s gold rush and by 1869 more than 2,000 Chinese people had settled here. Demographers now tell us that *'ours is one of the world's most globally super-diverse countries.'*

According to the 2018 census, more than a quarter of the people living in Aotearoa New Zealand were born overseas. Statistics New Zealand Tatauranga Aotearoa projects that by 2038 the ethnic percentages of the Aotearoa New Zealand population will be: 65.5 per cent European or other; 18.4 per cent Māori; 10.2 per cent Pasifika; 22 per cent Asian; 1.2 per cent Middle Eastern, Latin American, African (combined). The majority of Asian immigrants here have been people from China and India. Every group has its own culture and stories. Thus, our system of government must cater for a wide range of people with different cultures, different first languages, and different religions. We must govern with a set of values that provide a sense of security and a sense of community with which all can identify and relate to. This journey requires sensitivity, innovation, and policy changes. A major contribution everyone can make is to celebrate diversity.

Aotearoa New Zealand is a democracy. That means that the people are in charge. You have a strong personal interest in learning how to navigate the political system so that you can contribute to the decisions. In any democracy a citizen has both rights and obligations. You are obliged to obey the law; but you also have the right to have your say in the making of it. You have the right to participate in government decisions, especially those affecting you. You have avenues that you can pursue if you are unhappy with the policies being followed. There are avenues for complaint when you have been treated unfairly. You can ask for change.

This book is about putting the people back in politics and government, the *demos* back in *demo*cracy, and showing you how to make your voice heard. On the journey through it, remember the proverb:

He aha te kai a te Rangatira?

He kōrero, he kōrero, he kōrero.

What is the food for the leader?

It is knowledge. It is communication.

So, let's get to it!

References

RS Foa and others *The Global Satisfaction with Democracy Report 2020* (Cambridge, Centre for the Future of Democracy, 2020) at 1; Freedom House *Nations in Transit 2020 – Dropping the Democratic Facade* (Washington DC, Freedom House, 2020); A C Grayling *The Good State: On the Principles of Democracy* (One World, London, 2020); Paul Spoonley *The New New Zealand-Facing demographic disruption* (Massey University Press, Auckland, 2020); *Te Ara Encyclopedia of New Zealand*: https://teara.govt.nz/en/population-change/page-2

2 The beginnings

I have chosen that today we will embark together on a journey. It is not enough that we begin in the present that is the reality for Pākehā and Māori in New Zealand, for in order to understand where we are and to what we aspire for ourselves in the future, we must know who we are and how we got here.
—John Rangihau. Address to High Court Judges, 3 April 1987

Illustration by Huriana Kopeke-Te Aho

Aotearoa New Zealand has a rich and diverse natural environment. Its territory lies long distant from other countries, being some of the southernmost islands in the vast Pacific Ocean. It is part of what is known as Zealandia, a continent that broke away from Gondwana separating from Australia and Antarctica 80 million years ago. More than 90 per cent of the continental fragment went undersea more than 20 million years ago and Zealandia now runs from New Caledonia in the North to the Campbell Island in the South.

This territory is home to some truly incredible wildlife. It is often celebrated as a land of birds, such as the tūī frequently found sipping nectar from harakeke flowers, the kea – infamous in Te Wai Pounamu for their cheekiness, and the gorgeous little pīwakawaka fanning their tails as they flit about te ngahere. Aotearoa New Zealand is also home to an impressive 110 species of lizards and 80 per cent of our total biodiversity is actually found in the sea. However, the arrival of human settlers also saw the introduction of mammalian predators such as rats and stoats. This change in the ecosystem affected all species of wildlife here, with many facing extinction or becoming endangered.

Human beings arrived late to Aotearoa in comparison to all other parts of the world. Māori settled here after navigating double-hulled waka with sails across the oceans from East Polynesia, to arrive in about 1200–1300 CE. It is thought Māori came from the Society Islands (including Raiatea in what is now French Polynesia), the Cook Islands, and the Austral Island group. Many waka arrived, the names of which are known, and many are linked to iwi that exist now. These massive feats of navigation, using celestial methods including winds, tides, and star maps, brought significant numbers of people to this land. By the time of the big influx of British settlers starting in 1840, the population of Māori has been estimated to have been between 70,000 to 90,000 although evidence is unreliable.

Māori had Aotearoa New Zealand to themselves for the best part of five centuries. Māori communities were organised in hapū, described by Reverend Māori Marsden as communities that acted as an *'organism rather than [an] organisation.* Rangatira were the chiefs or leaders of hapū and their authority stemmed from the consent and respect of the entire group. They were seen as the weavers of people. Values such as aroha, utu, and whakapapa underpin tikanga, the customs and laws embedded in te ao Māori, although there is diversity in practices, customs, and values between hapū. Māori customs, culture and language are vastly different from that of the British. Cultural differences led to many difficulties in intercultural communication, misunderstandings, and conflicts when the British settlers first arrived. Values such as whanaungatanga contrasted with the British focus on individualism and linear hierarchy.

In 1642, the Dutch navigator Abel Janszoon Tasman, of the Dutch East India Company, set sail from what is now Jakarta in Indonesia. He was the first recorded European to see Aotearoa New Zealand and spent about a month in these waters. The expedition included a hostile encounter with Ngāti Tūmatakōriki at Golden Bay Taitapu and four of his sailors were killed after going ashore to get water. Much later than

Tasman's expedition, Dutch mapmakers marked the land Tasman had seen as 'Nieuw Zeeland' after a pre-existing Dutch Province, 'Zeeland'. This later turned into New Zealand, the English name for this country.

More than a century later, in 1769, Captain James Cook made the first of his three exploratory voyages to Aotearoa New Zealand, as well as to a number of other places. The two main purposes of this first trip were to observe the transit of Venus in Tahiti and to try to discover a southern continent thought to exist. The expedition carried out research, including mapping land and making detailed charts of coastlines, examining land resources, gathering, recording, classifying botanical samples, and collecting art and artefacts. Accounts of the life and customs of Māori were recorded, from the perspectives of Cook and his crew.

On a couple of occasions, Cook raised the British flag and claimed possession of the land, or parts of it, for George III, the British monarch. However, Cook had no consent from Māori to do so and no official step was taken to make Aotearoa New Zealand a British colony until many years later. Cook and his crew had many interactions with Māori during his expedition and despite instructions to avoid bloodshed, up to nine Māori men were shot within two days of Cook arriving onshore. Captain James Cook's three visits to Aotearoa New Zealand put it on the European map in more ways than one and thereafter greater contact between Māori and the rest of the world was inevitable. Those seeking to harvest whales and seals were amongst the early arrivals from Europe and the United States. Substantial connections developed over time between our shores and the colonial government of New South Wales, centred on Port Jackson/Sydney.

References

George Gibbs *Ghosts of Gondwana* (Fully revised ed., Potton & Burton, Nelson, 2016); Atholl Anderson, Judith Binney, and Aroha Harris *Tangata Whenua – An Illustrated History* (Bridget Williams Books, Wellington, 2014); J C Beaglehole *The Life of Captain James Cook* (A & C Black, London, 1974); Anne Salmond *Trial of the Cannibal Dog: Captain Cook in the South Seas* (Penguin, UK and NZ, 2004); *Tears of Rangi – Experiments Across Worlds* (Auckland University Press, Auckland, 2017); Ani Mikaere *Colonising Myths – Māori Realities: He Rukuruku Whakaaro* (Huia (NZ) Ltd, Wellington, 2013); Waitangi Tribunal Wai 1040 *He Whakaputanga me te Tiriti, The Declaration and the Treaty* (Legislation Direct, Lower Hutt, 2014). *Te Ara – Encyclopaedia of New Zealand* contains much information on New Zealand people and their arrivals.

3   He Whakaputanga and Te Tiriti o Waitangi

The Māori world that early Pākehā encountered was organised around hapū, autonomous political, economic and kinship units typically comprising a hundred or so people. Notwithstanding their independence, hapū were capable of rapidly aligning with and acting in concert with others, based on factors such as shared identity and common interest. The task of managing inter-hapū relationships and advancing hapū interests fell on rangatira, 'weavers of people', who were alternately economic managers, diplomats, military leaders, mediators, peacemakers, and much more. As encounters with Pākehā increased, the duties of rangatira expanded to encompass this new diplomatic and trading sphere.

A significant share of the early nineteenth century Pākehā trade and settlement occurred in the north of Aotearoa New Zealand, around Hokianga and the Bay of Islands, and from the early nineteenth-century rangatira from those districts began to deliberately cultivate alliances, trading relationships and technological exchanges with Britain and other foreign countries. Rangatira travelled to Port Jackson/Sydney and London, building relationships with missionaries and traders, and learning about European technology and farming methods. Māori also saw military potential in this new relationship, and in 1820 the Ngā Puhi leader Hōngi Hika visited London, meeting King George IV and initiating what his people came to see as a protective alliance with Britain.

During his return voyage, Hōngi Hika stopped in Port Jackson/ Sydney and acquired a large cache of firearms, sparking the so-called 'Musket Wars', which led to many Māori casualties and significantly reshaped the North Island Te Ika-a-Māui tribal landscape. The Musket Wars were fought in periods between 1818 and into the 1840s. It is possible that more Māori died during these wars than in the later New Zealand Wars. By the early 1830s, as old causes were addressed and military equilibrium achieved between major North Island Te Ika-a-Māui tribes, Māori attention increasingly turned away from warfare and towards the economic development opportunities arising from contact with Europeans. Rangatira, particularly in the north, took advantage of new farming methods to provide cargoes of food to Port Jackson/Sydney, and spars and flax to the British Navy. In turn, they sought British assistance to support trading relationships, manage unruly settlers, and protect them from any threat of foreign invasion. Britain responded by recognising a Māori flag which could be used for trading vessels, and by sending a Resident, James Busby, to mediate between Māori and Pākehā.

In 1835, a 19-century explorer with French heritage, Charles de Thierry, wrote to Busby saying he was on his way to Aotearoa New Zealand in order to establish a sovereign government there, with himself as Sovereign Chief. De Thierry had acquired interests in a parcel of Hokianga land, but had no military support and no hope of achieving his ambitions. Nonetheless, Busby took the threat seriously and organised a meeting with many rangatira in the northern region of Aotearoa New Zealand to deliberate on what the response should be. The result of this hui was he Whakaputanga o te Rangatiratanga o Nu Tireni – the Declaration of Independence of New Zealand.

He Whakaputanga was an agreement signed originally by 34 rangatira and later acknowledged by another 18 rangatira. It was recognised by the British Crown and signed by multiple British witnesses, although it was not a legal binding treaty in the context of English law. He Whakaputanga affirmed Māori independence and sovereignty over Aotearoa New Zealand. In Busby's English draft, Article 2 stated that *'all sovereign power and authority within the territories of the United Tribes of New Zealand is hereby declared to reside entirely and exclusively in the hereditary chiefs and heads of tribes in their collective capacity.'* The term 'sovereign power and authority' was translated as 'Ko te kīngitanga ko te mana' in the Māori text which the rangatira signed. Modern translators have variously translated these terms as together meaning sovereignty, kingship, and ultimate authority.

Article 3 outlined that the rangatira agreed to meet annually at Waitangi to make laws, and Article 4 dictated that a copy of He Whakaputanga was to be sent to the King of England, thanking him and asking for his protection against foreign threats.

Busby's hope was that the confederation would operate as a European parliament, meeting annually at his residence to make laws under his guidance. However, this was not how Māori saw the declaration; rather, they viewed it as an affirmation of the existing political structures in which mana was possessed by hapū. Although the chiefs met regularly in their own hui and hākari, they retained their autonomy and did not attend any more general gatherings called by Busby.

In 1838, the Permanent Under-Secretary of the Colonial Office, James Stephen, wrote that the agreement had failed to achieve its purpose since it had not unified hapū into a single independent state. This reflected a British belief that their culture and systems of political organisation were superior to those of Māori, and is one example of the British attempting to transpose their own customs upon Māori. This was often abhorrently seen as 'civilising' the native population, by imposing the British world view and system of government on Māori.

He Whakaputanga is a part of Aotearoa New Zealand's history that is often ignored and erased, perhaps influenced by the British understanding of the agreement as a failure. However, it is an important event in the colonial history of this country and one that provides the context for the later agreement of te Tiriti o Waitangi.

Te Tiriti o Waitangi, or the Treaty of Waitangi, was signed in 1840. This was an agreement between the British Crown and Māori rangatira. It has been described by the Aotearoa New Zealand jurist Lord Cooke as *simply the most important document in New Zealand history* and is often regarded as the founding document of the nation. However, there are great controversies surrounding te Tiriti including issues of translation and significant breaches of the agreement by the Crown.

The Treaty was drafted by Crown officials including William Hobson and James Busby, translated into te reo by Henry Williams, an Anglican missionary, and signed on behalf of the Crown by Hobson. According to Hobson's instructions, Britain's decision to intervene in and seek sovereignty over Aotearoa New Zealand was motivated by its desire to protect Māori from the harmful consequences of uncontrolled settlement. It was the British policy that Britain needed Māori consent before it could proclaim sovereignty. However, Hobson's hand was forced by the New Zealand Company's attempts to establish its own government in Port Nicholson, and in May 1840 Hobson proclaimed British sovereignty over the whole country. Te Tiriti was still being circulated at this time, and Hobson had no knowledge of any signatories from south of Auckland. Nonetheless, te Tiriti was ultimately signed by 540 rangatira covering much of the country – although, importantly, some powerful rangatira chose not to sign and significant areas were not represented.

In the British understanding of the English text of the Treaty of Waitangi, Māori ceded to Her Majesty the Queen of England all the rights of sovereignty which they possessed. In return, Her Majesty granted rangatira '... *the full exclusive and undisturbed possession of their Lands and Estates Forests Fisheries and other properties which they may collectively or individually possess*....'. They could dispose or sell their land to the Crown only. The Treaty also gave Māori the rights and privileges of all British subjects.

However, it is now generally accepted that the Māori text of te Tiriti did not adequately convey what Britain meant by 'sovereignty'. Instead, that text guaranteed Māori the *'tino rangatiratanga'* over their lands, homes and other taonga. Hobson reinforced the perception that Māori would retain their authority, giving a verbal assurance that they would retain their *'perfect independence'*. This statement reflected his instructions to assert British authority over settlers while for the most part leaving Māori communities alone on the assumption that missionary influence would eventually lead them to voluntarily assimilate.

In 2014, the Waitangi Tribunal found that there had been no legitimate cession of sovereignty and that instead *'Rangatira agreed to share power and authority with Britain. They agreed to the Governor having authority to control British subjects in New Zealand, and thereby keep the peace and Māori interests.'* Nonetheless, under English law and in the eyes of British officials, Hobson's proclamations meant that Aotearoa New Zealand became a British colony, part of a massive imperial system safeguarded by the British navy. The British Empire, at this stage, covered about a quarter of the world's population and about the same proportion of the earth's surface.

References

Claudia Orange *An Illustrated History of the Treaty of Waitangi* (Bridget Williams Books, Wellington, 2021); Ron Crosby *the Musket Wars – why the Musket Wars matter today* (Oratia, Auckland, 2020); Mark Hickford *Lords of the Land – indigenous property rights and the jurisprudence of Empire* (Oxford University Press, Oxford, 2011); Michael Belgrave, Mereta Kawharu, David Williams (eds) *Waitangi Revisited* (Oxford University Press, Melbourne, 2003); Matthew S R Palmer *The Treaty of Waitangi in New Zealand's Law and Constitution* (Victoria University Press, Wellington, 2008); F M Brookfield *Waitangi & Indigenous Rights: Revolution. Law and Legitimation* (Auckland University Press, Auckland, 1999); Waitangi Tribunal Wai 1040 *He Whakaputanga me te Tiriti, The Declaration and the Treaty* (Legislation Direct, Lower Hutt, 2014).

4 The British Empire arrives

Prior to the Treaty of Waitangi, British involvement in Aotearoa New Zealand was limited. Missionaries had been in the country since 1814, attempting to convert Māori to the Christian religion while also promoting European farming methods. Whalers and traders from Britain and elsewhere arrived in increasing numbers during the 1820s and 1830s. Britain recognised Māori possession of the country and was generally reluctant to involve itself in the country except in a protective capacity.

In 1823 the Parliament at Westminster in Britain passed a law giving the Crown authorities in New South Wales the power to prosecute offences committed by British subjects in Aotearoa New Zealand. There were, however, many practical difficulties in bringing prosecutions under the law, not least the fact that Britain had no authority over New Zealand. Māori had sufficient military force to respond to settler breaches of tikanga, but often chose lenience in order to sustain trading relationships. Britain increased its official presence by appointing James Busby as official British Resident in 1833, but he lacked both legal authority or practical power.

After te Tiriti o Waitangi was signed in 1840, the Crown first treated Aotearoa New Zealand as an appendage to the British colony in New South Wales in Australia, but it was made a separate colony on 16 November 1840. Proclamations of sovereignty were sent to Britain, approved by the British Government and published in the *London Gazette* on 2 October 1840, an action treated by British officials to be the final step in the cession of Aotearoa New Zealand by Great Britain.

As British authorities were well aware, this created a legal position that was well out of step with on-the-ground reality. Notionally, in the eyes of British officials, Britain possessed sovereignty and therefore an absolute right to govern over Aotearoa New Zealand as it wished. Māori vastly outnumbered Europeans in 1840, and the Crown initially had little hoped of extending practical authority over Māori communities. Containing settlers demands for land, resources and political authority was therefore a significant issue for early governors.

In 1847 the New Zealand Supreme Court discussed the Treaty of Waitangi and affirmed the common law legal doctrine of aboriginal title, guaranteeing Māori the continued use of their lands, fisheries, and traditions under British law. This also affirmed the Crown exclusive power to grant private title to land purchased from Māori, thereby excluding settlers from direct land dealings with Māori. Settler demand for access to Māori land was already a matter of considerable concern to Māori leaders.

Once Britain had secured sovereignty under its own law it set up a Parliament and a governmental system. There were three early constitutions drafted and implemented, or partly implemented. The first constitution, called a Charter, was written in 1840. It provided an Executive Council to run what government there was, a Legislative Council with seven members that was to write the laws, and three nominated Justices of the Peace to deal with minor legal issues. The Legislative Council met only on 10 occasions but passed 129 ordinances (laws). One of the most important new laws was the establishment of the Supreme Court which provided for a judicial system that promoted and applied the rule of law. In practice, the Governor was in full control of all matters, subject to what his London masters decided – something which many settlers criticised as they did not like this system of autocracy. Laws began to be made and administered in Aotearoa New Zealand in 1841. The approach was that the laws of England were to be applied to Pākehā settlers, according to a later statute, *so far as they were applicable to the circumstances of the colony.*

In 1846, Governor Grey was instructed to implement a new constitution with three tiers of governance, each with their own roles and jurisdictions. **Tier One** were communities organised around towns or small districts created as municipal corporations like English boroughs. The closest modern-day equivalent in the current governance arrangements of Aotearoa New Zealand would be district councils. **Tier Two** featured two provinces – New Ulster in the North and New Munster in the South – each with their own assembly nominated by each mayor, councillors from the municipalities, and appointed Legislative Councils. **Tier Three**, the proposed General Assembly of New Zealand, was to comprise of an overarching Legislative Council and a House of Representatives, elected by the provincial assemblies from among their own members. Steps were taken to set up the New Munster Provincial Council but it did not perform well, met only once, and was criticised by settlers. Grey also feared that settler self-government would provoke opposition from the Māori majority, unless significant safeguards were put in place to protect their rights and interests. Implementation of the constitution was suspended for five years.

A second attempt at a representative constitution for settlers was the New Zealand Constitution Act 1852, passed by the Parliament in Westminster. There had been considerable ongoing agitation from settlers advocating for self-government; constitutional associations were established and public meetings were held in various settlements. Governor Grey came under pressure and proposed a new constitution which was based on the 1846 constitution and tailored towards the scattered character of the Pākehā settlements of the time. This constitution created six provinces – Auckland, New Plymouth, Wellington, Nelson, Canterbury, and Otago – each presided over by an elected superintendent. An elected Legislative Council could make laws, although the New Zealand Governor could disallow these if he so chose. The nationwide body, the General Assembly, comprised a national Legislative Council of appointed men with life tenure and a House of Representatives that was elected every five years. In many cases, the Provincial Assemblies had joint powers with the General Assembly.

The colonial Parliament first assembled in Auckland Tāmaki Makaurau in 1853 which acted, at that point, as a capital city for the nation. The capital was later changed to Wellington Te Whanganui-a-Tara in 1865, a decision recommended by a panel of Australian politicians set up to inquire into the issue, as it was thought our own MPs could not provide an unbiased view. Over time, many elements of the 1852 Constitution Act that provided for both representative and responsible government were whittled away and became increasingly irrelevant. The provinces were abolished in 1876, greatly adding to the power of the Parliament, in what was then a unitary state.

Significantly, under that constitution, all dealings with Māori hāpu or tribes and land dealings had remained with the British Government and the Governor. Nonetheless, settler politicians exercised increasing influence over Māori affairs from the late 1850s, when the settler population began to rival that of Māori. Those matters did not pass on fully to Ministers in Aotearoa New Zealand until around 1870, after the New Zealand Wars. There were significant debates in the governing circles in London on how to strike a balance between the interests of Māori and the settlers. Similar debates often occur today – how do we represent Māori interests in our democracy, a system that is largely European, not Māori, in origin? As time went on, managing the inevitable intercultural tensions became more difficult and as the number of Pākehā settlers grew Māori power gradually ebbed away. The 1852 Constitution Act provided the power to proclaim 'native districts' where Māori could continue to govern themselves, but this power was never officially exercised despite the reality that – even well after 1870 – many Māori tended to live in areas remote from and outside the influence of the governmental authorities of British settlements.

References

Philip Temple *A Sort of Conscience – The Wakefields* (Auckland University Press, 2002); J G A Pocock *The Discovery of Islands – Essays in British History* (Cambridge University Press, Cambridge, 2005); James Belich *Making Peoples – A History of the New Zealanders to the end of the Nineteenth Century* (Allen Lane, the Penguin Press, Auckland, 1996); Michael King *The Penguin History of New Zealand Illustrated* (Penguin Books, North Shore, 2007); Gavin McLean *The Governors – New Zealand's Governors and Governors-General* (Otago University Press, Dunedin, 2006); A H McLintock *Crown Colony Government in New Zealand* (R E Owen government Printer, Wellington, 1958); Philip A Joseph *Joseph on Constitutional and Administrative Law* (5th ed., Thomson Reuters, Wellington, 2021), chapters 3–6; Michael Belgrave *Dancing with the King – the rise and fall of the King Country, 1864–1885* 9 (Auckland University Press, Auckland, 2017).

5 Colonisation and the New Zealand Wars

Let's remember, understand, embrace and own our history, because it is a big part of who we are as a nation.
—Vincent O'Malley,
The New Zealand Wars Ngā Pakanga o Aotearoa, 2019

Following the signing of te Tiriti o Waitangi, the government's attempts to assert its sovereignty and adjust the interests of Māori and settlers caused friction and conflict. Māori felt their mana slipping away as the settler population grew, land was lost, and the reach of colonial laws and institutions extended into their territories. British settlers brought additional resources and technology to Aotearoa New Zealand. However, the violence and destruction of colonisation, not only physical but also emotional and spiritual, should not be underestimated. Colonisation has left enduring harm among Māori that persists to this day.

The assertion of Crown authority over Māori occurred gradually, and took many forms. At times, the government negotiated with Māori to secure consent to public works or the establishment of institutions such as courts and magistrates, often promising economic benefits and some recognition of Māori autonomy in return. But the government also variously asserted its authority through warfare, land confiscation, economic neglect, the establishment of laws that undermined Māori communal authority, aggressive land purchasing activities that exploited Māori economic need, and rejection of Māori political and resource rights that had been guaranteed by te Tiriti o Waitangi.

In turn, as Māori saw their mana being threatened, they sought new forms of political organisation aimed at protecting their autonomy from the growing tide of Pākehā encroachment. Most notably, in the late 1850s the Kīngitanga or Māori King movement was established in the Waikato. A rangatira from the Waikato region – Pōtatau Te Wherowhero – became the king. Notably, this coincided with the Pākehā population outnumbering Māori for the first time, and with the increasing influence of the settler parliament over Māori affairs including land.

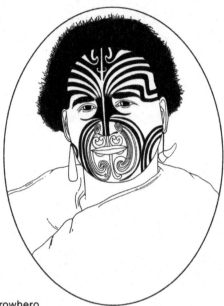

Pōtatau Te Wherowhero
Illustration by Huriana Kopeke-Te Aho

The growth of government and settler authority contributed to the outbreak of various armed conflicts between Māori and the Crown, which are collectively known as The New Zealand Wars. During the 1840s, violent conflict had erupted in the Wairau Valley, when Nelson settlers attempted to arrest Māori leaders and assert rights over an area of contested land.

Shots were fired, conflict broke out, and 22 of the settler party were killed along with four Māori. The government on that occasion sided with Māori, provoking outrage among settlers.

The first serious government-Māori conflict broke out in 1845, after the Ngāpuhi leader Hōne Heke made a series of symbolic attacks on a British flagstaff at Kororāreka in Northland. Heke, believed to be the first rangatira to sign te Tiriti, objected to the flagstaff flying a British flag, seeing it as a symbol of British sovereignty that Māori had not agreed to. This symbolic protest soon became more serious as the Governor sent troops and threatened military action against Heke and his people. In March 1845, Heke and his Ngāti Hine ally Te Ruki Kawiti cut down the flagstaff for the fourth time, attacking British troops who

Hōne Heke
Illustration by Huriana Kopeke-Te Aho

were protecting it. The Royal Navy then shelled the town, and Māori retaliated by sacking and burning the town. Several battles followed, which ended inconclusively. The Crown never put up that particular flag again. Around this time there were also several clashes in the Cook Strait area in Wellington Whanganui a Tara and Whanganui. Following the Battle of Boulcott's Farm, the Ngāti Toa leader Te Rauparaha was captured by Governor Grey and taken to Auckland Tāmaki Makaurau. Another attack was made on Te Rangihaeata at Pāuatahanui.

During the 1860s, several other conflicts occurred:

1860–61

The Taranaki Wars began over a dispute surrounding the purchase of 600 acres of land at Waitara the New Zealand Company thought it had made. The Pākehā Governor backed the validity of the purchase but Māori contested this and 400 troops marched on Waitara. Other clashes followed: British troop numbers were increased and Māori from Waikato and Ngāti Maniapoto travelled to Taranaki to fight in aid of the local hāpu. The British suffered a crushing defeat in Puketākauere in June 1860. There were several other conflicts and ambushes before matters sputtered to an end in 1864.

1863–64

The greatest conflict of the New Zealand Wars was the Waikato War. The Pākehā Governor delivered an ultimatum to the Māori King, demanding submission to British sovereignty and warning that Māori who defied the law would find the rights granted to them by te Tiriti forfeited. There were at least 10 significant military engagements and in some the British were seriously defeated. Although Māori lost some of these battles as well, they never surrendered and withdrew into Te Rohe Pōtae, the 'King Country', where they remained undisturbed until 1885. This was a pivotal war: it confirmed that the British demanded recognition of the Crown's authority and, despite the promises in te Tiriti o Waitangi, it would not accept sharing power or governance over Aotearoa New Zealand with Māori. The British expended great resources on the Waikato War, including fortified steamer gunships on the Waikato river and massive quantities of men and equipment.

1864

The War at Tauranga was also significant. There were two significant engagements before the events at Gate Pā on 29 April 1864. On one occasion, a heavy artillery barrage, including use of a 110 pounder Armstrong gun, made the British believe that they had pacified the pā, only to find when they entered it that they had fallen into a trap and their troops were cut to pieces by concealed warriors.

1864–66

The West Coast campaign occurred after the Pai Mārire, sometimes called the Hauhau, was founded by a Taranaki prophet, Te Ua Haumēne, who promised deliverance from oppressive Pākehā authority. Pai Mārire, which had emerged from the Taranaki War, was a new faith combining elements of Christianity and traditional Māori beliefs. Although Te Ua Haumēne preached peace, his supporters engaged in a number of violent acts on settlers and a number of conflicts under a series of British generals took place around New Plymouth Ngā Motu, Whanganui, and up the Whanganui River.

1865–66

The East Coast Wars began with the killing of a German missionary who was accused of passing information to the government about Pai Mārire. Those responsible fled to Ngāti Porou territories on the east coast, pursued by government troops. Ngāti Porou, defending their territories, fought several battles against Pai Mārire, assisted by government troops. The government then pursued some of the Pai Mārire leaders into Te Urewera, laying waste to several settlements and confiscating much of the district's productive land, despite a lack of evidence that the Tūhoe people of Te Urewera had any involvement in the killing or subsequent conflicts. Kereopa, a Pai Mārire leader caught and executed for the missionary's death, has since been pardoned.

1868–69

Tītokowaru's War was named after a man who is regarded to be one of the best generals Aotearoa New Zealand has ever produced. Following his attack on a garrison near Hāwera where 10 of the men were killed, 350 troops were sent to retaliate but were roundly defeated and humiliated. This situation was seen by the Pākehā government as threatening British power in the area. Tītokowaru's military reputation protected central Taranaki as an independent Māori state in effect for most of the 1870s. Only the invasion of Parihaka in 1881 ended his resistance.

1881

The Parihaka settlement was established in 1867 in Taranaki, as a base of passive resistance and peaceful protest. John Bryce, the Minister for Native Affairs, led 1,600 men into Parihaka arresting the leaders of Parihaka, Te Whiti o Rongomai, Tohu Kākahi, and Tītokowaru. Although there was no resistance, the Pākehā troops destroyed the village and there were multiple rapes. The people arrested were detained without trial and imprisoned in the South Island Te Waipounamu. In 2017, the Crown fronted up with a full apology, as is usual in such settlements, for these outrageous acts, and paid some compensation. Parihakatanga is still known as a philosophy of passive resistance and peace.

1865–69

The Ngāti Maru leader Te Kooti Kooti Arikirangi Te Tūruki was imprisoned without trial and sent to the Chatham Islands with about 300 others. After a spiritual awakening, he engineered an escape by capturing a supply ship; he and 298 prisoners arrived near Young Nick's Head on the East Coast. Troops attempted to capture them and Te Kooti responded with a number of attacks until a price was put on his head by the Pākehā government and his pā in Ngātapa was attacked in 1869 by 700 men, including members of Ngāti Porou. He fled and many of those left behind were executed without trial. Te Kooti managed to evade capture until he was pardoned many years later. He spent the final part of his life in the Bay of Plenty promoting the Ringatū faith he founded.

Māori were excellent warriors and skilled military tacticians. They won a significant number of military engagements – impressive considering that, at one point during the Waikato War, the Crown had more than 18,000 imperial and local troops under arms. The Crown had great difficulty in prevailing and essentially gave up. Imperial forces were withdrawn between 1867–1869. Throughout the wars, Britain was generally out-strategised although they had an advantage in more soldiers and bigger guns. Māori were never finally 'conquered' in the conventional sense of the term, but their capacity to further resist government authority and settler encroachment was seriously diminished.

Massive land confiscations against Māori, known as raupatu, were made by legislation enacted during and after the New Zealand Wars. The New Zealand Settlements Act 1863 gave power in Pākehā law for the Governor to declare districts within which a tribe or many members of a tribe were engaged in rebellion to define the areas. The preamble to this Act stated that Māori had engaged in open rebellion against Her Majesty's authority, and made it lawful for the Governor in Council to set aside the confiscated lands for settlement by the British. Confiscations took place in Waikato, the Bay of Plenty Te Moana-a-Toi, Taranaki, South Auckland Tāmaki Makaurau, Hauraki, Te Urewera, Hawkes Bay Te Matau-a-Māui, and the East Coast. One analysis states that 3,490,737 acres of Māori land were confiscated by the Crown, the two largest areas being in Taranaki and Waikato. The effects were traumatic for Māori. Some of the land was returned soon afterwards, but most was not.

By 1869 the British Government had had enough and the settler government in Aotearoa New Zealand thereafter took sole responsibility for colonisation of the country. With neither Māori nor Pākehā enthusiastic for more warfare, the government pursued a new strategy aimed at gradually breaking down Māori resistance and bringing them under the influence of the government's laws and institutions. The establishment of the Native Land Court in the 1860s was particularly influential: it broke down communal Māori authority over land, and supported a vast programme of government land purchasing, which in turn funded public works and assisted immigration that further swelled the Pākehā population.

There were many places within Te Ika-a-Māui where the Crown's authority did not extend until late in the 19th century or early in the 20th; Māori in these remote or isolated areas lived relatively undisturbed by the colony's governance arrangements.

As government authority was gradually extended into districts such as Te Rohe Pōtae (the King Country) and the Urewera district, Māori sought new means of asserting their autonomy. They variously appealed to the Queen for protection of their rights, and sought parliamentary recognition for various self-governing institutions at local or national level. During the 1890s, the Kōtahitanga movement established a Māori parliament with support from Māori in many parts of the country, and the Kīngitanga established Te Kauhanganui, its Great Council, which continues to operate today. The Kīngitanga movement remains a force in Aotearoa New Zealand with the King enjoying significant mana and leadership in issues of Māori interest.

The wars and associated extension of Crown authority condemned many Māori in Te-Ika-a-Māui to live a life of poverty. Māori never received what they thought, on reasonable grounds, that te Tiriti o Waitangi had granted them. The injustices inflicted upon them continue to have repercussions through entrenched inequality and mistrust of government institutions.

As time has gone by, some redress for wrongs has been made – the most important of which have been in the form of negotiated Deeds of Settlement between the Crown and Māori made possible by the Treaty of Waitangi Amendment Act 1985. Under these settlements, land and other assets including capital are handed over to Māori. A deadline of 2020 for the completion of historical settlements was established;

however this was not met and a number of claims are still being dealt with. It remains the law of Aotearoa New Zealand that te Tiriti cannot be enforced in the courts unless it has been incorporated in an Act of Parliament, but the Tribunal's work remains relevant in determining the law in the courts. Nowadays there are more than a score of Acts of Parliament that do refer to te Tiriti. Some big victories have been secured by Māori in the courts as a result, but the basic rule stands: te Tiriti remains half in and half out of the legal system. The establishment of the Waitangi Tribunal in 1975, and the extension of its jurisdiction 10 years later to make recommendations on compensation for breaches of the Treaty by the Crown, was a significant step in addressing colonial harms. It has made the possibility of securing some redress for historic injustices a reality. However, there is more to be done.

References
James Belich *The New Zealand Wars – and the Victoria Interpretation of racial conflict* (Auckland University Press, Auckland, 1986); Alan Ward *A Show of Justice Racial amalgamation in nineteenth century New Zealand* (Auckland University Press, Auckland, 1995); Vincent O'Malley *The New Zealand Wars Ngā a Pakanga o Aotearoa* (Bridget Williams Books, Wellington, 2019); Vincent O'Malley *The Great War for New Zealand-Waikato 1800–2000* (Bridget Williams Books, Wellington, 2016); Vincent O'Malley *Voices from the New Zealand Wars He Reo Nō Ngā Pakanga o Aotearoa* (Bridget Williams Books, Wellington, 2021); Richard Boast *Buying the Land, Selling the Land: Governments and Māori Land in the North Island, 1865– 1921* (Victoria University Press, Wellington, 2008); Danny Keenan *Wars without end – Ngā whenua o mua New Zealand's land wars – a Māori perspective* (Revised edition, Penguin Random House, Auckland, 2021).

6 Community

*Imagine there's no countries / It isn't hard to do / Nothing to kill or die for /
And no religion too / Imagine all the people / Living life in peace*
—John Lennon, *Imagine*

Illustration by Ursula Palmer Steeds

The Greek philosopher Aristotle famously wrote that *'Man is by nature a
political animal destined to live in a polis'* (city-state). People live together
in political and social communities. We talk with one another. We care
about how we fit into society, how we conform or do not conform. We
are interested in the decisions and rules that affect us – some of us more
so than others. We socialise, communicate, care for, love, and sometimes
hurt each other. As social animals, humans have various different ways
of organising ourselves in communities.

All social animals organise themselves in different ways. Meerkats,
for example, live in matriarchal 'mobs' where the alpha female is often
aggressive, especially to subordinate females and their pups, in order
to preserve her own status and reduce competition for her own pups.
About 20 per cent of meerkat deaths are murders, many of them in the
claws (or teeth!) of the alpha female. Chimpanzees live in complicated
'communities' or 'troops' with a patriarchal hierarchy. Challenges to
determine the alpha male can be vicious. Brown kiwi are predominately

solitary and territorial but usually mate for life and often share overlapping territories with their mate. Chicks become independent and leave their parents' territory after just four to six weeks.

A human political community can be a village, town, city, province, or a country. It can be an iwi or a hapū. It can be an association formed for a particular purpose; for example, to look after the interests of teachers, farmers or netballers. In some ways, the state itself can be looked at as an association of associations. Political activity takes place at many levels, in many ways. It concerns a multitude of issues. Concern about the conduct of public affairs generates discussion and deliberation. A majority may have one view, a minority another. The disagreements may become divisive. The adjustment of these differences in order to arrive at a decision is the challenge of democratic government.

Politics is about the achievement of collective public goals: how we, as social and political animals, can survive and thrive collectively. There are many contested views about what the most important goals are, how they should be addressed, and in what order. Priorities have to be established and decisions made. This is politics. No government can do everything at once. The machinery for making and implementing these decisions comes from the organisation of public power within the State.

But what exactly is a State?

References
Henry Milner *Civic Literacy – How informed citizens make democracy work* (Tufts University, Hanover, 2002); David Belgrave and Giles Dodson *Tūtira Mai-Making change in New Zealand* (Massey University Press, Auckland, 2021); Ernest Barker (translation) *The Politics of Aristotle* (Clarendon Press, Oxford, 1957) at 6.

Additional resources
To read stories of communities in action across Aotearoa New Zealand, see: https://inspiringcommunities.org.nz/stories/
To give back to your community, see if there are volunteer opportunities nearby here: https://www.volunteeringnz.org.nz/

7 The State

It is not simple to define what a 'sovereign state' might be. Essentially, the State is a political organisation that forms the foundation for government. There are three clearly identifiable features of a state. A state must have a **territory**, **people**, and a **government**. Beyond that, the definition becomes soggy. There is no requirement for a state to have any minimum geographic area or population, or any particular form of government. There is no stipulation as to what resources are required, hence, in the international system, massive states and tiny ones exist together in sovereign equality – at least in theory if not in reality.

Max Weber, a German sociologist and political theorist, defined the State as *'a human community that (successfully) lay claim to the monopoly of legitimate physical violence within a certain territory, this 'territory' being another of the defining characteristics of the state.*

In order for a state to organise and manage the people living within its territory, the State needs to have laws and the ability to enforce them. A state's territorial limit restricts the sphere in which its power can operate. In many cases, the State itself defines its own territory. Laws are, ideally, made to reflect the values and customs of society and create stability by holding people accountable to these values, allowing a population to live together in a territory in a way that is beneficial and effective for all. The State has a monopoly on the use of force in order to enforce the law. In many states, a common consequence of breaking the law is imprisonment, which can be enforced legitimately through physical force by arrest and detention.

A state has sovereign power. Sovereignty is a tricky word and means different things in different contexts – better not to use the term if you can avoid it; it's better to specify precisely what you mean. In this context, sovereignty means supreme power, and so, for example, the State of Aotearoa New Zealand has full, supreme authority over this territory and the people that live here. It is the most dominant influence and other states do not have power over our territory and people, nor can we interfere with what goes on in the territories of other states.

Sometimes states operate on a federal system. For this form of government there are state governments and federal governments with different powers. Examples are Australia or the United States. The states in a federation do not have 'sovereignty' in the sense of the word defined above. In such cases powers are divided between the state and federal governments.

In contrast to a state, the idea of a nation can be defined quite differently. A nation can be described as a social collective, a community that has a shared belief in a right to self-determination which requires territorial control. There can be more than one nation governed by a single state. Benedict Anderson famously described a nation as an 'imagined community', elaborating that: *it is imagined because the members of even the smallest nation will never know most of their fellow members, meet them or even hear of them, yet in the minds of each lives the image of their communion.*' For instance, even though it would be impossible to know each individual New Zealander there is some sense of community – a sense of solidarity surrounding rugby, pineapple lumps, and marmite between all of us kiwis.

But what gives the State its power? Why is it that most people tend to follow the law and do what the government says? Why should this abstract concept of a state have so much authority and play such a role in our lives?

Many political philosophers have made the argument that there is a social contract between the governors and the governed. Quite simply, this is the idea that the State has power because we all agree to give it power. The idea stipulates that there is a contractual relationship between the State and its citizens in which the State has to administer certain services, such as providing protection and guaranteeing liberties, and in return the citizens agree to submit to the State's power by following the law. The idea here is that people consent to the State's power, reasoning that living within the organised state is beneficial to us, our welfare, and livelihood. This is a political idea; it is not a legally enforceable contract.

However, the idea of a social contract paints the relationship between the governed and the governors as voluntary, when in reality this is not the case. In most states, there is no option to live outside the existing political organisation. Even if you explicitly dissent from the State you are still expected to follow the law and will be punished if you do not. The people's consent revolves around two big political issues: the type of government adopted by a state and the policy objectives to which that government is directed. Do the people who live in Aotearoa New Zealand consent to the existing governance arrangements? We have never been asked. Are we content to live in a democracy? Probably. However, recent global trends do indicate that dissatisfaction with democracy is increasing dramatically worldwide. Do we actually consent to the power of the State? Is true consent even possible in such a relationship?

An enormous study of why nations fail or succeed was published in 2014 by Professor Frances Fukuyama. It found that a successful state requires three elements. These are: **competence; a strong rule of law**; and **democratic accountability**.

First, for a state to be competent its administration must be efficient, and the authority of the State must be respected within its territory. There cannot be areas that act independently and undermine or make war on the State. Government officials cannot be bribed. Second, a successful state must have a strong rule of law, which means that the laws must be applied uniformly to the whole of society, including to the lawmakers and enforcers themselves. Third, a state must be accountable to the people it governs. This means that the State has to be responsive to the interests of the whole society, not just parts of it. There need to be strong institutions that hold decision-makers to account for their actions and power must be used in a way that most people find acceptable. There are many states in the world with significant levels of corruption and cronyism. Fortunately, so far, Aotearoa New Zealand is not one of them.

It is not contested that Aotearoa New Zealand is an independent sovereign state. One of the ways we know this is because it is recognised by other states as being one. We accredit our diplomats to other states, join international organisations that are only open to states, and enjoy other functions that are accorded by international law to sovereign states. Aotearoa New Zealand is a member of the United Nations, which only states can join. We were one of the 50 founding nations that established the United Nations in 1945 at the conclusion of the Second World War; there are now 193 members.

States have relationships with one another. International relations and agreements between states govern such issues as overseas trade in goods and services, freedom to travel, immigration and security alliances, international civil aviation, and the posting of items from one country to another. Aotearoa New Zealand is bound by more than 1,900 treaties or international conventions, with more sitting in the wings waiting to come into force.

Aotearoa New Zealand also has a clearly defined territory. This includes legal authority over three main islands – the North Island Te Ika-a-Māui, the South Island Te Waipounamu, and Stewart Island Rakiura – but also many offshore islands. Not only does it include the land, but the State also has authority to regulate some activities, particularly fishing, out to sea to the limit of 200 miles: in some circumstances beyond. Aotearoa New Zealand has also claimed sovereignty over the Ross Sea Dependency in Antarctica, but this claim is not necessarily recognised by other nations. The territorial claims that all nations have over Antarctica are currently, in effect, suspended – or put on ice – because of the 1959 Antarctica Treaty.

Only the State of Aotearoa New Zealand has the power to make laws that apply to this territory. It has the power to control the currency and regulate the economy, to determine who can visit or live here, and to decide what is unlawful. Laws can be enforced by the New Zealand Police Ngā Pirihimana o Aotearoa. The New Zealand Government controls the New Zealand Defence Force Te Ope Kātua o Aotearoa that can, in defined circumstances, come to the assistance of the Police to enforce the law. The State's power is wide and sweeping. In normal times, Aotearoa New Zealand enjoys a system of democratic government with human rights and freedoms protected by a system that respects the rule of law. Your rights cannot easily be taken away.

References

The World's Classics *Social Contract – Essays by Locke, Hume and Rousseau* (Oxford University Press, London, 1946); James Crawford *Brownlie's Principles of Public International Law* (9th edition, Oxford University Press, Oxford, 2019); Alberto Costi (ed) *Public International Law: A New Zealand Perspective* (LexisNexis, Wellington, 2020), Chapter 3; Francis Fukuyama *Political Order and Political Decay – From the Industrial Revolution to the Globalization of Democracy* (Farrer, Straus and Giroux, New York, 2014).

8 Types of government

For centuries, political philosophers have argued about the best method for organising power within a state. We've noted that humans often live together in political communities so they can survive and thrive collectively. Politics involves making decisions and setting priorities about the best way to organise and run this community. But how should the political system and decision-making mechanisms be structured? How should power and responsibility be organised? We've established that the State exists, but how should it be run?

Deliberation and disagreements in the discussion of how society ought to be structured started early. In ancient Greece, the birthplace of Western democracy (or *demokratia*), philosophy was ablaze. Two famous philosophers, Plato and his student Aristotle, developed dramatically different views. Plato believed that the ideal political community would be governed by a meritocratic system, where leaders are selected based on merit. For Plato, merit was defined as possessing and being driven by wisdom, or a 'love of learning and philosophy' and hence his ideal political community would be governed, essentially by 'philosopher kings'. These leaders would be carefully educated and brought up so that they would be wise, objective, and personally disinterested and would work together to serve the greater good of the collective. Plato believed that *'uneducated people who have no experience of true reality will never adequately govern a city'*. His basic premise that the wisest and most educated people should be those making decisions does have some advantages, especially when we consider how policy blunders and fall backs have occurred due to people being uneducated or ignorant about matters such as climate change.

Aristotle was unconvinced by the idealism of Plato's State. It is one thing to say that the State should strive to produce a just and harmonious society and another thing entirely to provide measures that would make it happen. Plato's idealism provides very few safeguards to combat the fickleness of human nature. Aristotle thought that politics should be studied as a science. It needed to be concerned with how states were ruled in reality, not just with how the ideal state would look. Theory was only one aspect – the mechanisms by which power was exercised were of predominant importance to Aristotle.

The relative benefits and advantages of the various forms of government are hard to judge because, according to Aristotle, all forms of government are capable of being abused. While the ideal state may be a useful touchstone, it must yield to the conditions of actual government on the ground. Politics is the art of the possible. Given the real political forces that exist, it is necessary to examine how things *actually* work. It is necessary to see what happens when a political community is put to the test. For Aristotle, politics is empirical, it is about what is the best option that is achievable in the circumstances.

History has witnessed versions of many distinct forms of government. Within each type, there are a number of possible variations. For example, no two dictatorships or democracies are likely to be organised in the same way. Elements of each of these forms of government can sometimes be found in another form. For example, a democracy can have a state religion, or a constitutional monarchy can have a different form of government where the monarch does not effectively rule.

Plato and Aristotle
Illustration by Ursula Palmer Steeds

So, what are some different types of government?

Meritocracy

A meritocratic system means that the leaders are not elected by the people, but instead selected based on merit. There are many possible definitions for what 'merit' would or could mean and it is not an easy concept to analyse when it comes to governance. Plato thought that the wisest people should rule, but are there other definitions of merit that could be considered? What makes a good leader?

Feudalism

Feudalism is a social and political system based on class organisation. It was a complicated method of ensuring that the lower orders or classes were constrained to follow the wishes of their lords, or the higher classes. It also functioned as a method of protecting people from invasion and disorder. This system dominated medieval Europe and there have been similar systems in Asia. There are many variations of feudalism dependent on the country and region.

In Europe, nobles typically held lands and property from the Crown in exchange for military service. For example, they might have to provide a certain number of knights and equipment to fight wars for the King. Some people were tenants of the nobles. Before a lord could grant land, known as a fief, to a person he made his 'vassal', they had to go through a process that involved oaths of fealty and loyalty. At the bottom of the feudal hierarchy were peasants, serfs and even slaves, who were obliged to live on their lord's land and give him homage, labour, and a share of the produce, in exchange for security and military protection.

Dictatorship, Autocracy, and Totalitarianism

In a dictatorship, one person holds a monopoly to make political decisions and create policy in any way they see fit. Autocracy is similar except a small group holds the power, rather than a singular individual. Both dictators and autocratic leaders are not elected and are not subject to the opinion and interests of the masses unless they become so unpopular that a coup is mounted, and the dictatorship topples. Totalitarianism is another way of describing dictatorship. This is characterised by strong central rule that attempts to control all aspects of individual life through coercion and repression.

Oligarchy, Aristocracy, and Plutocracy

Oligarchy, aristocratic government, and plutocracy are all related forms of government. An oligarchy is where power is in the hands of a few. Aristocratic governments are ruled by a small class of privileged persons identified by their heritage. These people are often referred to as the nobility, and they hold hereditary titles and offices. Monarchs can be regarded as aristocrats. A plutocracy is where a small group of wealthy people rule. A plutocracy is similar to an aristocracy as the decision-makers are a small group of elite people, but in this case, they are defined by their wealth, not birth or bloodline.

Monarchies

Monarchies are ruled by a member of a royal family who usually becomes a monarch by being born into the family. This is an inherited position, not an appointed one. The term 'absolute monarchy' refers to when the monarch has supreme power, so they have the right to make all the decisions and there are no restrictions on the monarch imposed by the law. Another type of monarchy is a constitutional monarchy, such as what we have here in Aotearoa New Zealand. Here, the Queen of New Zealand is Head of State and has great legal powers, although she does not personally exercise them. The Queen is represented here by the Governor-General who, like the Queen, must follow the advice of the Ministers who are elected Members of Parliament who have the confidence of the House of Representatives. Hence, monarchies can be either autocratic or democratic.

Theocracy

A theocracy is where a state is organised on the basis of a religion, so that the Church is responsible for political organisation and decisions following the tenets of the religion. The term literally signifies 'the rule of God'. The state religion influences the leadership and customs of the country and clergy or priests often rule or occupy leadership positions.

Indigenous Forms

Indigenous peoples in many countries around the world, including Aotearoa New Zealand had, and still have in varying degrees, their own forms of governance. Many of these systems include some aspect of tribal governance or organisation. Māori communities were organised in hāpu, described by the Waitangi Tribunal as *'not simply large whānau but political and economic groupings based on a combination of common descent and interest'*. Hāpu are led by rangatira whose authority arise from the respect and consent of the entire hāpu. These groupings held territory and resources, and rangatira were responsible for coordinating community activities and use of these resources within the territory. Cooperation between different hapū was common, with importance given to manaakitanga, although conflicts over territory did occur on occasion. Iwi were the largest political communities, although these groupings were not politically significant until after the 1850s. Iwi were normally made up of several hapū.

Democracy

Democracy is a form of government which holds that decision-makers should be accountable to the people. Many different types of democracy are possible. Direct democracy is where people can vote on laws, policies, and decisions themselves. Representative democracy is where people vote to elect decision-makers but the decisions themselves are made by those elected, not by the people directly. One possible variety of democracy could also be regarded as mob rule, or its relative, populism. The term 'totalitarian democracy' may also sometimes be encountered. This is a system in which lawfully elected representatives maintain the integrity of the State. The people have the right to vote but little or no involvement in the decision-making process of the government.

Voting for major decision-makers is the most salient sign of democracy. In some democratic electoral systems, including Aotearoa New Zealand, every person's vote is worth the same as every other person. Elections are regulated to ensure they are free and fair. In some democracies, political parties are formed, normally organised by ideology, and compete for votes in the elections. Some key features of a democratic system include freedom of speech to encourage public debate, freedom of expression, and an independent court system. There will also be the rule of law, the protection of human rights, and a constitution to delineate the powers of government.

Anarchy

Anarchy, in its purest form, is where there is no government at all. There is no rule of law, no institution or person has authority over any other, and even if there is a state, it has no means of social or political control. In the absence of government there is complete freedom for every individual. The theory is that self-government is based on voluntary institutions and that there should be no hierarchy of authority.

Stealing and looting of other people's property could easily occur in such a system. Violence could bring power to control other individuals and the system could turn into what is called a kleptocracy, where those in charge pursue personal wealth and power using stand-over tactics. Crime cannot be controlled because there are no legal consequences. There will be no civil peace, but rather conflict. However, anarchy can also mean that people have expressly decided and consented to there being no government, believing there should be no formal power hierarchies. In the 19th century, a strong movement was formed that believed that anarchy was the best way to organise human society.

References
F M Cornford (translation) *The Republic of Plato* (Clarendon Press, Oxford, 1955); Ernest Barker (translation) *The Politics of Aristotle* (Clarendon Press, Oxford, 1957).

9 Ideologies

Politics can be a polarising arena. Debates, disagreements, and disputes are constant. Many of these debates occur due to people having opposing beliefs of what they think will be best for society. These beliefs can often be organised into different ideologies. Political ideology plays a significant part in policy choices and there are numerous political ideologies that have been developed over the years. Belief in a political ideology is a bit like belief in religion: it requires a leap of faith. But what is an ideology?

Put most simply, an ideology is a system of beliefs. In the case of a political ideology, it is a system of beliefs relating to how the government should govern and serve its people to create the best life or opportunities available. What is the good life? What values are the most important? Should the State aim to provide equality for all? What about liberty? Or well-being? A political ideology will provide answers to such questions, but different ideologies may provide strikingly different answers.

How we respond to current issues and policies depends heavily upon ideology. Circumstances change over time. New problems emerge and new demands upon public policy occur. Different frameworks may be more responsive to different issues. Take climate change, for example – we could decide to ignore the current climate crisis. However, this will result ultimately in inundation of houses and property from rising sea levels, economic harm on a wide scale, as well as mass global immigration, due to changing weather patterns including fires, floods, droughts, and hurricanes. Alternatively, we could adopt policies to combat climate change. In the lead-up to the 2020 United States General Election, both Republican and Democrat voters were surveyed about what they believed the most important issues were: 68 per cent of Democrat voters saw climate change as an important issue, in contrast to a mere 11 per cent of Republican voters. Clearly political ideology has a great effect on how people respond to this issue. As well, Rebecca Solnit writes in a *New York Times* article: *'Since vaccines became widely available, counties that voted heavily for Donald Trump have had nearly three times the Covid-19 death rate as counties that voted for Joe Biden.'*

One of the most common ways of conceptualising ideology, what political parties or leaders believe, and where they sit in relation to one another, is the left-right divide. Ideas that are commonly categorised as more 'left-wing' include progress, freedom, equality, collectivism, human rights, internationalism, and reform. Political ideologies that are commonly referred to as being on the left-wing of the political spectrum include communism, socialism, democratic socialism, and more. 'Right-wing' leaning values may include duty, tradition, order, hierarchy, individualism, freedom, and market-values. Note that both sides claim 'freedom' but may define freedom differently. Ideologies seen as right-wing may include movements such as fascism, monarchism, and conservatism. However, the left-wing–right-wing scale is overly simplistic and may not actually provide proper representation of people's political views which are, after all, complicated and multifaceted.

In Aotearoa New Zealand, one of our two major parties, the National Party, tends to adopt policies that favour businesses, farmers, and free markets. In contrast, the Labour Party tends to favour the eradication of poverty, a strong social welfare system, and the protection of the working people. On some policies, however, there is agreement between these two major political parties. For example, on the issues of the importance of free trade and an international rules-based system.

So, what are some different ideologies?

Capitalism

Capitalism is an ideological system for organising the economy. The basic premise is that ownership over the means of production, distribution, and exchange is held by private individuals – not the State. The owners keep the profits. Some central characteristics of free-market capitalism include the accumulation of wealth and the existence of competitive markets for the supply of goods and services. This means that private individuals or companies sell goods and services to other private individuals or companies in return for a profit. Price varies depending on the supply and demand from society. Clashes between capital and labour, or between the owners and the working class, have been one of the common repercussions of capitalism.

What is described above is the purest form of capitalism, often not perfectly replicated in the real world. In modern times, many economies are mixed in the sense that they use a capitalist system for some activities, but not others. Even in a capitalist economy, governments will often regulate the economy in a myriad of ways. Governments will frequently intervene in markets to attain what they consider to be desirable social policies and with the implementation of a tax system. The State may own some industries themselves, especially if they are judged to be so vital to national interest that they cannot remain in private hands, such as the education or medical sectors. Such interferences would not occur under a 'pure' capitalist system. Different forms of capitalism may include laissez-faire capitalism, where there is a minimum level of State interventions, and State capitalism, where the State has the power to decide or guide investment decisions.

Communism

Communism developed as a response to capitalism. The ideas behind this economic ideology, especially in Western political theory, derived largely from the work of Karl Marx and Friedrich Engels. They developed a theory, or system of social organisation, in which all forms of property are owned by the community, instead of by private individuals or companies. Each person contributes and receives according to their ability and needs. They believed that under this system there would be no divisions between classes, and all would be equal. Communism involved violent revolution to bring it about.

Communism became a dominant political trend in the international socialist movement in the 1920s after the Russian revolution of 1917 led by Vladimir Lenin. However, many of these movements differed dramatically from the ideas of Marx and Engels. The Soviet model of Marxism-Leninism spread after the Second War to much of Eastern Europe as well as other countries, including China. In the contest with capitalism, communism lost, signalled by the end of the Soviet Union in 1991. Communist systems withered away in many countries that had adopted it. The dominant critique was that while the theory sounded attractive, the practical reality was different. Many capitalist democracies, however, took on some features of socialism, such as free medical care and a variety of other State-provided services.

Socialism

Socialism is also a system of economic organisation that responds to some of the injustices or weaknesses of capitalism. Socialism holds that most of the means of production, distribution, and exchange should be held by the collective or the State, rather than under private ownership. However, unlike in a communist system, private individuals or businesses can still own some property under a socialist economy. Socialism has many different variants. The ideology covers a wide range of different forms of government that give greater or lesser recognition to the need for the State to use its resources to aid the poor and dispossessed. One of our major political parties in Aotearoa New Zealand, the Labour Party, says in its constitution that it is a democratic socialist party. This can be quite different to a purer form of socialism. Parties of the left these days often describe themselves as advocating 'social democracy'.

Fascism

Fascism is a form of extreme right-wing government characterised by dictatorial power, forcible suppression of opposition, and strong regimentation of society and economy. Fascists believe that democracy is obsolete. Society needs to be reorganised as a totalitarian one-party state. The ideology holds that strong leadership is required, in the form of a dictator leading a martial government. It is necessary to prepare for armed conflict and to respond effectively to economic difficulties. The essential aim of fascism is to achieve national unity and a stable and orderly society. Fascists believe that the best way to organise the economy is with a mixed system that aims towards economic self-sufficiency. Fascist movements often use political techniques to arouse feelings of intense nationalism and use sophisticated and manipulative propaganda.

Liberalism

Liberalism is a political ideology that holds that freedom is of the utmost importance. Liberals tend to believe the government's main job is to strike a balance between keeping individuals safe and not threatening the individual's liberty. There are two predominant definitions of liberty in Western political philosophy. 'Positive liberty' is the presence of an individual's control or autonomy whereas 'negative liberty' is the absence of constraints restricting the individual. Political liberalism has generally centred around the definition of negative liberty. Over the years, liberalism has taken many different forms in many different countries. For example, liberalism is now closely linked with democracy, however before the 19th century, many liberalists objected to the dangers of majoritarian rule, especially in societies where people did not have access to proper education and information. Liberalism also views ideals such as reason, justice, property, and inclusivity or tolerance as important.

Libertarianism

Libertarianism is another political philosophy that holds the importance of liberty, particularly negative liberty, as a core principle. Libertarians believe that individuals should have the greatest possible amount of freedom and autonomy. The State should only have minimal powers so that it does not interfere greatly with the economy or the lives and autonomy of the people. This philosophy is related to anarchy, or anarcho-capitalism. The ACT Party could be considered a libertarian party, or classical-liberal party, and, according to its mission statement: *'exists to promote and implement better policy for all New Zealanders, particularly through reducing the role of government and increasing the role of free markets.'*

Conservatism

Conservatism favours traditional values and opposes change. Conservative political parties, of which there are many around the world, usually favour free enterprise, private ownership, and may be socially conservative. They respect authority, hierarchy, and property rights, and are not usually in favour of big government. The New Zealand National Party is a conservative party. Its constitution states that it believes in competitive enterprise, rewards for achievement, and limited government.

Progressivism

Progressivism is a political movement that favours reform. Humans have made great progress in science, technology, and in the improvements of the conditions in which people live. Change should be pursued. People in different countries identify with progressivism in different ways. These days, progressivism is normally equated with public policies that aim to lead to positive social change. These include reducing inequality, combating discrimination, improving the environment, and intervening to reduce the harsher effects of capitalism.

Environmentalism

Many political groups are rapidly emerging around the world that are concerned primarily with protecting the environment. These are seen as particularly important in modern times when responding to the current climate crisis. The New Zealand Green Party is an environmentalist party. Their Charter outlines the principle of ecological wisdom: *'The basis of ecological wisdom is that human beings are part of the natural world. This world is finite, therefore unlimited material growth is impossible. Ecological sustainability is paramount.'*

Feminism

Feminism is an ideology and a range of philosophical responses that critique the patriarchal social and political structure in society. It has become a political movement that fights for a change in how the idea of gender in our society is addressed and argues for a more equal worldview in this regard. It has tended within Western countries to have arrived in three distinct waves. Beginning in the 19th century with the votes for women movement, it moved on to ideas of effective equality and freedom. The third wave has addressed the experiences of transgender and non-binary people. It is important to realise that the patriarchy has negative effects on people of all genders – not just women. This may include the marginalisation of people who are transgender, non-binary, or gender non-conforming, as well as pressures from masculine gender roles on cisgender men, such as the expectation that men need to be strong creating a culture of toxic masculinity.

Multiculturalism

Put quite simply, multiculturalism holds that all cultures are, and should be seen, as equal. It is defined by Cohen, Matthews, & Nussbaum as *'the radical idea that people in other cultures are human beings too – moral equals, entitled to equal respect and concern, not to be discounted or treated as a subordinate caste. Thus understood, multiculturalism condemns intolerance of other ways of life, finds the human in what might seem Other, and encourages cultural diversity'.* Some political theorists have taken a liberal-individualist approach to multiculturalism – holding that membership in a cultural group is important for an individual's wellbeing and self-respect, especially for providing a context of values and opportunities that individuals can choose between to assert their autonomy.

Colonialism

Colonisation is the policy or practice of acquiring full or partial political control over another country or state, sending settlers to it, and/or exploiting it economically. For a large portion of our history, Aotearoa New Zealand was part of the British Empire, an enormous empire that ruled over many parts of the world for several centuries. This was, in a way, a method of international governance by the British. The journey from colony to independent state for Aotearoa New Zealand was a long and complicated one. Considerable injustice to Māori was inflicted in colonisation and significant harms still linger today.

Decolonisation

For Linda Tuhiwai Smith, *'decolonisation is a process which engages with imperialism and colonialism at multiple levels.'* This involves *'having a more critical understanding of the underlying assumptions, motivations and values which inform [. . .] practices.'* Many practices aiming to ameliorate the harms of colonisation in Aotearoa New Zealand have involved trying to incorporate elements of te ao Māori into the dominant Pākehā context, such as integrating tikanga principles in legislation, some Select Committee hearings being held on marae, changes to court procedures, and the ongoing process of Treaty settlements. While this is admirable work, whether this approach can effectively address the root inequalities in our institutions remains to be seen. Scholars have argued that decolonisation must dismantle these systems themselves to create equality at the root, rather than at the branches or leaves of the tree. Moana Jackson has argued that *'the ethic of restoration'* may be a better way of looking at these issues than the term decolonisation.

Te Pāti Māori The Māori Party's ideology contains many policies that would further decolonisation. Their constitution states: *'The Māori Party is born of the dreams and aspirations of tangata whenua to achieve self-determination for whānau, hapū and iwi within their own land; to speak with a strong, independent and united voice; and to live according to kaupapa handed down by our ancestors.'*

References

The full sources are too diverse and too numerous to be listed.
Linda Tuhiwai Smith *Decolonizing Methodologies: Research and Indigenous Peoples* (Zed Books, London, 2012); Rebecca Solnit *Why Republicans Keep Falling for Trump's Lies* (New York Times, Jan 5, 2022), Retrieved from: https://www.nytimes.com/2022/01/05/opinion/republicans-trump-lies.html
Alex Tyson *How important is climate change to voters in the 2020 election?* (Pew Research Center, Oct 6, 2020), Retrieved from: https://www.pewresearch.org/fact-tank/2020/10/06/how-important-is-climate-change-to-voters-in-the-2020-election/

10 Big brains

Political philosophy shapes our ways of seeing the world. Philosophers and great thinkers throughout history influence how we envision, interact, and construct our political communities. These people may have radically different ideas about what such things as power and human nature are. In Aotearoa New Zealand, as many of our political institutions and structures have developed from the British Westminster system, Western political philosophy has influenced our politics greatly. Below is a brief and simple account of what are truly complex issues and arguments, but you will get the flavour of the debates.

Niccoló Machiavelli (1469–1527)

The Renaissance diplomat Niccoló Machiavelli published *The Prince* in 1513, a book of advice to rulers about how to get political power and how to hold on to it. Some of his advice still shocks. It has given rise to the word 'Machiavellian,' which means a person who uses political methods that are cunning, scheming, unscrupulous and in bad faith. For Machiavelli, *'power is the pivot on which everything hinges. He who has the power is always right; the weaker is always wrong.'* He had a bleak view of human nature, believing that we are all *fickle, hypocritical, and greedy of gain'*. He thought that the ruler needed to assume that all people are evil and that they are always going to act in accordance with wickedness whenever they can. To secure power and hold on to it, it was necessary to be ruthless, use force, and have a good army.

Perhaps the most stunning feature of Machiavelli's advice lies in his basic indifference to the morality of the ruler's behaviour. He takes the view that the end – maintaining power – justifies the use of terrible means to accomplish it. A ruler is entitled to use cruelty and even murder if that is necessary. A ruler had to know how and when it was appropriate to behave badly. Machiavelli believed that ideally a ruler should be both loved and feared, however: *'Since love and fear can hardly exist together, if we must choose between them, it is far safer to be feared than loved.'* A ruler should not be good all the time, as this will lead to ruin, since those

Machiavellian dragon
Illustration by Huriana Kopeke-Te Aho

who he rules, the people, are not good. A ruler can and must do evil if good will come out of it. Machiavelli was dragonlike and ruthless in his approach.

The Prince speaks to political practice even today, even in a democracy. Indeed, Jonathan Powell, the former British Prime Minister's Chief of Staff, wrote a fascinating book in 2011 applying Machiavelli's doctrines to the real political life he experienced working for Tony Blair. Examples of the need to be ruthless, even cruel, to dissemble were all applied. Such issues of access to the leader, the allocation of offices, the relationship between the politicians and the public servants, the need for courage and emotional intelligence, the disasters of dithering, how to communicate, how to deal with issues of hubris, arrogance and losing touch with the real world within the political bubble are issues all run through the lens of Machiavelli.

Thomas Hobbes (1588–1679)

The English philosopher, Thomas Hobbes, believed that the power of the State, and the sovereign, was essential. Without a centralised power to keep us in check, he argued that we would live in what he referred to as the 'State of Nature' and believed that this would be *'consequent to a time of Warre, where every man is Enemy to every man'*. Hobbes is famous for saying that, in this state of nature, life would be *'nasty, brutish, and short'*. Hobbes conceptualised a pessimistic view of human nature, envisioning humans as essentially self-interested and power-hungry.

Nonetheless, Hobbes also believed that we have a natural inclination towards peace that compels us to harmonious living in a political community. Hobbes's ideas, along with John Locke and Jean-Jacques Rousseau, contributed to the social contract argument. This is the idea of a metaphorical contract between the rulers or state and citizens where those in power must provide certain services and, in return, the citizens agree to submit to the power. Hobbes explains that we must: *'conferre all their power and strength upon one Man, or upon one Assembly of men, that may reduce all their Wills, by plurality of voices, unto one Will'*. Hobbes argued that the prime obligation of the State was to provide security – security against invasion from other countries, and the security of the people in their person and their property.

John Locke (1632–1704)

Locke, a defender of the 1688 bloodless revolution in Great Britain, was determined to find an argument that explained the theory of divine rights of kings. This theory held that the kings, or monarchs, have the right to rule because of divine authority bestowed upon them by God. Locke argued that a high degree of freedom had to be surrendered to secure the benefits of living in an ordered society. He argued that the principal purpose of the State was to serve the collective and hence a government that behaved in a way that is contrary to the public good ceases to be legitimate. The people have a duty to overthrow illegitimate governments. Power is held in trust.

Locke asserted that people have the rights to life, liberty, and property. He believed these rights should not be surrendered to the State by any social contract. Instead, the system should be based on laws that are widely disseminated, applied by independent judges, and are capable of being enforced. If there is no explicit consent from the people that live under a particular system of government, then there need to be means to ensure that the system can be adjusted peacefully. This means that the political system will be able to meet the current expectations of the governed and will be able to deal effectively with new problems that arise, as they always do.

Jeremy Bentham (1748–1832)

Jeremy Bentham argued for a philosophy of utilitarianism, a theory based on the idea that actions should be evaluated by what results or consequences they produce. Pain and pleasure were two crucial elements that must be balanced. In his definition, happiness meant pleasure, and its absence meant pain. If an action brought pleasure, it was meant a positive, and an action, and its doer, should be judged by these standards. He believed that the purpose of government was to produce the greatest happiness for the greatest number of people. Following on from this idea, Bentham advocated for the maximisation of individual liberty, as he viewed any restriction of liberty as something that brought pain, and therefore was an evil.

John Stuart Mill (1806–1873)

John Stuart Mill was also a utilitarian. His philosophy focuses primarily on the importance of liberty. Mill believed that maximising liberty was of paramount importance to ensure that individuals were able to live as they saw fit, rather than having 'the good life' prescribed for them. He was adamant that liberty meant that the free expression of all opinions should be permitted. Restrictions to liberty suppresses individuality and debilitates challenges to the fallible status quo, therefore reducing chances for progress or refining the understanding of the truth. For Mill, there is great benefit in the contestation of ideas as deliberation may either prove our original viewpoint wrong or right or reveal a previously unconsidered partial truth. However, Mill also argued that one case in which one's liberty could be restricted is when it caused damage or harm to others or had a definite risk of doing so.

John Rawls (1921–2002) and Robert Nozick (1938–2002)

John Rawls and Robert Nozick both have opposing views on the idea of justice. Producing a just society in difficult circumstances is not an easy goal to accomplish. Such idea of equality of opportunity must compete with ideas of equality of outcomes: whether the State should aim to provide equal opportunities for everyone so that they start on equal footing at birth or attempt to provide equal results for all. Individual and class interests must be balanced with the collective good. John Rawls believed that justice is fairness. He believed that a just society should secure fair distribution of resources, opportunities, and rights and liberties. Robert Nozick contests the Rawlsian view. He developed a more libertarian approach and wanted a minimalist state, conceptualising a just society as one where individuals have rights that cannot be interfered with. For Nozick, justice should uphold the idea that *'from each as they choose, to each as they are chosen'.*

Amartya Sen (1933–)

Amartya Sen, the Indian philosopher, argues for a more practical means of producing justice, not confined to arguing what the ideal state looks like. In its perfect form, the ideal state was probably not attainable anyway. Instead, we need a theory that can provide guidance on comparative justice – analysis that tells us whether we are moving closer or further away from the idea of justice in a globalised world.

Sen wants to have a direct impact on policy choices. We need a practical set of reasoning about justice and injustice in the real world. This means the feeling, concerns, and mental abilities that we share as human beings must be considered. The general pursuit of justice resides in human beings, even where they may disagree on its features. He concludes: *'Because of these basic human abilities – to understand, to sympathise, to argue – people need not be inescapably doomed to isolated lives without communication or collaboration.'* Deprivation is bad enough, but it would be worse if we could not communicate and respond. We must continue to work to cure redressable injustice. For Sen, there is a connection between seeking justice and seeking democracy, that is government by discussion.

Martha C Nussbaum (1947–)

Professor Nussbaum is one of the most interesting philosophers writing today. She is a Distinguished Service Professor of Law and Ethics at the University of Chicago. With Amartya Sen she developed a framework to set out the of goals and conditions for human achievement and happiness known as the 'capabilities' approach. She is a feminist and has written in a compelling way about the links between feminism and social justice. Her 1998 book on sex and social justice was a pioneering work.

Her most recent book, published in 2021, is entitled *Citadels of Pride: Sexual Abuse, Accountability, and Reconciliation*. The book analyses the #MeToo movement building on her earlier work and finds the movement was overdue. She finds that three occupational areas in the United States have not made the necessary changes: the judiciary, the performing arts and sport.

She wrote in conclusion:

Just as women demand that their voices be heard, so must we resolve to hear one another in all our differences, and to hear the voices of men, both those who agree with us and those who do not, both those who have behaved well and those who have not, creating a dialogical culture that is also a culture of empathetic imagination. . . . Only that new freedom, and that love, can really create a just and lasting peace.

References

A C Grayling *The History of Philosophy* (Penguin Random House, London, 2019); George H Sabine *A History of Political Theory* (3rd ed.,George Harrap & Co. London, 1951); Niccolo Machivaelli, Quentin Skinner (ed), Russell Price (ed) *The Prince* (Cambridge University Press, Cambridge, 1988); Niccolo Machiavelli *The Prince and The Discourse* (The Modern Library, New York, 1950); Jonathan Powell, *The New Machiavelli: How to wield Power in the Modern World* (Vintage, London, 2011); Thomas Hobbes, Michael Oakeshott (ed) *Leviathan or the Matter, Forme and Power of a Commonwealth Ecclesiasticall and Civil* (Basil Blackwell, Oxford, 1957); John Locke, Peter Laslett (ed) *Two Treatises of Government* (Cambridge University Press, Cambridge, 1960); John Stuart Mill *Utilitarianism, Liberty and Representative Government* (Dent, London, 1964); John Rawls *A Theory of Justice* (The Belknap Press of Harvard University Press, Cambridge, 1971); Amartya Sen *The Idea of Justice* (The Belknap Press of Harvard University Press, Cambridge, 2009); Robert Nozick *Anarchy, State, and Utopia* (Basic Books, New York, 1974); Jeremy Bentham *A Fragment on Government* (Blackwell, Oxford, 1948).

Part Two

Institutions

11 Who has what power?

The essence of the system of government in Aotearoa New Zealand is simple. The complexity arises from the relationships of each institution to one another and how they work. Who exercises the public power of the State is the issue to keep your eye on. The term 'power' needs to be understood. Legal power to make the decisions is in the hands of government institutions; the Prime Minister, Cabinet and MPs are the principal actors. But power and influence are not restricted to politicians. Prominent public figures, including sports people and celebrities, can often influence public debate and decisions made in the political arena. So can pressure groups and the media. This 'soft' power needs to factored in to the reality of decisions made by the institutions. It seems to be a growing phenomenon. The media enjoys 'soft'power.

GOVERNMENT INSTITUTIONS

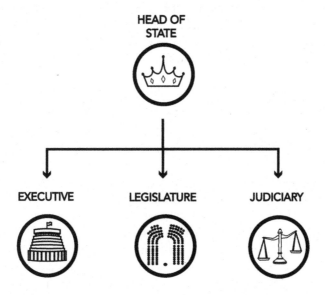

HEAD OF
STATE

EXECUTIVE   LEGISLATURE   JUDICIARY

Public power tends to be divided between various institutions that the State establishes. A frequent division used in many countries is the division between the Executive, the Legislature, and the Judiciary. There is often also a Head of State. Essentially, the Legislature makes the law, the Executive applies the law, and the Judiciary interprets and enforces the law.

The Queen and the Governor-General – The Head of State

The Queen of the United Kingdom is also the Queen of New Zealand by New Zealand law and is therefore our Head of State. She lives in the United Kingdom, but she is represented here by the Governor-General who can carry out her functions here in her absence. The Governor-General, like the Queen herself, must follow the advice of her Ministers in the exercise of her official powers.

The Governor-General functions as an important symbol of national unity and remains politically neutral. Although not a member, she presides over the Executive Council, which is a council comprising of all ministers. Her role includes being informed and consulted by ministers so she may offer advice, as necessary. Ministers of the Crown, by law, must be elected Members of Parliament.

This feature makes Aotearoa New Zealand a constitutional monarchy, nothing like the absolute monarchies of the old. This means that although we have a monarch as our Head of State, her powers are largely ceremonial and constitutional.

The House of Representatives – The Legislature

The House of Representatives refers to all of the Members that have been elected to Parliament. It provides the central democratic institution for Aotearoa New Zealand.

Its functions are to:

- provide a government. The party, or group of parties (such as in a coalition or confidence and supply agreement), that has the majority of seats in the House forms the government. The government must enjoy the confidence of the House to survive
- scrutinise proposals for new laws and agree on Bills to become law
- raise money by which the business of government is conducted and approve the rates of taxation

- scrutinise public expenditure and approve the spending of public money
- provide a forum for the redress of grievances
- provide a forum for political contest.

An especially important function of the House is to hold ministers to account for their stewardship through a variety of parliamentary mechanisms, including:
- Parliamentary questions – both written and oral
- Select Committee hearings, including the conduct of inquiries by those Committees
- the scrutiny of departmental expenditure
- motions of confidence – which may result in the defeat of the government
- raising issues for parliamentary debate on matters of public interest
- setting up by legislation watchdogs, such as the Ombudsmen, to which the public can complain.

Parliament – The Legislature

Parliament refers to the House of Representatives plus the Head of State. The Constitution Act 1986 says that the Parliament of New Zealand continues to have full power to make laws. It is the supreme law-making body.

The government – The Executive

The government comprises the ministers, the Cabinet, and the Public Service. This is sometimes referred to as the Executive. The government governs the country. This entails making a myriad of decisions every day. The House of Representatives refers to **all** the Members elected to Parliament, and Parliament refers to **both** the House and the Head of State – the government refers to the party or group of parties (such as in a coalition or confidence and supply arrangement) that hold the majority of seats in the House.

Ministers are a top source of authority in government departments. Ministers have to be members of the House of Representatives. They make policy decisions. The Cabinet is a key-decision making group made up of the Prime Minister, the Deputy Prime Minister and other senior ministers. The Public Service employs many people and is tasked with the job of carrying out the decisions made by cabinet ministers.

The Public Service is governed by a number of principles contained in law:

- *Politically neutral* – to act in a politically neutral manner
- *Free and frank advice* – when giving advice to Ministers, to do so in a free and frank manner
- *Merit-based appointments* – to make merit-based appointments (unless an exception applies)
- *Open government* – to foster a culture of open government
- *Stewardship* – to proactively promote stewardship of the Public Service, including of—
  i.   its long-term capability and its people; and
  ii. its institutional knowledge and information; and
  iii. its systems and processes; and
  iv. its assets; and
  v.   the legislation administered by agencies.
- Public Service chief executives are responsible for—
  i.   upholding the Public Service principles when carrying out their responsibilities and functions; and
  ii. ensuring that the agencies they lead, or carry out some functions within, also do so.

There are more than 50,000 public servants working in 32 departments. Beyond the Public Service itself, there are a collection of government agencies that the government is responsible for, including: State-owned enterprises, government scientific agencies, public hospitals, and the whole education system. More than 400,000 people work in the wider public sector.

The courts and the judges – The judiciary

Judges are an important part of the system of government. Their decisions are made independently from Members of Parliament, ministers, and the Public Service. The law, the courts, judges, and lawyers make up a significant industry involved in delivering justice.

The judicial processes for decision-making, appointment, and accountability are different from the other branches of government. They are not elected and it would be a disaster for the rule of law if they were. The judiciary also differs from the other branches of government because judges are obliged to give reasons for their decisions, and those decisions can be appealed. In Aotearoa New Zealand, two appeals are as of right provided for, for most judgements of the courts, and there is a third possibility of an appeal to the Supreme Court.

Judges are the Queen's Judges, expressing the point that the Queen is the fountain of justice, and all that means in historical terms. There are many more judges in Aotearoa New Zealand than there are Members of Parliament. Their numbers, however, are capped by law and Parliament must agree if the cap is to be increased. Judges are invested with great powers by the State. They preside over criminal trials that find people guilty or not guilty in prosecutions for criminal offences. Judges sentence those who are convicted. They can imprison people for lengthy periods and decide important civil disputes between citizens, or between citizens and the government, according to law. We have different types of judges with different expertise and experience for the various courts that each handle different classes of case. For example, family law is a different legal world from commercial law.

To some, court procedures seem quaint and antiquated. Many people regard the law as mysterious – it may be better to say that the law is often highly intricate. The law has a long tradition, stretching back centuries, and customs that were established long ago still survive. The courts have many rituals that have symbolic importance. People would like the law to be clear and certain in its application all of the time. Often it is. But not always. Either the facts are unclear and contested, or the law is unclear and ambiguous, or sometimes both. When these things happen, litigation in court occurs.

Institutions and people

Trusted institutions are a necessity for any political system to work effectively. The quality of those institutions will depend, to a great extent, upon the quality of the people who work within them. These institutions need to operate in a transparent manner and their functions must be properly understood by the public. Such continuing knowledge of their behaviour is essential for a healthy democracy.

Key decision-makers need to be identifiable and capable of being held to account – for the actions they take in both legal and political terms. Further, the public must have the capacity to participate in the system and be convinced that their views are heard.

The institutions outlined in this chapter have all been around a long time. Despite this, they constantly evolve and change. Our political institutions must remain fit for purpose. If they degenerate and decay the stability of the State itself will be imperilled. Its citizens will suffer. The institutions must be constantly kept up to the mark, reviewed, and tested. Political polarisation could cause rot and decay. In that event, it is likely that the institutions will lose their legitimacy in the eyes of the public.

The needs and resources for each of these institutions differ dramatically. The Executive employs many thousands of people whereas the Governor-General's office is small. The judiciary is big too: there are more judges than MPs, and large numbers of support staff. How these institutions are led, how they adjust to circumstances, and how they attract the best people to work for them determines the continuing health of the system of government.

Key professional career officials carry out critical tasks in the system. Their remits are not well understood, but they influence the system of government greatly and help it to follow proper processes and uphold high standards. It is not only the elected politicians who keep the ship of state afloat, but also the hundreds of people rowing alongside them in the background.

Such officials and offices include:

- The Public Service and the Chief Executives of departments and ministries
- The Ombudsmen
- The Parliamentary Commissioner for the Environment
- The Controller and Auditor-General
- The Clerk of the House of Representatives
- The Solicitor-General
- The Secretary of the Cabinet and the Clerk of the Executive Council
- The Judiciary
- The Privacy Commissioner
- The Public Service Commissioner
- The Reserve Bank
- The Human Rights Commission
- The Children's Commissioner
- The Independent Police Conduct Authority
- The Electoral Commission

THE SOURCE OF POLITICAL AUTHORITY

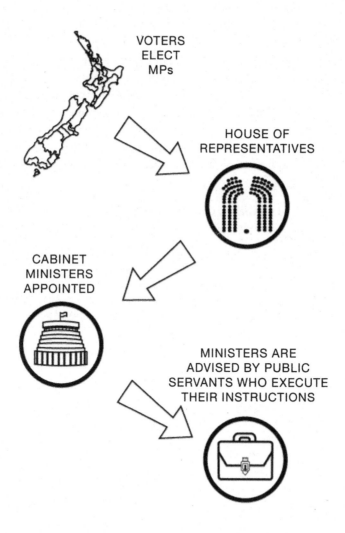

VOTERS
ELECT
MPs

HOUSE OF
REPRESENTATIVES

CABINET
MINISTERS
APPOINTED

MINISTERS ARE
ADVISED BY PUBLIC
SERVANTS WHO EXECUTE
THEIR INSTRUCTIONS

- The Representation Commission
- Inspector-General of Intelligence and Security.

The people – you!

The most essential element of a democracy is that power flows from the people. While much of the legal authority within the system flows from the monarchy, it is exercised in fact as a result of the political authority that flows from the voters in the electorate.

Within the Aotearoa New Zealand system of government, there are many highways and byways filled with multiple complexities. The vibe of politics drives the system. This is driven by events and the reaction of the public to those events. It is never easy to anticipate where that is going. Civics requires an understanding of the essential characteristics of the system as a whole. Citizens can then appreciate how the system can serve them and how they can contribute positively to it.

References

Janine Hayward, Lara Greaves, Claire Timperley (eds) *Government and Politics in Aotearoa New Zealand* (Oxford University Press, New York, 2021); Geoffrey Palmer and Matthew Palmer *Bridled Power* (4th ed, Oxford University Press, Melbourne, 2004); Les Cleveland *The Politics of Utopia New Zealand and its Government* (Methuen Publications, Wellington, 1979); Matthew S R Palmer and Dean R Knight *The Consitution of New Zealand – a Contextual Analysis* (Cambridge University Press, Cambridge, 2022); Raymond Miller *Democracy in New Zealand* (Auckland University Press, Auckland, 2015); Joanna George, 'The rise of the celebrity as politician' *Prospect* 23 June 2020.

12 Catastrophes, power and Covid-19

All changed, changed utterly. —W B Yeats

Emergencies

This chapter takes a dive into Aotearoa New Zealand's experience with the international Covid-19 pandemic. The material is complicated. It aims to show how our system of government dealt with the issues and demonstrates something of the relationships between the various institutions – how each cog turns, works together, and holds the others accountable. The institutions of government had an enormous workload. The quantity of law and new policy made in the course of two years relating to Covid-19 is truly astonishing. The disruption to people's lives was profound. Not within living memory has such a large amount of law with such heavy consequences been made so quickly in Aotearoa New Zealand. Few parts of life here remained unaffected by the pandemic.

A great challenge for any system of government lies in how it responds to unexpected emergencies and challenges. Heavy demands fall on the shoulders of political leaders. Emergencies of one sort or another occur quite frequently in Aotearoa New Zealand: floods after a deluge of rain, big fires in a time of drought, and sudden earthquakes have always been a feature of life here. Over the years we have developed **a system of civil defence** to mitigate the effects and put things right. This system involves both central and local government and often stimulates the whole community to pull together. For this reason, there is a **ministerial portfolio for Emergency Management.**

Some disasters, or calamities, are of a higher order of magnitude and may warrant the name catastrophe. Some in recent history include:
- The Christchurch Ōtautahi earthquakes in 2010 and 2011 which caused great devastation to houses and infrastructure. 185 people lost their lives and many others were injured.
- The shooting of worshippers at two Mosques by one terrorist gunman in Christchurch Ōtautahi on 15 March 2017. 51 people

died and 40 more were injured.

- The Whakaari White Island volcanic eruption on 9 December 2019 killed 22 people and injured 25 people who were visiting the island at the time of the eruption. The survivors suffered horrific burns.
- The Covid-19 pandemic has caused not only deaths but massive disruptions to the health system, the economy, and the whole community. Life has to be lived differently now.

Pandemics are known to history. The great influenza pandemic of 1918–19 killed about 9,000 people here in two months. The bubonic plague, the so-called 'Black Death', spread by fleas throughout Europe, Africa, and Asia in the 14th century killed an estimated 50 million people. Infectious diseases are not the hazard they once were. Noncommunicable diseases – such as heart attacks, strokes, and cancer – have each killed more people in Aotearoa New Zealand each year than has Covid-19 so far. Accidental death and injuries also kill many more people in a year.

The government has the responsibility to foresee adverse events and pandemics, to make preparations to stop them happening, to lessen the effects if they do occur, and then plan and execute the recovery. Devising appropriate policies is extraordinarily difficult. An infectious disease pandemic, where the nature of the virus changes, makes predictability hard and calculating risks difficult, if not impossible. Plans for the future are often dashed. Fear in the population spreads.

In such circumstances, people rely upon their governments. The most fundamental obligation of a government is to protect and safeguard its people. While sickness and disease vulnerability are part of life, catastrophes throw the spotlight on the policies of government. This includes the adequacy of their administrative processes and the level of foresight exercised to take steps to combat or prepare for disasters before they happen. In many ways the advent of Covid-19 in Aotearoa New Zealand has brought about war-time conditions. Public cooperation and disciplined behaviour was, and remains, critical to success. How it will all conclude is unknown as we finish this book.

The government response to the Covid-19 pandemic, demonstrates the great power of the State to limit people's liberties in order to protect the health and welfare of wider public. Few experiences can tell us more about the methods, capacity and competence of our system of government than how it responds to exceptional events.

The challenge of Covid-19 – Phase 1

On 29 December 2019, China advised the **World Health Organisation (WHO)** that cases of a dangerous respiratory illness from an unknown cause had occurred in Wuhan. On 7 January 2020 the Chinese authorities announced they had isolated a novel coronavirus that later became known as Covid-19. It did not take long for the pandemic to spread like wildfire around the world. On 30 January, the WHO declared the epidemic a global health emergency. On the same day Aotearoa New Zealand made **an Infectious Diseases Order** which added the disease to the list of notifiable diseases and required doctors to notify cases to the **Ministry of Health Manatū Hauora**, a vital step in knowing where the disease was spreading. Aotearoa New Zealand had its first case on 28 February 2020. The government, on 21 March 2020, announced a four-level alert system to manage the pandemic:

• Level 1 – Prepare
• Level 2 – Reduce
• Level 3 – Restrict
• Level 4 – Eliminate

Each level placed different restrictions on the population, escalating to Level 4 where people were required to stay at home in their bubble unless essential personal movement was required, all public venues and businesses except for essential services were closed, and travel was severely limited. The features of the various levels were adjusted as circumstances changed. In the initial stages of the pandemic, the government had legal powers to respond and combat the spread of the virus as authorised by **the Health Act 1956, the Epidemic Preparedness Act 2006**, and **the Civil Defence and Emergency Management Act 2002**. While these proved sufficient to get through the initial stages of the spread of the disease, they were later replaced with better directed legislation.

Alert Level 4 was first imposed on 25 March 2020 and the whole country went into lockdown. We moved back to Level 3 on April 27 and down to Level 2 on 14 May 2020. In August, there were new cases detected in the community which meant that the Auckland Region moved up again to Level 3 while the rest of the country remained at Level 2. Auckland Tāmaki Makaurau moved to Level 2 on September 23, and then to Level 1 on October 7, after the rest of Aotearoa New Zealand.

Illustration by Huriana Kopeke-Te Aho

The initial strategy was to keep Covid-19 out – prevention rather than management. International flights were controlled and people were prevented from entering Aotearoa New Zealand. Citizens and permanent residents were allowed back but had to go into government-managed isolation for 14 days before being released. Contact tracing was set up and people downloaded an app and scanned in wherever they went. Later, scanning or signing in and contact tracing became compulsory and masks had to be worn in public with social distancing required. Freedom of movement was curtailed, and internal travel restricted. Education at schools and tertiary institutions was interrupted. The State imposed stringent restrictions on personal freedom of movement, commerce, transport, travel, and more. Never in the history of Aotearoa New Zealand have such severe restrictions on the freedom of people been imposed, except in times of war.

The measures caused substantial damage to commerce, especially the tourist and hospitality industries. Supply chains for food and goods around the world and internally were seriously disrupted. The government paid billions of dollars to businesses and others to prevent hardship and the government itself had to borrow substantial sums to keep the economy afloat. Credit was eased by **the Reserve Bank of New Zealand Te Pūtea Matua**. Meanwhile, various new community cases were met by regional lockdowns in the areas where that was necessary.

Preparing policy and legal changes, drafting them, and ensuring they were within the powers granted by Parliament created a massive workload. The whole of the Aotearoa New Zealand government was involved in this concerted effort to keep the population safe. Ministerial action of a type quite extraordinary compared with traditional methods of law-making was required. Speed was essential. Many technical issues had to be solved. The science had to be understood by ministers. The risks had to be weighed quickly. Complex legal drafting had to be carried out by **the Parliamentary Counsel Te Tari Tohutohu Pāremata** and **Formal Orders-in-Council** had to be made. The **Governor-General** needed to sign many of the documents produced. Cabinet government is a flexible system but for the pandemic it had to be adjusted to be more agile, due to the emergency character of the public health decisions that had to be made. The ordinary Cabinet processes were too ponderous for the demands of the situation. A rapid but considered decision-making system was developed. An ad hoc **Cabinet Committee** was superseded by a group of eight ministers, headed by the Prime Minister and Deputy Prime Minister. The Secretary of Cabinet, Michael Webster, wrote that a 'battle rhythm' for meetings emerged. He describes the process:

Ministers were, at incredibly short notice, regularly provided with information, analysis and advice and, in a collective setting, after robust discussion in a virtual environment, made decisions that were accurately and clearly recorded, and quickly promulgated. The longstanding principles of best practice decision-making, as set out in the Cabinet Manual, were effectively combined with modern technology the adaptation of systems and processes with a dash of Kiwi pragmatism, to deliver a decision-making approach that supported Ministers to respond to one of the most significant crises New Zealand has ever faced.

One feature stood out clearly during Phase 1. The system prevented widespread transmission of the disease in the community; unlike many other countries where deaths were widespread, Aotearoa New Zealand suffered just 27 deaths in the first phase. We were helped in some respects by our remoteness, allowing the government to learn from what happened in other countries.

The main method of communication between the government and the public during the Covid-19 crisis were **the daily televised media conferences** held in the Beehive Theatrette. These were usually fronted by the Prime Minister Rt Hon Jacinda Ardern or the Hon Chris Hipkins, Minister for Covid-19 response and the Director-General of Health, Dr Ashley Bloomfield, or the Director of Public Health, Dr Caroline McElnay. The Deputy Prime Minister and Minister of Finance Hon Grant Robertson also appeared on economic effects and the assistance being offered. People watched and listened avidly as they were given information about the cases of Covid-19 in the country and how to protect themselves. Communication by government during this crisis was constant. The evolution of the virus and the revision of measures to contain it required constant official advice and people had to pay close attention to see if they were affected by developments. Leading the public debate were epidemiologists, such as Professors Michael Baker and Rod Jackson, microbiologist Dr Siouxie Wiles, modellers such as Professor Shaun Hendy, virologists, and other experts. They provided accurate information to people in an understandable way. Aotearoa New Zealand was unusual in this compared with many countries. Here people listened to the experts in the science. It proved the value of the universities and their research skills for the benefit of the community. Nevertheless, the experts were on tap, not on top: the decisions were made by ministers.

The general election date, announced by the Prime Minister, had to be delayed because of Covid and the election was finally held on October 17, 2020. The result was a convincing victory for the incumbent New Zealand Labour Party. Although restrictions were extensive, with limitations on individual liberty, people were apparently largely convinced that the steps being taken were in the interests of their own health and that of the country. The 2020 election results showed the bulk of the voters supported the measures that had been taken. They responded to the leadership of the Prime Minister, who had become, in 2017, the youngest Prime Minister here in 150 years. Remarkably, the general election was not a source of polarisation or division as in some other countries during the pandemic. All of this demonstrated a real sense of togetherness and unity in the community, or the 'team of five million', as the Prime Minister put it.

For the first time since the introduction of MMP in 1996, a single party, Labour, won a majority in the House of Representatives. The National Party suffered political fallout, seemingly caused in part by reaction to their criticism of the Covid-19 policies. The Leader of the Opposition, Simon Bridges, was removed as Leader in May 2020 and replaced by Todd Muller. On 14 July, Muller resigned and was replaced by Judith Collins, an uncomfortably short time before the general election. She later suffered a vote of no-confidence in her caucus and new leader Christopher Luxon was elected on 30 November 2021.

Phase 2

The next phase of the virus proved to be more difficult to combat than the first. In 2021 the virus mutated and became more easily infectious in its Delta phase, resulting in more serious health consequences. Further regional Level 3 lockdowns occurred in Auckland in February-March of 2021. There was a reprieve until 17 August 2021 when all Aotearoa New Zealand was put in lockdown at Level 4, after a single Delta case brought by a traveller from Sydney spread in the community.

Testing went through the roof. On 21 August, 41,464 swabs were processed. The rest of Aotearoa New Zealand went down again to Alert Level 3 on 31 August, but Auckland Tāmaki Makaurau remained at Alert Level 4 as cases continued to occur there. On 7 September, Aotearoa New Zealand, except for Auckland Tāmati Makaurau, moved to Level 2. On 21 September Auckland dropped to a revised Alert Level 3. Cases in the community continued to occur. Auckland Tāmati Makaurau remained in lockdowns of various intensities for more than three months, and some restrictions still applied.

Arrangements were made to vaccinate people against the disease, initially requiring two jabs of the Pfizer vaccine, starting with those over 60 and some essential workers. The rollout began in February 2021. Supplies purchased by government were slow in arriving. More supplies of the vaccine were procured from Spain and Denmark, in addition to those being supplied by the manufacturer. Vaccination rates increased rapidly although rates were low among Māori and in some areas of the country. It became a race against time to secure adequate rates of vaccination to prevent the hospital Intensive Care Units being overwhelmed by sick people.

The extended lockdown in Auckland Tāmati Makaurau in 2021

caused disquiet. People became restless and wanted to go out and to socialise in bars and restaurants. The hospitality industry wanted their businesses to be able to open. Some people broke the rules by travelling out of Auckland Tāmati Makaurau without permission to holiday houses in the South Island Te Waipounamu. The extended Covid-19 public health measures involved many complications, and issues changed almost daily.

It created a sense of unease in the community, who wondered whether it would ever end. Outbreaks in the Waikato and Northland Te Tai Tokerau caused fresh lockdowns and community infection rates in Auckland Tāmati Makaurau stayed high. People began to say Aotearoa New Zealand would have to stop the restrictions when vaccination rates were high enough to do so safely. But there was resistance to vaccination in some quarters. Some false and misleading statements about vaccination spread through social media, and conspiracy theories abounded. Meanwhile, there were 202 new cases of Covid-19 on 12 November 2021, most of them in Auckland Tāmati Makaurau.

Serious issues developed about the plight of New Zealanders overseas not being able to return because of the limited numbers of spaces in managed isolation facilities. Many were unhappy they could not return at the time they wished. A lottery system was introduced, which many disliked. The Ombudsman Kaitiaki Mana Tangata received more than 200 complaints and is investigating whether the allocation system administered by the Ministry of Business, Innovation and Employment Hikina Whakatutuki was lawful, unfit for purpose, unfair or poorly managed. A legal challenge was filed in the High Court Te Kōti Matua and will be determined in 2022.

A big effort all over the country called a 'Vaxathon' was organised and a 'Super Saturday' vaxathon event on October 16 resulted in 130,000 vaccinations given in one day nationwide. Nevertheless, a small minority demonstrated against the lockdowns and defied Covid orders in doing so. Prosecutions were brought. The methods adopted by these groups featured some of the divisive and polarising tactics that characterised the Trump presidency in the United States. A serious demonstration took place in Wellington Te Whanganui-a-Tara on 9 November 2021 when Destiny Church's Freedom and Human Rights Coalition organised a large-scale anti-vax protest. The quantity of misinformation posted on social media was increasing and the encouragement of vaccine hesitancy obvious. The group later adopted a strategy of blocking major roads in the major cities and slowing traffic down. On December 16, the day after Parliament adjourned for the year, the same group conducted a further demonstration at Parliament, although rain fell on its parade.

Phase 3

During late October and early November 2021 transition away from lockdowns began. The Delta variant could not be successfully eliminated, and the government changed its policy to the 'traffic light' system, or the **New Zealand Covid-19 Protection Framework**. Once a vaccination level of 90 per cent of the eligible populations had been reached, the old system of lockdowns would be abandoned and this new one substituted. Three levels are involved:

- **Green** – There are sporadic cases throughout Aotearoa New Zealand. Community transmissions are limited. Hospitalisations from Covid are at a manageable level. The whole of the health system is ready to respond, including primary health care public health and hospitals. Retail outlets, workplaces, and education institutions are all open. Specified outdoor community events are allowed. No limits on hospitality if vaccination certificates are used. Gatherings for weddings, places of worship, marae etc, are limited to 100 people with social distancing.
- **Orange** – Increasing community transmission with increasing pressure on the health system. Whole of the health system focusing resources but can manage, including primary care, public health, and hospitals. Increasing risk to at-risk populations. Record keeping and scanning required. Face coverings mandatory on flights, public transport, taxis, retail public venues, and encouraged elsewhere. Public facilities open with capacity based on social distancing. Retail open with capacity limits based on social distancing. Workplaces and education open with public health measures in place. Specified outdoor events allowed. No limits on general settings where vaccination certificates are used for hospitality and gatherings, weddings, places of worship, marae etc. More restrictions where no vaccination certificates are used.
- **Red** – Action needed to protect health system. Systems facing unsustainable number of hospitalisations. Action needed to protect at-risk populations. Record keeping/scanning required. Face coverings mandatory on flights, public transport, taxis, retail,

and recommended whenever leaving the house. Public facilities open with up to 100 people based on social distancing, seated, and separated. Retail open with capacity limits based on 1-metre distancing. Workplaces working from home encouraged. Education and schools open with public health measures and controls. With vaccination certificates, hospitality up to 100 people based on 1-metre distancing seated and separated. Gatherings, such as weddings, places of worship, marae, up to 100 people based on social distancing. Indoor and outdoor events up to 100 people based on social distancing seated and separated. Close contact businesses, public health requirements in place. Gyms up to 100 people based on 1-metre distancing. Tertiary education vaccinations required for on-site delivery. Specified outdoor events allowed with social distancing. For those without vaccination certificates tighter restrictions apply.

The framework envisages factors to be weighed when deciding to move from one level to another, including: the capacity of the health and disability system, testing and contact tracing, case management capacity, community transmission level of Covid and its impact on populations. Localised lockdowns can be used, like the old Alert Levels 3 and 4. Vaccination certificates are available for those who are fully vaccinated and, while optional for many locations, they will be mandatory in some legally mandated situations.

The new traffic light system began to operate on 3 December 2021, although 90 per cent vaccination rates had not been met everywhere, with Auckland Tāmaki Makaurau, Northland Te Tai Tokerau, Taupo, Rotorua Lakes, Kawerau, Gisborne Tūranga-nui-a-Kiwa, Wairoa, Rangitikei, Whanganui and Ruapehu in the Red setting. The rest of the North Island Te Ika-a-Māui and the whole of the South Island Te Waipounamu was in Orange. Auckland Tāmaki Makaurau came out of lockdown on December 15, 2021, and people could travel out of the city with proof of double vaccination or a recent negative test.

Restrictions for entry to Aotearoa New Zealand at the border remained controlled under the new policy. On 13 December summer traffic light settings were announced. All of the country moved to Orange, excluding Northland Te Tai Tokerau which remained Red until 30 December. From 15 December, people could travel within Aotearoa

New Zealand for any reason, and people could leave Auckland Tāmaki Makaurau with some restrictions.

Meanwhile, the new Omicron strain of Covid arrived in managed isolation from overseas and by 21 December, 22 cases were here. Omicron was rampant in more than 70 countries. As a result, new measures were announced, designed to keep Omicron out of the community for as long as possible. The reopening of the border previously announced was pushed back until the end of February 2022 and the managed isolation rules were increased for a period up to 10 days for those arriving from overseas. A third booster jab of vaccine was made available to people sooner by reducing the period from six months to four from the time of the second jab. It was decided to roll out paediatric doses of the Pfizer vaccine for five- to 11-year-olds starting from 17 January 2022. This was a classic example of how the mutations in the virus forced adjustments in policy. The pandemic is not over until it is over.

By Christmas 2021 the percentage of the eligible population who were double vaccinated reached almost 91 per cent.

Making of policy and law at speed

Since the Covid-19 pandemic arrived in Aotearoa New Zealand, 22 separate Acts of Parliament bearing on Covid were passed between 15 May 2020 and 21 December 2021. More than 220 pieces of secondary legislation containing orders and regulations on many matters of detail affecting many businesses, occupations, and activities have been made. The volume of law was enormous, it was complex and much of it technical. Finding out what you had to do became difficult because of the changing circumstances, especially after the arrival of Delta.

Making policy and law in a rapidly developing situation poses grave problems:

1. What should the policy be in a situation where the science may be unknown?
2. How should the policy be adopted and what legal changes must be made?
3. How can the public be informed about what is going on and the actions they need to take?

There are so many moving parts, and Covid caused a challenge to lawmaking process of unprecedented proportions. It is not surprising there were difficulties.

Large amounts of both **statute law** and **secondary legislation** (law made by someone other than Parliament under legislative power given by the authority of Acts of Parliament) were made in both phases of the pandemic. Most people probably know little about secondary legislation, but they were subject to it. Many of the detailed orders and rules were made by secondary legislation by the Executive not by Parliament itself. The most important piece of privacy legislation was the **Covid-19 Public Health Response Act 2020** that was passed quickly with no scrutiny by a Select Committee. Parliament at this time was conducting its business in a manner brought on by the pandemic itself. The then Leader of the Opposition, Hon Simon Bridges, chaired a special parliamentary committee that met remotely through Zoom where MPs questioned officials and heard the views of experts and members of the public. These hearings were televised so the public could understand the issues at play. The House of Representatives itself met with a reduced number of MPs.

Later, after the 2020 general election, a Select Committee took submissions on the rapidly enacted 2020 Covid Act and proposed amendments to remedy defects and ensure the powers available were appropriate and fit for purpose. These amendments were passed into law by the House. Accountability was strengthened by improving Parliament's express power to bring to a halt the application of secondary legislation that it considered defective. Defects were fixed later, a most unusual back-to-front legislative process.

Even that was not enough. As the virus mutated and the experience in combatting it increased, the legal framework had to be adjusted further. In late September 2021 two Bills were introduced to Parliament to further refine and tighten the law. The **Covid-19 Public Health Response Amendment Act** was enacted in November 2021. It dealt with dates and the vexed issue of managed isolation facilities and increased the penalties for breaches. It extended the time the law was set to expire from 13 May 2022 to 2023. The statute contained such exceptional powers over people it was thought it must be repealed when it was no longer needed.

Two more Bills were enacted under urgency within 24 hours of introduction in controversial circumstances in November 2021. There was no Select Committee scrutiny of them. These were the **Covid 19 Response (Vaccinations) Legislation Act 2021** and an Act providing for Working for Families Tax Credits and support payments. Much of the first measure dealt with protections against Covid in the workplace and in public venues. One of the key changes was to provide statutory authorisation for measures involving vaccine requirements for certain occupations thereby strengthening the authority that would otherwise have relied on secondary legislation which is more vulnerable to attack in the courts. The Act provides specific workers must not carry out specified work unless they are vaccinated or are exempt and exemptions are dealt with in the Act. After the Acts were passed a massive 115-page Order, **the Covid-19 Public Health Response (Protection Framework) Order 2021**, was made. It contains the extraordinarily detailed rules relating to the traffic light system.

The lack of parliamentary scrutiny of the Bills before becoming law was roundly criticised in several quarters as a constitutional outrage. In normal circumstances it was certainly exactly that. Could it have been avoided? There was not even any commitment to review it afterwards, as had happened in 2020. No real reason was advanced for the stopping of scrutiny. The Speaker of the House complained about it, although he did remark that the Select Committees could have taken up the issue when the policy was announced but did not do so. The most likely explanation was that so much was going on within the system the government just ran out of time before the policies had to be in place before the holiday break. This was a most unfortunate blemish in legislative process.

Secondary legislation can be disallowed by the House as authorised by the Standing Orders of the House and by **the Legislation Act 2019**. It is done by resolution of the House of Representatives after a single debate, compared with the elaborate multiple readings received by Bills that become law. The governing party does not lose its power to make secondary legislation because Parliament has been prorogued (dissolved) before a general election. The key constitutional issue is that even with secondary legislation Parliament remains in control and can disallow orders.

The **Regulations Review Select Committee,** Parliament's watchdog against excessive or wrongful use of secondary legislation, worked hard in 2020 and 2021 examining the regulations, Orders, notices and Bills introduced concerning Covid-19. The Committee is also empowered to receive complaints against secondary legislation on several grounds – these can be summarised to the effect that the instrument is an improper use of the power delegated to the Executive by Parliament or is unfair. The Committee is, by constitutional convention, always chaired by an Opposition MP, to reflect that the government party MPs are parliamentary colleagues of the Ministers, whose regulations are being scrutinised. The current chair is Chris Penk MP, who is a lawyer. Complaints have been made against some Covid orders. The Committee holds hearings and makes a report to the House.

A sessional order of the House requires the Committee to report on all Covid orders made. In 2020, it reported to the House that it had scrutinised 110 instruments made under 42 different Acts of Parliament. In the new Parliament it continued its scrutiny and reported in September 2021 on seven Covid orders presented between 18 and 21 August 2021. The Committee held hearings and engaged in dialogue with officials and ministers and secured alterations on occasions to what was proposed. In its work, the Committee considered the unauthorised sub-delegation of the power to make secondary legislation – that means handing on legislative power to someone other than those who have been given the authority to make the law by Act of Parliament. There was one issue that the Committee found was unacceptable – a regulation made to provide temporary financial support to people on the expiry of benefits paid under the authority of the Social Security Act. For the most part, however, it found that what was done, after adjustments, met the proper standards for secondary legislation in the circumstances of the pandemic that required rapid and significant action.

After the 2020 legislation was refined in 2021, the work of the Regulations Review Committee increased. The Act gave the responsible Minister, Hon Chris Hipkins, the power to make orders 'to do things or not do things' depending on the needed public health response. The law provides that orders are automatically revoked after a certain lapse of time. Where necessary to continue orders, they were referred to the Regulations Review Committee and a debate took place in the House on its report on whether such orders should be confirmed. This became quite a common proceeding and showed how the House remained in control of the content of the law even when it was secondary legislation made under the authority of an Act of Parliament. All the reports of the Regulations Review Committee are available on its website and debates are held regularly. On 16 November, 13 orders were approved by a vote of 118 to two. In the reports of the Regulations Review Committee, it possible to trace how each issue was handled and how the issues were resolved. Parliament through the Regulations Review Committee was holding the Executive to account.

Court challenges

The Covid-19 response from the government demonstrated the immense power of the State, but also tested the extensive accountability measures in place to ensure that power is being exercised appropriately. The rule of law is a serious restraint upon the power of government. Another significant check and balance are the judges. The courts are the custodians of the rule of law to a considerable extent. The actions taken to prevent the spread of the virus were challenged in the courts on several occasions by taking a judicial review. Decisions made under secondary legislation are more vulnerable to judicial review than those that are made to decisions made under Acts of Parliament. Here we deal with only a few of those challenges. More will occur.

A former Parliamentary Counsel Te Tari Tohutohu Pāremata's first challenge concerned the first nine days of lockdown. This succeeded, but nothing practical turned upon it. The second challenged the lawfulness of two orders made by the Director-General of Health that, it was argued, exceeded the reach of the emergency powers contained under section 70 of the Health Act 1956. The third concerned the lawfulness of the Director-General of Health delegating his powers to determine what premises needed to be closed to members of the public. The second and third causes of actions failed as the judges upheld the powers that the government had used were legally valid. The court rejected the arguments advanced and held that the exercise of the powers under the Health Act were necessary, reasonable, and proportionate to the threat. There was no invalid delegation of legislative power. The case lost in front of a full court of three High Court Te Kōti Matua judges. The applicant then appealed and lost in the Court of Appeal Te Kōti Pīra. In both courts there are long judgments, going into significant analysis of the reasons for the government's decisions. The law under which the challenge proceeded had been superseded by the time of the Court of Appeal Te Kōti Pīra decision.

In September 2021, Justice Churchman dealt with a case where an employee of the New Zealand Customs had her employment terminated because the Vaccinations Order had been made that such a person had to be vaccinated. The Order had been approved by resolution of the House of Representatives. The Judge held the Vaccinations Order was neither ultra vires the empowering Act nor irrational. The public health group interest to prevent the spread of Covid overcame the individual rights of the employees not to be vaccinated.

Justice Venning set aside an exemption that had been refused for an applicant under the International Quarantine Order and directed it should be reconsidered. The Chief Executive of Ministry of Business, Innovation and Employment Hīkina Whakatutuki was required to consider the applicant's need to attend a board meeting in Boston, the right of New Zealand citizens to enter Aotearoa New Zealand without unreasonable limitation, and the need to avoid the risk of contracting Covid-19 at a MIQ facility including any characteristics that make them especially vulnerable.

Two decisions made by the High Court Te Kōti Matua in November 2021 upheld the validity of government decisions to make orders requiring employees in some occupations to be vaccinated. The first by Justice Cooke held that Aviation Security Service employees were required to be vaccinated or be dismissed. Another by Justice Palmer reached similar conclusions in respect of some midwives, doctors, and teachers. The argument there was that the Vaccination Order was legally valid because the Act does not empower it to be made, if interpreted consistently with the right to refuse medical treatment under the New Zealand Bill of Rights Act and the principle of legality. The argument failed. An appeal from the decision straight to the Supreme Court Te Kōti Mana Nui, cutting out the Court of Appeal Te Kōti Pīra, also failed. These decisions are long and need to be read to understand fully how the law works.

A later 2021 challenge case brought by Māori interests was successful. A Māori health provider, Whanāu Ora Commissioning Agency (WOCA), had sought individual details from the Ministry of Health Manatū Hauora of Māori who had not been vaccinated, so they could be approached and helped to get the jab. High Court Te Kōti Matua judge Justice Gwyn held that the provider was entitled to more information than was given. Māori rates of vaccination were lagging behind those of the general population and the applicants were part of the government-funded, Māori-delivered, whanau-centred approach to helping get people vaccinated. The law relating to privacy was central to the case as health information is sensitive. The Health Information Code of Privacy 2020 promulgated by the Privacy Commission Te Mana Mātāpono Matatapu made that clear.

The judge decided that the Ministry was wrong in its application of the Code. It had not correctly considered whether the disclosure of the information was necessary. The judge also held that the applicants had a legitimate expectation that the Treaty of Waitangi should have been applied in the circumstances in which the Crown had specifically decided to uphold and honour the Treaty in its vaccination programme. The judge set aside the Ministry's decision and declared that the power to disclose information had to be exercised in accordance with the Treaty of Waitangi and its principles. She directed the decision be retaken within three working days. Limited information was released as a result of the case, but not enough to satisfy the applicant.

Remarkably, after the first case the Director-General of Health refused to provide the information requested for all the North Island Te Ika-a-Māui Māori. A consultation conducted by the Ministry did not involve the applicant. But the Director-General decided to *'decline the request for access to all Te Ika/North Island individual level Māori Health Information sought by the applicants.'* This led to a journey back to the court before the same judge. In a lengthy and persuasive decision, Justice Gwyn held on 6 December 2021 that the Ministry had made several errors of fact and of law in reaching its decision. Worse still, it breached the applicants' right to natural justice contained in the Bill of Rights Act in the way it conducted the consultation. Justice Gwyn ordered the Ministry of Health Manatū Hauora to consider and decide on provision of data in those areas where it had not yet agreed to provide data to the applicants. Further, the Ministry should review its decision to provide data in relation to those Māori who had only a first dose of the vaccine.

These findings of legal and factual errors and the appearance of bureaucratic stubbornness in the face of the law did not look good in the same week the Waitangi Tribunal began hearings on whether the policy on the vaccine rollout in respect to Māori was in breach of the Treaty of Waitangi. Within the time frame laid down by the court the Director-General changed his decision and, while there were some qualifications, undertook to provide most of what had been originally requested.

On 20 December 2021, The Waitangi Tribunal published a report after urgent hearings, finding the government's policy on the vaccination rollout breached the Treaty of Waitangi in several important respects.

Haumaru: the Covid-19 Priority Report found the government's Covid-19 response had breached Treaty principles such as active protection, equity, partnership and tino rangatiratanga. It recommended the Crown urgently provide further funding, resourcing, data, and other support to assist Māori providers and communities with localised responses, including continuing vaccination efforts.

The report said Cabinet breached te Tiriti principles when it rejected advice from officials, such as Director-General of Health Dr Ashley Bloomfield and the Ministry of Health Manatū Hauora, to adopt an age adjustment for Māori in the vaccine roll-out due to the population's greater risk of infection and health inequities. It was also considered a breach of the Treaty when Cabinet ignored calls from Māori health leaders and iwi not to move into the Covid-19 Protection Framework. Under te Tiriti, the Crown has a duty to adopt rational, scientific and equitable policy choices for Māori, the Tribunal said, and a moral and ethical duty to defend those choices against unreasonable public backlash: *'Failing to perform these duties for the sake of political convenience does not reflect the Treaty partnership and, in fact, threatens the fundamental basis for it.'*

Such a rapid response from the Waitangi Tribunal was another important mechanism of accountability.

Accountability

In 1979 Geoffrey Palmer published a book with a chapter headed 'The fastest law in the west,' characterising the Aotearoa New Zealand law-making system as it then was. Recent events have seen again a remarkable spate of new statutes and secondary legislation made at speed. This was because the pandemic has been so unusual and posed great threats to people. To combat this, a great deal of new policy and law of necessity had to be decided upon quickly and the established processes were set aside to some degree. The Covid legislation is specific, it does not abridge rights generally in an enduring way. When Covid goes, the ability to restrict will go.

Here we try to summarise the constitutional protections that were at work. It is an intricate story of the interaction between Cabinet, the public, the House of Representatives, the Regulation Review Select Committee, the New Zealand Bill of Rights Act 1990, and the courts. It is a story of how the Aotearoa New Zealand constitution works when under extreme pressure.

Cabinet made decisions and was advised by a wide range of officials and experts from both inside and outside the government system. The decisions were communicated to the public through widespread methods and there was plenty of public debate on the measures.

The quantity of Covid law is vast, and it was altered often. The methods of scrutiny of the legislation were on occasions truncated, due to the need for speed and because of changes concerning the disease and its spread. The legislation that imposed the greatest restrictions required renewal by parliamentary vote on a regular basis to avoid its automatic expiry. Parliamentary debates were held on measures. The legislation passed was not general legislation giving the government wide powers, but it was restricted to the Covid situation. Ministerial accountability was enhanced because orders made by the Minister for Covid were made subject to Parliamentary debate and disallowance.

No steps were taken to abridge the rights of people to test the legality of the measures taken and their consistency with the New Zealand Bill of Rights Act 1990. All Covid legislation must be made, like other legislation, considering the Bill of Rights and the courts must also strive to give an interpretation that is consistent with the Bill of Rights. The key Covid statute in 2020 made protection of the Bill of Rights explicit and the law said that restrictions on civil liberties should be undertaken only to the extent required.

The Attorney-General Hon David Parker managed on behalf of Cabinet the 2020 principal piece of Covid legislation, and he handed over responsibility for vetting the consistency of the legislation with the Bill of Rights to the Minister of Justice, since the Attorney-General could not provide a legal opinion with propriety on his own legislative work. The vaccination Bills in 2021 received positive vets from the Ministry of Justice Te Tāhū o te Ture which are publicly available.

The Regulations Review Select Committee was highly active in scrutinising secondary legislation that made up many of the restrictions imposed and on occasion they caused measures to be altered. The amount of work carried out by the Committee was prodigious. It performed its watch-dog functions regarding the improper exercise of secondary legislation and caused material improvements to be made to pieces of it.

The superior courts have decided cases that tested the legality of the Covid measures and, so far, the main features of the framework have been upheld by the courts. The rule of law has been followed and no block imposed upon its exercise. The mechanisms of a liberal democracy were at work. That continues.

Many people involved in opposing government policy on Covid-19 repeated the mantra that the policies were contrary to the New Zealand Bill of Rights Act 1990 that guarantees fundamental rights and freedoms. However, no rights conferred can be regarded as absolute. It is not correct that the Bill of Rights cannot be overridden by legislation. Section 5 of the Act says the rights are *'subject only to such reasonable limits prescribed by law as can be demonstrably justified in a free and democratic society.'* This is a similar test as appears in Canadian law upon which much of Aotearoa New Zealand's Bill of Rights was based. Many other countries with which Aotearoa New Zealand identifies have adopted similar policies for Covid-19. Section 5, however, does **not** permit the government to do anything it likes, the steps must be 'reasonable' and must be able to be *'demonstrably justified.'*

The State has the capacity to be all-powerful when it needs to be within the limits of the law. Opinions will differ on the exercise of such great powers. Both the Courts and Parliament acted as a restraint upon the powers being exercised by the Executive. Accountability was clearly present. How power is exercised is the product of politics and the controls that exist over its unbridled existence. The examples here show Cabinet, Parliament, the Courts, and the Waitangi Tribunal all fulfilling their constitutional roles.

A reprise

This narrative stops with the announcements that came into effect on 21 December 2021, at which point the Covid-19 saga was not over. What can be confidently said so far is that the Covid virus has brought unprecedented challenges to the entire system of government in Aotearoa New Zealand. These challenges sprang up on multiple fronts and placed great strain on the machinery of government to adjust to so many issues so quickly and for so long. Challenges included:

- Medical and science issues concerning the nature of the virus, diagnostic issues concerning its detection, the changing research on the means of combatting it, and treating it, dealing with the levels of uncertainty and the risks present.
- Medical treatment delivery issues and how hospitals and the public health system can be organised to keep the death rate low.

- Border control issues as to how to prevent the spread of the disease from people returning to Aotearoa New Zealand from overseas, involving immigration issues, enhanced border controls involving Customs, Police, and the development of government quarantine facilities for new arrivals where the New Zealand Defence Force Te Ope Kātua o Aotearoa took an important role.
- How to deal fairly with the numbers of New Zealanders returning to the country when the spaces available for quarantine could not accommodate them all in a timely fashion, and adjusting the system over time.
- The development of policy and law to adjust for changes in the virus and, passing of many statutes and secondary legislation containing large quantities of technical detail and the development of a new framework at speed following the impossibility of stamping out the Delta variant.
- Measures to ensure compliance with the detailed rules that restricted liberties and the role of the New Zealand Police Ngā Pirihimana o Aotearoa and development of methods encouraging compliance without being too heavy-handed, including regarding illegal demonstrations in breach of the new measures.
- A communication strategy so the government could communicate its messages to the public on a continuing basis in a rapidly developing situation to influence their behaviour and tell them how to best protect themselves. This involved a massive multi-media advertising programme, leaflets, telephone helplines and detailed information on the Covid-19 government website to get accurate information out and to combat the false information on social media.
- The development of detailed policies for segments of the economy, such as retail, hospitality, and public events, including funerals, to prevent the spread of the disease. The development of such rules required a great deal of consultation with affected groups.
- The development of a vaccination strategy once vaccines were available, choosing the most appropriate ones, procuring them, taking steps to ensure they were available all over Aotearoa New Zealand and people were vaccinated in a timely fashion.
- Developing and delivery of policies for the protection of people in schools and tertiary education facilities, including universities and

their halls of residence.

- Adjusting the practices in justice facilities, including prisons, and the operation of the courts to protect people there. There were big disruptions in the working of the courts and the measures taken were led by the Chief Justice.
- The development of a new system of protection when it became clear that the Delta variant could not be permanently eliminated from Aotearoa New Zealand.
- Much financial and Treasury advice was required to ensure measures were taken to prevent the economy from collapsing due to Covid. Colossal sums of public money were handed out to assist and subsidise employers and the self-employed with taxpayers' money and this required increased government borrowing.
- Adjustments had to be made to the system of social welfare benefits to cushion people against poverty due to Covid.
- Planning steps to reopen Aotearoa New Zealand when safe to do so.

It is important to appreciate how all these steps, and indeed many more, placed an enormous strain on ministers, officials and indeed every element of the public service. It was a case of all hands to the pump. By Christmas 2021, exhaustion was a real issue within the system. Despite the nature of the emergency and strains it placed on the institutions, they functioned, and many would say they functioned well. By 21 December 2021 Aotearoa New Zealand had sustained 49 deaths due to Covid-19. This is a low mortality rate for the disease, a record that few countries can match. Yet the pandemic is not over. Whatever lies ahead, it seems clear that the Aotearoa New Zealand's system of governance can deliver complex protective policies in time of a prolonged emergency. Yet no final conclusions are possible. We do not know how it will all end. The yearning for normality after Covid may in the end prove to be a delusion. Many things have changed. Some of them may have changed permanently. People critical of what was done need to consider the counterfactual: how many people would have died had the measures not been adopted?

A brief update: 1 April 2022

Between 21 December 2021 and 1 April 2022 there were a multitude of new developments around Covid. The Omicron variant spread rapidly, and the infection rates became high. Efforts were made to delay the spread, but it was never going to be possible to eliminate it. Vaccinations continued and the rates became higher. Booster rates increased and they were continuing with 2,123 boosters given on 31 March. Restrictions had been gradually but drastically reduced. Plans to resume overseas travel were announced. Rapid Antigen testing has become widespread, there were more than 30,000 RAT test results on 31 March. There were 15,250 new community cases that day and 8230 cases in hospital. There were 22 deaths reported that day, including people who had died over the past four weeks. This increased the total death toll from Covid to 338.The authorities were encouraged that case numbers were continuing to decline. How things will go into the future is no easier to predict than it was in December 2022. In terms of international comparisons New Zealand continues to do well.

References

Niall Ferguson, *Doom – The Politics of Catastrophe* (Allen Lane, London, 2021); Adam Toose, *Shutdown: How Covid shook the world economy* (Allen Lane, London, 2021). The government websites contain much information about the policies and the events, including links to many of the media conferences: https://covid19.govt.nz. *Borrowdale* v *Director-General of Health* [2020] NZHC 2090,[2020] 2NZLR 864 (High Court); *Borrowd*ale v *Director-General of Health* [2021] NZCA 520 (Court of Appeal); *Te Pou Matakana Limited* v *Attorney-General* [2021] NZHC 2942 (High Court); *Te Pou Matakana Limited v Attorney General* [2021] NZHC 3319; *Bolton* v *The Chief Executive of the Ministry of Business, Innovation and Employment,*(High Court*); Four Aviation Security Service Employees* v *Minister of Covid-19 Response* [2021] NZHC 3012 [8 November 2021]; *Four Midwives, NZDSOS and NZTSOS v Minister for Covid-19 Response* [2021] NZHC 306; *GF v Minister of Covid-19 Response & Ors* [2021] NZHC 2526 [24 September 2021]; Steven Levine *Politics in a Pandemic Jacinda Ardern and New Zealand's 2020 election* (Victoria University of Wellington Press, 2021); Michael Webster, 'Government decision making during a crisis' 17 Policy Quarterly, Issue 1, February 2021, page 11; Dean R Knight 'Stamping our Covid-19 in New Zealand : Legal pragmatism and democratic legitimacy [2021] *Public Law*, April 2021, 241; Hon David Parker, 'The Legal and Constitutional Implications of New Zealand's Fight Against Covid' Speech to the New Zealand Centre for Public Law, 2 December 2021; Waitangi Tribunal, *Haumaru: The Covid-19 Priority Report, Prepublication version*, (Wai 2575, 2021); New Zealand Law Commission, NZLC R22, *Final Report on Emergencies* (December 1991).

https://www.lawcom.govt.nz/sites/default/files/projectAvailableFormats/NZLC%20
R22.pdf.
Regulations Review Committee Reports: Final report (Examination of COVID-19
orders presented between 18 and 31 August 2021); Final report (Briefing to review
secondary legislation made in response to COVID-19)
History of the Covid-19Alert System: https://covid19.govt.nz/alert-levels-and-updates/
history-of-the-covid-19-alert-system/; https://www.worldometers.info/coronavirus/
country/new-zealand/

13 Elections, MMP and political parties

The election of major decision-makers is fundamental to the idea of democracy. In Aotearoa New Zealand, representatives are elected every three years. Elections are fundamental to our constitution since they provide its basic democratic element. Voting acts as a way for citizens to have their say in how they are governed, enabling public opinion to hold elected representatives to account by answering for their actions.

But how exactly do elections work? What are the rules of the game?

In Aotearoa New Zealand, elections are held for Members of Parliament, as well as for mayors and councillors who make the decisions for local government. Parliamentary elections and local government elections are not held in the same year and local government elections operate under different electoral law. The restrictions on who is eligible to vote for MPs are simple and liberal by international standards. Those 18 years or older, who are a New Zealand citizen or permanent resident, have lived in Aotearoa New Zealand continuously for 12 months or more at some time in their life are all eligible. There are a couple of exceptions to this such as those currently serving an imprisonment sentence of three years or more.

The only way that one can become a Member of Parliament is by democratic competitive election. Parliamentary elections are seen as crucial to our constitution. The only laws that cannot be changed by a majority vote in Parliament are six provisions relating to elections. To amend a limited number of the electoral law provisions requires a 75 per cent majority in Parliament or a majority vote in a national referendum. These restrictions: limit the parliamentary term to three years; give the powers to set the electoral boundaries to the independent Representation Commission instead of politicians; define the general electoral population and electorate boundaries; define an adult as a person aged 18 years or older; and protect the secret ballot method of voting. These unique safeguards first appeared in Aotearoa New Zealand law in 1956.

The Electoral Act 1993 sets out the principal rules for the conduct of elections. It is very technical, long and complicated in many respects.

Some of the fundamental topics dealt with in the Electoral Act include: the rules for the registration of political parties; the processes for counting votes; methods parties can use to establish their party lists; the rules for registering voters; provisions for Māori electorates and how and when Māori may transfer from the Māori roll to the general roll if they wish. Māori can also transfer from the general roll to the Māori roll. This Act also deals with the establishment of the Electoral Commission Te Kaitiaki Take Kōwhiri. As well, it outlines controls over how much can be spent by political parties and candidates during an election. There are various regulations for political advertising that include restrictions on who may authorise political advertisements.

MMP and FPP

For many years, Aotearoa New Zealand had a First-Past-the-Post (FPP or 'plurality') electoral system, which almost always resulted in a single political party forming the government, even though this governing party did not usually receive the majority of votes cast. The last occasion before 2020 when an incoming government received a majority of the votes cast at a general election was in 1951. In 1978 and 1981 the Labour Party received more votes than National but did not become the government. In 1996 we switched to a mixed-member proportional (MMP) system. Under FPP voters had one vote: for a party representative in their electorate. Under MMP you have two votes: one for a representative candidate for the electoral district that you live in and a second for a political party. It is this party list vote that primarily determines parties' overall strength in Parliament, and therefore the political flavour of the government. MMP has usually resulted in governments formed by more than one party and governments often depend on negotiated agreements with other parties for confidence and supply or the formation of a majority coalition.

MMP aims for proportional representation so that the overall number of Members of Parliament a political party secures corresponds to the number of votes that party received across the whole country. For example, under MMP, if a party receives 20 per cent of the party vote they are entitled to a total of 20 per cent of the seats in Parliament, which would be 24 seats. If 14 of their members win their electorate vote, then the party is entitled to 10 more Members of Parliament. These are selected from the party's list, which is a ranked list of candidates nominated by the political party. To secure representation in Parliament a party must receive 5 per cent of the party vote or one electorate seat.

Many more political parties compete in parliamentary elections than ever manage to succeed in electing a member to Parliament. This is partly due to parties being subject to the 5 per cent threshold of the party vote. However, if a party wins an electorate seat it can bring in more members into the House as an exception to the 5 per cent rule. This is known as the coat-tailing effect and has been criticised. A good example is what happened in the 2008 general election:

- The Green Party did not win any electorate seats but did receive 6.7 per cent of the nationwide party vote, exceeding the 5 per cent threshold. It secured nine of the 122 seats in that Parliament.
- The ACT party won 3.6 per cent of the nationwide party vote but because one of its candidates won an electorate seat it was entitled to a proportional share of seats in the House. This gave ACT five seats – one electorate seat and four list seats.

The Electoral Commission Te Kaitiaki Take Kōwhiri in a report in 2012 recommended that the coat-tailing law be repealed and that the 5 per cent threshold for the party vote be reduced to 4 per cent. These recommendations have not been acted upon. As well, the number of seats available in the House of Representatives can vary because of what is known as an 'overhang'. This is where more seats are allocated above 120 because more electorate seats have been won by a political party compared with the seats it is entitled to under the party vote. This has occurred four times since the introduction of MMP: in 2005, 2008, 2011 and 2014.

Parliamentary representation is not easy to achieve. Since the introduction of MMP in 1996 only once has a single political party alone won a majority in the House of Representatives. This happened in the 2020 general election, conducted in the most unusual circumstances caused by the Covid-19 pandemic, when the Labour Party secured 65 of the 120 seats. In 2020, 17 political parties competed in the general election, and only five of them secured any seats. Smaller parties sometimes tend to lose all representation in MMP elections. Both registered and unregistered parties can have members run as electorate candidates at general elections. However, only parties registered with the Electoral Commission Te Kaitiaki Take Kōwhiri can contest the party vote, have their registered logo on the voting paper, access public broadcasting funds for advertising on television and radio and, since 2017, on the internet.

The change in electoral system from FPP to MMP was one of the most important changes in Aotearoa New Zealand's constitutional history. MMP altered the political incentives. The old two-party duopoly disintegrated. A surprising feature about the introduction of MMP is not how much the Cabinet government has changed, but how little. However, what has changed is the style of management and the development of techniques to deal with coalition, and confidence and supply agreements. The need to hunt for support for the introduction of Bills becomes uncertain compared with FPP. Another reason for the switch may have been that the voters were tired of the powerful executive government that did not heed their desires sufficiently. The executive branch used to control virtually everything that Parliament did; not what was said, perhaps, but certainly what was decided there. MMP put the brakes on the system, to a degree, because the chance of one party securing a majority alone under the new electoral system was reduced.

Under MMP, the diversity of representation in Parliament has also become much greater, in terms of age distribution, gender, and ethnicity. There are now more Māori MPs than ever before, as well as more Tagata Pasifika MPs. However, we still have a distance to go to ensure that our Parliament accurately reflects what our community looks like.

First-Past-the-Post functions quite differently from MMP. It is not always appreciated how recently FPP voting in single-member electorates was developed. In early English elections for Parliament, voting was all done in public; there was no secret ballot and, if necessary, heads were counted. In ancient Greek city states votes were determined either by raised hands or by the loudest shouts. At one point, as a recent history of proportional representation in Britain states, most electorates returned two members each. In England at one point there were only five single member electorates. Essentially Aotearoa New Zealand had a two-party system since the 1890s, although there was a transitional phase between 1911 and 1931. Until 1903 there were multi-member constituencies and between 1908 and 1911 a second ballot procedure was used.

FPP was the essence of simplicity from the 1950s onwards in Aotearoa New Zealand: put quite simply, the candidate with the most votes won. In each of the 99 electorates, political parties put forward one candidate for election. During the election campaign (usually lasting about three months), each party would try to convince voters to make them the government by voting for their candidate in each electorate. In this way, parties provided the link between popular consent and representative government, actively encouraging the inactive portion of the population to think about public issues and take part in elections.

In each electorate, the candidate with the most votes won the seat. If there were only two candidates, the winner needed more than 50 per cent of the votes cast to win. However, there were often candidates from four or more parties. The candidate who received the most votes won, even if they had fewer votes than their opponents combined. So, elected candidates frequently earned a minority of the valid votes cast, say 30–40 per cent, while together the other candidates would have received 60–70 per cent between them. This meant results often did not reflect the views of much of the electorate. This was often criticised and seen as unfair.

The outcome of the election was that one party controlled the power of government in the country. Results were almost always decisive. Either a party controlled all the power of government or none of it. One of the few 'laws' of political science is that the FPP system has a bias toward the existence of two parties. There was little point in voting for a third party because only one of the two main parties had a realistic chance of forming the government. Furthermore, it was only voting in the 'marginal' seats, where the fight between the two main parties was close, that would matter and that parties would heed. This is comparable to 'swing states' in the American political system where gerrymandering occurs that is legally impossible in Aotearoa New Zealand because independent officials set the boundaries and MPs cannot not do so. The outcome of the contests in 'safe' seats, where most people would vote for Labour or for National, was virtually assured.

The primary catalyst for the change from FPP to MMP was that FFP often produced results that were not proportional to the vote. In 1972 and 1975 the difference in voter support for National and Labour was 6.8 per cent and 7.7 per cent respectively. Yet on both occasions those differences produced a disparity of more than 26 percentage points in seats gained. Quite small changes in the level of relative support produced a landslide in parliamentary seats. In 1978, however, both major parties were supported by the voters nearly equally, but there was a disparity of 10 percentage points in seats secured. In 1978 and 1993, a third party obtained more than 50 per cent of the votes obtained by each of the two main parties, yet received 2 per cent of the total seats in Parliament.

In 1985 the Labour Government established a Royal Commission on the Electoral System, chaired by Sir John Wallace, a High Court Judge. In 1986 it recommended a mixed-member-proportional electoral system based on that of Germany. The new system was opposed by the two main political parties National and Labour. It took years for it to be adopted, being finally approved by referendum in 1993. In 2011, MMP was once again put to a referendum and almost 58 per cent of voters wanted to keep it, which was an increase of about 3.9 per cent over the support it received when initially passed by referendum.

Elections in Aotearoa New Zealand are designed so that those in power are held accountable and are responsive to the people. They are meant to produce results that are proportional, fair and reflect the needs of the general citizen body overall. Democracy is intended to be government by the people, for the people and elections are a fundamental way in which this vision is realised in modern democratic representative systems. Elections open a channel of influence regarding how the country should be run; what we want, what we don't want, and what we see as important. Voting is an invitation for you to have your voice heard in this conversation, and while it is not the only way you can engage in politics and democracy, it is an important one.

The fluctuating fortunes of MMP on political parties

An examination in detail of the nine MMP election results demonstrate a pattern: small parties come and go while National and Labour continue to be dominant. Those two parties have led every MMP government that has been formed since 2006.

Local support for an electorate MP has been strong in several instances, for example, for the ACT party in Epsom and for United Future's Peter Dunne who held the Ohāriu seat from 1996 to 2017. In both instances the party vote for those parties fluctuated considerably, sometimes bringing in more members and sometimes none. New Zealand First did well in the first MMP election with 17 seats and entered a Coalition with National that later broke up. The level of support for the Green Party has been relatively consistent since 1999, when they first contested an election on their own. The Alliance led by Jim Anderton did well in 1996 with 13 seats and at that time included three Green MPs, but the Alliance later imploded. Jim Anderton held his Sydenham seat and joined up again with Labour. While MMP has given minor parties the possibility of a political life in Parliament it has not made it easy for them to remain there.

Election results

2020

A Labour majority government, with a cooperation agreement with the Green Party.
Seats: Labour 65, Green Party 10, National Party 33, ACT Party 10, Māori Party 2
Number of seats in House: 120

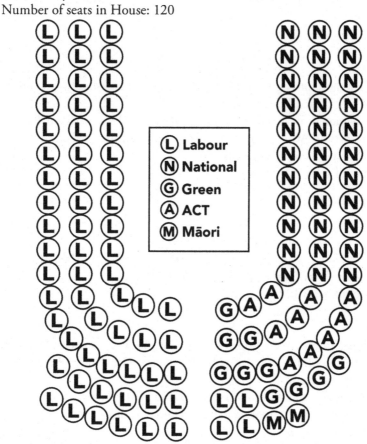

2017

A Labour New Zealand First minority coalition government with confidence and supply agreement with the Green Party.
Seats: National 56, Labour 46, New Zealand First 9, Green Party 8, ACT 1 (David Seymour)
Number of seats: 120

2014

A National minority government with confidence and supply agreements with ACT, United Future, and the Māori Party.
Seats: National 60, Labour 32, Green Party 14, New Zealand First 11, Māori Party 2, ACT 1 (David Seymour), United Future Party 1 (Peter Dunne)
Number of seats: 121

2011

A National minority government with confidence and supply agreements with ACT, United Future, and the Māori Party.
Seats: National 59, Labour 34, Green Party 14, New Zealand First 8, Māori Party 3, ACT 1, (John Banks), United Future 1, (Peter Dunne) Mana Party 1, (Hone Harawira).
Number of seats: 121

2008

A National minority government with confidence and supply agreements with Act, United Future, and the Māori Party.
Seats: National 58, Labour 43, Green Party 9, ACT 5, Māori Party 5, Progressive Party (Jim Anderton) 1, United Future 1
Number of Seats 122

2005

A Labour minority coalition government the Progressive (Anderton) Party with confidence and supply agreements with United Future and New Zealand First.
Seats National 48, Labour 50, New Zealand First 7, Green Party 6, ACT 2, Māori Party 4, Progressive Party 1, United Future 3.
Number of seats 121

2002

A minority Labour Progressive Coalition government with a confidence and supply agreement with United Future.
Seats: Labour 52, National 27, New Zealand First 13, Green Party 9, ACT 9, Progressive Party 2, United Future 8.
Number of seats 120

1999

A Labour Party and Alliance Party minority coalition with a confidence and supply agreement with the United Future Party.
Seats: Labour 49, National 39, Alliance 10, ACT 9, Green Party 7, NZ First 5, United Future 1 (Peter Dunne)
Number of seats: 120

1996

A National Party and New Zealand First majority coalition.
Seats: National 44, Labour 37, New Zealand First 17, Alliance 13, ACT 8, United Future 1 (Peter Dunne)
Number of seats 120

Māori seats

A unique aspect of our electoral and governance system is the existence of Māori seats. This is a mechanism to ensure that there is Māori representation in Parliament. In Aotearoa New Zealand, voters can be enrolled in either the general roll or people of Māori descent can choose to be enrolled in the Māori roll. Under MMP, the Māori roll has the same options for the party vote but will have different options for the electoral candidate. There are currently seven Māori electorate seats. However, they are not an entrenched element of our electoral law and could be abolished by a majority vote in Parliament.

The Māori seats were established in the political context of the Kīngitanga movement and the end of the New Zealand Wars. The pan-tribal development of the Kīngitanga movement made the British authorities nervous. In 1867, the colonial Parliament determined to end Māori self-government and bring Māori under the colony's authority. To this end, Parliament voted to establish four Māori seats in the House of Representatives, initially as a temporary experiment. All Māori males over 21 could vote. At this stage, Pākehā males were still subject to a property qualification to be eligible to vote. However, since Māori held lands as hāpu, iwi, or whānau groups and did not have the same te ao Pākehā signification of property where land was owned under individual freehold or leasehold titles, this property requirement was waived to simplify things. These seats became permanent in 1876 and are still a part of our electoral system despite being the subject of controversy from time to time.

The role of political parties

Political parties play a vital role in the function of our democracy. They provide much of the machinery of political organisation and discussion in the communities, select candidates to run for the party in elections, and they decide party policy and promote it.

Political parties are neglected by our constitutional law in a similar way to how Cabinet is treated. Parties profoundly influence public decision-making, yet they are treated to a large extent by the law as private organisations. The two major parties have no corporate personality; they are not even incorporated societies which makes them harder to sue in the courts and to enforce any judgment. Parties are only slightly regulated by the need to be registered. There is one provision in the Electoral Act section 71, that prevents the worst types of abuse and candidate rigging:

Requirement for registered parties to follow democratic procedures in candidate selection
Every political party that is for the time being registered under this Part shall ensure that provision is made for participation in the selection of candidates representing the party for election as members of Parliament by—
(a) current financial members of the party who are or would be entitled to vote for those candidates at any election; or
(b) delegates who have (whether directly or indirectly) in turn been elected or otherwise selected by current financial members of the party; or
(c) a combination of the persons or classes of persons referred to in paragraphs (a) and (b).

What has happened over time is that MPs now arrive in the House as members of a political party to which they have pledged loyalty and they will try to carry out its policies that they have been sent there to promote. People are free to join political parties but many fewer do than was the case up until the 1960s. Those who do belong nowadays tend to be passionately interested in politics and may wish to become parliamentary candidates. Party members are active in fund raising and canvassing the electorate to see where the support lies and getting the vote out at election time.

Party rules are also important in determining who may become the Leader. This is most pronounced in the Labour Party where the Leader must be determined by the votes cast in a preferential election by an electoral college in a system of weighted voting:

- Members of the parliamentary Labour Party 40 per cent
- Party members 40 per cent
- Affiliated members (trade unions) 20 per cent.

With the National Party it is simpler. The Parliamentary Party elects the Leader who, upon receiving the approval of the Board of the Party, becomes the Leader. The political parties all have quite elaborate constitutions and rules that need to be read carefully by people wishing to become members.

Despite the importance of political parties, membership has declined drastically since the 1950s. Nonetheless National and Labour remain the two main political parties in terms of voting behaviour in recent elections. But, to a large extent, they are now both cadre parties rather than political parties with a mass membership base. They are dominated by an elite group of political activists. This has consequences for citizen engagement with the machinery of government and governance. Fewer people have a direct involvement these days with the issues that concern political parties, and many feel less connection with the system.

Review

In October 2021 the government announced a review of electoral law. It is in two stages. The first changes aim to help the delivery of the 2023 election. The second is an independent review of electoral laws ahead of the 2026 General Election, with an independent panel to report by 2023. The longer review will look at: voting age and overseas voting; funding of political parties, the length of the parliamentary term; and the 1996 Electoral Commission Te Kaitiaki Take Kowhiri's recommendations on MMP. These are specified as changes to party vote threshold, the one seat electorate rule, ratio of electorate seats to list seats, and the overhang rule. Outside the scope of the review are: online voting; a return to First-Past-the Post; the future of the Māori electorate seats; fundamental constitutional change, such as becoming a republic or having an upper house.

References
Keith Jackson and Alan McRobie, *New Zealand Adopts Proportional Representation* (Ashgate Aldershot, 1998); Neill Atkinson *Adventures in Democracy – A History of the Vote in New Zealand* (University of Otago Press, 2003); Raymond Miller, *Democracy in New Zealand (Auckland University Press, 2015);* Ryan Malone, *Rebalancing the Constitution – The Challenge of Government Law-Making under MMP* (Institute of Policy Studies, Wellington, 2008); Claire Robinson, *Promises, Promises—80 years of wooing New Zealand voters* (Massey University Press, Auckland, 2019); Report of the Royal Commission on the Electoral System , *Towards a Better Democracy* (December 1986, Appendices to the Journals of the House of Representatives H3 14.

Additional resources
Henry Cooke from *Stuff* wrote a four-part series published in October 2021 on 25 years of MMP: https://www.stuff.co.nz/national/politics/300426115/mmp-at-25-how-an-academic-dream-from-west-germany-changed-new-zealand-forever

14 Your vote

Do not think your single vote does not matter much. The rain that refreshes the parched ground is made up of single drops. —Kate Sheppard

Voting is one of the most crucial elements of representative democracy – it's the lifeblood of the system. By international standards, the percentage of eligible voters who vote in Aotearoa New Zealand is high, but it has fallen in recent years. In 2020, 82.2 per cent of enrolled voters turned out to vote, but in 2011 only 69.57 per cent of people eligible to enrol voted. The Electoral Commission Te Kaitiaki Take Kōwhiri reported that this was the lowest recorded turnout for a Parliamentary election in this country since the adoption of universal suffrage in 1893. The turnout, however, increased in the next three elections. Turnout in the Māori electorates in 2020 was 69.1 per cent; the highest since 1999 when it was 70.65 per cent.

In Aotearoa New Zealand, unlike Australia, it is not compulsory to vote, although everyone is legally required to register as an elector with a registrar of electors, which means to enrol. The Electoral Commission Te Kaitiaki Take Kōwhiri estimated that 94.1 per cent of eligible voters were enrolled in 2020, up from 92.4 per cent in 2017, and the highest enrolment rate since 2008. Youth turnout also rose with 80 per cent of the eligible 18 to 29 years enrolled in comparison with 75 per cent in 2017.

It can often be tricky to work out how to vote but the process is quite easy. This chapter will act as your ultimate how-to guide for how to vote in a Parliamentary election in Aotearoa New Zealand. There are four basic steps that you need to follow:

1. Enrol to vote
2. Decide who you are going to vote for
3. Plan where and when you're going to vote
4. Vote!

Let's go through these steps in a little more detail.

How do I enrol to vote?

For your vote to count, you need to be enrolled on the Electoral Roll. If you are concerned about your safety or privacy, you may also apply to be enrolled on the confidential unpublished roll. This keeps your enrollment details secure and private. You can enrol in advance of election day, or you can enrol in a voting place when you go in to vote, although the former is normally recommended.

Before you enrol you will need to check your eligibility. You can enrol to vote if you are 18 years or older, are either a New Zealand citizen or permanent resident, and have lived in Aotearoa New Zealand for more than 12 months continuously at any time. To enrol you will also need to know which electorate you live in. You can find this out on the vote.nz website. If living overseas, you should enrol in the electorate where you last lived in Aotearoa New Zealand for one month or longer. If you're of Māori descent and enrolling for the first time you can choose whether to enrol on the Māori roll or the general roll. If you are enrolled in the Māori roll you will vote in a Māori electorate but will still have the same choice of political parties for your party vote.

Currently, there are four main ways that you can enrol before an election period:

- Go to **vote.nz** online and follow the online enrolment form instructions. To enrol online, you will need a current valid New Zealand Driver's license, passport, or RealMe ID.
- **Download, print, and complete** an enrollment form from the vote. nz website. Sign and return the completed form by email, post, or by uploading on the vote.nz website.
- **Call 0800 36 76 56** to have an enrolment form sent to you in the mail. Sign and return the completed form by email, post, or by uploading on the vote.nz website.
- **Text 3676** to have an enrolment form sent to you in the mail. Sign and return the completed form by email, post, or by uploading on the vote.nz website. This is a free text.

You should email your form to enrol@vote.nz or post it to:
Electoral Commission
FREEPOST 2 ENROL
PO BOX 190
Wellington 6140

If you have enrolled to vote at least a month prior to the election day you will receive an EasyVote card and an information pack in the mail. If you bring your EasyVote card with you on the day you vote, then the process will be quicker. The information pack will include information on how to vote and who the candidates and political parties are.

How do I decide who to vote for?

There are several ways that you can make sure that you are informed and decide whom you would like to vote for. The easiest way to learn more and figure out your own views is simply to engage with politics. You could do this by paying attention to the news or by discussing politics with your friends, family, and other people you know. Public debate and deliberation help fuel democracy. You can look up political parties' websites to discover more about their candidates, policies, values, and ideas. There are also online resources that can help you compare political parties' views to your own including Vote Compass, On the Fence, and Policy.nz.

Remember, you have two votes: party vote and an electorate vote. Your electorate vote is for which candidate you would like to represent your local electorate area and your party vote is your political party preference. The percentage of people who cast a party vote for a certain political party will be proportional to the percentage of seats in the House of Representatives that party receives. You can vote for one political party in your party vote and a candidate that comes from a different political party for your electorate vote. There are various ways to be strategic about this.

How do I vote?

You can normally vote from two weeks before the election date up to 7pm on election day, although sometimes this changes. Voting places may have different voting hours in the two weeks lead-up but generally will be open from 9am-7pm on election day. You can easily search online to find a nearby voting place. They are often in community centres, churches, or schools, and there should be one close to wherever you are in Aotearoa New Zealand. Although you can vote at any voting place it is quicker if you vote in the electorate where you live.

You do not need to bring your ID or anything else with you when you vote but the process is quicker if you bring your EasyVote card. When you arrive, someone will explain the process, answer your questions, and give you a voting paper. You will fill out your voting paper behind a screen so that the process is private. The secret ballot is a fundamental feature of the electoral system. You tick next to the name of the electorate candidate you would like to vote for on the right side of the paper. You tick next to the name of the party you would like to vote for on the left side of the paper. If you make a mistake, you can take your paper back and ask for another one.

Once you have filled out your paper you put it in the ballot box and your vote is cast!

You can also cast a postal vote or vote from overseas. You can apply to register for postal voting by calling 0800 36 76 56 and you will be sent voting papers to return either by post or by dropping them off at a voting place. If overseas, you can download your voting papers and can cast your vote either by posting or delivering them to an overseas voting place, by fax, or by uploading them to the vote.nz website. They can also be posted back to the Electoral Commission Te Kaitiaki Take Kōwhiri. The Electoral Commission Te Kaitiaki Take Kōwhiri also offers in-person voting at overseas voting places, for example at embassies or High Commissions. If you vote from overseas, from outside of your electorate, or if you enrol when you vote or are on the unpublished roll, your vote will count as a 'special vote' and may be counted after provisional election results. It will still count.

References

Electoral Commission *Enrol or update online*. Retrieved from: https://vote.nz/enrolling/enrol-or-update/enrol-or-update-online/; Electoral Act 1993 https://www.legislation.govt.nz/act/public/1993/0087/latest/DLM307519.html

Additional resources

See also for special voting rules: Electoral Regulation 1996 (SR 1996/93)s
The Spinoff *Make Me Tick* [series] (The Spinoff, 2017) https://www.youtube.com/watch?v=3mgdtKG40ZM&list=PL-xxT3W4uRNZwM2yCrRoKK4qZDrCM80Rv

15 Cabinet

Cabinet is the powerhouse of our system of government. It occupies the pinnacle of political power and makes the decisions that govern the country. Cabinet typically comprises 20 Ministers of the Crown presided over by the Prime Minister. Cabinet's purpose is to discuss and make decisions on significant policy issues, proposals that would affect constitutional arrangements or the structure of the public service, draft government bills, and more. Most important decisions are made by the Cabinet, although some are made by individual ministers.

Although not all ministers are part of the Cabinet, they are all part of the Executive Council. The Executive Council holds regular meetings with the Governor-General, following the Cabinet meetings. Because our Head of State acts on ministerial advice these meetings are the mechanism by which much of this advice is given. The Cabinet itself has no legal powers of its own. The government works through individual ministers within their own portfolios, or areas of responsibility, for the most part. Ministers supervise and direct the work of public servants in accordance with Cabinet decisions.

All ministers are also required to be elected Members of Parliament. This means that, unlike countries with greater separation of powers, Aotearoa New Zealand has very strong executive power. The legislative branch, our Parliament, is joined to the executive branch, meaning our ministers and public service, through Cabinet. An Australian constitutional lawyer once opined that Aotearoa New Zealand was an 'executive paradise' because of the relative lack of checks and balances on executive power.

The Cabinet must enjoy the confidence of the House of Representatives. If its support declines, for whatever reason, and it cannot command a majority of the House then there will likely be a new administration or an early general election. Confidence votes can occur about six times a year and the government can also move a confidence vote on itself in the House and secure a vote on it.

Cabinet must also secure 'supply' from Parliament, which means the approval to spend public monies. Parliament – both the Head of State and the House of Representatives – are obliged to ensure that Acts of Parliament control taxes, loans, and the spending of any public money. The Constitution Act 1986 requires Parliament to agree on these measures. Government cannot carry on without money and it is Parliament, not the government, that has the ultimate control of public finance. If the government cannot get their budget approved by the Parliament, it will fall. Under the MMP electoral system that we have had since 1996, minority or coalition governments will often rely on confidence and supply agreements where other political parties promise to support the government on these two matters. It is a good approach to understanding politics to find out where the money is being spent. If in doubt follow the money!

Strangely, Cabinet is unknown to the law. The Constitution Act 1986 contains no mention of it nor is it set up under the authority of any other Acts of Parliament. It is founded, for the most part, on constitutional convention. Conventions are recognised norms, practices, or customs that are generally followed. They are rules of political obligations rather than rules of law. The most important constitutional conventions arose to ensure the democratic nature of the constitution. For example, the convention that the legal powers of the Governor-General and the Queen are exercised on the advice of the ministers was put in place gradually, since the powers of the monarchy were established a long time ago when hereditary kings had real political power, which is incompatible with modern democracy. Conventions are somewhat slippery and can change over time: one British writer likened them to the 'procreation of eels'.

You can find out who the ministers are and what they're responsible for by consulting the ministerial list. Ministers are given an official ranking which may act as a guide to their political influence and importance. This can be changed at any time, even if there has not been an election. The ministerial list is on the Cabinet Office website: https://dpmc.govt. nz/our-business-units/cabinet-office/ministers-and-their-portfolios/ ministerial-list

It is important when examining the ministerial list to keep in mind the minister's ranking, whether the minister is in Cabinet, and the nature of the minister's portfolio responsibilities. We set out three entries from the present ministerial list as examples, for the ministers ranked 2nd, 11th, and 20th. After number 20 they are ministers outside

Cabinet or under-secretaries, who have fewer responsibilities than ministers, but are members of the Executive. Associate ministers have areas of responsibility delegated to them by the principal minister. The delegations are in writing and publicly available. Remember, Cabinet can be reshuffled from time to time, and it is important to check who is responsible for what as time goes on.

2 Hon Grant Robertson
Deputy Prime Minister
Minister of Finance
Minister for Infrastructure
Minister for Racing
Minister for Sport and Recreation.

11 Hon Damien O'Connor
Minister of Agriculture
Minister for Biosecurity
Minister for Land Information
Minister for Rural Communities
Minister for Trade and Export Growth

20 Hon Dr Ayesha Verrall
Minister for Food Safety
Minister for Seniors
Associate Minister of Health
Associate Minister of Research, Science and Innovation

How Cabinet works

Cabinet meets in the private Cabinet room at the top of the Beehive most weeks of the year to make major decisions. There are various rules surrounding the processes and procedures of Cabinet that protect the integrity of the decision-making process and ensure that it is orderly and well-considered. The Prime Minister, however, is the final arbiter of Cabinet procedure.

Cabinet submissions are papers that ask Cabinet to consider a proposal or issue in their discussions. Ministers sign off on Cabinet submissions that relate to their areas of responsibility. They must be filed on time. Usually they are written by officials, but ministers can write their own. Typically, they are distributed to ministers at the end of the week for consideration at the Monday Cabinet meetings. Ministers, both those in and out of Cabinet, often spend quite a portion of their weekend reading and considering Cabinet submissions so that they can engage in a collective discussion about them. When this discussion is complete the Prime Minister sums up the nature of any decisions and the Secretary records it.

Cabinet's decisions are recorded in meeting minutes, which are approved by the Secretary of the Cabinet, currently Michael Webster. He and the Deputy Secretary sit in on the meetings. The minutes are closely scrutinised and faithfully followed. These minutes are known as the 'Cabinet greens' because they are printed on green coloured paper. Minutes are not distributed to all ministers. Instead, they are accessible to: the responsible minister; ministers who are members of the Cabinet Committee that the paper was submitted to; and to ministers and chief executives with an interest in or responsibility over the issue involved. This is to avoid inadvertent disclosure or 'leaks'.

Since 2017 a more streamlined system involving modern technology has been in use. It has a slightly different set of protocols, known as CabNet, which is a secure digital platform for supporting Cabinet and Cabinet Committee processes. It is the workflow system for Cabinet and its committees and the central repository of Cabinet papers and minutes of decisions. This electronic system of filing Cabinet submissions and appendices has many advantages for remote access for authorised people and facilitating rapid decision-making, as required for Covid-19. The system is fully explained in the Cabinet Guide: https://dpmc.govt.nz/publications/cabguide

Much of Cabinet's business is transacted before Cabinet Committees. These are smaller committees made up of Cabinet members and are designed to encourage detailed deliberation over particular issues. Other officials can be invited to Cabinet Committees to explain proposals and be questioned on them. Meetings are held in a special room designed specifically for the purpose. Ministers also have the opportunity of conducting discussion among themselves. How much interaction there is with officials at these committee meetings varies. When the committee has arrived at a decision this is reported at the next full Cabinet meeting for confirmation.

In 2021 there were 10 Cabinet Committees:

- Appointments and Honours Committee
- Business Committee
- Priorities Committee
- Economic Development Committee
- Environment, Energy and Climate Committee
- External Relations and Security Committee
- government Administration and Expenditure Review Committee
- Legislation Committee
- Māori Crown Relations: Te Arawhiti Committee
- Social Wellbeing Committee.

Individual votes are rarely cast in Cabinet and it is usual that an overall consensus decision is made. It may be that some Ministers inside of the Cabinet are opposed to some of the proposals that are accepted. However, they must accept the Cabinet decision. This is known as collective responsibility and it is a principle which is at the heart of Cabinet. Once a decision has been taken, all ministers are obliged to support it, regardless of their personal views. One of the founders of the United States, Benjamin Franklin, once said, *'we must indeed all hang together, or, most assuredly, we shall all hang separately'*, and this sentiment holds true of the nature of Cabinet government in Aotearoa New Zealand. This principle is important because the government can only have one policy, not competing policies. Otherwise there is confusion.

However, when there is a coalition government, as there are frequently now under MMP, the smaller party or parties in the coalition may wish to preserve their distinctive policy ideas and express disagreements with Cabinet-agreed policies. Coalition governments may, therefore, establish 'agree to disagree' processes which may allow ministers to maintain different positions on particular issues in public. However, collective responsibility will still apply to the areas of portfolio responsibility of these ministers. Portfolios are the particular areas of responsibility assigned to a minister. For example, in this present government, the Green Party MP Hon. James Shaw is the Minister for Climate Change but not a member of Cabinet. There is a detailed cooperation agreement between the Greens and Labour currently. This means that James Shaw is bound by collective responsibility in issues regarding Climate Change, and therefore must agree on Cabinet decisions regarding this issue, but not in other areas where the Green Party may have different policies.

Ministerial responsibilities are divided into portfolios, although all major policies must be agreed upon by the full Cabinet. The names of these portfolios can vary from time to time depending on the preferences of the government of the day. Ministers outside Cabinet do not attend Cabinet meetings unless asked to by the Prime Minister but have the same overall duties and responsibilities as Cabinet Ministers. Individual ministers are responsible for deciding on policy priorities and objectives within their portfolio area(s). They are usually responsible for one or more government departments or agencies. They have considerable influence over the public service. They have individual ministerial responsibility over their decisions, their actions, and the decisions and actions of individuals and organisations they have responsibility over. Ministers supervise and direct the work of public servants in accordance with Cabinet decisions.

In the 2020 general election, for the first time since the introduction of MMP, a single party – the Labour Party – won an overall majority in Parliament. They hold 65 seats out of a total of 120. This meant Labour did not need to make arrangements with other parties in order to form a government but nevertheless does have an agreement with the Green Party. In the present government, there are 20 Ministers in Cabinet, all of whom are Labour Party MPs. There are four Labour Party Ministers outside of Cabinet and two Green Party Ministers, described as co-operation agreement ministers. There are also two Labour Party Parliamentary Under-Secretaries who assist designated ministers. These two are also bound by collective responsibility.

References

Geoffrey Palmer, 'The Cabinet, the Prime Minister and the Constitution: Constitutional Background to Cabinet' (2006) 4 New Zealand Journal of Public and International Law 1; M S R Palmer, 'What is New Zealand's Constitution and who interprets it? Constitutional Realism and the Importance of Public Office-holders' (2006) 171 Public Law Review 133; Elizabeth McLeay *The Cabinet & Political Power* (Oxford University Press, Auckland, 1995).
Cabinet Office, Department of Prime Minister and Cabinet, *Cabinet Manual 2017.* https://dpmc.govt.nz/our-business-units/cabinet-office/supporting-work-cabinet/cabinet-manual This document is under revision at the time of writing and is the essential document to get to grips with how Cabinet is organised.
Cabinet Guide: https://dpmc.govt.nz/publications/cabguide

16 The Prime Minister's power

The Prime Minister's duties include command over important levers of power. As a key player in the world of politics and government in Aotearoa New Zealand, the Prime Minister must fulfil a wide variety of roles and responsibilities. The Prime Minister must lead the Executive government, manage a political party, communicate with the media and with the country, represent the country internationally, and more.

Prime ministerial power is not limitless and its exercise is circumscribed by a number of boundaries: the government must continue to enjoy the confidence of the House of Representatives; the Prime Minister's actions must be within the law; all big decisions must go through Cabinet – and it is not unknown for Prime Ministers occasionally to be against a collective decision that Cabinet makes.

So, what are the sources of Prime Ministerial power? What exactly does a Prime Minister do?

The Prime Minister is the head of government and, as such, is the principal adviser to the Head of State – the Queen, represented by the Governor-General. The Prime Minister is also the leader of their political party which means chairing the weekly caucus meetings that are held in secret in order to decide on issues and to enable a party to present a unified face to the Parliament and to the public. The extent of electoral support a leader of a political party maintains among the country at large is an important ingredient in the authority wielded.

The Prime Minister is also the principal political manager of the government and is in charge of coordinating its activities and super-intending the work of Cabinet – the primary engine of the government. Prime Ministers sit at the apex of a very large system of public service agencies in which many public servants work. In broad terms, they are responsible for how the system functions, alongside Cabinet Ministers. The Prime Minister is the ultimate guardian of the constitution.

One essential element of the role is also the responsibility for the norms and values of our uncodified constitution being upheld. The Prime Minister is the judge of ministerial behaviour, whether standards have been transgressed and dismissing a minister. Only the Prime Minister can give that advice to the Governor-General. The Prime Minister also recommends the appointment of ministers and the allocation of their portfolios to the Governor-General.

Another role is to be the chief spokesperson for the government. The office is a primary source of news and the Prime Minister's views, utterances, speeches, and actions are reported widely in every type of media. The Prime Minister must make speeches in and out of Parliament, give frequent media interviews and conferences, and, nowadays, be active on social media. As a source of hard news, the position is unrivalled.

The Prime Minister is the sole person who can advise on the date of a General Election and can cause an early election as long as there is confidence of the House. Since many MPs do not wish to face an early general election, this can be a source of political leverage.

An especially important part of the job is to promote the interests of Aotearoa New Zealand and speak on its behalf at the United Nations and other important international meetings on the world stage. This involves developing positive relationships with other heads of governments worldwide. The Prime Minister is also the overall supervisor of the country's security and safety and has many sources of intelligence and advice available in order to make judgments.

To fulfill all of these responsibilities, the Prime Minister is assisted by the Department of the Prime Minister and Cabinet. She has as well an Office (which is not part of DPMC), to provide personal support, media services, and advice of a party political nature. The Office handles the more political side of things and includes a Chief of Staff and media advisers headed by a Chief Press Officer, as distinct from the public servants that staff the Department.

The Department of the Prime Minister and Cabinet's mission statement describes that its *overall area of responsibility is helping to provide, at an administrative level, the "constitutional and institutional glue"' that underlies our system of parliamentary democracy.* It employs about 275 people and includes the Cabinet Office, the Honours Secretariat, a Policy Advisory Group and a Security Group, a Child Wellbeing and Poverty Reduction Group, a Health Transition Group and most recently a Covid-19 group. These groups change over time somewhat, depending on the other portfolio responsibilities of the Prime Minister and the country's changing needs.

Reference

Guyon Espiner and Tim Watkin (eds) *The 9th Floor-Conversations with five New Zealand Prime Ministers* (Bridget Williams Books Ltd and Radio New Zealand, Wellington, 2017).

17 The view from the 9th floor: Interview with Prime Minister, Rt Hon Jacinda Ardern, November 2021

Illustration by Ursula Palmer Steeds

Q: The first question we'd like to ask you is just what is the role of the Prime Minister?

A: The role of Prime Minister I would describe as being both routine, but also unexpected. Every Prime Minister will enter into office with a list of policy changes, programmes and initiatives that they would like to see implemented. Their role will be ensuring that, whether or not it's them that's driving it individually or ministers, this agenda progresses. The essence is coming in with that agenda and seeing it through. Then, a large part of the job is also governing through everything, in spite of what you plan. That can, to varying degrees, take up more or less time dependent on your good fortune. The unexpected can be everything, from managing the fact that your team are humans and we all make mistakes. It means managing these politics always, and managing whatever the global or domestic environment throws at you – whether it's international events or domestic natural disasters. Different parts of my term have been more heavily weighted to the latter, so it's been about how you then govern without losing sight of the things that you wanted to come in and change for the long term. That's been the challenge of my time in office.

Q: To what extent has your term as Prime Minister been dominated by unexpected emergencies, such as the mosque shootings, the Whakaari White Island volcanic eruption, and the COVID 19 pandemic?

A: When I was considering your questions, I wrote the word 'overwhelming' – these emergencies have dominated my term to an overwhelming degree at times. I think the only template that you can draw on to anticipate what your time in office may be like is the experience of those before you. And it's fair to say, having looked at the last long term period prime ministers had in office – and for me the predecessors were Bill English and John Key – they had the experiences of the Christchurch earthquakes, Pike River, and the Global Financial Crisis. On anyone's measure, those were substantial and nation-shaping events. And so I think if you took that as a rule of thumb, you'd think, well, over a nine-year period, you might have that number of events. But I don't think I necessarily anticipated the range that we've experienced in the past few years.

New Zealand is not unique in that. I look at Spain recently experiencing volcanoes, Australia and the horrific bush fires . . . But we've had some particularly devastating events: 15 March 2019 in Christchurch is one that, particularly when it comes to place-shaping events, I think will leave a mark for a long, long time. As will the pandemic on the world.

But as I say, governing is what you do in spite of those things. I feel a duty and a responsibility – when we reflect back on anyone's time in this place, I absolutely accept now that my time in this job will be defined by those things. I accept that. But I also feel a duty of care to make sure that that doesn't become a reason why we don't make progress on fundamental issues like child poverty and climate change.

Q: Yes, of course. We'd like to ask, so the Prime Minister's role is sometimes described as 'the minister for coordination', 'the government's prime communicator' and 'the political leader of the government'. Do you agree with these interpretations?

A: I do, and I think the degree to which a Prime Minister at any given time is seen to be any one of those things will depend a little bit on what drives and motivates them. If you're a Prime Minister who has been motivated by politics, and the sport of politics, then you might take a particular approach to what the idea of governance is. And what greater position from which to govern is there than being a Prime Minister? But if you are, like me, driven by ideas and change and policy, then you might see yourself as fitting into a range of those different pieces of the puzzle.

I would like to think that first and foremost, I'm a policy wonk. I'm sitting in the company of probably one of our prime policy wonks though, so I can't quite claim that degree. But I've got such huge satisfaction from coming in and being able to, in that first term, implement the Best Start payments, which was something that myself and a few others designed from Opposition. Mana in Mahi was also from something that we designed in Opposition. And now I hear our Ministry of Social Development officials say that's how we are now getting more and more young people into training and apprenticeships. I find that so satisfying!

So, I think it depends on the person. Political leader – that's if you really love the politics. Prime communicator, I think that, actually, that's probably the least flattering of all of them. Minister for coordination – that's a given, everyone has to be that part, and play that role. I feel like I do a bit of all of it. Less emphasis on the last one. But I like to think most Prime Ministers also have an interest in solutions and policy ideas. Maybe add that to the list!

Q: In your day-to-day work, how do you work alongside ministers and public servants in your role?

A: I like to be quite direct. I don't like to have too many layers between me – certainly not between me and ministers. One of my lasting memories of working in the British civil service was how much time I used to spend on things that I felt could be so easily remedied with closer relationships and even cohabitation in buildings. I could spend half a day setting up a call between ministers! Because over there, ministers sit within their departments rather than in a Beehive setting, for example, where you could just walk downstairs and resolve an issue like that. For me, the direct relationships that we can all have as a Cabinet lead to greater cohesion and greater efficiency, it just removes layers of bureaucracy.

I feel the same way about public servants, having the ability to really give direct and quick feedback so that you don't slow down processes. In a Covid environment, that's been so key. When working with Ministers and public servants directly, I like to engage in that detail of issues. I don't feel as if I can communicate ideas to the public unless I go through that process myself. So, that's why probably more public servants get to see my handwriting than perhaps in other places. It's probably, again, a reflection of what I've said before, if you're really interested in ideas, then being really engaged like that is just how I tend to work.

Q: How do you conduct Cabinet meetings?

A: I guess if I was stepping back a bit to provide an explainer for people around how ideas are generated in government or decisions are made: we have layers that a decision needs to go through, and some people would call it bureaucracy. I call it refinement. By having people who are coming at any issue from different experiences from outside of Parliament and different portfolios from inside – where they're getting advice from their officials around needing to think about everything from the perspective of a disability lens, or be it a fiscal lens, or be it a children lens – a Cabinet committee brings in many, many different perspectives. Then it goes up again and to Cabinet where we, again, have even more ministers engaging with it. That is just good policy making. Because unless you test these ideas with different ministers in different roles, but also backgrounds and experience, then you're just not road testing things properly. And so that, to me, is a really critical part of a process.

So, that then brings to me, how do I conduct cabinet meetings? I put papers and decisions into two different categories. Often they'll have gone through a really rigorous process, everyone's kind of really had their say. And so we'll present the paper, take it as read, to have a final round to see that everyone's content with it. Other times, actually, we might genuinely have not resolved the issue, it might be a vexed issue with multiple options. Often I'll either, if I've got a strong view, start by putting mine forward and saying, what's everyone else's or I'll just put the issue out there and I'll let it go around the room, which is quite often the case. From there, then I'll listen and think, okay, I can feel a bit of consensus forming around this option, I'll propose this as a way forward. So, that is often how we will work in the room.

I actually asked our cabinet secretary once, so how did other Prime

Ministers lead these discussions? And I think there's real variation, but for me, I would want to use the experience in the room because often we come out with a solid way forward just by being willing to let it play out and hear people's views and perspectives. And if we don't land on it, then I'll just make a decision and then we move on. But it is a solid process and it serves us well.

Q: Can you outline the role of the government caucus, and then your role in it as well?

A: I had the benefit of sitting in a caucus for the better part of a decade and then deciding what I felt like: what I had always wanted to see in a caucus. One thing that I hope is an indication of the way that we run it, when we're in the Cabinet room, I refer to everyone as Minister. It's a way of us just acknowledging the magnitude of the roles that we have and the respect we need to treat everyone and their perspectives with when we're in that room and with the decisions that we make. When I'm in the caucus room, ministers drop the 'Minister' title and we all just go by our first names. I can't quite get everyone to strip back and call me Jacinda, they still call me Prime Minister. For me, that's indicative of the environment that I want in our caucus – that we feel less like there's a hierarchy in that room – that we're all Labour MPs and we're all elected to be, first and foremost, Labour representatives. Caucus is the place where I expect that ministers bring policy and ideas to, to add to the process. So ideas start there and then goes up through the Cabinet process, sometimes the process flips around, but no matter what, our caucus need to be involved.

The most important job that I feel like I have there is to keep the unity, the cohesion, and people's sense of fulfilment by being part of that team. That's the thing that I really felt sometimes was hard in my time in opposition. That when you don't have unity and cohesion, then that's a really hard starting point for a team in an already difficult environment. So, I see my role as just keeping the team together, keeping us rolling through hard times, supporting one another, and making the most of the amazing experience in that room as well.

Q: How do you decide, and what criteria do you use, to recommend the appointment of ministers and the allocation of their portfolios?

A: This is one of those areas that no one can write a rule book for you around – what you need to do in order to make these very individual decisions. There's a couple of parts of the processes of Prime Minister that are very direct to you. One is your Cabinet – there's no one that sits down and gives you the policy advice to direct you on how to establish the Cabinet or who to put in different roles, that's all on you. And the other is the honours role, they're very clear, that process is at your discretion.

My way of making these decisions is that the Cabinet office prepare for me a bunch of portfolio cards and then every potential candidate's name. And literally I sit down either on my floor or with a whiteboard and I do a first cut of moving people and portfolios based on two criteria: the strengths of that individual, both in their experience in portfolio knowledge, but also in their personality and the way of operating. I try to match that based on whether or not I believe a portfolio needs to be a place where we need to direct change through putting that new person in that spot and how their personality will match with that, or, where we need just the ability to roll out a large programme or a tough programme, one that requires additional policy work. Either I'm signalling something with my choice or I'm pushing an agenda through with it. That's the process that I loosely go through.

I know that in some cases, Prime Ministers have not talked to the different members about the decisions until they're made. I don't do that. I will call and talk through my proposal. I'll hear a minister out on whether they're content. In fact, my first iteration often is to ask 'What's your bid? What would you like to do?' Then I call back and say, this is what I'm thinking. And I might make changes as a result, or I might stick with it, but we do have a conversation. So it's quite iterative, lots of moving around on the board.

Q: I wonder if you could describe the relationship the Prime Minister has to the Governor-General?

A: This is a part of the role that I think, probably unless you've already been in Cabinet, will be the one that has probably the most mystique to it. Most parts of the political process are quite public, and this one has a layer of a behind-the-scenes process and formality that is not otherwise seen or necessarily well understood. In some ways, ministers will have sometimes more of a day-to-day relationship with the Governor-General, in that when they have certain instruments that go to Executive

Council, they will appear and be questioned by the Governor-General, and be really a part of that final process where the Governor-General is essentially seeing off that final decision into confirmation. I, as Prime Minister, don't experience that as much, of course, because I don't have the policy responsibility for those instruments.

So instead, my relationship is one level up again. I engage with the Governor-General around elections – election dates, elections being called, and I, of course, confirm when I've been able to establish a government. Then there's the formal engagement around the swearing in and the speech from the throne. That's the level at which my relationship sits with the Governor-General. However, there's also the engagement that you have through the experiences that the nation's going through. During events such as memorial events and through times of crisis, I will talk to the Governor-General and explain the big decisions that we might be making because that is our ballast – the Governor-General is the ballast in our governance, that's how I see the role.

Q: And what about the Palace? Do you have much to do with that?

A: More so than I probably expected. So, again, when New Zealand has gone through times of tragedy and difficulty, despite us being one of many nations within the Commonwealth, the Palace has taken, I think, particular care of an interest in New Zealand. I've spoken to Her Majesty, since the pandemic, twice. She just wanted to see how New Zealand was. I've spoken to Prince Charles on a number of occasions. He's incredibly interested in what we do on environmental issues, very engaged. And I've met Prince William and Prince Harry a number of times. So I didn't expect that level of engagement. Nor did I expect the level of interest and knowledge in New Zealand and its affairs. It's quite striking for me. I have a philosophical position on New Zealand's future. But undeniably, I see the role that the Royal family plays for New Zealand here and now.

Q: Now, coming on from that, how much of your time do you have to spend with foreign leaders, foreign governments, and foreign policy issues?

A: Probably one of the most unexpected things for me was, not the engagement that you have, but the proportion of time that it takes up. I remember having a conversation with a minister, I proposed that they take on the role of foreign affairs and they sought to have additional portfolios. I said, you will be surprised by the weight of this portfolio. And after taking it on for a period of time, they acknowledged that I was right with that advice.

The same goes in this role. It takes up much more time than I expected. All my foreign affairs briefings come in a yellow folder. There is not one evening where I do not receive a yellow folder.

Bilateral engagements are constant. I have two bilaterals tomorrow, one next Tuesday, I think I've got maybe three or four in the lead up to APEC, and of course the chairing of APEC – it is substantial. Perhaps a surprising thing to me is the degree to which New Zealand sees it as a bit more of a 'nice to have' though. It is a challenge because I would travel far less than many of my counterparts. They're often surprised when they'll talk about different engagements, you know, will I see you at X or Y? And I always say, I'm very careful about what I travel to or what I'm a part of. Because New Zealand's strong view is, and rightly so, first and foremost, that we have to be focused on domestic affairs. Absolutely. No disagreement there for me. But there's a view that those international engagements are not as relevant and yet they are the ways that you lay the ground for your FTA [Free Trade Agreements] and your other important instruments. They're all about relationships, you know. I think about the foundations of those engagements over the Christchurch Call when we worked together with countries like France; it all, in the end, bears fruit.

Q: Do you think that, over the years, the Cabinet government system in New Zealand has become something more like Presidential government?

A: Perception? Perhaps yes. Practice? No.

From a practice perspective, the only thing that I think has adapted would probably be in the way that within the policy process now there's much more consultation with either coalition partners or supply and confidence partners. So you build that into your policy development. But otherwise, the perception is probably that it's much more presidential because of things such as quick media cycles that are constant, a social media world, and probably less focus generally on different ministers or different MPs. I think in the past, New Zealand's exposure to different ministers was probably a bit more than now, with the exception of this current period where they're seeing much more of our team. So I would say there's a presidential perception just based on the fact that there's a focus on a figurehead, but in terms of the way our system functions, we are well served by the fact that our Westminster system allows us to make very quick and nimble decisions when we need to. Coalitions can slow it down a bit, but not like the US. And this is not too dissimilar to the philosophy around having a Cabinet – you make, by and large, for the most part, better decisions as a result of going through a process that involves a range of people and experiences, and the same holds for political parties, for the most part. Sometimes where I would say that it doesn't apply as much is if you no longer have a debate on the issue itself, but it's used as leverage to get what you want, as a trade-off.

Q: The interesting thing is that the New Zealand government evolves constantly. It has to. It evolves to deal with COVID, it evolves to deal with MMP, it's changed a lot over the years. But what hasn't changed is that people still regard government as something that they want to do things for them. And they have not lost faith in government here, the way they have in many countries. And I wonder why that is. Is it because we're small?

A: Yeah. I mean, I do find it interesting sometimes, that sense of 'Ugh, government, ergh, nah, but my local MP is good! Yeah, nah, he's a hard working chap.' I think it's all about proximity – I think so long as we have a sense that there's a proximity to our political representatives, where they don't feel too disconnected, where you feel at least that they're of your community, that they have some understanding of your experience. I think that is really key to the way that we operate in New Zealand. So long as you can see your politicians in common places, supermarkets and your local dairy! Then we feel connected.

Q: It's a sense of community in some ways, isn't it, and in a big country with millions of millions of people, you lose that. Well now, I wonder, how do you ration your time? Because there's far too much to do, the demands on the Prime Minister are extraordinary. So how do you manage to ration your time and rest?

A: I would say, I don't martyr sleep. When I first came into the job, people would often ask me, oh, you mustn't sleep and I almost felt like that it would look like I was somehow not working hard enough, if I said, no, actually, I do prioritise getting a good night's sleep. My last

Labour predecessor was Helen Clark, who famously slept very little. So I thought, oh, will people think I'm not working as hard? But I've since been very open about the fact that I'll sacrifice many other things, but I try not to sacrifice that. Because I noticed it impairs my decision-making. And so that's not good for the country! Certainly, I don't get a huge amount, I wouldn't say that, but I don't run on three to four hours.

Q: What do you think the best features of being Prime Minister are?

A: There's no other job in the world where you can simultaneously be making decisions that you know will change the long-term future of a country whilst also getting the joy of seeing the impact of the little things. And that's, to me, the privilege of the job. To give you an example, I know the architecture we've created for climate change will make a long-term difference, but at the same time, I get the same joy from that legislation passing as I do from going out on the road and seeing a young person make the decision to be vaccinated. I get the same satisfaction. How many jobs do you get to see things at both levels?

Q: On the other side of that coin, what are the worst things about it?

A: The grinding anxiety.

Q: Yes, quite, and quite a lot of abuse too?

A: Yeah, do you know what, I always thought that would have a bigger impact on me than it does. I remember my dad being quite concerned about me choosing to enter into politics because he knew how thin-skinned I am. And I am; I'm a very sensitive person, I take everything to heart, I worry about everyone. I expected, you know, comments about the way I look or those superficial things to upset me, but they genuinely don't.

Instead, the thing that I find hard is the grinding anxiety of the 'what if?' A pandemic is the worst for that.

Q: Well, the thing is that the science isn't settled yet, you can't predict what's going to happen. And it's so difficult to navigate your way through that. There's no road map.

A: And all we've got instead is countries doing their own version of things, and you're sitting left feeling like, well, what is my option if that doesn't feel right for us? When people just want certainty in an uncertain environment.

When we have a situation that arrives on our doorstep, I'm very quick now just to kick into the mode of action, pulling together a team, working very hard to get things in order, designing our response, and getting on with it. But in between times, there is just this constant feeling of 'what if?' What might come our way next? And that never goes away.

Q: Now, is there anything you would like to say about anything that is on your mind, or what you are planning to do maybe next year ?

A: Next year I would like to get back to our non-Covid agenda. So, particularly next year, it will be very climate focused for us. We are on a steep curve where we built the architecture and now we need to roll out the plan. So that's a big focus for us.

What I hope though is that, whenever my time comes to leave this job, that those who might be sitting either in a classroom or somewhere thinking about maybe whether they'd like to do this job in the future, I'd like to think that there's a wider group now of people who might think they could, than perhaps before.

I don't say that from a gendered perspective. For me, I'd like to think that anyone who sees themselves as maybe being quite driven by empathy, or a bit sensitive, or maybe a bit on the anxious side, or not overly confident, or not driven by ego or power – I just hope a wider range of people can look at leadership and say, well, actually you can do it a bit differently. I hope that exists once I leave.

18 The Public Service and the State Sector

Pretty much without exception, all the people I have met over the course of my career as a public servant have been focused, committed and passionate about making a difference in our country. They, at the very least, deserve our respect.
—Peter Hughes, Public Service Commissioner, 2021

Modern governance is extraordinarily complicated and logistically tiresome. Parliament makes the most important decisions, enacts laws, and decides how money is spent. Important as they are, ministers would not achieve much if they had to do everything alone. It is one thing to adopt a policy, it is another to have it implemented. It is the unsung heroes in the public service that actually make the system work and ensure that the decisions are converted into operational reality. Not only do they provide administrative grunt in the implementation of policies but they also provide substantial advice on what new policies should be adopted.

It is fair to say that the public service is the most important ingredient in the development of policy, not merely its execution. Policy ideas can come from many quarters – spurred from debates in Parliament, to petitions, to conversations out on the street – but they all must be tested under close examination and analysis to see whether once put into practice they will achieve what has been intended. It is hard indeed to foresee what the unintended repercussions of changes may turn out to be and policy blunders are not uncommon. Consequently, this tends to make policy analysis in the public service a cautious and careful practice rather than visionary. However, independent inquiries, such as from a Royal Commission, deliberations amongst political parties, MPs, and other actors may bring fresh thinking to bear, and if ministers agree then new ideas may prevail. The public service has nothing like a monopoly on policy, which is a great deal more contested than it once was.

The core principles that govern the public service are set out clearly in the Public Service Act 2020:

The public service supports constitutional and democratic government, enables both the current government and successive governments to develop and implement their policies, delivers high-quality and efficient public services, supports the government to pursue the long-term public interest, facilitates active citizenship, and acts in accordance with the law.

The Act declares that *'[t]he fundamental characteristic of the public service is acting with a spirit of service to the community.* It is also tasked with the role of *'supporting the Crown in its relationships with Māori under the Treaty of Waitangi (te Tiriti o Waitangi).* The public service must provide free and frank advice to its ministers. The ministers decide what advice to adopt and what to reject.

The public service of Aotearoa New Zealand enjoys a long tradition of political neutrality going back as far as 1912. This means that if the government changes and a new political party rises to power the public servants do not lose their jobs. Such disruptive change does occur in some countries. Here public servants are promoted on the basis of merit, rather than on a political basis. The public service is also, by law, required to exercise stewardship in relation to its long-term capabilities, knowledge, systems, and processes.

As with all our political institutions, the public service must act within the law. It is also meant to foster a culture of open government, as its purpose is to serve the community, not only the ministers. It is the job of the Public Service Commission Te Kawa Mataaho, headed by a Commissioner, but supported by a staff, to lead the public service so that it works as a system to deliver better services and achieve better outcomes for the public. The Commissioner is also required to promote integrity, accountability, and transparency through the agencies in the State Services – a category that is wider than the public service itself, as we shall see. The Commissioner acts as the employer of the public service chief executives and appoints them and reviews their performance. Appointment procedures at the top are thorough and rigorous.

The public service is a career service, but in more recent times it has become increasingly common to use private sector consultants and experts under contractual arrangements. This trend has probably increased because of emergencies that have arisen, such as the earthquakes and terrorist attacks in Christchurch Ōtautahi, the volcanic eruption at Whakaari White Island and the Covid-19 pandemic. These novel and exceptional situations have required rapid responses and the system has had to pivot quickly. People may also move in between private and public sector roles during their careers, a phenomenon known as the 'revolving door'.

The public service is made up of a collection of departments, some are called ministries but it is the same thing. Each of them is headed by a Chief Executive. Each department has extensive responsibilities that are not always evident from their names. For example, the Department of Internal Affairs Te Tari Taiwhenua was the original agency in the early days from which many others were later derived. It still has a wide variety of disparate tasks. For example, Internal Affairs supplies passports, deals with local government, gambling regulation, racing, the National Library, and Archives. This sole Department reports to six ministers over seven ministerial portfolios. The Ministry of Business Innovation and Employment Hīkina Whakatutuki has an even wider range of responsibilities. It reports to 14 different ministers occupying 18 different portfolios. This involves topics as diverse as immigration, work-place safety, business regulation, space law, energy, and other topics too numerous to set out. Below is the official list compiled by the Public Service Commission Te Kawa Mataaho of what are known as departments, which includes some called ministries. There is no magic in that name distinction.

- Crown Law Office Te Tari Ture o te Karauna
- Department of Conservation Te Papa Atawhai
- Department of Corrections Ara Poutama Aotearoa
- Department of Internal Affairs Te Tari Taiwhenua
- Department of the Prime Minister and Cabinet
- Education Review Office Te Tari Arotake Mātauranga
- government Communications Security Bureau Te Tira Tiaki
- Inland Revenue Department Te Tari Taake
- Land Information New Zealand Toitū Te Whenua
- Ministry for Culture and Heritage Manatū Taonga
- Ministry for Pacific Peoples Te Manatū mō ngā Iwi ō te Moana-nui-ā-Kiwa
- Ministry for Primary Industries Manatū Ahu Matua
- Ministry for the Environment Manatū Mō Te Taiao
- Ministry for Women Manatū Wāhine
- Ministry of Business, Innovation, and Employment Hīkina

Whakatutuki
- Ministry of Defence Manatū Kaupapa Waonga
- Ministry of Education Te Tāhuhu o te Mātauranga
- Ministry of Foreign Affairs and Trade Manatū Aorere
- Ministry of Health Manatū Hauora
- Ministry of Housing and Urban Development Te Tūāpapa Kura Kāinga
- Ministry of Justice Te Tāhū o te Ture
- Ministry of Māori Development Te Puni Kōkiri
- Ministry of Social Development Te Manatū Whakahiato Ora
- Ministry of Transport Te Manatū Waka
- New Zealand Customs Service Te Mana Ārai o Aotearoa
- New Zealand Security Intelligence Service Te Pā Whakamarumaru
- Oranga Tamariki Ministry for Children
- Public Service Commission Te Kawa Mataaho
- Serious Fraud Office Te Tari Hara Tāware
- Statistics New Zealand Tatauranga Aotearoa
- Te Kāhui Whakamana Rua Tekau mā Iwa Pike River Recovery Agency
- The Treasury Te Tai Ōhanga

The New Zealand Defence Force Te Ope Kātua O Aotearoa and the New Zealand Police Ngā Pirihimana O Aotearoa

There are several departments that do not fall under the power of the Public Service Commissioner, although they are part of the Crown. The two largest of these are the New Zealand Defence Force **Te Ope Kātua O Aotearoa** and the New Zealand Police Ngā Pirihimana O Aotearoa. Both of these are uniformed and organised under command hierarchies. The ordinary working methods of the public service are not appropriate for these uniformed services – the NZDF sometimes has to operate in hostile warlike situations in which it is obliged to kill people. According to the 2020 Report of the NZDF there are 15,232 personnel in the NZDF of whom 3,179 are civilians. They are divided up between the Army, Air Force and Navy. The armed forces also have substantial numbers of people in the 'reserves' who can be called upon when circumstances require it. Over the Covid-19 period, these forces have been helping to combat the pandemic. It is the role of the Ministry of Defence Manatū Kaupapa Waonga to provide civilian advice to the Minister of Defence, and the government, to balance the advice of the military itself. Both civilian and military defence officials enjoy equal status as servants of the minister and the Crown.

The New Zealand Police Ngā Pirihimana O Aotearoa are a nationwide organisation, not locally controlled as in some countries. It is essentially a law enforcement organisation consisting of about 14,000 people. This number includes several thousand non-sworn staff. Sworn constables are invested with special coercive powers that ordinary citizens do not have, such as the ability to arrest people suspected of committing offences, detaining them, and bringing them before the courts.

The Policing Act 2008 sets out the principles that govern the Police and the functions they perform. The Act states the following core principles:

(a) principled, effective, and efficient policing services are a cornerstone of a free and democratic society under the rule of law;
(b) effective policing relies on a wide measure of public support and confidence;
(c) policing services are provided under a national framework but also have a local community focus;
(d) policing services are provided in a manner that respects human rights;
(e) policing services are provided independently and impartially;
(r) in providing policing services every Police employee is required to act professionally, ethically, and with integrity.

The Act also outlines the functions of the Police:
(a) keeping the peace;
(b) maintaining public safety;
(c) law enforcement;
(d) crime prevention;
(e) community support and reassurance;
(f) national security;
(g) participation in policing activities outside New Zealand;
(h) emergency management.

The wider state sector and Quangoland

As well as the institutions covered above, there are a number of other entities that make up our State Services. A third non-public service is the Parliamentary Counsel Office Te Tari Tohutohu Pāremata (PCO) that drafts Bills to be introduced to Parliament. This Office consists of highly trained specialist lawyers with particular expertise in statute drafting and interpretation. There are also a small number of agencies attached to host departments which carry out specialist tasks, such as the Cancer Control Agency attached to the Ministry of Health or the Social Wellbeing Agency attached to the Public Service Commission Te Kawa Mataaho.

The wider State sector encompasses many more agencies tied to the Crown and the government to varying degrees. Many of them are independent from government, although members may be appointed by it. Others act as agents for the government. These are sometimes known as Quangos or quasi-autonomous non-governmental organisations. They tend to multiply rapidly over time. The Crown Entities Act 2005 sets out the law relating to them, and they are divided into a number of categories:

• Crown agents
• Autonomous Crown Entities
• Independent Crown Entities

The official list of Crown entities number exceeds by twice the departments in the public service:

Crown Agents

• Accident Compensation Corporation Te Kaporeihana Āwhina Hunga Whara
• Callaghan Innovation
• Civil Aviation Authority of New Zealand Te Mana Rererangi Tūmatanui o Aotearoa
• District Health Boards (of which there are 20 around the country)
• Earthquake Commission Kōmihana Rūwhenua
• Education New Zealand
• Energy Efficiency and Conservation Authority Te Tari Tiaki Pūngao

- Environmental Protection Authority Te Mana Rauhī Taiao
- Fire and Emergency New Zealand Whakaratonga Iwi
- Health Promotion Agency Te Hiringa Hauora
- Health Quality and Safety Commission Kupu Taurangi Hauora o Aotearoa
- Health Research Council of New Zealand Te Mahere Whakamātāmuatanga a Rangahau Hauora Aotearoa
- Kāinga Ora – Homes and Communities
- Maritime New Zealand
- Antarctica New Zealand
- New Zealand Blood Service Te Ratonga Toto O Aotearoa
- New Zealand Qualifications Authority Mana Tohu Mātauranga o Aotearoa
- New Zealand Tourism Board Manaakitanga Aotearoa
- New Zealand Trade and Enterprise Te Taurapa Tūhono
- New Zealand Walking Access Commission Ara Hīkoi Aotearoa
- Pharmaceutical Management Agency (PHARMAC) Te Pātaka Whaioranga
- Real Estate Authority Te Mana Papawhenua
- Social Workers Registration Board Kāhui Whakamana Tauwhiro
- Sport New Zealand Ihi Aotearoa
- Taumata Arowai The Water Services Regulator
- Tertiary Education Commission Te Amorangi Māturanga Matua
- Waka Kotahi NZ Transport Agency
- WorkSafe New Zealand Mahi Haumaru Aotearoa
- Autonomous Crown Entities (ACEs)
- Accreditation Council
- Arts Council of New Zealand Toi Aotearoa
- Broadcasting Commission
- government Superannuation Fund Authority
- Guardians of New Zealand Superannuation
- Heritage New Zealand Pouhere Taonga
- Museum of New Zealand Te Papa Tongarewa Board
- New Zealand Artificial Limb Service Peke Waihanga
- New Zealand Film Commission Te Tumu Whakaata Taonga
- New Zealand Infrastructure Commission Te Waihanga
- New Zealand Lotteries Commission
- New Zealand Symphony Orchestra Te Tira Pūoro o Aotearoa

- Public Trust Te Tari Tiaki Iwi
- Retirement Commissioner Te Ara Ahunga Ora
- Te Reo Whakapuaki Irirangi Māori Broadcasting Funding Agency
- Te Taura Whiri I Te Reo Māori Māori Language Commission
- Independent Crown Entities (ICEs)
- Broadcasting Standards Authority Te Mana Whanonga Kaipāho
- Children's Commissioner Manaakitia a Tātou Tamariki
- Climate Change Commission
- Commerce Commission Te Komihana Tauhokohoko
- Criminal Cases Review Commission Te Kāhui Tātari Ture
- Drug Free Sport New Zealand
- Electoral Commission Te Kaitiaki Take Kōwhiri
- Electricity Authority
- External Reporting Board Te Kāwai Ārahi Pūrongo Mōwaho
- Financial Markets Authority Te Mana Tatai Hokohoko
- Health and Disability Commissioner Te Toihau Hauora Hauātanga
- Human Rights Commission Te Kāhui Tika Tangata
- Independent Police Conduct Authority Mana Whanonga Pirihimana Motuhake
- Law Commission Te Aka Matua o Te Ture
- Mental Health and Wellbeing Commission
- New Zealand Productivity Commission Te Kōmihana Whai Hua o Aotearoa
- Office of Film and Literature Classification Te Tari Whakarōpū Tukuata, Tuhituhinga
- Privacy Commissioner Te Mana Mātāpono Matatapu
- Takeovers Panel
- Transport Accident Investigation Commission Te Komihana Tirotiro Aitua Waka

The Crown also owns or controls many other entities, more than a hundred. They are on the list on the Public Service Commissioner's website. Some are organised as companies under the Companies Act or under separate statutes. Others are trusts. Some are mixed ownership model companies, such as three energy companies that generate electricity. Seven carry out research for the government, others carry out commercial activities, and State-owned enterprises are businesses. There are 12 State-owned enterprises, some of them like Transpower, which reticulates electricity around the country, and the Airways Corporation which deals with air traffic control have vital public functions. The Reserve Bank Te Pūtea Matua has critical economic functions over the money supply and has its own statute. Radio New Zealand Te Reo Irirangi o Aotearoa and Television New Zealand Tātaki o Aotearoa are companies. Many tertiary education institutions of various types are set up under statute and in other ways are largely financed and controlled by the Crown, although more remotely and less directly than government departments of the public service. This includes eight universities and 16 polytechnics. And do not forget the 2,416 school boards of trustees. Just to complicate matters further, many of the entities mentioned in this chapter also have subsidiaries.

Conclusion

From the extensive range of topics and areas outlined above one can tell that the State, the Crown, and the ministers have their tentacles in many different activities. The degree of ministerial control varies substantially, but the financial connections are present. The wider responsibilities for the State sector provided to the Public Service Commissioner by section 44 of the Public Service Act 2020 are to: *'promote integrity, accountability, and transparency throughout agencies in the State services, including by setting standards and issuing guidance.'* This provision gives some power to the Public Service Commissioner over most, but not all of the agencies beyond the public service. Making such a large and diverse structure of organisations function effectively and efficiently is no tiny task. The house of governance of Aotearoa New Zealand contains many mansions.

References
Public Service Act 2020; Crown Entities Act 2005; Defence Act 1990; Policing Act 2008.

19 Parliament

Parliament is a noisy place at the best of times, but an experiment by National Foundation for the Deaf boss, Louis Carroll yesterday showed just how deafening it can be. A device to indicate that noise levels in the House during question time showed MPs, who have the assistance of microphones, regularly topped 90 decibels – the same as a lawnmower, and a level considered harmful.
—News item, *The Dominion Post*, 24 March 2011

Parliament is more than just a talking shop – it is the central democratic institution in Aotearoa New Zealand. As established, the term 'Parliament' refers to the House of Representatives plus the Sovereign.

Members of Parliament are elected to the House of Representatives in a democratic vote once every three years. The Prime Minister and ministers, who are important actors in the Executive branch of government, must also be MPs. This unique fusion distinguishes Westminster-style government from other systems, where power is more divided between the different branches. The celebrated editor of *The Economist*, Walter Bagehot, wrote in the 19th century:

The efficient secret of the English Constitution may be described as the close union, the nearly complete fusion, of the executive and legislative powers. . . . A Cabinet is a combining committee – a hyphen which joins, a buckle which fastens, the legislative part of the state to the executive part of the state.

This feature makes for a powerful government that can act decisively and rapidly when confronted with emergencies.

The first essential function of the Parliament must be to provide the government. This includes determining its identity, providing it with the confidence of the House, and granting supply so that the government can reach its financial obligations. It is a cardinal principle of our system that Cabinet is responsible to Parliament so that Parliament can act as a check and restraint if need be.

Parliament physically meets in Wellington Te Whanganui-a-Tara, our capital city, and transacts most of its business there. Most MPs must travel from their homes to attend, and when Parliament is sitting (which means it is in session), they will spend three nights a week in Wellington. However, the extensive parliamentary precinct accommodates many more people than simply MPs and has hundreds of people working on its grounds. It has produced an extraordinary and unique human sub-culture or community that revolves around politics and government.

When Parliament moved from Auckland Tāmaki Makaurau to Wellington Te Whanganui-a-Tara in 1865, it took over the Wellington Provincial Council Buildings, part of which still exist and remains in use as the Parliamentary Library. However, much of this complex was destroyed by fire in 1907 and a new building was erected, using Takaka marble. Only half of the new design was ever built and what was built could not be used until 1922. Later, the Beehive, a circular building made to accommodate the ministers, was opened by the Queen in 1977. The Parliament also occupies a few other buildings nearby. The original design for the Beehive sprang from a pencil sketch by distinguished British architect Sir Basil Spence done on a napkin at a dinner with Prime Minister Sir Keith Holyoake in 1964.

The various people and activities that need to be accommodated within the Parliamentary precinct are:

- MPs and staff for MPs
- Ministers' offices and ministerial staff
- The Speaker's offices and staff
- The Prime Minister's office and staff
- The Leader of the Opposition's offices and staff
- Rooms for meetings of the party caucuses
- The research units of the political parties
- Hansard reporters – who produce the published record of the parliamentary debates
- Select Committees and the staff that service them
- Department of Prime Minister and Cabinet
- The Office of the Clerk of the House and staff
- The Parliamentary Service that provides administrative support services to the House and MPs
- Catering by Bellamy's staff to produce food and service the bar

- Security and reception staff
- Parliamentary Counsel Office that drafts most of the legislation
- The ministerial and secretariat services of the Department of Internal Affairs
- A swimming pool and gym for MPs
- A travel office
- The Press Gallery of media reporters.

Parliament's role and functions

In a nutshell, Parliament's functions are to:
- **consider and pass Bills into law.** Before becoming Acts of Parliament, and therefore a part of our law in Aotearoa New Zealand, Bills must go through a process which includes being considered by the whole of Parliament to debate and deliberate;
- **provide a place for the airing of grievances;**
- **raise money** by which the business of government may be conducted. This includes setting the taxation rates;
- **approve the expenditure of money** – Parliament must approve the government's budget;
- **act as a check and restraint** on how government is carried out; and
- **serve as a forum for party political contests and debates**.

Out of these, the core twin principles of Parliament are to make the laws of the country by passing Acts of Parliament and to approve the levying of taxes and spending of public money. Both will be elaborated on further into the chapter.

Nothing in our constitutional arrangements says that Parliament is a forum for political party contest, however, in modern times, that is what it has become. Question Time in the House has become a forum where parties jostle for political advantage by attempting to embarrass one another. Much of the debating time is spent on the same pursuit. This is a poor substitute for real efforts to hold the government to account. Although this element of party-political contest is not going to disappear, it is our view that it should receive less emphasis. While politics can be seen as a theatre or a game, that is hardly its most important aspect. Incessant attempts to secure political advantage are quite distinct from carrying out the classical functions of Parliament.

Although the outline above explains the general functions of Parliament, the role of individual Members of Parliament is more difficult to describe. There is not an adequate job description for what precisely an MP does. This is difficult for both MPs themselves and the public and could potentially lead to great confusion. What are MPs supposed to do? How do we know if they're doing a good job? What skills are most helpful to the job? With each new batch of MPs arriving in the House, only a few will have much grasp of what it is they should be doing or how to do it.

Nonetheless, it could be said that the primary role of an MP is to represent their electorates and the people who voted. This is the oldest function of elected representatives in a democracy. MPs are meant to make representations to the Executive about unfairness, weakness in administration, and anomalies that have occurred because of decisions of government. However, this classical function has become masked to a degree in recent years, due to the proliferation of complaints bodies in Aotearoa New Zealand, such as the Ombudsman Tari o te Kaitiaki Mana Tangata, Independent Police Conduct Authority Mana Whanonga Pirihimana Motuhake, the Health and Disability Commissioner Te Toihau Hauora, Hauātanga, and more. These authorities also make investigations to hold the Executive to account.

In Parliament, MPs inhabit a different world. They take part in parliamentary debates, sit on parliamentary select committees, meet with lobbying groups and constituents, give speeches, and talk with and inform the media and contribute views on social media. MPs visit all sorts of businesses, places of employment, schools, prisons, and other publicly-owned institutions. They want to keep in touch with public opinion and must do a considerable amount of travelling around the country and talking to people to do that. They learn a great deal about what is happening in the community, what people do, and what their problems are. Indeed, being an MP is an excellent crash course on how Aotearoa New Zealand ticks.

In short, the leading tasks of MPs are to:
- participate in the **law-making process** – scrutinising legislation, bringing anomalies to the attention of the House, and contributing policy ideas;
- participate in **determining government expenditure** and taxation levels, and scrutinising public finance;
- act as **local troubleshooters** who help people in their electorates when they are in difficulties. They hold regular clinics with their

constituents and take up problems on their behalf with responsible ministers;
- act as **representatives of the people** – obtaining their views and speaking for them in Parliament, thereby moderating the actions of the Executive;
- act as a **watchdog** for the people on the actions of the Executive;
- be a **member of a political party** – the MP in Parliament can be regarded as a soldier in the political battle between the parties;
- **gain experience** to prepare to become a minister.

Despite their great service to the community, the behaviour of MPs and the performance of Parliament does not always engender feelings of widespread respect through the community. Parliament is not very outward-looking or user friendly. Updated and simpler terminology would help, as would simpler procedures.

Worldwide, political trust, and the belief that governments will act in accordance with public interest and expectations, has fallen. According to a 2021 Roy Morgan poll, 57 per cent of those surveyed believed that Aotearoa New Zealand politics was moving in the right direction, and the Public Service Commission reported in 2021 that 79 per cent of New Zealanders trust our public services. In comparison to many other established democracies, these figures look quite good. Nonetheless, political cynicism is still a threatening trend.

MPs are the representatives of the people and spend most of their time advocating on behalf of the public. The public's preferences are the key incentive that drives MPs' behaviour, both in aiming to represent communities and earning votes. They were voted in by the same people who say they distrust them. In a representative democracy, if the people do not like their representatives, it either suggests that they do not like themselves, or they do not like the system.

Members of Parliament also become celebrities of a sort. Their opinions ever-changing are sought after by the media constantly and this exposure gives MPs political oxygen and attention. Despite this, what goes on in Parliament is subject to much less analysis, reportage, and attention from traditional media than it was 40 years ago. It is to be hoped that this does not reflect a lessening of public interest in political issues and how we are governed. In the social media age, Parliament is in danger of becoming something of a side-show. Social media has given exposure to many more points of view than can be easily expressed, accessed, and debated in the formal political process. In a democracy, unless there is adequate communication between the governors and the governed, democratic accountability breaks down. Perhaps the processes of Parliament must change to ensure that people can relate to them better? People need to be able to understand and access Parliamentary debate as easily as they can access debates about the latest reality TV show, TikTok trends, and pop stars on Twitter. Parliament's Standing Orders Committee is not the most outward-looking, progressive, or transparent reform institution in this regard. It is easier to legislate by majority than it is to secure the high level of consensus needed to change Standing Orders. Parliament's procedures and changes to them are therefore inherently limited and conservative. A recent illustration might be the failure to achieve enough consensus in 2021 to adopt the proposed rules for an online Parliament to allow remote participation in the sittings of the House because of Covid-19.

But members of the public can access Parliament in Aotearoa New Zealand simply: the proceedings in the Chamber are broadcast on radio and television, radio since 1936 (being the first Parliament anywhere to do so), and television since 2007. The Parliamentary website is full of helpful information. Select Committee hearings are open to the public (including by webcast) and members of the public can go and listen to the parliamentary debates and sit in the public gallery. The Office of the Clerk of the House funds the Radio New Zealand Te Reo Irirangi o Aotearoa programme called the House: https://www.rnz.co.nz/national/programmes/the-house.

Acts of Parliament

The journey through which policy ideas travel to generate a new Act of Parliament is long and difficult. The process for passing Bills into Act can be regarded as a series of hurdles that have to be jumped before the proposal becomes law. Or it may be thought of as an ever-changing dance that is never the same from one piece of legislation to another. Making law is a bedrock function of the Parliament and legislating is a task that Parliament carries out in partnership with the Executive. The Executive has a monopoly on the legal drafting carried out by specialist lawyers, called the **Parliamentary Counsel**. Drafting resources are scarce and the **Cabinet Legislation Committee** determines the government's legislative programme: what Bills will be drafted and in what order. The Inland Revenue Department Te Tari Taake has a Law Drafting Unit that drafts tax legislation.

There are four different types of Bills that go through Parliament: **Government Bills, Local Bills, Private Bills,** and **Members' Bills.** Some Members' Bills are passed, but the vast bulk of the Acts are Government Bills. **Members' Bills** are introduced by MPs who are not ministers. Every second Wednesday the House gives precedence to Bills that are not Government Bills and Members' Bills are debated. To decide which Bills will be debated there is a ballot. Since the 1980s, numbers, that each represent a Bill, are drawn out of a biscuit tin! However, if 61 or more back-bench MPs indicate support for a members' Bill then it can be introduced without being balloted. Important issues of public policy can result from Members' Bills. For example, Louisa Wall's Marriage (Definition of Marriage) Amendment Bill, passed in 2013, amended the Marriage Act 1955 to ensure that all people regardless of sex, sexual orientation, or gender can marry if they wish. Then there was David

The Members' Bills Ballot Box/Biscuit Tin
Illustration by Huriana Kopeke-Te Aho

Seymour MP's End of Life Choice Act 2019 that, after being put to referendum, gave terminally ill persons the option of receiving assisted dying. The danger with Members' Bills lies in their likely inadequate policy development. There are not the same pre-introduction checks as there are with Government Bills. The PCO examines and reports on Members Bills only if the Attorney-General so directs.

For **Government Bills**, Cabinet must agree on the policy before any drafting commences. They are introduced by ministers and shepherded through the various stages of the legislative process by the government. To become law, there must be agreement by the House of Representatives and then the Governor-General, on ministerial advice, must sign them into law. This process is a perfect illustration of Bagehot's point about the fusion of Executive power and Legislative power within Aotearoa New Zealand's system.

There is, however, now a procedure in Standing Order 280 that allows the government to write to a Select Committee to say it wants to develop a law-change engagement plan for the legislation. This allows greater Opposition involvement at the beginning and may help in securing consensus and support. There is also a developing practice of introducing exposure drafts of Bills and referring them to a Select Committee before the Bill to be enacted is introduced. This was done in July 2021 for the replacement legislation for the Resource Management Act 1991: *Inquiry on the Natural and Built Environments Parliamentary Paper, 5 July 2021*, upon which the Select Committee took submissions from the public.

Once the Bill reaches Parliament, there are six stages a Bill must travel through to become law. But even before then, ministers and public servants have been hard at work, devising the policy, overseeing the drafting, and securing the agreement of Cabinet that the Bill should be introduced. A Bill may fail by being voted down, but the government will not persist with Bills where that is likely to occur. The whole process can take a long time from introduction to passage – sometimes years. On the other hand, in the case of emergencies, measures can be passed with lightning speed. When the House agrees to an urgency motion this cuts down the length of time required, and the House will sit for longer hours until the business has been resolved. Short of taking urgency the House sometimes sits extended sitting hours to progress its business.

The Legislative Process for Government Bills and Members' Bills

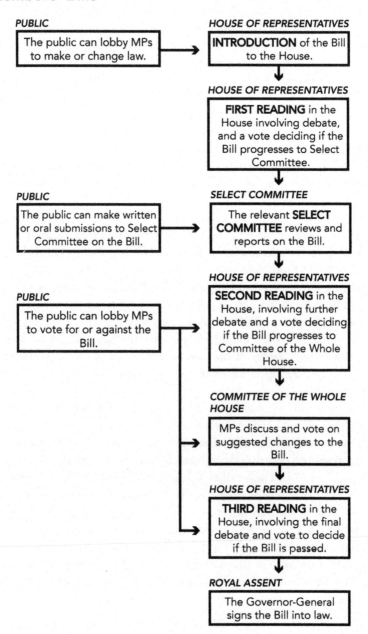

Stage One: Introduction – Bills can be introduced on any working day. Copies of the Bill must be provided to each Member. The Leader of the House will send notice to the Clerk of the House and, once announced, a Government Bill will be set down for the First Reading three sitting days after its introduction. Once a Bill has been introduced it becomes available on the New Zealand legislation website. (It should be noted that the process is slightly different for Local Bills and Private Bills. There are also different processes for making different types of secondary legislation.)

Stage Two: First reading – This stage is the first opportunity for MPs to debate what they think of the Bill. The debate is led by the minister in charge of the Bill and this minister will move a motion at the end of the debate, specifying the Select Committee to which the Bill will be referred for public submission and scrutiny. There is a limit of 12 speeches in this stage, each of which can be up to 10 minutes in length.

Stage Three: Select Committee consideration – Almost all bills go to a Select Committee (unless they are introduced and have first and second readings together under urgency or are Imprest Supply Bills or Appropriation Bills). Usually, the Bill is referred for more than four months, and public submissions are called for. It is not unknown for Bills to be introduced and spend a very short time at Select Committees. The Committee will hold hearings on these submissions and sometimes MPs will travel out of Wellington to hear them. Nowadays, submissions are often heard remotely by video conference. They will hear reports from officials, committee staff, and perhaps the minister, about the Bill. The Committee will consider the Bill and deliberate on it. In Covid-19 circumstances, these steps may also occur by video conference. If the Committee recommends amendments, these will be drafted by Parliamentary Counsel and printed in the Bill. As well, a commentary will be added to the Bill explaining what the Committee concluded and why. The Office of the Clerk also provides legislative scrutiny memoranda to assist MPs.

Stage Four: Second reading – This is the main debate on the Bill. When the Bill has been read a second time it means that it has been adopted by the House, in principle. In addition, amendments recommended by the Select Committees are adopted at the end of second reading. Wide discussion is permitted, including on the work of the Select Committee, and there is a limit of 12 speeches. Sometimes during this debate or the next stage, Supplementary Order Papers or Table amendments are moved or proposed, which contain further amendments.

Stage Five: Committee of the Whole House consideration – The purpose of this stage is to consider the Bill's provisions in more detail and ensure that it contains the principles agreed upon in the second reading. Speeches, at this stage, are in proportion to the representation of the political parties in the House (for example, if a party has 20 per cent of the seats it would get around 20 per cent of the allocated time for speeches). There will be debates on every section of the Bill to find out whether they will work properly and be fit for purpose. These debates often involve points being made to the minister responsible for the Bill who will then respond, and discussions will take place. Amendments can be moved at any time before the closure motion is accepted.

Stage Six: Third reading – At this final stage, the debate is much narrower. Speeches must be confined to the general principles of the Bill, as it was left in the previous stage. Again, there is a limit of 12 speeches, each of which can be up to 10 minutes in length. Once this debate is finished, the Bill is prepared for the Governor-General to sign, which occurs on the advice of both the Prime Minister and the Attorney-General. This is called Royal Assent. Only then will it become law.

However, matters can become much more complicated than indicated above. For example, the Attorney-General can table reports that say a Bill may be inconsistent with the Bill of Rights Act 1990 if it limits the rights and freedoms guaranteed to us all. This would lead to a Select Committee examining the Bill in some serious work to make the Bill compliant. There are a myriad of procedural issues that could arise at each stage.

The House makes a great deal of law. The quantity of statute law enacted by Parliament adds up to many thousands of pages. There are large quantities of secondary legislation as well. Reforms implemented on 28 October 2021 flowing from the Legislation Act 2019 and the Secondary Legislation Act 2021 provide a single category of secondary legislation with clear rules for parliamentary oversight and publication. This is an important change to improve access to the law and has taken a long time to achieve. It is recognition that legislation is part of the public infrastructure and requires constant maintenance. It will take some time for the full programme to be completed: http://www.pco.govt.nz/sl/

Here is the information supplied by the Parliamentary Counsel Office about legislation on the legislation website as at 3 November 2021. (This excludes secondary legislation published elsewhere, such as on agencies' websites).

Acts of Parliament	Number	Pages
Principal Public Acts	967	60,611
Amendment Public Acts	1,800	27,699
Total Acts	3,679	96,114
Principal Legislative Instruments, secondary legislation	2,463	33,339

Managing the money

Power over expenditure has always been a core concern of Westminster-style Parliaments. A large part of the historical development of constitutional relations between the English Crown and Parliament can be seen as a struggle over who has the power to tax and to spend. Magna Carta and the 1688 Bill of Rights, both of which are part of the law in Aotearoa New Zealand, were vitally concerned with this. Securing accountability for the spending of public money is always a challenge. There are always too many ideas and not enough money. Everyone has different ideas about what money should be spent on. It is infinitely more complicated than creating a household budget. Measuring child poverty reduction or health and justice outcomes is not straightforward.

The financial procedures of the House are elaborate and extremely complicated. They revolve around the annual Budget cycle. The Budget cycle requires a massive amount of work from both officials and ministers and many documents and reports are produced – which probably do not receive the attention they deserve. The process has two stages. First, the Executive prepares the Budget itself. After it is presented, there is a Parliamentary process relating to it. The Parliament authorises the spending of money for certain purposes. In return, the government must report back to Parliament, giving an account of what has been achieved with the money. There is therefore reciprocity between the Executive and the Parliament.

Parliament has two key functions regarding public expenditure. Firstly, near the start of each financial year, the Parliament must scrutinise and approve appropriations for the annual expenditure the government proposes:

- On the afternoon of **Budget Day,** the Finance and Expenditure Committee allocates Votes and appropriations in Estimates of Expenditure to subject Select Committees. 'Appropriations' give authority for the government to spend money up to specified limits. 'Votes' here are an appropriation, or group of appropriations, and correspond to ministerial portfolios (e.g., the Conservation Vote or the Public Service Vote would include the Budget estimates for those areas).
- Select Committees have 10 weeks after the Budget Day to scrutinise the allocated Votes and appropriations and report on them to the House.
- The House has until four months after the Budget Day to complete the Estimates debate (which lasts for 11 hours in which MPs consider each Vote individually) and the three-hour-long third reading debate on the main Appropriation Bill.

Secondly, after the end of each financial year, Parliament must review the government's annual financial statements, the performance and current operations of each government agency, and what has been achieved with expenditure from the appropriations approved for that financial year:

- The Finance and Expenditure Committee allocates to subject Select Committees, annual review of departments, Offices of Parliament, Crown entities, State enterprises, and bodies the House has resolved to be public organisations.
- Each annual review starts when the annual report of the agency concerned is presented to the House.
- Select Committees have until 31 March to complete their allocated annual reviews and report on them to the House.
- The House debates these annual review reports in the 10-hour annual review debate, which must be completed before Budget Day.

There are some key provisions that the government finance system functions around. The main appropriation in each year is included in the

Appropriation Bill that accompanies the Budget. It must be introduced before the end of July each year, unless the House makes a resolution to the contrary, as the government's financial year runs from the 1st of July until the 30th of June. When the government requires money, in anticipation of the Budget being passed by Parliament, it can introduce an **Imprest Supply Bill** to be passed by Parliament to tide the government over. Parliament may authorise spending through a permanent legislative authority by inserting the words 'without further appropriation than this section' into legislation where it decides it is appropriate to do so, such as to cover debt servicing costs or judges' salaries.

The Minister of Finance plays a key role in the Executive as government ministers are all dependent upon that Minister for what funds they are allocated in the annual Budget. Even after a lot of negotiations, ministers often fail to get the allocations they bid for and there can be tension. The Minister of Finance's delivery of the Budget speech, with the release of all the accompanying documents, is the big financial event of the year.

In 2019, the government delivered what was called a 'Wellbeing Budget' and made changes in the law requiring wellbeing objectives, as well as fiscal objectives, to guide the government's Budget decisions. The Child Poverty Reduction Act 2018 and the Public Finance (Wellbeing) Amendment Act 2020 are both indications of that expanded fiscal approach. These were efforts to try and connect wellbeing objectives into the fiscal strategy, while, at the same time, ensuring public finance remained sustainable. The Covid-19 pandemic has imposed strains on public finances that are likely to continue in the future, requiring greater effectiveness in public spending to ensure that value is obtained for the money spent.

The Finance and Expenditure Select Committee is the big parliamentary beast on expenditure and financial controls issues. This committee oversees overviewing and scrutinising all things related to economic and fiscal policy. Other Select Committees also become involved in looking at the expenditure issues as well, and all receive investigatory assistance and technical help on these issues from the Auditor-General's staff in the Audit Office. The Auditor-General is an Officer of Parliament and is the independent watchdog over the spending of public money. Auditing all the government accounts is a massive task. Value for money audits are also carried out.

Parliament also engages in an annual review debate concentrating on financial issues. This requires the consideration of the financial position of the government, as reflected in the report of the Finance and Expenditure Committee on the annual financial statements of the government for the previous financial year, and Select Committee reports on annual reviews.

The Fiscal Responsibility Act 1994 (now part of the Public Finance Act) introduced a comprehensive regimen of reporting requirements of the government's fiscal and economic policies. The genesis of the Act was the desire of the former Minister of Finance, the Hon. Ruth Richardson, to entrench principles of fiscal responsibility for a future government to follow. However, it is difficult to stop governments from doing what they want if they have a majority in Parliament and so the Act had few substantive requirements; rather, it relies on publicity and reporting requirements on governments to tell Parliament and the public what fiscal and economic policies they propose to pursue, what effects they are likely to have, and to justify any departures from specified principles of 'responsible' fiscal management.

The Act requires the Minister of Finance to present the fiscal strategy report immediately after delivering the Budget for the financial year to which the report relates. The report must:

- state the government's long-term objectives for fiscal policy
- explain how these long-term objectives accord with the principles of fiscal management
- state the period to which the long-term objectives relate
- assess the consistency of the long-term objectives with the most recent fiscal strategy report
- justify any departures from the long-term objectives
- detail the government's strategy for managing expenditure, assets, and liabilities for the next three financial years
- detail how the government's wellbeing objectives have guided the Budget decisions.

One of the most interesting and innovative changes to Standing Orders in 1996 was the establishment of a financial veto procedure. This was introduced in recognition of the long-standing constitutional conventions surrounding the Crown's financial initiative — that it is for the Crown, not ordinary MPs, to propose expenditure increases. The result is that ordinary MPs can initiate a Bill, amendment or motion involving expenditure or taxation, but if the government certifies that it does not concur on the grounds that it 'would have more than a minor impact on the government's fiscal aggregates', or a change to a Vote would have 'more than a minor impact on the composition of the Vote', then Standing Orders provides that it will not be passed. Financial vetoes have been given on several occasions and the mechanism appears to be achieving its desired object.

If the financial reporting requirement and the Budget process are added together there flows a stream of details, performance updates and reporting that permits observers to examine what the state of the government's finances are and how matters are trending. The data, however, requires expert analytical ability and probably few members of the public follow these issues closely. The picture is a complex web of principles and processes mixed in together.

The Auditor-General

The essential watchdog over financial expenditure is the Auditor-General, who audits the accounts of the government, conducts inquiries, and reports to Parliament on mal-administration in financial matters. The Auditor-General is also the Controller, who checks the legality of issuance of money to the Crown. The Public Audit Act 2001 sets out in details the powers and features of the office. The functions aim to ensure public finance is treated with integrity, and financial corruption is guarded against. The Auditor-General is an Officer of Parliament, with special protection against removal, protection (similar to that of a High Court Judge) on an address of the House of Representatives for 'disability affecting performance of duty, bankruptcy, neglect of duty or misconduct. Appointments are for a term of up to seven years but are non-renewable. The Auditor-General is not accountable or responsible to the Executive but to Parliament and the Speaker. The Auditor-General and their staff also assist Members of Parliament in carrying out financial scrutiny functions. The extensive Auditor-General's reports are often of topical interest. They can be accessed through the Auditor-General's website: https://oag.parliament.nz

For 2021–22, unsurprisingly, the Auditor-General's plan is to concentrate on:
• The Covid-19 response and recovery
• How well the public sector is improving the life of New Zealanders

- How well the public accountability system is working as a whole
- Keeping New Zealanders informed about public sector performance and accountability
- Sharing insights about what 'good' looks like.

MPs' pay and support

Members of Parliament do not decide upon their own pay and conditions. Their remuneration is set by the Remuneration Authority, which is an independent body. It has power to make law by making determinations on the levels of remuneration for various public officials.

Under the Members of Parliament (Remuneration and Services) Act 2013, the Authority determines the remuneration for MPs. It also makes determination of the accommodations services for Members and travel services for their family members. Under the October 2020 determination, an ordinary back-bench MP receives an annual salary of $163,961. Ministers receive more, with the Prime Minister's remuneration set at $471,049. Other ministers receive substantially less. The Speaker receives $296,007, the same as a minister who is in Cabinet. The Leader of the Opposition receives the same amount. Various responsibilities for other MPs with extra responsibilities such as party leaders, whips and chairpersons of Select Committees receive more than MPs who do not have these extra responsibilities.

Allowances are also determined by the Remuneration Authority. Each MP receives a tax-free allowance of $16,980 to cover out-of-pocket expenses in the pursuit of parliamentary business. The Authority also makes determinations on the level of superannuation support for MPs, the last determination having been made in 2003.

The Speaker of the House, under the law, is also responsible for giving directions as to the entitlement of MPs for travel services, administrative support services such as offices and staff for MPs in their electorates, the communication services such as printers, internet, and other communications equipment. The Speaker's Directions No 2 of 2020 cover 33 pages of detailed specification of the support available to MPs. It deals with travel services, communication services, political party and MP support funding, and support for members with impairments. It also deals with budgeting, monitoring and certification. All the relevant statutes and directions are available on the website of Parliament.

When Margaret Wilson was the Speaker, from 2005 to 2008, she found considerable difficulty in making the arrangements for MPs' entitlements transparent and clear. She made changes to ensure transparency and openness to ensure that the public could have confidence in the integrity of the democratic system. After considerable work, greater clarity was achieved, and the entitlements are now contained in the Speaker's directions. The Speaker is independent but occupies a post that in effect is the same as that of a Minister for the Parliamentary Service, being accountable as a minister would be for the expenditure. This involved essentially what she felt was a conflict of interest and that issue has yet to be addressed.

References

Matthew S R Palmer and Dean R Knight *The Constitution of New Zealand* (Cambridge University Press, Cambridge, 2022); Mary Harris and David Wilson (eds) *McGee's Parliamentary Practice in New Zealand* (Oratia, Auckland, 2017); Ross Carter *Burrows and Carter Statute Law in New Zealand* (6th ed., LexisNexis, Wellington, 2021.); John E Martin *The House – New Zealand's House of* Representatives, 1864– 2004 (Dunmore Press, Palmerston North, 2004); Mai Chen *Public Law Tool Box* (2nd ed., LexisNexis, Wellington,2014); Margaret Wilson, *Activism, Politics and Parliament* (Bridget Williams Books ,Wellington 2021); Philip A Joseph, *Joseph on Constitutional and Administrative Law* (5h ed., Thomson Reuters, 2021).

20 The politicians' umpire: Interview with Rt Hon Trevor Mallard, Speaker of the House of Representatives, June 2021

Illustration by Huriana Kopeke-Te Aho

Q: What are your duties in your role as Speaker of the House of Representatives?

A: Well, I think they break down into a couple of main areas: one is the constitutional role of the presiding officer in the House – that's the most public part of it, looking after the House's procedures – and secondly, there's an administrative role looking after the buildings, services and the people who work here.

So, the Speaker is the spokesperson for the House – I lay claims, in a very traditional way, before the Governor-General for the rights and privileges of the House, and present addresses to the Governor-General that have been adopted by the House. Indeed, that is something which under the older systems used to happen quite a lot more than it does now. I preside over deliberations in the house, keep order or attempt to, and make determinations on points of procedure. The Speaker makes decisions and rulings. He or she decides how practices and precedents should be interpreted and applied and how to proceed when new situations arise, ones that are not clearly within previous precedents. Although MPs try to contest them, the rulings by the Speakers are final and can't be challenged. If there's significant disagreement, then the Standing Orders Committee of the House can look at issues. If the majority of Members of the House believe the Speaker has an interpretation which is not appropriate there is this way of reversing decisions, but it's a slow process.

There's also the administrative side, looking after the buildings and grounds; the services for staffing, travel, accommodation and communication services for which MPs have entitlements. I have responsibility for the expenditure for the parliamentary agencies and for the Officers of Parliament, including:

- The Clerk's Office, a smallish organisation whose people are the procedural advisers to the House
- The Parliamentary Service, which is quite big, and includes offices for MPs around the country
- The Office of the Ombudsman
- The Parliamentary Commissioner for the Environment; and
- The Controller and Auditor-General

I have parliamentary responsibility, effectively ministerial responsibility, for those offices. Although, I can't interfere in a way that many ministers can in their agencies.

I also chair committees in this job, including:

- The Business Committee
- The Parliamentary Service Commission – that's not a Select Committee, but it's an important advisory body to the Speaker
- The Offices of Parliament Committee
- The Standing Orders Committee.

There is also an international role, coordinating the relationships between New Zealand Parliament and other Parliaments. These are relationships between Parliaments, not governments. That is an important distinction. There are official parliamentary visits overseas and there are a couple of important inter-parliamentary associations that meet regularly to which delegations of New Zealand MPs are sent.

Q: Isn't it true that the Speaker, in terms of the order of precedence, is a very high-ranking officer in New Zealand?

A: Well, the position is regarded internationally as important, and it does sit in our Order of Precedence between the Prime Minister and the Chief Justice and above the Dean of the diplomatic corps. This is something which can be useful to the country. For example, if there are trade negotiations occurring and our officials are having trouble seeing people, on a number of occasions I've been sent to places with the agreement of the government and the Opposition – because I don't travel without being part of a program that the Opposition is part of – my office can help get access. We find this opens doors for our officials and almost miraculously we make progress on things that we might not have otherwise because an 'important' visitor is coming.

Q: Can you say anything about the history of the Office? It goes back a long way into English Parliamentary history.

A: Under the Westminster tradition, the Speaker's role is to convey the view of Commons and our Parliament, to the Crown and to the House of Lords. That is not relevant here now, having abolished our Legislative Council in the 1950s. Originally, the Speaker was seen as an agent of the Crown, but that changed in 1642 when King Charles the First tried to arrest some MPs for treason and the Speaker intervened to try and speak on behalf of the House. In New Zealand, the Speaker still represents the Parliament and its relationship with the Crown. This is usually by mediating between the House and the Governor-General, but that is not nearly as frequent as it used to be, even 20 or 30 years ago; it is more about symbolism now.

Prior to MMP, the Speaker used to only vote on a casting vote basis in the House and generally voted for the continuation of the status quo or the elongation of debate, or to further discussion. With MMP and party votes the Speaker now has a vote by proxy, cast by the party. There is no longer a casting vote, so effectively a tie in our Parliament is a loss for the proposition being put. So, the real position hasn't changed much.

George Maurice O'Rorke was the longest-serving Speaker of the House. He served two separate periods, amounting to 19 years, beginning in 1879. Interestingly, since 1984 no Speaker has served two full three-year parliamentary terms. The Honorable Peter Tapsell was the first Māori Speaker in 1993, and Margaret Wilson was the first woman Speaker in 2005.

Q: How is the Speaker appointed?

A: Members of Parliament elect the Speaker. Effectively, it is the first confidence vote after the Prime Minister has formed a government after an election. But if the Prime Minister's party put up someone for Speaker and they were not elected, in the New Zealand system, that would be a very bad sign. Candidates must be nominated and seconded by other members. If there's only one candidate, the Clerk, who is effectively the chair at this point, declares that person elected Speaker. If there are multiple candidates, then a vote is held. Members must vote by going into either the Ayes or Nos lobby. A lobby vote is unusual under our system these days.

There have been other Commonwealth Parliaments, quite recently in Canada, a situation in their House of Commons, where the government's nomination for Speaker was not elected. This was a little bit of trickery as a small group of disaffected government members were enticed to vote for one of their own, who was from the Prime Minister Party. I have to say this slightly carefully to be diplomatic, but it is fair to say he didn't have the same reputation and probably intelligence as the person who was the previous Speaker and whom the government would have preferred to continue. When the Speaker is appointed, the Speaker-Elect goes to the Governor-General and the Governor-General confirms the person in office.

Q: There was always a reluctance for the Speaker to go to the Chair, he had to be forced into it by other members, is that correct?

A: Yes, well, certainly that was the tradition up until 2017. The candidate at that stage decided it might be a breach of privilege to indicate reluctance. The tradition came, of course, from the UK. Several Speakers in England were beheaded when the Crown didn't like the message being conveyed.

Q: What is the relationship between the Speaker and the Governor-General?

A: The Speaker represents the House, the Governor-General, symbolically at least, embodies the Crown. So, the Speaker lays claims to the privileges of the House, presents addresses that have been adopted by the House to the Crown, or to the Governor-General on behalf of the Crown, and reads out messages from the Crown to the House. But, as I indicated, that used to be a very frequent occurrence and under our modern conditions, it has been dispensed with for the most part.

Q: There is only one address-in-reply debate about once every three years now, is that correct?

A: Yes, I think there were some financial measures that required addresses from the Crown as well. Now, I think it's assumed that if the government gets a money bill through, then it has the numbers and it has support of the Parliament.

Q: So, you don't now need that part of the Constitution Act that used to exist and was repealed in Dr Michael Cullen's time, as Minister of Finance, so that you do not need a message from the Governor-General before you could get on to an appropriation Bill?

A: That's right, that's right. That doesn't happen anymore.

Q: Can you tell us a bit about how you go about looking after the Parliamentary Precinct?

A: We have a very good tradition of good public access to the grounds. This is much, much easier than most Parliaments overseas. However, in the last 15 years or so we have been much more worried about security matters than previously. We've been trying to get that balance right. Unlike most Parliaments, who put a barrier around the outside of their grounds, we have an effective barrier in the buildings using cameras, scanners, and technology. Hence, we have balanced peaceful assembly access with safety.

The Precinct covers the Parliament House, the library, the Beehive, the forecourt, the gardens, and other areas which we, from time to time, determine should be part of the Precinct. Under the Treasury Building we have two Select Committee rooms which are our emergency temporary Parliament under Number 1 The Terrace; people used to think they're in Bowen House, they're not, they're under the Terrace. We also have areas in the Reverse Bank building where the Department of Prime Minister and Cabinet reside as part of the Precinct so that ministers who are there are regarded as being on Precinct for the purpose of voting, so they can have meetings over there.

The Speaker allocates the working spaces to MPs, and it's not always easy. In fact, we sort of allocate them to parties rather than necessarily to individual Members of Parliament. We leave to the whips or the Prime Minister, as far as ministers are concerned, the responsibilities for the individual room allocation, but even that is not that easy. This also includes where ministers work – the Beehive is the Executive Wing but it is part of the Parliament. In most Westminster parliaments ministers work out in their departments rather than centrally within the parliamentary Precinct.

Access and accreditation of media is my responsibility and sometimes a bit controversial. Most weeks I make decisions about the media. Recently, there was a certain Australian programme where we had some journalists who behaved in a manner not typical for New Zealand journalists. They had a temporary accreditation that I have given them on the recommendation of our Press Gallery. But I don't tell anyone when I do it.

Access of the public to the building can raise issues. I make the recommendations for trespass orders to exclude people when required. We do not have many of those in place now. We have a group of people who have access more than the public does through having swipe cards and they miss the current scanning systems. Some of them are lobbyists, some of them are party officials, former members, and parliamentary staff who have access. It is a public list so there is transparency.

Q: I'm just wondering how much ceremonial material there is, or duties there are – whenever you go to a parliamentary sitting these days, there's a little procession isn't there?

A: At the beginning of each sitting of the House we do have a procession. Now, the procession has changed over the years. It used to go through a back route and in through the Speaker's door without being at all public. Under the Speakership of Dr Smith, it became quite a lot grander with a slow march to the centre of the Chamber. This continued with his successor Mr Carter. I can't quite bring myself to do that, a serious ceremonial, a sort of slow goosestep, and, therefore, I amended it. I nick through the lobby but come back down through the Opposition Lobby through the Speaker's door. I've also stopped the business of the public being excluded from the corridors, and members are not held back as I do my walk. In fact, I like having a chat with the members as we go in.

So, it's a bit less formal than it used to be. But the Mace is still there. That's placed in the middle of the table when the House is sitting, that's quite symbolic. The doors are shut. I also read a prayer, a prayer which evolved in 2017. I changed the prayer, effectively to make it meaningful for those of all faiths, as opposed to being a Christian prayer. That step was controversial at the time but seems to have settled down now. You know, we can each believe we want.

Q: What is the Black Rod?

A: The Black Rod is a person who summons MPs when the Governor-General or the Queen wishes them to go to be spoken to. The Usher of the Black Rod used to be the Sergeant of Arms for the Upper House. But since the Upper House was abolished in 1950, the role of that officer is now much more limited. The Black Rod itself, until 1931, was a billiard cue. The Governor-General at that time presented the Parliament with an ebony rod instead. So, when the Black Rod approaches, we shut the doors to keep him, or now her, out – we now have our first woman Black Rod in New Zealand, since 1892 when the first Black Rod was appointed. So, the Black Rod knocks three times and delivers a message asking us to go into the Legislative Council Chamber to hear the speech read by the Governor-General to open the Parliament. It is written by the government. This dates back to 1642 in the United Kingdom. The fact that the doors are shut and then there is a deliberate decision made to open them symbolises the reluctance of MPs to be ordered around by the Crown.

Q: These things you've been talking about are largely English practices. How has Parliament accommodated the Māori element of society into the House?

A: I think the answer is not well . . . yet. Over time we have been changing the approach to use of Māori language. Earlier in my time, if MPs wanted to speak in Māori, they had to provide their own translation and it was deducted from their speaking time. Later, some extra time was allocated and now we have simultaneous translation in the House and through our television channels as well. I think that's a good thing. We are trying to better approach incorporating or working with Māori. There have been some recent discussions about Standing Orders and Speaker's Rulings around how members address each other and the attitudes they take to one another, and whether a more marae-based approach would be better – where basically you can say anything, but you have to put up with anything coming back at you. There's a view that it might be appropriate amongst some members. In my opinion, it wouldn't totally help the dignity of the Parliament to be so loose. Further, on lots of Bills, Select Committees sit on marae to hear submissions, and tikanga Māori gets picked up that way. All the Treaty of Waitangi Bills get done that way, but also with a lot of the other committees now, when they can travel. Although they're not travelling quite as much as they used to before Covid-19. We've also got some modernisation now around Select Committees and for submissions using Zoom and Facebook Live. It makes Parliament more accessible.

Q: Can you talk about the relationship the Speaker has with Parliaments of other countries?

A: At the high level, all our parliamentary relationships work through the Speaker's office. I have the practice of working through a program for travel and meetings with a group of senior members, mainly whips, and people who are involved in the Inter-Parliamentary Union and Commonwealth Parliamentary Association. I've tried hard to do an allocation which reflects the non-executive proportions of Parliament, to get people away, and that appears to work quite well. When MPs come here from offshore I identify and introduce them to the House.

I am also, it's more nominal than anything else, the President of the Inter Parliamentary Union and our branch of the Commonwealth Parliamentary Association.

Q: Those organisations have regular conferences, don't they?

A: Yes, they do. Each of those organisations have conferences, IPU has multiple conferences, but certainly a big one every year, the Commonwealth Parliamentary Association now has one every two years. We are generally involved in the executives of both organisations. I think New Zealand is seen as a trusted, honest, and clean Parliamentary system compared to a lot of others. So, people do rely on New Zealand more than most countries for some of these executive roles. My former colleague Hon Anne Tolley, the Deputy Speaker in the last Parliament, was women's vice president of the IPU. She was a member of several international committees for the promotion of women parliamentarians and did a fine job there.

Q: How does the Speaker keep order in the House of Representatives?

A: Unevenly, I think. The Speaker calls members, but that's probably less important than it used to be. There is a much tighter allocation by the Business Committee of speaking times and party proportionality in Standing Orders than there used to be. The calling of members is mainly important on procedural matters, on points of order, and on conscience votes. When there's a controversial conscience issue, there are often more people who want to speak then there are slots available. Although one of the things that I have tried to do on that is extend times so that, within reason, members who want to speak at a second reading or a third reading of a conscience vote, can, even if we run over the times which are set down. I generally quietly seek out the Leader of the House and see if the House is prepared to make some extra allowance. In my view, members should have a right to get their views on the record at one reading or another.

Q: And I suppose, if members are disorderly, you can throw them out?

A: I can. Generally, the first point where people are disorderly in a minor way is to require them to withdraw and apologise. That's normally when it's in debate or by interjection and generally calling them out is enough to settle it down. There's a new mechanism which I have developed for question time. As a minister for nine years, I was always anxious about the next question that might be asked by the Opposition and whether it might get right to the heart of the matter. And as an opposition MP for even longer, I always felt if I had one or two more supplementary questions I would get to the heart of the matter and put the minister on the spot. One of the most valued resources for accountability in our question time are supplementary questions, because, unlike primary questions, the minister is not given notice in advance of what the supplementary questions are going to be.

Another innovation that I've made is not to allow interjections while members are asking questions. I think everyone should have the respect of having the question heard, no matter how unfortunate it is – just let them run. So, I insist on silence during that time. I started off by taking questions away, but then worked out there was no problem for the government to lose a few supplementary questions since there was no value in their supplementaries anyway. I then started adding supplementaries to the Opposition if the government offended. This has worked quite well for discipline and having order during question time compared to how it was previously.

If members are highly disorderly, then I can order them to leave the Chamber. That does not happen frequently now. I specify the time for their return, normally sometime during that afternoon, it just depends on the level of the offending. If there's gross disorder such as someone persistently defying the Chair, then I can use the procedure of naming a member. A naming involves an automatic recommendation to the House that someone is suspended and that's put to a vote. I think I've only done it twice in the time that I've been here. It happens infrequently. A period of suspension involves a reduction in pay, as well; it is one day for the first offence, seven days for the second offense, and 28 days for the third offence. There was once an ability for them to be suspended for a longer period. That's been taken out.

Q: Following on from keeping order in the House, how does the Speaker determine when to bring a debate to the end?

A: Much more now than previously, debates are structured. They go naturally according to a pattern, and even the order of calls is allocated. They're generally proportional to the parties, however, the government was previously quite generous to ACT, giving them a five-minute call in a two-hour debate, which was much more than proportionate. They have been similarly generous to the Māori Party in the current Parliament. There's an order, but there are some debates, for example, in the Committee of the Whole House, procedural motions, generally to shorten a report-back period for a Bill, so that a decision must be made, and a closure motion put to the vote. Now the Speaker or the Chair decides whether to accept the closure motion.

There are several factors which we take into account – one is just the scope of the question: is it a big question? Is it an important question? Is it a broad question? How long has the debate been going on for? Have parties or members had a chance to put their view to the House? We generally consider proportionality and try and preserve that. We also look at relevance and repetition, which is one of the bigger tests. A lot of members, especially for technical motions, have trouble being relevant.

Another thing we consider, which is relatively new and comes from a ruling that I did when I was an assistant Speaker, is whether the government has been engaged in the debate during the committee stage of a Bill. I found that the government was sometimes not engaging and not answering the questions that were being asked and just expecting when time went passed that the debate would be concluded. My practice was, and we worked it into the Speaker's rulings, that if the government had engaged properly, answered the questions well, the chances were that the closure would be accepted early. That was an encouragement to always go back to the older days of the committee stages here and so that was effective. But the Speaker doesn't decide – in the end, the House decides, so all the Speaker is doing is accepting a closure motion and the House makes the decision. It is very, very rare for the government not to support a closure motion.

Q: This connects quite well to what you were talking about earlier. What exactly is the role of question time in the House, and how effective is it at holding government to account?

A: It depends on the quality of the questioning. Over the years we have lost any semblance of government back-benchers really trying to hold the ministers to account. I've felt like we had a little bit of it in my time. And I can remember one meeting with the Deputy Prime Minister where there was a minister who was unhappy with a supplementary question that had been asked in the House. But I don't think we have much of that anymore. Parties all get a proportional allocation of questions, based on the number of non-executive members, similarly with supplementary questions. The best questions are short and clear. It's much easier for the Speaker then to insist that the questions are at least properly addressed, and even better if they're answered. Some questions are asked of MPs who are not ministers, about Bills or other items of business that they have responsibility for, maybe as a member in charge of Member's Bill or member in charge of a Select Committee.

The quality of the accountability mainly depends on the preparation of the members who are asking the questions. I often advise members to have a good look at Helen Clark in Opposition. I used to sometimes sit very close to her and I would see sort of four or five lines of typed questions and then a lot of handwritten possibilities, almost like a flow chart. Helen would look very carefully at the possibilities in advance and then have alternative supplementary questions available, sometimes going out to about four different sets of alternatives. I think that Helen probably spent about an hour of preparation for every question she asked in opposition. Then as Prime Minister, when she was answering them, she would be equally well prepared.

There are a number of other members who were seen as nimble-on-their-feet as askers of questions but later, when they get into very senior ministerial or opposition roles, now find themselves quite heavily scripted, probably by staff. They may not have been able to spend the time on preparation that they should. As a result of that, they are often very flat-footed when they give an answer. Occasionally, people have ended up looking quite silly because they either haven't listened, or haven't understood, or haven't been nimble enough to respond when an answer is not what they expected. Preparation for question time is important.

In the last review of standing orders we made, we provided for the possibility for more pressure to go on ministers in questioning them. This was for several processes, including at the Committee of the Whole House. We took out the limit of the number of speeches that members could make in the Committee. It was previously four. What we found was that people were making four five-minute speeches but weren't properly interacting with the minister. So, by removing it we have now a slowly developing practice of people getting up, asking questions and the minister answering them. That might go on for 10 minutes and results in a better quality of discussion. It produces more accountability than making speeches at each other for 10 minutes, which is not really adding much value, especially because people often come close to simply reading their speeches prepared by the research units.

With ministerial statements, there is now an ability for Opposition members to ask questions and ministers to respond. What I roughly do is give them about three quarters of the time that they would get to speak, to ask the questions, but it often means that the time is doubled or tripled because the minister's responses do not come out of the Opposition's time. The other thing is, in Select Committees, we have expectations that ministers will attend on Bills, which means that now there is more questioning than previously. Some of it is public and some of it technical and in private. We had a meeting of Select Committee chairs, talking about providing the opportunity for members to ask their ill-informed questions, when they really don't understand what the minister is trying to do. In more recent years, I think departmental officials have become much more agents of ministers and have been reluctant to give opinions. Certainly, in my day as a minister we would have Cabinet papers which would say this is my preferred option, the Associate Minister prefers this one here, the Department prefers this one, the Treasury prefers this one, and here are the four other options . . . If you couldn't convince a Cabinet Committee that you're doing the right thing by providing them with all the choices then the chances are you'd have some trouble out in the public.

So, I think it's good, in the Select Committees, to have the ministers interrogated about the reasons for going in a particular policy direction. I hope that will assist the level of Select Committee understanding. It might be they want to get the minister when they first get the Bill so that they can get a bit of understanding before they head into hearings. It might be when they've got some choices to make in their consideration phase, that might also be a good time to get the ministers back in and to get their opinion. With the current shape of the House, the government members vote as a block, and at that point the submission process becomes ineffective. You might still get changes from the government but having any real impact on the decisions is harder. This new approach may help committees be more independent.

Q: Can you tell us about parliamentary privilege and contempt of Parliament as well?

A: The core idea is that Parliament's proceedings should be free from judicial control or challenge. Unlike what most people think, privilege isn't about perks, it's a historical term which has been used to describe the powers and protections associated with the Parliament, coming from Westminster. Our law recognises the fact that Parliament continues to hold the privileges, such as the freedom of speech, the freedom of debate, the control over the House's proceedings, reports, and its precincts, and importantly, the ability for the House to set its own rules and standing orders. The Courts can't do that. The House has rules that protect the freedom of speech of members, but it also restricts members from using those freedoms to diminish the House's relationship with the Courts.

For example, if there is a Court order, under some recent changes of Standing Orders, no one is allowed to breach those in the House without first notifying the Speaker of their intention, something which can be blocked.

So, contempt of Parliament refers to Acts, or sometimes submissions, which obstruct or impede the House or the performance of its functions. So, if it stops a member or officer of the House in the discharge of their duties, or even has a tendency, even indirectly, to produce such a result, that can be a contempt. I have no powers to punish people for contempt and only the House does, but the way that it works is always the result of a Privileges Committee hearing. For example, if a person sought to mount a legal challenge to the House's proceedings, that would be seen as a breach of privilege. If a member failed to comply with an order of the House to attend the House or a committee, or, in fact, if a member of the public were to do that, that would be a breach.

We have pecuniary contempts these days, which requires members to declare a pecuniary interest. If someone accepts a bribe or a fee, that would probably be dealt with in the courts under the Crimes Act these days. If you misrepresent a report or a record of Parliament, there is risk of contempt. We have loosened some of our rules over time – certainly, there is a satire exemption.

One of the important ones is punishing or disadvantaging people who have participated in parliamentary proceedings or taking action against a person who's made a submission to the Committee. We had some quite recent involvement with the situation when an academic from Canterbury University made a submission to a committee, which was extensive, quite controversial, and not liked by another nation. Pressure was put on universities to complain about it and an inquiry was set up at the academic's university to investigate the matter. This resulted in me writing to the Vice Chancellor of the university, pointing out that there was a danger of the university being subject to contempt procedures. So, it is an interesting area and one of which, within the last 12 months we've had a practical example. I decided it was better to send a warning shot across the bows of the university, as having a formal privileges hearing which would go right to the relationship between New Zealand and one of its major trading partners would probably not be in the best interest of the country. Better to stop the breach before it happened.

Q: Can Parliament itself imprison and fine people, and why should it be able to do so?

A: It can. It's never used its power to arrest, but it still exists. It hasn't been abolished. We've severely restricted our fining ability to $1000, which I think for most individuals and companies, or for many individuals, is symbolic. Enforceability is a bit of a question. I think the general view is that would be treated like a fine under the Summary Offences Act in the same way as for a contempt of court. I think the reason for those powers is just to stop people ignoring decisions of Parliament.

Q: What is the role of the Business Committee in organising the parliamentary agenda? And can you describe the function of party whips?

A: The Business Committee is a forum for members to discuss the organisation of business at the House. All parties are represented, but any member can attend and it's not unusual for that to occur. Meetings are held just about always at a set time of 4:30pm in the Speaker's office. It's not unusual for members who have an interest in a particular area to come and to make representations to the other members. Decisions are made on the basis of near unanimity, which means that they have the support of parties representing the overwhelming majority. We've never put numbers on it, but part of my role is to ensure that it's not unfair on small parties. There's always a danger of two big parties disadvantaging smaller parties. So, I am the person who decides if there's near unanimity or not. As it happens, people work things through, they talk a lot, and sometimes there's a minor party unhappy. I'd be concerned if two of the bigger minor parties were unhappy, or the three minor parties.

The Business Committee has extensive powers. It can adjust the sitting calendar, adjust the hours on a sitting day, it can determine the order in which business is dealt with, it can allocate calls, determine the length of particular debates and, after some recent changes to the standing orders, it has been encouraged to set up, on a fairly regular basis, special debates. So, recently, we had a debate on petitions concerned with immigration. We also had a local issues debate, where members had up to five minutes to talk about an issue that was important to them. We're going to have another one soon. There's a report which a group of members have facilitated outside the Select Committee process on mental health, on a cross-party basis, so we're going to allocate an hour and a half to that. The Education and Workforce Committee has done an inquiry into student accommodation, following the death in Canterbury. They produced a report, and we will allocate an hour for that to be debated. It's a good way of bringing things together.

Sometimes a bit of horse trading goes on because you do need both parties agreeing. I think it's a good way of running the place. Unless the Business Committee decides otherwise, the order of government business is something for the Leader of the House to decide. You're not going to override the Leader of the House because the leader's party must be part of the Business Committee consensus. But it is a place where those discussions take place. Sometimes members have personal or electorate appointments which are important and as part of discussions of the Business Committee, the business can be reordered to facilitate the attendance of the members who otherwise might be away. Members are more generous about doing that now than used to be the case.

The whips, sometimes called musterers in New Zealand now, do some negotiation of the passage of business through the Committee of the Whole. This is probably not as much as they used to do now that we have the Business Committee, but they do function within the Business Committee as well. I think what we refer to as being behind the Chair, you know, they have their discussions . . .

The Bell rings

Q: Oh, is the Parliament meeting?

A: Parliament has just finished meeting. We have new hours! We now only have one hour for dinner, and we finish at 5 o'clock on a Thursday, which means there are members who can catch planes that make it home tonight who couldn't otherwise. That was one of the recent standing orders changes. It has occurred as part of the family-friendly initiative we have been developing around sittings of the House.

So, the whips arrange speaking orders within their parties. They can give permission for members to be absent – with the current standing orders, with our proxy voting system, any party can have up to 25 per cent of its members absent at any time. I have a compassionate leave override with that, which I have been using automatically at the moment for anyone who is having a Covid test. I'm not prepared to have people trading off political appointments for a Covid test. So, if you've got a Covid test, go and have it, and your vote will still count. The other thing with compassionate leave is that we do have people with family circumstances. I use it for family leave, paternity, maternity leave. It's part of being family-friendly. I don't want someone having to not do something which is important for their family just because someone else has something which is seen as more important politically. It's a matter of trying to get that balance right.

The whips come to me quite often. They ring me and tell me why someone may be absent, and I say I will approve that, and they send me an email and no one other than me, the individual, and the whips know the reason for it. Well, when people have babies it's pretty bloody obvious, but most of the time people don't know. Today we've got four members away. There's a bit of the sniffles going round, and we are very strong on having the Covid tests done so we've got three members away who've have had their Covid tests today or yesterday. This place could be an awful vector for the pandemic if we did not take care.

There's a whole pastoral thing with whips too, which is not much to do with the running of the House, but the pastoral care of their members. More recently, the whips are taking some leadership in professional development of members. One of the parties, probably because they have more resources at the moment, have appointed someone full-time who is effectively a professional development coordinator. They work with members, mainly backbench members and especially the new members for the last two Parliaments, on programs to improve their capability. This is a good development.

Q: You've talked about this quite a lot previously in the conversation, but can you describe the functions of Parliamentary Select Committees?

A: We're a bit different from some Parliaments in that our committees are not as specialised as they used to be, or as they are in other places. They should be more important because we have only one House in the Parliament, not two as many democratic countries have. I'm not convinced that the Select Committees are working well. Part of the problem is the size of the government. It's a serious problem. But our Select Committees do a lot more work than in any other Parliament that I know of – dealing with Bills, and petitions, and estimates, and annual reviews, and all the international treaties go through the Foreign Affairs Committee. They meet more than Select Committees do in other places. Some are specialist.

We have reinstated a Petitions Committee, which we are regarding as a triage committee. If a petition comes in, if there's a real issue it should go straight to the minister, and we should get a response back quickly on some of them. If one deserves an inquiry at the Select Committee level, we will refer the petition to the subject Select Committee to do the inquiry. If a petition is a pile of nonsense, we will report and say thank you very much.

Scrutiny by the Regulations Review Committee is an important task. The committee must make sure that secondary and tertiary level legislation is consistent with the law passed by Parliament and made properly under the powers delegated by Parliament.

The Officers of Parliament Committee is both quite important and interesting. It works on the basis of consensus to make recommendations to the House on the appointment of the officers of Parliament, and the funding which, again, I think is really important. So, the Minister of Finance has no role in the setting of the funding for the Officers of Parliament. Theoretically, he or she could, at the committee stages of the Estimates Bill, cut the funding but it would be a really big thing since it has been determined unanimously.

The Standing Orders Committee recommends changes to the rules and practices of Parliament. We do have a regular three-year cycle of the sittings of the Standing Orders Committee although sometimes things take longer than some of us want. Sometimes it takes a few cycles to get matters through. Internationally, that three-year cycle is unusual. The thing I really like about it is that we will set up the committee and think: well, we might be in government, we might be in Opposition, and therefore we must have a system which is fair to both. If we're making changes, let's make some which advances government and efficiency of business and things like that, and some others which gives the Opposition more power to secure accountability. There were some changes in 2011 that were quite radical. The last set of changes were good, and part of it was because several members had been quite clear in the changes wanted when in Opposition and followed through on that in government, which some found surprising. The accountability changes have been useful and have not made the government unduly nervous.

The Finance and Expenditures Committee is an important committee because of the vital parliamentary role of financial scrutiny. It makes decisions about which committee looks at what and it examines any of government financial directions that the government makes.

The Foreign Affairs and Trade Committee looks at the international treaties, which again I think is something which is important. And when those Bills are enacted, the first reading and the report of the Select Committee are generally done together. So, the Select Committee is earlier in the process than generally is the case. I think that's successful. It's not just that the changes to the law are made, but the level of understanding about what's being signed up to increases.

Q: Do you think that the House of Representatives is large enough to discharge all the responsibilities it has?

A: This is going to be an unpopular view with the public, but no. Our Parliament hasn't grown since MMP, but the population of the country has grown by about a third since that time. I found as a local Member of Parliament that MMP made a big difference because of the major increase in the size of the electorates. It made my ability to know and understand the people I was representing as an electorate MP much harder. And the current increase in population has made it harder still as the uneven increase has meant that several of the electorates are so big, in my opinion, it's very hard to represent them well.

The other issue has to do with the small size of our Parliament but also the large size of the Executive. We don't have a proper role for a senior backbencher who is not a minister. I think that if we had a bigger Parliament there would be more scope for that. I also have a view that the big and important Select Committees should be chaired by Opposition members. I would not give up most of the committees to the Opposition, but I would entrust the chairing to an Opposition member. I've a good friend who used to be Secretary of Education in England, Margaret Hodge, who then chaired the Public Expenditure Committee for I think six or seven years. And it just means that the agenda was well set, there was proper time for their hearings, people had their say, and the process was seen to be not controlled by the government. I think if we had a bigger Parliament, it would improve things.

We have, in the last standing order review, encouraged the reduction in the number of members on committees. We're still not back to what

I think is desirable. The problem when you have a committee that is too big and rapidly moving through issues is our members know that they are unlikely to be able to make much of a contribution. The danger is that they don't properly read the material and are not well prepared. But if you have a small committee and there's an expectation that all members will be asking questions and will understand things, then I think you get better quality for both legislation and inquiries out of that. We have several committees of only five members, which I think is a better number.

The other change that we've made as part of the Standing Orders changes, was to allow parties that are not represented on the committees to attend – not to vote, but to ask questions, to contribute, and put in the minority report, even if they're not members of the committee. That was designed to keep the numbers down, but where parties thought there was an important issue they can still get in there and make a contribution. That's a good thing. If we had made some more progress, there would be other committees that I would set up. I'd rather have more and smaller.

I think we need something around legislative quality. I don't believe we do that function well. The Governance Administration Committee doesn't look properly at public governance and some of the longer-term issues. One of the better changes that we made, was to require the departments or ministers to put in what are effectively five-year plans every three years, which will be referred to Select Committees. Select Committees will be required to have hearings on them and to report on them. I think that will get members of committees much more familiar with what's coming up and the bigger, longer-term issues for the departments and will make them much better prepared to become ministers.

Can I say, Mr Speaker, that this has really been a wonderful experience for us because you have prepared so diligently that it has made a real contribution to this book. We just want to thank you so much.

21 The other side of the House: Interview with Hon Judith Collins, Leader of the Opposition, June 2021

Illustration by Ursula Palmer Steeds

Q: The first question I'd like to ask is what is the role of the Leader of the Opposition?

A: Well, it's actually to ask questions – to be a bulwark, for want of a better word, against a government that has a majority, or any government, really. To ask the questions, to hold the government to account. That means, basically, to ask the questions that people don't want us to ask, to say to the Prime Minister: 'You promised to do this, why haven't you done it?' It's not for me to work out why they haven't done it, it's for me to ask those questions. It's also an important role, I see, wherever possible, that we can support the government when there are issues, policies, or actions that we agree with. And, for as much as possible internationally, to try to keep an understanding of New Zealand being a small but unified country. If we are entirely opposed to something that we in New Zealand are doing, we'll say so, but we try not to give too much comfort to any foreign power as such. The role is also to have alternative views and policies so that the people can say: 'Well, I didn't vote for that government, so this other party, this Opposition, they have some ideas I like.' So, we've got to develop policies – we've got to look like and become a government in waiting.

Q: Now, it might be very difficult to answer this, but what's a typical work week of the Leader of the Opposition?

A: Haha! It's a good question! Well, it's a very, very long working week. But there's no point complaining about it because nobody will give any sympathy, and sympathy is not what we want – votes are what we want! We want to hold an alternative vision for the country. I think Mondays are the slowest days for me normally because I probably wouldn't start work until about 9am or 10am, but then I'll go through to reasonably late at night. I'll be in both Wellington and Auckland that day, or in some other part of the country. I work very long hours on Tuesdays, from early in the morning, like 8am until 10pm that night. Then, Wednesday is a shocking day! It's a 5am start, and I don't finish until 10pm at night. It's ridiculous! Thursday is normally a bit calmer, but then I've got plenty of media and other things to do, like going to some other part of the country. Last week on Thursday I finished at 10pm that night and was giving a speech somewhere in the Bay of Plenty. The next day, Friday, I'll be doing various things and it's just a long day overall. Both Saturdays and Sundays are often consumed with work, but if I can get one day off in the weekend, I'll be very happy. That's the day I get to do the washing!

Haha, people laugh about it but it's actually those normal things of life – like the washing, or going to the gym, or for a walk – that help to keep a sense of balance and understanding. Even though it's a really tough job it's actually not life. I think that's one of the things that I've learnt in my experience in politics: this is a really hard job, you have to do your best, but it's actually not your life.

Q: Now, you've been a minister for a lot of your years in politics. How does this job compare with being a minister?

A: Well, there are similarities. I do not have enormous government departments full of large numbers of highly intelligent people, all trying to do the best job. What I do have now is a very small, but talented group of people in the National Leader's Office. I have to manage the MPs and I have a very close relationship with the National Party itself, and the board – I'm a member of the board. In terms of responsibility, I think it's right up there, or probably more so, with being a very busy minister. Having been a very busy and senior minister was good training for being Leader of the Opposition because you understand the time that it takes, and you understand that you cannot please everyone – you can only do what you can do. But it's much harder than being a minister.

Q: Can you give us some clue as to how much of the job you dedicate to the House itself and how much you spend engaging with the public outside the House?

A: So, for the House itself, there's Question Time on Tuesdays and Wednesdays, and so there's obviously preparation for that, some days more than others. I probably speak on issues such as the Budget debate and the major debates, but I'm not involved as Leader of the Opposition on every piece of legislation that comes through the House. So, there's maybe not much more than eight to 10 hours a week that I spend in the House itself.

I spend more time in the Parliamentary Precinct. I'm here on Monday afternoons, Tuesdays, Wednesdays, and Thursdays in the morning – so that would be a full week for most people at least. Of course, I also have engagements with the electorates and with the MPs who hold shadow portfolios. I have given myself some portfolios, such as Pacific Peoples, which may seem odd to people, but I'm pretty much the closest thing in the National Party caucus that we have to a Pacific person; just simply because my husband is Samoan, my son is Samoan, and I've been involved with the Samoan community for 40 years. I also have the portfolio for Technology, Manufacturing, and Artificial Intelligence as well as for Space. I've taken that because I'm very excited about technology and the way forward for the country. So, I have to do a lot of engagement around both of those things and then also engage with electorates.

I also manage MPs and help to guide them. When I first came in, I felt that we could do better with guiding MPs, so I introduced a system of management very much like what many businesses have. I first had a meeting with each MP to determine where their interests were and then I tried to give them one portfolio that they were interested in and one that they weren't interested in. From this, they had to produce a plan for each portfolio: what they're going to do and how they should be judged on that. Afterwards, I had a meeting with every single one individually to go through each of those and they have meetings booked in with me in August and September to go through them again. This is a very hands-on approach, but I've found it is necessary because, even for some very experienced MPs, sometimes they don't quite know what is available to assist them or they might struggle with a particular issue, or others are experienced in some ways but have never been a minister. I found that when I first became an MP in 2002 that the best people to give me advice on what I should be asking a minister were former ministers who knew where things got hidden and what things to do. All of this is quite time-consuming, but I feel it is something I have to do, and people do seem to quite like it. It's giving some structure and some help – a bit of a matrix on what the MPs can do.

Q: I do want to ask, how do you divide things up with your Deputy?

A: Well, Dr Shane Reti is the very kind and caring face for the National Party, which is excellent, but he's also someone who has quite a role when it comes to keeping me to meet with and manage MPs or get information about what people are doing. He also has a disciplinary role, but a lot of his role is getting out to electorates as well. I'm trying to get out to at least an electorate a week, sometimes more than that, but he can do more of that than me. He also does a lot of the pastoral care side of things and often knows more about what's happening in an MP or staff person's life than I will because he's the sort of person who knows those things.

Q: The next question I would like to ask is what is your role in caucus discussions?

A: Right, so I lead those. What I do is run a very tight ship in caucus. The meetings start at 10.30am, and I don't have any meetings that have gone past 12.30pm and I try to get them under that. I keep them controlled in terms of time; I think that's important. I'm fortunate because I had previously been a chair of boards before I came to Parliament, and I've always felt that I know how to chair things efficiently and effectively. I like to let everyone in caucus who wants to have their say and then I sum things up. I will not tolerate bullying in caucus. I will never attack people in caucus verbally or allow people to do that. I've been in a lot of caucus meetings over the years, and I've thought that was one of the worst things I've seen.

Q: So, you are the Leader of the Opposition, but you're also the leader of a political party. How do you manage your relationship with the National Party organisation?

A: The leader of the National Party is also a board member of the National Party, although some previous leaders of the National Party have not been particularly engaged with the board. I try to go to almost all the meetings of the board, even if it's only for part of it or I can only Zoom in. I think that's very important as it's very easy for the board to become disconnected from the caucus. We also allow the President of the National Party to attend our caucus meetings and when we have one-day or two-day caucus meetings to discuss bigger issues, like policy issues, we will normally invite the local board members and often the local chairs of the electorate. I play more of an active role than some leaders have in the party itself before, but I also try to respect the boundaries.

Q: This next subject is quite a big one, and you've already covered this to some degree, but what is the role of the Opposition in terms of holding the government to account?

A: We often talk about the role of the media to hold the government to account, but if the media doesn't do that, then our role becomes even more important. Accountability is necessary because we're in a democracy and we are supposed to have a contest of ideas. We are supposed to question those in power and to refuse to do so, or to simply go along, makes us not only surplus to requirements but it also fails the people of the country who believe very firmly in a democracy. Sometimes we get questions like: 'Why can't you just have a grand coalition with Labour and have everyone in Parliament work all together?' Well, yes, that's worked very well in North Korea . . .

People sort of look at this and say . . . 'But, but, but!!' However, this sort of thing, this grand coalition, is the sort of thing you do during a war – if you're under attack. Democracy requires a contest of ideas. It needs and it requires the courage to have ideas that one believes in and to have principles and visions for the country. It does not mean that the role of the Opposition is just to agree with whoever is in charge. That's not the way it works. That's not a democracy! That's called a dictatorship, and we're not having it! I think that people don't always understand what that role is, normally because they don't learn about it. The number of emails I've had complaining about the government and asking if I can fix things that the government's done is astounding. Well, you know, it's in your hands. It's a democracy – you vote for us and then I'll fix it!

Q: How important is the role of the Opposition for the democratic responsibility of the State, if I can put it that way?

A: I think it's crucial. I think that an Opposition that does its job makes for a better government. It encourages transparency and it encourages people to do their best. And an Opposition that doesn't do its job of holding the government to account fails its people; it fails the country because it's not doing the role it's meant to. Having been a minister, I know fully well that when we've got a competent person shadowing from the Opposition you watch exactly what's going on – you should be watching anyway, but departments pay careful attention when they're being shadowed. I think that a good Opposition makes for a better minister.

Q: I'd like to ask how many people communicate with you or want to see you, and how you prioritise your time?

A: I have a diary committee that meets once a week and decides. I do have some time to myself, and, on occasions, I make decisions such as 'yes, I will see so and so' and then I simply ask Lucy, who's my executive assistant to help organise them and to make it happen. But a lot of what I do has to go through a process primarily, so I don't commit to something when there's already a team organising for me to go to Gisborne at that same time, for instance. And how many requests do I receive? Just hundreds! I particularly like the ones that say: 'If only you would take up my idea, then you will win the next election.' There are an endless number of helpful suggestions like that, and sometimes they would be very good ideas and other times I think: yep, I've never thought of that one . . .

So, I am not in charge of my own diary, and I cannot be because of the pressure of it. There are too many people with the ability to put things in my diary. Some people think that it's ridiculous, that I should have control over my diary – and in the real world you would, but we live in the world of politics. A back-bench MP generally has control over their own diary, but I'm not a back-bench MP.

Q: So, it's sometimes said that the Opposition is Her Majesty's Loyal Opposition. What does this mean?

A: I think it's loyal to the sovereign, that's the way I take it. But I also think it means loyal to the country as well. In New Zealand, that's probably how most people interpret it. This means, like I said, we wherever possible support the country on anything we can, and when we're opposing things it's not just for the sake of it, it's because we think it's the right thing for the country. We may not agree with the government, but our view is that we think we've got a better way for the country as a whole and we need to represent that as well.

Q: Could you please discuss the role of the media and your interaction with them?

A: I think that the role of the media has become a little confused over the last year or so and that it is at risk of losing more influence than it might think it should have. I say that because the media has had a large amount of money given to it by the government, in a way that I look back and think – I can't imagine if we had given the media $110 million over two years whether that would have ever been acceptable to the populace. You're starting to see the odd little moment where they're doing their job properly and holding the government to account – because that's their job: to speak truth to power. But, actually I've become a little concerned. I don't think it's a good idea for governments to pay media money, particularly with strings attached. I think that's very unfortunate.

Q: In your opinion, what is the most difficult aspect of the job?

A: It's really hard watching us occasionally come out with something where you look at it and think 'That's a really good policy' and then the government says 'Oh, that's terrible' and a week later they've adopted and funded it. That's so annoying. It's something I experienced before last time we were in Opposition, and I learned that that's the game. The trouble is, you can't spend your whole time in Opposition just being negative, you actually have to propose things from time to time. This runs the risk the government will come along and say, 'Yes, I'm going to do that too.' You've got to do a lot of work with people beforehand so that they understand it's your idea, not the government's. So that is quite hard, it is annoying.

Q: What do you find the most satisfying?

A: Making a difference, actually. Knowing that sometimes we can advocate for people, or issues, or policies and we can get the right result. Sometimes we can do things for individuals more so than when we're in government. You hear different issues when you're in Opposition than you do when you're the minister. We can often advocate with ministers for things from our position and I've noticed sometimes government ministers are nicer towards their Opposition counterparts on constituent issues than they are to their colleagues.

Q: What do you do in order to develop new policies?

A: Well, we listen to a lot of people, and being in Opposition is a good time to listen. In government, it's hard to come up with new policies in many ways because you have incredible vested interests in government agencies, industries, and contact. For ministers who have taken a particular stance, Opposition is a good opportunity to take back and reflect on what one would do differently if starting again. So, when it comes to policy, we have policy advisory groups from the National Party who are interested in policy as well as policy teams within our caucus that meet every week about various things such as the economy or environment. However, we often get our best ideas when we go out and listen to people. Some of my best policy work that I did in government, in terms of changing things, came not from the people I worked with in government in Wellington, but from people, when I went out and saw things myself.

For instance, I'm very proud of being able to stop smoking in prisons. Everybody thought I was mad to try this! Steven Joyce came and told me I was being brave . . . which is a terribly dangerous thing to be in politics! I got this idea because I went to visit a prison and they showed me the shanks, the prison knives, that were being made – they showed me plastic spoons that had been melted with things and other things that had razor blades stuck inside them. I asked how they got these things, and the answer was that they had matches and lighters because we let them smoke. I said, 'What about the health and safety of the staff working here?' They said they couldn't do anything about it and I asked, 'Why not? Why don't you think about it?' As well as that, in those days they used to have around 70 fires a year in prisons. If you think about being locked up in a prison cell or working as a staff member and someone next door starts to make a fire with their mattress . . . well, just imagine the fear!

I thought that we should stop this – it seemed ridiculous! – but no country, no entire jurisdiction had ever done it before. The federal system in Canada had, and some other places had, but not an entire country's system. So, I sent the Department of Corrections off to go and do some work and they came back with a solution! They did a brilliant job. It is one of the best executed policy changes of that nature that has ever been seen, that I can think of. And all they really needed from me was the courage to back them to do it. It was also easier because they said I didn't need to have legislation to do it because the prison managers had particular powers. Later that was challenged in Court, but by that stage it was a success and the whole Parliament voted for it, I think, other than possibly the ACT party. This actually saved shanks being made, now they have to grind them all down with concrete and stuff, so it takes a lot longer and they don't have the same access to razors. The Corrections Officers were just amazed. It was actually them that gave me the idea and, yeah, that's one of the best policies I've helped with.

Q: Our last question is, quite simply, is there anything else that you would like to add?

A: I think Leader of the Opposition is a remarkable position because it's the one that is expected to be able to produce the best with the least. Particularly as parties go from government to Opposition there's always a significant churn – there are difficulties for every Opposition I can think of, and Oppositions have to find their way and stay true to what they believe is right. It's a tough job. But that's why it helps to have a bit of experience in government, in Opposition, and in life to be able to stay relatively even tempered through it all.

Well, it's been a wonderful interview! From our point of view, it has encapsulated the nature of this office in the way we could never have done ourselves. Thank you very much.

22 Courts, judges, lawyers

Aotearoa New Zealand has a judicial system based on what the British brought here from England. To many people, how courts conduct their business sometimes seems strange. The law has a long tradition stretching back centuries and customs established long ago still survive. The courts have many symbolic rituals and customs – judges wear robes; lawyers who wear gowns bow to the judges and the judges bow to members of the bar; on ceremonial occasions wigs are worn. Some complain about the rather formal way in which courts conduct their business, others contend that lawyers speak in a strange language that only confuses, and that the expenses associated with going to law are too high. Although the inaccessibility of law is a valid concern, whatever charges are levelled against our system of justice, the courts enjoy a high reputation for fairness and impartiality.

What judges are asked to do by the State to is best shown by the oath or declaration that all judges take when they take office: *'that I will well and truly serve Her Majesty, her heirs and successors, according to law, in the office of Judge [name of judicial office] and I will do right to all manner of people after the laws and usages of New Zealand, without fear or favour, affection or ill will . . .'* Note, it is the usages of New Zealand, not somewhere else.

Although the courts have been increasingly incorporating elements of Māori culture and tikanga, our legal system remains Pākehā-centric and its historical roots are based on understandings of law and justice from a British perspective. In te ao Māori disputes were not solely between two individuals but involved one's entire community. Disputes were often settled on marae with rangatira mediating the consensus of the hui and taking community views into account. The value of utu in tikanga Māori meant that balance and reciprocity must be maintained or restored, especially with regards to mana. The colonial government established a legal system here based on English law. They did not recognise Māori customary law and tikanga. That is changing.

There are more judges in Aotearoa New Zealand than there are

Members of Parliament. Their numbers, however, are capped by law and Parliament must agree if the cap is to be increased. Judges are invested with great powers by the State. They preside over criminal jury trials that find people guilty or not guilty of offences in prosecutions for criminal offences, sentence those who are convicted, and can imprison people for lengthy periods. They also adjudicate upon a wide range of other issues not involving crimes. The law, the courts and lawyers make up a significant industry involved in delivering justice. There were almost 15,000 practicing certificates issued to lawyers in 2020. This means one lawyer for every 356 people who live here. This is a generous ratio by international standards.

It has been said *'the judiciary, from the nature of its functions, will always be the least dangerous'* branch of government. Not only is the judicial branch of our government the least dangerous branch, but it is also probably the most reliable in its adherence to principle, neutrality, and rationality. Judges are the guardians of the rule of law, an essential role in a democratic government. If members of the Executive take actions without lawful authority the judges will correct them. Judges may be regarded as acting as the constitutional boundary riders. The judiciary differs from the other branches of government in two important respects. Judges are obliged to give reasons for their decisions. And those decisions can be appealed.

When most people think of the courts, they think of criminal justice trials that are conducted in court in public. The criminal trial, of course, remains central to our system of justice. It provides fundamental protections for the accused person against the might of the State. However, the courts also carry out a wide range of other duties. They hear civil cases which are disputes usually involving money, between one citizen and another, or between a citizen and the government. A great many important matters come before the civil courts: questions relating to taxation; business contracts; a wide range of commercial affairs; questions about wills, trusts, and inheritance; family disputes over divorce, custody, separation, and matrimonial property; cases where negligent conduct has caused another to suffer and experience loss; disputes over land and other property.

The two arms of what the courts do can be divided generally between civil and criminal cases. It is necessary to give priority to criminal cases, and this may mean sometimes delays in civil cases can be lengthy. The courts had great difficulty with Covid-19 in scheduling their work and keeping people in courts safe.

The judiciary has an essential role in upholding the law. The judiciary acts both as our society's formal method of dispute resolution and as a check and balance on the power of the other two branches of government. The judiciary's independence from Parliament and the Executive is one of its most crucial elements. The courts must operate autonomously to hold political decision-makers to the law. The law applies to everyone equally, including the government. Any person can bring a claim against the Executive to the High Court if the government has acted unlawfully or unfairly under what is known as administrative law. The courts and the laws can and do protect the vulnerable from exploitation.

Courts

There is more than one type of court. Different types of judges with different expertise and experience work in the various courts that handle different classes of cases. For example, family law is a different legal world from commercial law. The part of the court system where most people have dealings with the courts is the District Court Te Kōti Ā Rohe. As the District Court Te Kōti Ā Rohe website says: *'Most New Zealanders who go to court will go through the entire justice process in the District Court. Each year, 183 Judges in 58 courthouses deal with approximately 200,000 criminal, family, youth and civil matters.'* His Honour Judge Heemi Taumaunu has been the Chief District Court Judge since 2019. The District Court Te Kōti Ā Rohe sits in 58 locations around the country. These are the places where most judicial business is dealt with. Most people who end up in court will see only the District Court Te Kōti Ā Rohe or perhaps the Tenancy or Disputes Tribunals, the latter two of which are presided over by Tenancy Tribunal adjudicators and referees.

The District Court Te Kōti Ā Rohe is extraordinarily busy. For example, the majority of criminal cases are dealt with there: as many as 130,000 a year. And they have an extensive civil jurisdiction to deal with disputes involving up to $350,000. In the busiest areas, Community Magistrates function as part-time judges who are selected for their skills and knowledge to help with cases of more minor significance. Others who have been District Court Te Kōti Ā Rohe judges hold temporary warrants to help with the quantity of work. Some selected and trained

Justices of the Peace, who are appointed to take oaths and declarations and swear affidavits, can also sit in court to deal with minor offences and some traffic cases. Court houses are a significant investment, as are the support services for all the courts administered by the Ministry of Justice.

More than 50 District Court Te Kōti Ā Rohe judges hold Family Court warrants and spend most of their time sitting in the Family Court. Other specialist courts include the Environment Court Te Kōti Taiao that deals with environmental issues, usually those that arise under the Resource Management Act 1991. There are nine Environment Court judges who, while not part of the District Court Te Kōti Ā Rohe, are treated as if they were. The Māori Land Court Te Kooti Whenua was created in the 1860s and deals with Māori land. Its role is to provide a court service for owners of Māori land, their whānau and their hapū to promote the retention and use of Māori land and facilitate the occupation, development and use of that land.

The Coroners Court continued under the Coroners Act 2006 consists of the Chief Coroner and 20 other coroners whose purpose is to help to prevent deaths and to promote justice through investigations, and the identification of the causes and circumstances of sudden or unexplained deaths, or deaths in special circumstances; and the making of recommendations that may reduce the chances of further deaths occurring in similar circumstances. Another important court is the Employment Court Te Kōti Taiao. It hears and determines cases relating to employment disputes. These include challenges to determinations of the Employment Relations Authority, questions of interpretation of law, and disputes over strikes and lockouts.

The High Court Te Kōti Matua sits above the District Court Te Kōti Ā Rohe and as part of its work hears appeals from the District Court Te Kōti Ā Rohe, the Family Court Te Kōti Whānau, and the Environment Court Te Kōti Taiao. The High Court Te Kōti Matua also has responsibility for conducting the most difficult and important criminal trials, murder being the most obvious example. It also deals with judicial review of administrative action, tax cases, and big commercial disputes. Judicial review cases are where the High Court Te Kōti Matua tests whether the Executive followed the law correctly when making individual decisions. The High Court Te Kōti Matua has a wide range of duties, and its jurisdiction is not limited like the District Court Te Kōti

Ā Rohe. For example, it can hear civil cases up to unlimited amounts. The writ of habeas corpus that deals with detention of people is available only through this court. There were more than 40 High Court Te Kōti Matua judges in October 2021 and seven associate judges. Hon Justice Susan Thomas has been the Chief High Court Judge since April 2020.

The Court of Appeal Te Kōti Pīra sits above the High Court Te Kōti Matua in the hierarchy and is an intermediate appellate court. In the Court of Appeal Te Kōti Pīra and the Supreme Court Te Kōti Mana Nui there are no trials except on the rarest of occasions. Instead, there are what are known as legal arguments, which are like debates about the correct application of the law. The appellate courts are there to correct errors that may have occurred in the court being appealed from, and hear appeals on both civil and criminal matters. Ten judges are permanent members of the Court of Appeal but on criminal appeals sometimes a High Court Te Kōti Matua Judge will sit with two permanent members. There are ten judges in the Court of Appeal Te Kōti Pīra. They are presided over by a judge who is called the President, Hon Justice Mark Cooper, appointed in April 2022 after the former President Justice Stephen Kós was promoted to the Supreme Court. Usually, three judges sit on a case in the Court of Appeal Te Kōti Pīra but in particularly important cases five will sit. There were 663 appeals filed with the Court of Appeal Te Kōti Pīra in the 2021 year.

The final court for Aotearoa New Zealand is the Supreme Court Te Kōti Mana Nui. It was established in 2003 following the decision to abolish appeals to the Privy Council in London. In its later years, the Privy Council sat with one judge from Aotearoa New Zealand sitting with four of the United Kingdom Law Lords. The Supreme Court Te Kōti Mana Nui has six permanent judges, with five sitting on each case. It is presided over by the Rt Hon Dame Helen Winkelman, the Chief Justice of New Zealand who was appointed in March 2019. The Chief Justice is also, by statute, head of the Aotearoa New Zealand Judiciary. The Supreme Court Te Kōti Mana Nui hears fewer cases than the other courts, but they are usually cases of public importance. In 2020–21, the Supreme Court Te Kōti Mana Nui received 118 applications for leave to appeal. It delivered 21 substantive judgments in cases where leave was granted. The appellate courts for the most part do not conduct trials. They wrestle with difficult points of law and try to make the law clearer and easier to apply. They are more concerned with difficulties in the law, not finding out the facts, which is the task of the trial courts.

Unlike the other courts, the Supreme Court Te Kōti Mana Nui has a broad discretion as to whether to hear cases at all. The law states:

(1) The Supreme Court must not give leave to appeal to it unless it is satisfied that it is necessary in the interests of justice for the court to hear and determine the appeal.

(2) It is necessary in the interests of justice for the Supreme Court to hear and determine a proposed appeal if—

    (a) the appeal involves a matter of general or public importance; or

    (b) a substantial miscarriage of justice may have occurred, or may occur unless the appeal is heard; or

    (c) the appeal involves a matter of general commercial significance.

(3) For the purposes of subsection (2)(a), a significant issue relating to the Treaty of Waitangi is a matter of general or public importance.

In criminal trials, the accused person has the right to be represented by counsel. They have the right to have the evidence against them heard in open court and tested by cross-examination. The case against the accused person must be proved by the Crown to a high level: beyond a reasonable doubt. The nature of the charge must be clear – it must be an offence against the law as written down in an Act of Parliament. Upon conviction the person will be sentenced in accordance with the law. There is a right of appeal against both conviction and sentence.

Trial by jury is an important element of the justice system. It means that 12 people drawn from the community decide upon the issue of an accused person's guilt, after being directed on the law by the judge presiding at the trial. The right to trial by jury is protected in the New Zealand Bill of Rights Act 1990. A defendant has the right to elect a jury trial where he or she is charged with an offence punishable by a maximum sentence of two years' imprisonment or more. Most jury trials take place in the District Court Te Kōti Ā Rohe.

People who lose cases in court may not want to accept its judgment, but the State provides machinery to compel them to do so. This means that when a court makes a judgment it can be enforced. The Rules of Court provide detailed provisions on the topic. The law called contempt of court is also important and can take many different forms. So be warned, it is prudent to be careful with your behaviour when dealing with the courts and judges. Contempt powers extend to protecting

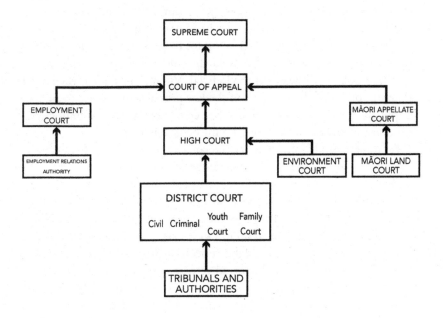

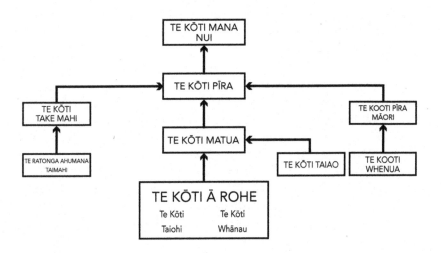

a person's right to a fair trial. Traditionally, the law of contempt has been developed by judges as part of the common law, but over time it became fearsomely complex. Recently, a serious effort has been made to simplify it and put most of the rules in a code. The Contempt of Court Act 2019 sets out its purpose of being to: (i) promote and facilitate the administration of justice and uphold the rule of law; (ii) maintain and enhance public confidence in the judicial system; (iii) reform the law of contempt of court. This branch of the law provides the power to punish people, including lawyers, who disobey court orders, such as injunctions and non-publication orders, or who misbehave in court.

A fundamental limitation on the courts' power to check Executive decisions results from the government's influence over legislative machinery. The government can change any legislative secondary legislation made by the Executive, at will. It can also pass new Acts of Parliament. Statutes can always be amended so long as Cabinet can secure the numbers in Parliament to do it. On occasion governments can react swiftly and decisively against judicial decisions that are unacceptable to them. One recent example involved retrospective legislation to deny a vulnerable group in the community human rights that they had secured through court action. For years, there had been a policy that parents (and resident siblings) who acted as caregivers for their adult, disabled children were not eligible to be paid for the care they provided. So, while non-relatives who undertook such care could be, and were, paid by the Ministry of Health Manatū Hauora for what they did, parents were not.

After years of seeking to have the policy changed, in 2008 a group of parents challenged the lawfulness of the policy under the Human Rights Act 1993. They argued that the policy discriminated against them on the grounds of family status and the policy could not be justified as a reasonable limit on that right in a free and democratic state like Aotearoa New Zealand (that being the test set out in section 5 of the New Zealand Bill of Rights Act 1990). The parents won before the Human Rights Review Tribunal (2010), the High Court Te Kōti Matua (2010) and the Court of Appeal Te Kōti Pīra (2012).

Then, out of the blue, and with no notice, the government introduced a Bill into Parliament which went through all stages of the legislative process within a single sitting day! The legislation was the New Zealand Public Health and Disability Amendment Act (No 2). Its principal effects were, first, to prevent anyone ever making a complaint to the

Human Rights Commission or bringing a court proceeding against any government family carer policy no matter how discriminatory; second, in effect, retrospectively to exclude the provision of remedies for past discrimination; third, permitting the ministry to adopt a paid family carer policy using whatever criteria it considered appropriate.

There was no warning that the Bill was to be introduced and there was no public consultation nor select committee consideration on it. It was declared to be a Budget issue and as a result the then government's support parties were duty-bound to vote in favour of it or else see the government collapse. The Act in effect took away rights from some of the disabled and family members who cared for them. Yet it passed in a single sitting day, despite almost immediate public concern about it. The Parliament has sometimes passed legislation contrary to the Bill of Rights Act 1990. Fortunately, a late remedy did arrive in 2020 when an Act was passed changing the offending 2013 legislation after a change in government. And it should be said this sort of legislation is not common.

The maw of the law

There are many different sources of law that the Aotearoa New Zealand Courts apply. First, they have the power to interpret all the statutes passed by Parliament and secondary legislation made by the Executive. Their interpretations are authoritative and binding on the other branches of government. Court decisions, however, must be faithful to the intention of Parliament as expressed in the legislation.

There are also many pieces of English statute law that are still part of our law. The list can be found in the Imperial Laws Application Act 1988. One such law is part of Magna Carta, a royal charter that resulted from the revolt in England of the Barons against King John in 1215. One part of the 1297 version of Magna Carta remains in our law. It contains a promise not to deny or delay justice to citizens:

C 29I Imprisonment, etc contrary to law. Administration of justice. NO freeman shall be taken or imprisoned, or be disseised of his freehold, or liberties, or free customs, or be outlawed, or exiled, or any other wise destroyed; nor will we not pass upon him, nor condemn him, but by lawful judgment of his peers, or by the law of the land. We will sell to no man, we will not deny or defer to any man either justice or right.

It is far from easy to ascertain how this medieval measure applies to modern Aotearoa New Zealand, but there are plenty of cases where Magna Carta has been cited in our courts. Magna Carta is more important as a symbol than a measure containing real legal application these days, although it could apply in an appropriate case. These days in most common law countries Magna Carta is revered as a foundation of the principle of liberty according to law and so relates to the rule of law, a powerful strand in a long legal tradition. For these reasons it forms part of our constitutional rhetoric and is frequently mentioned in parliamentary debate.

The courts' power to interpret statutes is a significant and important constitutional power. It would be wrong for ministers to decide disputed cases, as they are not independent of the Executive. Providing the courts with the power to interpret the statutes passed by Parliament is an aspect of the separation of powers between the three branches of government.

Second, the judges apply the common law. Originally the common law was the law of England. Common law systems are established in Australia, Canada, the United States, and many Commonwealth countries. The common law is not the product of parliamentary enactment. It is established by the judicial decisions the judges make. In this way, precedents are built up over many years. Think of it as a building being built by the judges, brick by brick. Once a precedent has been set by the superior courts, it must be followed by the courts further down the hierarchy. The role of precedent is a vital part of the system and promotes certainty. Much of our law is judge made, including almost all the law of negligence and much of that is known as tort law, or the law of civil wrongs and much of contract law. For this reason, cases are published in law reports and can also be found on Ministry of Justice websites. Lawyers need to keep up to date with the case law to be able to correctly advise their clients. Parliament can change the common law if it is so minded, and frequently does so. Over time, statute law has become much greater in volume, leaving less room for the common law.

The courts may also apply custom and tikanga Māori. One such case came before the Supreme Court in 2012. In 2007, a Māori man died in Christchurch where he had lived 20 years and his relatives from his Whakatōhea and Tūhoe whānau buried his body in the whānau urepā in Kutarere, against his spouse's wishes (and she was the executor of his will). A majority of the court held that the personal representative had the exclusive right under Aotearoa New Zealand law to determine the manner of disposal of the deceased's body. However, views that arise from customary cultural or religious practices could be considered and the representative must refer to *'tikanga, along with other important cultural and religious values, and all other circumstances as matters that must form part of the evaluation.* The court found that the spouse's decision had priority in the circumstances. Yet the case establishes that tikanga Māori has weight in the New Zealand legal system and it will be interesting to see how that develops. More decisions on the issue are expected early in 2022. We deal with these issues at greater length in Chapter 23.

Qualifications and appointment of judges

Judges are appointed by the Governor-General on the recommendation of the Attorney-General. For the Chief Justice the advice is given by the Prime Minister. To be eligible for appointment the candidate must have had a practicing certificate as a barrister or solicitor for more than seven years. For appointments to the Supreme Court Te Kōti Mana Nui, the Court of Appeal Te Kōti Pīra, and the High Court Te Kōti Matua, the Attorney-General also receives advice from the Chief Justice and the Solicitor-General. There will also be consultations with the New Zealand Law Society and the New Zealand Bar Association. As a matter of courtesy, the Attorney will mention the appointment in Cabinet so Cabinet ministers are not caught unaware. But ministers have no control over the decision as to whom to recommend as political considerations should not play a part in judicial appointments. Judges' salaries and allowances are set by the Remuneration Authority, which is independent of the government. As of 2021, The Chief Justice is remunerated with a salary of $560,100 plus an allowance. Other judges are paid less, with District Court Te Kōti Ā Rohe judges receiving $358,100.

The Senior Courts Act requires the Attorney-General publish information explaining his or her process for (a) seeking expressions of interest for the appointment of judges and associate judges; and (b) recommending persons for appointment as a judge or an associate judge. This development means that the process is much more open and transparent than it used to be. It is seldom that appointments of judges attract public, political or media criticism.

The most important aspect of judicial protocol are the criteria for appointment for High Court Te Kōti Matua judges because of their constitutional importance. Appointment of a High Court Te Kōti Matua judge must consider a candidate's *legal ability* in sound knowledge of the law and experience in its application; *qualities of character* including honesty, open mindedness, common sense, and other relevant qualities; *personal technical skills* which may include communication and organisation; and *reflection of society* being socially aware. These are rigorous criteria and people who can meet them are accomplished and skillful. Further, in recent years there have been many more appointments to the judiciary from people from diverse ethnic and social backgrounds. In 2020 Mike White wrote in *Stuff* that *'when it comes to ethnicity, 79 per cent of District Court judges are New Zealand European, 16 per cent Māori, four per cent Pasifika, with just two of the judges being Indian, and one Māori/Chinese'.* This is not entirely representative of the population of Aotearoa New Zealand, but the diversity of the bench can be expected to increase over time.

In practice a judicial appointments register is maintained by the Ministry of Justice. When a vacancy arises, the Solicitor-General reviews the names and consults the Attorney-General, the Chief Justice, and the President of the Court of Appeal Te Kōti Pīra as to whether an additional name should be added to the list. There are further consultations with the President of the Law Commission, the President of the Bar Association, the President of the New Zealand Law Society, and sometimes other professional legal organisations. A short list of no more than three names is prepared by the Attorney-General with the agreement of the Chief Justice. The Attorney-General then selects the candidate from the list and recommends the appointment to the Governor-General. The procedure is similar for District Court Te Kōti Matua judges.

Because of the extent of their power and responsibilities, it is essential the judiciary are subject to accountability mechanisms. An important principle is that the government should not exert any form of pressure on any judges to make decisions in a particular way. It would be quite wrong for a minister to tell a judge how to decide a case, especially as the legality of ministerial actions frequently falls to be decided by the courts. Political attacks on the judiciary would weaken the authority and standing of the courts, especially their reputation for impartiality. The *Cabinet Manual* also restricts ministers from public comment on judicial decisions that could be understood as *'reflecting adversely on the impartiality, personal views, or ability of any judge'*. There are also several rules in the Parliament against members making offensive remarks or using unbecoming words against any members of the judiciary. There is another side to this constitutional convention: judges must refrain from politically partisan activities and refrain from taking public sides in matters of political controversy.

There is a long-standing principle inherited from England contained in the Constitution Act 1986 which protects judges against dismissal from office. First, their salary cannot be reduced while they are in office. Second, a High Court Te Kōti Matua judge can only be removed from office by the Sovereign or Governor-General, acting upon an address of the House of Representatives. This can only be moved on the grounds of a judge's misbehaviour or incapacity to fulfil the duties of their office.

No such motion has ever been moved in the New Zealand Parliament. The same protection does not apply to District Court Te Kōti Ā Rohe judges. They can be removed by the Governor-General on ministerial advice if guilty of 'misbehaviour'. Misbehaviour was interpreted by the Solicitor-General in 1997 as *'conduct that is so morally wrong and improper that it demonstrates a judge lacks the integrity to continue to exercise judicial office'*.

In 2004, a Judicial Conduct Commissioner and Judicial Conduct Panel Act was passed that provides that complaints may be made about the conduct of judges in the exercise of their judicial functions. The Commissioner must receive and deal with every complaint made under this section and as many as 150 complaints a year have been common in recent years. In the case that there was an address in the House moved to remove a judge, there would first be an investigation under the Act and a decision made to set up a Judicial Conduct Panel. One of the statutory functions of the Commissioner, in appropriate cases, is to recommend to the Attorney-General that a Judicial Conduct Panel be appointed to inquire into any matters concerning judges' conduct. Such panels have been appointed, but so far, no panel has recommended removal, although one judge resigned before its work was completed.

Lawyers

Becoming a lawyer starts with about five years at university and qualifying for an LLB or LLB (Honours) degree. The law courses at the universities must be approved by the Council of Legal Education. After earning a law degree it is necessary to undertake formal professional training that may last several months. After this, a candidate must satisfy the High Court Te Kōti Matua, they are of a good character to be admitted as a barrister and solicitor of the High Court Te Kōti Matua. They must obtain an annual practicing certificate and pay the annual fee. There are restrictions upon practicing on your own account until you have sufficient experience. Lawyers are officers of the court. This imposes obligations on them not to mislead or bring false evidence before the court. The Law Society operates a system of discipline for lawyers who can be struck off the rolls if they are found to have been guilty of professional misconduct. They can also be censured or fined. The obligations that lawyers must care for their clients are set out in the rules made under the Lawyers and Conveyancers Act.

Aotearoa New Zealand lawyers are admitted as barristers and solicitors. When they have had some experience, they can practice on their own. They may then choose to practice as barristers and solicitors or as barristers only, this is sometimes called 'barrister sole'. Perhaps the best way of looking at the distinction is that barristers specialise in litigation, and also give legal opinions on difficult issues. The essence of a barrister's duty is to give independent legal advice in the matter, without any influence from extraneous considerations.

Senior, experienced, and exceptional lawyers can apply for 'silk' which means they can wear a silk gown in court not a stuff gown. They are admitted to the rank of Queen's Counsel (if a King ascends the throne, they automatically become King's Counsel). To become a QC, a lawyer must make a written application. These are carefully reviewed and there is consultation about them. Appointments are made under the advice of the Attorney-General, concurred in by the Chief Justice. The rank of Queen's Counsel is awarded to barristers-sole who have demonstrated excellence in their careers. The standard is high and will not be reached merely by completing a certain number of years in practice, according to the guidelines issued by the Attorney-General in 2019. The comparative rarity of the rank is illustrated by this April 2019 statement of the New Zealand Law Society: *'Over 35,000 people have been admitted as lawyers in New Zealand since the beginning of the 20th century. In that time just 317 members of the profession have been made Queen's Counsel.'*

Going to law

The law is complex. Disputes can be costly, last a long time and be emotionally draining. The processes of the law are not quick. People need lawyers to find their way around complicated transactions and issues. However, lawyers can be expensive and often must spend many hours on research, making inquiries, drafting documents, and appearing in court. They usually charge by the hour. Then again, lawyers can also save you a lot of money in the right circumstances. Lawyers tend to specialise more than they used to, and it is important to secure a lawyer who knows the field in which your issues arise. It is not wise to ask a specialist in tax law to make an application to the court for bail on a criminal charge, for example. People can represent themselves in court rather than hire a lawyer, but it is unwise to do so. Procedure is intricate and laid down in rules of court and certain documents must be drawn up and filed with the court. All of this may be confusing and demanding for those not legally educated. The risk is that in an adversarial system the unrepresented will be at a disadvantage. If you are taking a dispute to court, be sure it is the best step to take. Mediation can be a useful alternative.

Legal aid for people who cannot afford a lawyer is available, but not on very generous terms. According to the Ministry of Justice's website: legal aid is considered a loan. You may have to repay some or all of your legal aid, depending on how much you earn, what property you own and whether you receive any money or property as a result of your case. Legal aid may be available for people who need a lawyer but cannot afford one, and are:

- charged with a criminal offence
- involved in a family dispute that goes to court (such as care of children)
- involved in a civil matter (such as a dispute over money, housing, ACC, or a job)
- a victim of a violent offence wanting to apply for a civil non-contact order.

The present system of legal aid has been heavily criticised both by the judiciary and the New Zealand Law Society. The system fails to provide sufficient help in civil cases and is rather minimalist in the criminal arena. Many lawyers will not take legal aid cases because the remuneration is insufficient.

Disputes Tribunal

If you have a dispute that is relatively minor and do not want to go to the court, you may think about using the Disputes Tribunal, established by the Disputes Tribunal Act 1988. This tribunal was established to deal with small civil claims between people, where the value does not exceed $30,000. These may include such matters as contractual disputes, and disputes concerning the wrongful destruction or loss of any property, any damage or injury to property, or the recovery of property. Lawyers cannot be used when dealing with disputes through the Disputes Tribunal, which may make things more equitable in cases where one party cannot afford legal representation. The people making decisions are called Referees and they are carefully selected for their skills and are not required to be lawyers themselves. This scheme is administered through the District Court. When orders are made, they are enforceable, although there is a very narrow possibility of appeal to the District Court if the proceedings have been conducted unfairly or were prejudicially affected. There are several cases that can be viewed on the Disputes Tribunal website for those who want to get a flavour of what can be done within the Tribunal.

Conclusion

The key outstanding issues concerning the place of the courts in the Aotearoa New Zealand system of government relates to access to justice. How user friendly is the legal system? How can people engage with the system? How do people get information about the process? Will the legal process be accommodating to an individual's needs? How much will it cost? Too often, access to justice depends on the wealth of the individuals seeking it. A 2004 Law Commission Report entitled *Delivering Justice for All: A Vision for New Zealand Courts and Tribunals* made a set of recommendations to make the system more accessible. Few of them were implemented. The full report is available on the Law Commission's website. The Commission made a telling statement on the responsibility of the State for access to justice. It remains to be fulfilled. The judiciary is a necessary, but complicated, aspect of our system of governance. Hopefully, all going well, you will never have to go to court.

References

Grant Morris *Law Alive – the New Zealand Legal system in Context* (3rd ed., Oxford University Press, Melbourne, 2015); Jacinta Ruru, Duncan Webb, Paul Scott *The New Zealand Legal System – Structure and Processes* (6th ed., LexisNexis Wellington, 2016); Stephen Winter and Chris Jones *Magna Carta and New Zealand* (Palgrave Macmillan, Cham Switzerland, 2017); Alexander M Bickel *The Least Dangerous Branch* (Bobbs-Merrill, Indianapolis, 1962); Rosemary Riddell *To be Fair: Confessions of a District Court Judge* (Upstart Press, Auckland, 2021); District Court Act 2016; Senior Courts Act 2016; Disputes Tribunals Act 1988; Coroners Act 2006; Family Courts Act 1980; Environment Court; Part 11 of Resource Management Act 1991; Employment Court, Employment Relations Act 2000, Part 10.

23 Te Tiriti o Waitangi, tikanga Māori and law

Our current legal and governance systems are based on those set up during the first 20 years of government by the Crown – the 1852 New Zealand Constitution Act and the granting of responsible government. However, Māori tikanga also has a significant place here in Aotearoa New Zealand. This chapter explores the ways that te Tiriti o Waitangi and tikanga are currently represented in our legal system and how that relates to our historical context as a nation. Few aspects of our system of government are more complicated, contested, and untidy than the two intertwined concepts that are the subject of this chapter. Trying to make clear the current situation presents many challenges, not least because it is an area that has undergone rapid development in the last few years and the field continues to alter. The Executive, the Courts, Parliament and the Waitangi Tribunal are all active in this space. It is a changing scene.

Te Tiriti o Waitangi in the legal system

The British Empire's colonisation of Aotearoa New Zealand meant disruption and harm for Māori as the tangata whenua. Māori understood both He Whakaputanga o te Rangatiratanga o Nu Tireni and the te reo text Te Tiriti o Waitangi as cementing their authority and tino rangatiratanga in Aotearoa New Zealand. As the Waitangi Tribunal concluded, the te reo text Te Tiriti o Waitangi also granted kāwanatanga to the Crown, essentially allowing the Crown to have authority and impose law on British subjects and settlers in Aotearoa New Zealand. However, the Crown understood the English text of the Treaty of Waitangi to mean that Māori ceded sovereignty to the Crown while guaranteeing Māori property rights and rangatiratanga. This meant the law could be made through the mechanisms of the Crown and then became binding on everyone.

Māori found themselves in conflict with the Crown principally because, as the number of settlers increased, they wanted land and the colonial government wanted to exercise authority over Māori. These pressures ultimately led to wars breaking out. The government insisted that its power would predominate, rather than the shared power that Māori thought te Tiriti o Waitangi had provided for. The consequences of these developments for Māori were devastating. Historian Vincent O'Malley wrote in 2019 that Māori suffered a long history of *'invasion, dispossession and confiscation'* of land. These aspects of colonialism explain much about the inequities that afflict Māori to this day. Article 3 of te Tiriti gave Māori the 'privilege' of being British subjects.

Prior to the Treaty, Britain recognised Māori hapū as sovereign over their territories. When Britain sent Captain Hobson to negotiate the Treaty of Waitangi, the Colonial Secretary's instructions were clear that Māori tribal sovereignty was 'indisputable' and could be given up only with the 'free and intelligent consent' of Māori leaders. Britain's intention was to obtain sovereignty over New Zealand. Its immediate purpose was to obtain the legal power to control British settlement and, in particular, to head off the New Zealand Company, which intended to establish a colony at Port Nicholson/Wellington.

Modern experts in international law are in broad agreement that the Treaty of Waitangi was a valid Treaty under international law. As the international law expert Professor Ian Brownlie wrote in 1991:

There can be no doubt . . . that the Treaty of Waitangi presupposed the legal and political capacity of the chiefs of New Zealand to make an agreement which was valid on the international plane.

As such, the Treaty created real rights and obligations in international law. This means the rights and obligations the Crown took up in 1840 now belong to the Crown in right of New Zealand. Under the international law, the Crown had obligations to honour its guarantees of tino rangatiratanga and equal rights. Under Aotearoa New Zealand's current constitutional arrangements, rights and obligations arising from treaties cannot be specifically invoked and enforced in the New Zealand courts unless they have been incorporated into domestic law by Act of Parliament. Currently, te Tiriti is referred to in some Acts, but not all – making it both half in and half out of our legal system. However, our courts can and have used te Tiriti o Waitangi both as a source of principle and as an aid to interpretation of both statute and common law.

In the early years of the Aotearoa New Zealand colony, the Treaty had some influence over Crown actions in New Zealand. Although the Crown's interpretation differed from that of Māori, the Crown nonetheless took its obligations to protect Māori lands and customary rights seriously. The New Zealand Constitution Act 1852, which established the House of Representatives, also made provision for autonomous districts in which Māori laws would prevail within limits. In the event, these provisions were never used. Over time, as settler politicians persuaded Britain to hand over responsibility for Crown-Māori relations to the colonial government, Treaty rights faded from view. For a very long time, the Treaty received little recognition in New Zealand statute law and little recognition in public policy. English law as applied in Aotearoa New Zealand gave little weight to Māori views of law.

The Treaty of Waitangi Act 1975 was the most significant step towards reversing that trend. It established the Waitangi Tribunal and empowered it to inquire into claims that the Crown had caused harm to Māori people by breaching the Treaty and its principles. This measure was, however, limited, because it could only address Treaty breaches from 1975 onwards. In 1985, the Fourth Labour Government extended the Treaty's statutory reach by empowering it to inquire into historical claims as far back as 1840. Those claims have led to numerous settlements. Historic claims are not too far from completion; however, contemporary breaches will remain to be dealt with on a continuing basis. However, many Māori issues were dealt with by the Parliament which passed a Māori Purposes Act just about every year.

The Fourth Labour Government also incorporated Treaty principles into several other statutes. An early example was the Conservation Act 1987, which in section 4 lays down: *'This Act shall so be interpreted and administered as to give effect to the principles of the Treaty of Waitangi.'* Section 4 applies to all decision-makers under the Act. Even more significant was section 9 of the State-Owned Enterprises Act 1986, which provided: *'Nothing in this Act shall permit the Crown to act in a manner that is inconsistent with the principles of the Treaty of Waitangi.'*

The Treaty provision in the State-owned Enterprises Act 1986 led to a most significant legal case known as the *Lands* case, in which the Court of Appeal unanimously held that the Crown could not transfer assets to State-owned enterprises without establishing a system to consider whether such a transfer would be inconsistent with the principles of the Treaty of Waitangi/te Tiriti o Waitangi and therefore be unlawful. The result of this legal declaration was a negotiation with Māori followed by the passage of a statute that permitted transfers so long as the titles to the lands in question made it clear they were subject to Treaty claims. This meant the rights of claimants were expressly protected.

About 30 New Zealand statutes contain Treaty references of varying weight, which need to be considered carefully when dealing with Māori issues that arise under those statutes. Some statutes require government agencies to 'give effect to' te Tiriti principles; other statutes require agencies to 'have regard to' or 'take into account' those principles, or to consult Māori and involve them in decision-making. Some require government departments or local authorities to comply with Treaty obligations, while others set out specific processes for compliance.

The courts have had many cases over the years that interpreted Treaty clauses in statutes. These sometimes also include issues of tikanga Māori. For example, in 2021 the Supreme Court decided, in a case involving a Treaty clause in s 12 of the Exclusive Economic Zone and Continental Shelf Act (EnvironmentalEffects) Act 2012, that a broad and generous construction of such Treaty clauses, which provide a greater degree of definition as to the way Treaty principles are to be given effect, was required. *An intention to constrain the ability of statutory decision-makers to respect treaty principles should not be ascribed to Parliament unless that intention is made quite clear.* It followed that tikanga-based customary rights and interests had to be given weight. This meant that a decision of the Environment Protection Authority to allow seabed mining was unlawful.

Over the years, courts have interpreted these statutes and, in doing so, developed a series of Treaty principles which can be applied to other cases. Those principles include **partnership** (te Tiriti/the Treaty was a partnership between the Crown and Māori, in which both must act reasonably, honourably, and in good faith); **active protection** (the Crown's right to govern involved a corresponding obligation to actively protect Māori interests, in the nature of a fiduciary duty); and **redress** (past wrongs give rise to a right of redress). The Waitangi Tribunal has also identified other principles of **reciprocity**, **mutual benefit, self-government** (the right of Māori communities to manage themselves and their territories and resources), **options** (the right of Māori to choose whether to live according to tikanga or assimilate into European communities), and **equity and equal treatment**. \

So, the present situation is that te Tiriti o Waitangi and its principles are part of statute law for some purposes in Aotearoa New Zealand and not for others, and the application of te Tiriti is inconsistent from one statute to the next. Furthermore, under some circumstances, courts can consider the Treaty when interpreting a statute even when it is not specifically mentioned. In a 1987 decision, Justice Chilwell concluded that the Treaty was *'part of the fabric of New Zealand society'*, and that the Treaty obligations had been explicitly and implicitly recognised in statute law. Therefore, where legislation impinged on Treaty principles, te Tiriti is nonetheless considered part of the context in which that legislation could be interpreted, in accordance with existing principles of statutory interpretation.

In recent decades, starting in 1985–86, te Tiriti o Waitangi has also come to form a more important element in government decision-making. Decision-making processes set out in the Cabinet Manual require attention to be given to the consequences of decisions that affect Māori interests. For example, it is necessary for ministers who seek Cabinet approval of Bills to be introduced to Parliament to draw attention to any features of the Bill that *'have implications for or may be affected by [. . .] the principles of the Treaty of Waitangi.* While there has been increasing consensus within Parliament on these issues in the last 20 years, recognition of te Tiriti is still dependent to a large degree on the political decisions of the government of the day. In order to achieve more stability further steps may be needed.

Treaty Settlements

Since 1985, when the Waitangi Tribunal's jurisdiction was extended back to 1840, it has built up a series of enlightening reports about Crown-Māori relations in districts around Aotearoa New Zealand. Many of those reports have been followed by significant settlements of historical claims. In other cases, the Crown and Māori have negotiated directly without waiting for a Tribunal inquiry. All of these settlements become part of Aotearoa New Zealand law. Between 1992 and 2018 Parliament enacted 73 substantial Treaty of Waitangi Settlement Acts, which settled claims, apologised for the Crown's past wrongs, and transferred assets of various types to the claimants. The value of the transfers from all Treaty settlement was more than $10 billion as at the end of 2021. The nature of settlements differ from one region to the next.

One of the most recent settlement Acts passed by Parliament is also one of the most innovative. The Te Awa Tupua (Whanganui River Claims Settlement) Act 2017 not only declared the Whanganui River a living person, but also recognised the river and its tributaries as an indivisible whole which provided both physical and spiritual sustenance to its communities and environment. The Act also recognised the 'inalienable' connection between the river and its iwi and hapū, for whom it was a source of both identity and responsibility. This initiative, which grabbed headlines around the world, was an unprecedented recognition of traditional Māori values and laws in Aotearoa New Zealand legislation.

Another important and ground-breaking settlement was that concluded with the Ngāi Tūhoe settlement, an iwi that had never signed te Tiriti o Waitangi and had nonetheless suffered confiscations and other injustices. The historic treatment of this iwi, which occupied a large area in a remote part of the country including Te Urewera, has been atrocious to say the least. The settlement reached was creative and extensive. The key to the solution was that the former land in Crown ownership would be changed so that Te Urewera became its own legal entity under legislation. The members of the governance board, both Crown and Tūhoe nominees, act in the interests of Te Urewera, like trustees or directors of a company, instead of on behalf of either the Crown or Tūhoe. Redress to the value of $170 million was provided for the benefit of the iwi, and the Crown apologised to Tūhoe for past dealings that breached Treaty obligations. These included:

- indiscriminate raupatu, wrongful killings, and years of scorched earth warfare
- denying Tūhoe the right of a self-governing Urewera Reserve by subverting the Urewera District Native Reserve Act 1896
- excluding Tūhoe from the establishment of Te Urewera National Park over their homelands
- wrongly treating Lake Waikaremoana as Crown property for many years.

Another one of the recent and most notable settlements concerned the events that occurred at Parihaka. In 1881, John Bryce, the Minister for Native Affairs, mounted on a white charger and led 1,600 troops into the pacifist settlement Parihaka, arresting their leaders Te Whiti o Rongomai, Tohu Kākahi, and Tītokowaru. There was no resistance because the leaders were practitioners of the arts of passive resistance. The village was destroyed and there were multiple rapes. The people arrested were detained without trial and imprisoned in te Waipounamu (the South Island). A special Act of Parliament had to be passed to permit such an illegal action. In 2017, the Crown made a full apology for these outrageous acts and paid compensation.

The settlement process has undoubtedly had profound impacts on Aotearoa New Zealand in many ways. As Professor Janine Hayward has written, it has *altered New Zealand's political, economic, and social landscapes*, laying bare the nation's colonial history, acknowledging the harm done to Māori, establishing new relationships between the Crown and Māori, and re-establishing the base for future Māori development. Many of the iwi who have settled now operate major business ventures, in turn providing employment, paying dividends, and supporting education, housing and other community development projects for their people.

Yet the settlement process also has significant limitations, as Māori have pointed out. From beginning to end, it is a process that is defined by the Crown. The Tribunal that inquires into claims is part of the Crown's legal system, and the settlements that follow occur largely on the Crown's terms. Although settlements are negotiated between the Crown and iwi, the power relationship is unequal, and the Crown determines the parameters for negotiation. It determines who it will negotiate with, which claims it will negotiate over, how much it is willing to pay, and which lands and other resources are available as redress. The settlements are not intended to fully compensate Māori for lands taken or harm done, merely to acknowledge the grievances, and take some steps to restore Crown-Māori relationships and support Māori economic development.

Perhaps most significantly for Māori, the settlement process addresses elements of some harms arising from colonisation, particularly those to do with land and resources; but it does not address the process of colonisation itself. That is, it does not address the Crown's assertion of power over Māori who had not freely consented; nor does it overhaul political power structures. According to Professor Margaret Mutu: *'Despite government assertions that Māori are happy with settlements . . . research shows conclusively that they are not.'* In her view, many iwi regard the Crown's apologies as meaningless, and settlements as a pragmatic transitional step towards more comprehensive reform.

According to Associate Professor Maria Bargh, this reflects fundamentally different expectations about what the settlement process should deliver. While the Crown is, in essence, seeking to clear away historical grievances so it can get on with the business of governing, Māori are seeking fundamental changes to the ongoing relationship, including the manner in which Aotearoa New Zealand is governed and political power is shared.

Customary title and the foreshore and seabed case

The Treaty is not the only source of rights in law for Māori as the indigenous people of Aotearoa New Zealand. In fact, there is a long common law tradition in English law of recognising the rights of indigenous peoples.

When English common law arrived in Aotearoa New Zealand, one of the principles it brought with it was the principle of aboriginal or native title to land. The essence of this principle is that indigenous people have rights to possess and use land, and those rights cannot be taken away except with consent. It was this principle that led the Crown, in Article 2 of the English text of the Treaty of Waitangi, to recognise that Māori had rights to land which could not be extinguished except with their free, informed consent. This principle was also part of the reason Article 2, in the English text, granted the Crown a right of pre-emption, which meant only it could buy Māori land. Under English law at the time, only the Crown could extinguish native title. This was done, among other reasons, to protect the requirement for free consent, but it also meant the Crown could control the sale of land to settlers.

The so-called 'foreshore and seabed case' in the 1990s arose not from Treaty rights, but from this doctrine of native title. Under English common law, it was assumed that the Crown holds rights to the foreshore and seabed, and could therefore assign rights to others (including, in this particular case, marine farmers). A group of Northern South Island iwi challenged this assumption, arguing that they had pre-existing customary title. The Court of Appeal found that aboriginal or customary title (as it is now called) in common law remained in force until lawfully extinguished. The Crown's land title therefore depended on it proving that to be the case.

The Fifth Labour Government responded in 2004 with legislation that declared the Crown to own the foreshore and seabed, while also making provision for customary activities that had continued since 1840 to be protected. The subsequent National-led government repealed that Act in 2011, substituting it with a new statute that replaced the Crown ownership title with no ownership, and provided a mechanism for hapū and iwi to negotiate with the Crown for recognition of customary rights, and providing for ultimate determination by the courts. Among other things, the 2011 statute aimed to 'acknowledge' te Tiriti o Waitangi and 'recognise' the traditional authority of hapū and iwi as tāngata whenua over the foreshore and seabed (now known as the marine and coastal area) in their territories. The 2011 Act repealed the earlier Act that had extinguished those Māori rights. This provided for yet another form in which Treaty rights may be acknowledged in statute and has already acted as a precedent in many other similar cases.

The whole judgment in *Re Edwards (Te Whakatōhea No 2)* [2021] NZHC 1025 of Justice Churchman sets out the details of the processes that must be gone through. It is available on the High Court website.

Tikanga Māori

Sir Hirini Moko Mead explains that *'Tikanga are tools of thought and understanding. They are packages of ideas which help to organise behaviour and provide some predictability in how certain activities are carried out. They provide templates and frameworks to guide our actions. . . .'* Tikanga is not like English law, however, tikanga is nonetheless a system of law, which may including customs, traditions, procedures, norms, and practices. Tikanga Māori are based on traditional and customary precedents, but nonetheless adapt and can evolve to suit different and contemporary times. Tikanga may differ between iwi, hapū, and marae. As one Māori scholar, Ani Mikaere puts it:

I regard tikanga as the first law of Aotearoa. It arrived here with our ancestors and it operated effectively to serve their needs for a thousand years before Pākehā came. It was the only system of law in operation when the first Pākehā began living here amongst us. Had the reaffirmation of Māori authority in the second article of Te Tiriti o Waitangi been adhered to, the relationship between Pākehā and Māori would have been regulated by tikanga Māori throughout our shared history. I believe it would have resulted in a far healthier relationship than the one we currently have.

The relationship between tikanga Māori, te Tiriti o Waitangi, and the rest of the legal system is ever complicated. One example of an approach that the courts could take is set out in the following paragraph from a judgment of Justice Matthew Palmer in a case decided in February 2021:

Tikanga Māori was the first law in Aotearoa. It is recognised by Acts of Parliament. It is also recognised by the common law of New Zealand. Tikanga Ngāti Rehua-Ngātiwai ki Aotea lies at the heart of this dispute. But a court must be very careful about 'finding' tikanga as a fact, even where it is requested by the relevant iwi or hapū to do so. Any recognition by a court can only be a snapshot at a certain point and only for the particular purpose of the particular case before it at the time. What is recognised by a court cannot change the underlying fact of tikanga determined by the hapū or iwi, exercising their rangatiratanga.

Justice Palmer therefore determined that, as there was no conflicting law in the case at hand, he was bound to rule in accordance with tikanga Ngāti Rehua-Ngāti Wai ki Aotea – though he also determined that it was not the court's role to determine the tikanga involved or the relevant whakapapa. 'That is for Ngāti Rehua-Ngātiwai ki Aotea.'

Justice Joseph Williams, the first Māori Supreme Court Judge, has also described tikanga as New Zealand's first law, *'brought across vast ocean distances by Kupe and Toi and others from their respective home islands in the tropical Pacific to these shores a millennium ago'.*

Understanding this law (more accurately these laws for the laws were distinct in each source island) and its cultural drivers, helps to explain why this first law continues to force its way to the surface in the unimaginably different circumstances of modern New Zealand.

The Waitangi Tribunal has described Kupe's system of law as follows:

Its defining principle, and its life blood, was kinship – the value through which the Hawaikians expressed relationships with the elements of the physical world, the spiritual world, and each other. The sea was not an impersonal thing, but an ancestor deity. The dots of land on which the people lived were a manifestation of the constant tension between the deities, or, to some, deities in their own right. Kinship was the revolving

*door between the human, physical, and spiritual realms. This culture
had its own creation theories, its own science and technology, its own
bodies of sacred and profane knowledge. These people had their own ways
of producing and distributing wealth, and of maintaining social order.
They emphasised individual responsibility to the collective at the expense
of individual rights, yet they greatly valued individual reputation and
standing. They enabled human exploitation of the environment, but
through the kinship value (known in te ao Māori as whanaungatanga) they
also emphasised human responsibility to nurture and care for it (known in
te ao Māori as kaitiakitanga).*

As Justice Williams elaborated:

*Of course, in the beginning things were a little more complicated than
that. A score of ocean-going waka followed Kupe from both his island and
different islands and villages throughout eastern Polynesia. So the detailed
systems of tikanga they brought with them varied between waka. And those
variations remained with the descendants. As Buck said many years ago,
iwi are, in heart and mind, a series of islands connected by land. But the
underlying values of these old island cultures were, and remain, universal
and simply stated. They melded, adapted and changed in important
ways after arrival, in response to the very different environment of these
temperate islands located at the hinge of the southern hemisphere's weather
systems. In that sense Māori culture and Māori law is, in its distinctive
aspects, entirely a product of the interaction between those old Hawaikians
and this place. Te reo Māori was imagined out of the whenua, flora and
fauna of this place as new words were needed to explain things newly
experienced. The canoe and longhouse technology Kupe's descendants
developed was possible because of the great forests and necessary because
of the cooler climate in this place, and so on. The economy changed to
accommodate a place with four distinct seasons and a growing period for
gardens of only a few months.*
    *The system of law that emerged from the baggage Kupe's people brought
and the changes demanded of his descendants by the land itself have come
to be known as tikanga Māori: 'tika' meaning correct, right or just; and
the suffix 'nga' transforming 'tika' into a noun, thus denoting the system by
which correctness, rightness or justice is maintained. That said, tikanga and
law are not co-extensive ideas. Tikanga includes customs or behaviours that*

might not be called law but rather culturally sponsored habits. Where the line is to be drawn between the two need not deter us here. That is a legal anthropological debate for another time.

Sir Hirini has described tikanga in the following way:

Tikanga embodies a set of beliefs and practices associated with procedures to be followed in conducting the affairs of a group or an individual. These procedures are established by precedents through time, are held to be ritually correct, are validated by usually more than one generation and are always subject to what a group or an individual is able to do . . .

Tikanga are tools of thought and understanding. They are packages of ideas which help to organise behaviour and provide some predictability in how certain activities are carried out. They provide templates and frameworks to guide our actions and help steer us through some huge gatherings of people and some tense moments in our ceremonial life. They help us to differentiate between right and wrong and in this sense have built-in ethical rules that must be observed. Sometimes tikanga help us survive.

Tikanga differ in scale. Some are large, involve many participants and are very public . . . Other tikanga are small and are less public. Some of them might be carried out by individuals in isolation from the public, and at other times participation is limited to immediate family. There are thus great differences in the social, cultural and economic requirements of particular tikanga.

In Justice Williams' view:

. . . to understand tikanga one must first understand the core values reflected in its directives. It must be remembered that tikanga Māori is law designed for small, kin-based village communities. It is as much concerned with peace and consensus as it is with the level of certainty one would expect of normative directives that are more familiar in a complex non-kin-based community. In a tikanga context, it is the values that matter more than the surface directives. Kin group leaders must carry the village with them in all significant exercises of legal authority. A decision that is unjust according to tikanga values risks being rejected by the community even if it is consistent with a tikanga-based directive.

While there *is 'considerable debate about what should be in the list of generally applicable core values the holders of the first law brought, adapted and still hold'*, Justice Williams' identified the following:

- **whanaungatanga** or the source of the rights and obligations of kinship;
- **mana** or the source of rights and obligations of leadership;
- **tapu** as both a social control on behaviour and evidence of the indivisibility of divine and profane;
- **utu** or the obligation to give and the right (and sometimes obligation) to receive constant reciprocity; and
- **kaitiakitanga** or the obligation to care for one's own.

Of these, whanaungatanga is the glue that held, and still holds, the system together; the idea that makes the whole system make sense – including legal sense. Thus the rights in cultivable land and resource complexes such as rivers, fisheries, forests, swamps and so on are allocated by descent from the original title holder (take tupuna – literally ancestral right or source). There is a form of legal interest created by conquest (raupatu – literally the harvest of the war club) and even, though more rarely, transfer (tuku – literally to give up). But these variants are better understood as the foundation of a right rather than rights in themselves. They were, in practice, fragile until consummated (literally) by creating a connection to, and then spring-boarding off, the line of the original ancestral right holder. So a 'conquest' always involved formal making of peace through inter-marriage and assimilation of the old descent line into the new in order to remove later contestation about whether the newcomer held the primary right (history taught the makers of custom law that conquered hapū rebuilt and reasserted their rights unless properly accommodated in the new order of the conqueror). Tuku was never a one-off transaction in the way a contract is, but rather a means of incorporating the transferee into the community of the original title holder.

So whanaungatanga might be said to be the fundamental law of the maintenance of properly tended relationships. The reach of this concept does not stop at the boundaries of what we might call law, or even for that matter, human relationships. It is also the key underlying cultural (and legal) metaphor informing human relationships with the physical world – flora, fauna, and physical resources – and the spiritual world –

the gods and ancestors.

Thus the story of what happened to Rata when he felled his totara tree without proper procedure confirms that good relations must be maintained with the forest itself as a related descent group in order to maintain the human right to be a user of forest resources.

In a more prosaic context, the requirement to maintain ahikā (literally burning fires) – to continue to use resources in order to maintain the descent-based rights in them – makes the same point.

No right in resources can be sustained without the right holder maintaining an ongoing relationship with the resource. No relationship; no right. The term that describes the legal obligation is kaitiakitanga. This is the idea that any right over a human or resource carries with it a reciprocal obligation to care for his, her or its physical and spiritual welfare. Kaitiakitanga is then a natural (perhaps even inevitable) off-shoot of whanaungatanga.

The point is that whanaungatanga was, in traditional Māori society, not just about emotional and social ties between people and with the environment. It was just as importantly about economic rights and obligations. Thus rights depended on right holders remembering their own descent lines as well as the descent lines of other potential claimants to the right. Whakapapa was both sword and shield wielded by Māori custom lawyers. It remains so today.

Conclusion

Dr Hope Tupara makes the point that *'the law is intended to represent the value system of New Zealand society, determined by the beliefs and ideas that arise from society or, more accurately, dominant society.* The situation is, however, in the process of changing. New developments are expected in this space in the years to come. An important judgment is expected from the Supreme Court in early 2022 on the subject. Law schools will begin teaching tikanga in the university law schools soon, as required by the Council of Legal Education. Over time, Māori legal traditions are likely to seep into the common law of Aotearoa New Zealand to a greater degree and the place of te Tiriti o Waitangi in legislation will also likely be further addressed.

The Speech from the Throne delivered by Her Excellency the Rt Hon Dame Patsy Reddy after the 2017 election sheds a hopeful light on what the future might look like:

When our forebears signed the Treaty of Waitangi more than 170 years ago they did so in a spirit of cooperation.

Whatever else that agreement might have meant, it was supposed to bring opportunity and mutual benefit for tāngata whenua and settlers alike. It was supposed to provide a place for all peoples in this country. Instead what followed was a long process of colonisation, in which one of the Treaty partners acquired most of the power and the resources, and the other was side-lined.

For almost 40 years, New Zealand has been addressing past injustices. Most of New Zealand's major iwi are now involved in Treaty settlements. This government is committed to bringing others to completion as quickly and fairly as it can.

It is time to start considering what the Treaty relationship might look like after historical grievances are settled. To consider how we, as a nation, can move forward in ways that honour the original Treaty promise.

A promise of a nation in which Māori values—diverse as they are—stand in their rightful place alongside those of European New Zealanders and other more recent arrivals.

A nation in which manaakitanga and kaitiakitanga and whanaungatanga inform our decision-making.

A nation in which fairness and equality of opportunity are not just aspirations but facts. And a nation in which all communities are empowered.

References

Hope Tupara *Ethics, Kawa, and the Constitution: Transformation of the System of Ethical Review in Aotearoa New Zealand* (Cambridge Quarterly of Healthcare Ethics, 20(3), 2011); Helen Potter and Moana Jackson *Constitutional Transformation and the Matike Mai Project: A Kōrero with Moana Jackson* (Economic and Social Research Aotearoa, 2018); Ani Mikaere *Colonising Myths and Māori Realities* (Huia Ltd, Wellington, 2013); Margaret Mutu *The Treaty Claims Settlement Process in New Zealand and Its Impact on Māori* (Land 8, no. 10, 2019); Hurini Moko Mead *Tikanga Māori: Living by Māori Values* (Huia Publishers, Wellington, 2003); Janine Hayward 'Treaty of Waitangi settlements: Successful symbolic reparation' in Joannah Luetjens, Michael Mintrom and Paul Hart *Successful Public Policy: Lessons from Australia and New Zealand* (Australian National University Press, Canberra, 2019); Renika Siciliano *Iwi histories in te Tiriti o Waitangi settlements: the impact of a Crown framework on our narrative histories* (New Zealand Journal of Public History, 2020); Māmari Stephens, *Kārearea* (Bridget Williams Books, Wellington, 2021); *Trans-Tasman Resources Ltd* v *Taranaki-Whanganui Conservation* Authority [2021] NZSC 127(30

September 2021); Justice Joseph Williams 'Lex Aotearoa: An Heroic Attempt to Map the Māori Dimension in Modern New Zealand Law', the Harkness Henry Lecture (2013) 21 Waikato Law Review 1; Maria Bargh, 'The Post Settlement World(so far):Impacts for Māori' in Janine Hayward and Nicole Wheen (eds) *Treaty of Waitangi Settlements* (Bridget Williams Books, Wellington, 2012); Ian Brownlie ,(edited by F M Brookfield) *Treaties and Indigenous Peoples* (Clarendon Press, Oxford, 1992); Rex Benton, Alex Frame, Paul Meredith *Te Mātāpunenga-A compendium of references to the concepts and institutions of Māori customary Law* (Victoria University Press, Wellington, 2013).

24 In the engine room of justice: Interview with Rt Hon Dame Helen Winkelmann, Chief Justice of New Zealand, June 2021

Illustration by Huriana Kopeke-Te Aho

Q: We would like first to ask, what is the role of the Chief Justice in New Zealand?

A: The Chief Justice is first among equals amongst all the judges. I am not in any meaningful sense the boss of the judges, although some judges do call me boss – their idea of a joke. But I do have a number of important leadership roles and a number of important administrative roles.

In terms of leadership, I am a spokesperson for the judiciary. I am the principal public face, but by no means the only public face, of the judiciary. This means I will speak on behalf of the judiciary publicly on issues. I also am the spokesperson for the judiciary when engaging with the Executive. (The judiciary does not directly engage directly with Parliament). We engage with the Executive through the office of the Attorney-General, at the moment the Hon David Parker. I try to be very diligent about that point of contact, keeping the Attorney informed of contact with other parts of the Executive. We often have dealings with the Ministry of Justice (part of the Executive) as they support the operation of the courts, and with the Minister of Justice and the Minister for Courts.

I have responsibility on the administrative side for the orderly and efficient conduct of judicial business. That is my statutory responsibility for the Supreme Court, but not for the other courts. Each Head of Bench has that statutory responsibility. However, the judiciary needs oversight. If you think of the judiciary as an organism with over 200 judges, all independently operating – it is obvious you need some sort of directing mind for the judiciary as a branch of government.

So, I see my role as supporting the Heads of Bench in the work they do to facilitate their courts to operate in an efficient, orderly, and just fashion. I also see it as my role to create a vision for the courts – which I suppose is a vision for what justice before the courts should look like in our society. And that's a vision that is communicated to the judges. It is also the role of the Chief Justice to communicate this vision to our society so that the public can have confidence in the judiciary and the courts.

I think it's also the role of the Chief Justice to enunciate standards of conduct for judges and to model them. The judiciary has Judicial Conduct Guidelines which are published. You can read them on the New Zealand Courts' website. Issues do arise from time to time in relation to judicial conduct, but the Chief Justice does not have a disciplinary role. The Judicial Conduct Commissioner is in charge of disciplinary issues.

Having said that, the Chief Justice may have to respond to disciplinary issues in public. We saw that a little while ago when a survey of lawyers came out that showed that around 65% of participants had experienced bullying by judges. My predecessor, Chief Justice Dame Sian Elias, spoke out and said that bullying by judges was not acceptable. The then Chief Justice created a protocol that operates with the Law Society which allows lawyers to raise concerns of bullying by a judge which can be passed on to the Head of Bench or the Chief Justice.

Q: As the head of the judiciary, can you tell us about the extra responsibilities that you have compared with a judge who is not the Chief Justice?

A: I have responsibility for all the tasks which come with the administrative load I just discussed. I convene and run the Heads of Bench, which is a committee where all the Heads of Bench come together and discuss the issues for their court and work out how each court will address those issues. In reality, when you come together as a group in this way you discover that the issues are in fact common from court to court. So, that situation naturally lends itself to creating a plan for the courts as to how we will address these issues.

I also see myself as responsible as for conceptualising and putting into action the ways in which we will address the issues the courts face. For instance, we face an issue with facilitating open justice – access by the public to information about the work of the courts. We have formed a committee called Huakina kia Tika, the Open Justice Committee, which thinks about the ways the courts can themselves support a public understanding of the work the courts do and their role in society, given that the media play only a very limited role in that regard.

Another issue we have identified for all courts is to have a judiciary fit to judge in such a diverse society. One aspect of diversity is who the judges are. I don't have responsibility for judicial appointments, but I do have responsibility for encouraging people from diverse backgrounds to think of themselves as fit for judicial appointment and to put themselves forward for appointment. The judiciary can play a leadership role in that regard. For that reason, we have Te Awa Tuia Tangata, the Diversity Committee. The Chief Judge of the Employment Court, Judge Christina Inglis, chairs that committee. It's a very important committee from my point of view.

Then there's the operational aspect. The judiciary doesn't have its own money. It's the third branch of government, but it doesn't have and cannot raise its own funds. So, the judicial branch of government depends upon Parliament for the money and the Executive (the Ministry of Justice) for its operations.

It is my task to develop a functional relationship with the Ministry of Justice, reaching a consensus about what support for the courts needs to look like, what issues need to be addressed in relation to that, and how we are going to accomplish those goals. The relationship with the Executive in terms of the operational side is incredibly important. And I think it's a really important role for the Chief Justice: a very important aspect of the role is relationship building.

I have to manage relationships with the Executive. The Chief Justice doesn't have a relationship with Parliament. This is an issue of constitutional interest for me – whether the Chief Justice should have some forum in which she speaks to Parliament to give the judiciary's view as to the support the judiciary needs. In England, the Chief Justice has constructed ways of engaging with Parliament. Having said that, one must be very careful because judges must not become accountable to Parliament for their judicial decisions, or their independence will be eroded, but I think whether there should be a relationship with Parliament is an interesting area to explore.

I also need to form relationships with what one might call stakeholders, particularly the legal profession. And nowadays the legal profession is represented by many groups. The New Zealand Law Society, which represents all lawyers, is our principal point of engagement, but there's also the New Zealand Bar Association, Te Hunga Rōia Māori, the Pacific Lawyers' Association, and now there's also the recently formed New Zealand Asian Leaders (NZAL) lawyers group. It is important that the judiciary has a good working relationship with the profession. Judges are engaged in a collaborative enterprise with lawyers and at times we very much need to depend upon them.

There was a good example of that in the Covid-19 pandemic response when we relied on this working relationship to respond in a very agile way to the shut-down of some court operations consequent on Alert Level 4, and then to achieve the staged opening up at other levels.

Q: To expand on something you said, Chief Justice, what are the courts doing to try and assist Māori, Pacific Islanders, and Asians – those three groups that the Law Society has committees with which to engage with the court system?

A: I'll answer this in two categories because the response to Māori is slightly different. The courts recognise Māori as one of the two founding cultures of New Zealand: as the Treaty partner, they have a particular right to have their culture represented in government, including in the courts. And so, over the last 10 years, the courts have really been evolving the look and feel and procedures of the court, incorporating elements of Māori culture.

I think it's quite lovely how judges' gowns have changed. Judges have cast aside the scarlet ceremonial robes and full bottomed wigs we used to

wear. We have retained the black robes still worn by counsel before the
courts, (a reference to the medieval robes worn by barristers in England),
but for judges those gowns have a poutama pattern trim in red, black,
and gold down the side reflecting New Zealand's two founding cultures.
Embroidery on the shoulders feature the three baskets of knowledge of
Māori tradition set in fern fronds, representing the common law method
which is to work with knowledge of the past and an eye to the knowledge
of the future. And there is a kauri cone woven into the fabric.

If you look at our courthouses, they are slowly evolving into buildings
more appropriate to the South Pacific nation we are. We are also changing
how we conduct hearings in court rooms and embedding more of the
Māori language, te reo Māori, into the courts.

This is more than just symbolic – it is important also that our courts
have a greater New Zealand feel for people who come into the court, so
it does not seem to them such a strange and alien environment.

The law is also beginning to develop to be fit for this nation. When
English law and courts began to arrive here, they evolved quite quickly
to meet the circumstances. But then came the explosion of the settler
population. From the late nineteenth century, the law became frozen in
lock step with English law. It was around the 1960s that this began to
change, initially quite slowly but nevertheless the law was developing a
distinctly New Zealand character. We had people of great vision, intellect
and character who began this process, people like Lord Cooke and Sir
Owen Woodhouse. They identified themselves and felt themselves to
be of *this* place. They saw the need to develop a law for New Zealand.
That change gained pace in the 1980s with the development of Treaty
of Waitangi jurisprudence – largely in response to legislative provisions
which gave the Treaty a place in our law.

I think today we are seeing a fresh burst of creativity with the
realisation that the common law should, in fact, reflect the values,
culture and customs of the place where it is being administered.

In that discovery, we've also reminded ourselves that tikanga Māori
has always been part of the custom and values of this place. Tikanga is
now starting to find its way into the common law. As usual, Parliament
got there first, including references to tikanga in the statute law which
was a spur for the courts, but now the courts are finding their own way
as well.

The judiciary is also increasingly engaging with communities. We're doing that in two ways. For some time, we've recognised the need to educate judges about the society in which they operate. We have Te Kura Kaiwhakawā, which is the Institute of Judicial Studies – it's really like a university that's run for judges. A significant stream of judicial education focuses on understanding the diversity within our society. We run courses which engage judges in learning about the history of the different peoples who came to New Zealand, particularly Pasifika and Asian – Asian in the broader sense – and about their cultures and how those cultures fit and operate within New Zealand society. This is important for the courts because we must decide cases in which significant cultural issues are at play, but which would be beyond the knowledge of judges without this education.

Another aspect of our work lies in community outreach. The courts have traditionally sat in their Victorian structures and seen themselves as necessarily constrained within them – it was not exactly an ivory tower, but more of a masonry tower: it was traditionally thought that part of the necessary behaviour of a judge was to keep themselves apart from their community. Judges were appointed and then kept themselves away from society. This was thought to ensure the judge was not affected by any extraneous or improper influences. Nowadays, we don't see the judiciary that way. Judges must be in and part of society and the society that they have to be part of is not merely their own community – they have to be able to reach beyond their own backgrounds and understand every part of society.

We now seek connection with communities because that connection is important to how we conduct judicial business. This is the thinking behind Te Ao Mārama, which is the new model for criminal and family justice in the District Court. This model involves the mainstreaming of therapeutic justice and bringing communities into the courtrooms to support the work of the courts. Communities have knowledge about the people that are before the court – what is needed to support them, to rehabilitate them, and to support victims. This is knowledge that the judiciary just cannot have. Professor Ronald Dworkin's ideal of the superhuman Herculean Judge with all relevant knowledge and perspectives is an unreachable ideal. To judge well is the most extraordinarily difficult task. So, the idea of Te Ao Mārama is to bring in an element of co-management – the notion of allowing the community to support you in providing effective justice. No human being can really encompass all the knowledge required to judge well. To do the task well, we do need to rely on the strength of the community.

Q: I wonder if we could now look at the Supreme Court over which you preside. How does it conduct its business?

A: There are six judges, but we sit in a panel at five. Often there's one judge who can't sit because they're unavailable in some way, perhaps they have a conflict of interest having been involved with the case in a lower court. I'll talk functionally about how we operate first.

We are all independent in how we work and the decisions we make. Every judge operates in their own way. Some judges like to read every last thing and some judges like to take a more targeted approach to their preparation as they don't want to reach too much of a concluded view beforehand. But every judge will have prepared, so they have a strong understanding of the judgments under appeal, of the pleadings and of the evidence. Some will have read all the relevant precedent cases.

The judges have a discussion before every hearing, but we try not to reach or express views. We're human beings, sometimes views are expressed, but we try to discipline ourselves not to. That is because we see the hearing as an extremely important part of the process. And it is quite remarkable how much an oral hearing changes your view about the merits of the case. It is important not to become too committed to a view before the hearing because, if you do, then you can become an antagonist in the courtroom.

Before we hear the case, we discuss what particular issues we want the barristers to focus on, whether there is something we think that they've overlooked, whether there are cases we want to bring to their attention. Afterwards, we come back out and we discuss the case. This usually happens straight after the hearing. Then each judge expresses a view about the different issues. And at the end of discussion, there will be an apparent grouping of people, a majority/minority. Sometimes it's more complex than that. It's my task to assign judgment writing responsibilities, and to ascertain majority/minority views.

It's a tricky thing being a judge on an appellate court because you do not want to compromise your own views. The particular perspectives you have in the law are part of why you've been appointed there. All the same, you do need to have some sort of coming together of the law. If, in every case we have five separate lengthy judgments which don't really speak to each other, the law can become incoherent.

And the role of the Supreme Court is to create and enable a more New Zealand flavoured law to develop – a law which is fit for New Zealand. That was the thinking behind the establishment of the Court in 2004. The Supreme Court Act 2003 records this purpose:

(a) to establish within New Zealand a new court of final appeal comprising New Zealand judges:
  (i) to recognise that New Zealand is an independent nation with its own history and traditions; and
  (ii) to enable important legal matters, including legal matters relating to the Treaty of Waitangi, to be resolved with an understanding of New Zealand conditions, history, and traditions; and
  (iii) to improve access to justice.

That Act was repealed in 2016 and this purpose was not carried forward, but the vision remains.

Part of the court's task is to clarify the law. That means that as a group of judges we must work to make clear what the law is as it emerges from the case. And that's something I think, is my particular role as Chief Justice. I can't and won't tell people what to think, but what I can do is to try and make us work hard to reduce the areas of disagreement and to ensure that when we produce a judgment, it speaks clearly as to where the law stands.

Q: We have in Aotearoa New Zealand a great many judges, many more than there are Members of Parliament. What is the best description of the role of the courts in the system of government?

A: Well, there are two different things – there's the role of the courts in the system of government and there is the role of the courts in society. The judiciary is the third branch of government. Its constitutional function is to uphold the rule of law which means that every person exists equally under the law, the law applies to all equally, and that includes the powerful. The most powerful of all, of course, are Parliament and the Executive. The judiciary ensures that government is conducted in a lawful fashion, and it does that through holding the Executive (ministers and government departments) to the law, primarily through the procedures of judicial review.

Any citizen has a right to bring a claim to the High Court that the Executive has acted unlawfully, unfairly, or irrationally. The courts must be prepared to rule that a member of the Executive has acted outside what is legally permissible when satisfied that is so. When that occurs, the decision may need to be remade or it may simply be set aside. That is the power of judicial review of Executive action. Judicial review is so constitutionally important that it has never been allowed to be captured in its entirety within a statute. Although there are statutes which set up judicial review processes, the power to judicially review sits outside statute. It is a power that is derived from the common law – judge-made law. Any kind of attempt by Parliament to entirely capture judicial review within statute (we would call that codifying it) in New Zealand would I think be met with a great deal of resistance.

The rule of law is an absolutely fundamental feature of democratic government. It goes beyond the government. Everybody must be subject to the law, and equally, everybody must be entitled to its benefit. The law does not just constrain the powerful from wrongdoing, it should protect the poor and vulnerable from oppression and exploitation. The poor and vulnerable in society do not have the personal means to assert their rights or hold the rich and powerful to their obligations.

For that reason, they must be able to come to court to do that. In that respect, it is vital we have something called access to justice. If you can't come to court to hold the Executive to the law, or if you can't come to court to hold say, for example, your rich and powerful landlord to their responsibilities under the law (to ensure, for example, that the place you are renting under a lease is a fit home), then you may end up pushed to the margins of society excluded from the normal benefits of living in a community – perhaps all of the economic benefits, but maybe also the ability to develop safe and nurturing human relationships.

The other thing I was going to say about the role of the courts sits beyond the normal legal analysis. There is a sociological function for the courts: it is society's method of dispute resolution. So instead of just being the law of the jungle out there, people should be able to come to court to have their disputes resolved without resort to violence. The courts' judgments are not enforced with violence. People usually accept the decision of the courts. They accept it because they can see they have had a fair hearing. The notion of fair hearing lies absolutely at the heart of our system of justice. This is the idea that people can bring their disputes to court. The parties will be heard, the judge will listen carefully, and the judge will then issue a judgment. This produces a peaceful final resolution of a dispute between them.

Q: What makes a good judge?

A: Knowledge of the law! We wouldn't expect you to be a judge unless you were learned in the law because the thing that judges do is administer the law. But a judge must also be knowledgeable about their society. The common law really is a distillation of the values and customs in a society that we wish to carry forward into our laws and if the law is to embody those values and customs the judges must have that knowledge.

So, when I say knowledge about this society, they don't only have to know about the communities. The judge must also know about all sorts of things that bear upon the people who come before them and courts. We teach judges about the various cognitive disabilities that may affect a person's ability to participate in a hearing or understand what is going on. We teach judges about how family and sexual violence impacts upon people, the impact of a hearing upon them and their ability to engage in it. There are many necessary aspects to the education provided to judges.

Q: How would you state the qualities?

A: They have to know about the people in front of them and the communities they come from. This is important in many ways – for example, how can you know what is reasonable conduct in a circumstance if you don't really understand that circumstance? What may be reasonable for a person who lives on $400,000 a year may not be so reasonable for someone who is living in abject poverty.

A judge must have the temperament to enable them to conduct a fair hearing. They need to be good listeners and good communicators. And they also have to have the humility to treat everybody in front of them with dignity. Humility is one of the most important attributes. Why do I say humility is important? If you think you're a very powerful, important person, you can often be slighting of others or minimise their significance. I also see courage as important.Judges may be called upon to make a decision, which they know will be very unpopular. That's true often in the sentencing realm where the law requires that they sentence in a way which in a particular case may be against the flow of public opinion. Judges must be prepared, in keeping with the judicial oath, to make the hard decisions.

And independence as well! Judges have to be very conscious of the need to stand apart from others when they're making their decision. They must be impartial, and impartiality is something you must actively construct. It depends upon all of those things I've talked about earlier. You actually have to know about your society so that you can effectively do the mental exercise to make necessary adjustments so that you are conducting yourself in that hearing in a way which is completely fair.

Q: Now how does the appointment of judges work from your point of view and how does the process of consultation that goes on about judicial appointments work?

A: There is a Protocol that is currently in place between the Attorney-General and Chief Justice. It was negotiated by my predecessor as Chief Justice and the former Attorney-General Hon Christopher Finlayson.

The Governor-General appoints judges on the advice of the Attorney General. But the Attorney General consults with me for the Senior Courts appointments (the Supreme Court, the Court of Appeal, and the High Court). Different considerations apply to the specialist jurisdictions and the District Court, so I'll just speak for the Senior Courts. I see it as my role to encourage appropriate people to express an interest in judicial appointments. The Solicitor-General seeks expressions of interest for judicial appointment. She also asks the profession, the Law Society, the Bar Association, Te Hunga Rōia Māori and now the NZ Asian Lawyers group and the Pacific Lawyers Association to nominate people they believe are fit for judicial appointment. We hope to have applicants drawn from a wide catchment.

As to process, in consultation with the Attorney-General a short list of three people is created. From there, the Attorney-General will consider that shortlist and make a final recommendation for appointment to the Governor-General. It is the Governor-General who makes the appointment itself, in keeping with her role as the Queen's representative in New Zealand.

Different Attorneys-General take different approaches to this process of consultation. Some are knowledgeable about the legal profession and have their own particular views. Some are much more consultative. I've only had the opportunity to work with one Attorney-General so far and

I find the process is extremely consultative.

I talk to the Chief High Court Judge, who is currently Justice Susan Thomas. I talk to the President of the Court of Appeal, Justice Stephen Kós. And when the issue is about Supreme Court, because it's such a small court, I talk to all the judges of the court. The Heads of Bench have a very good understanding of the skill sets that the judiciary requires and what the bench needs at that particular time. I take into account these points of view before I go and work with the Attorney-General to create the shortlist.

Overall, in relation to appointments I see a need for long term planning to ensure we have applicants from a variety of backgrounds and with a variety of experiences so that through the judicial appointment process we can achieve a diverse balance.

Q: Can you help us with this expression that New Zealand is often called a common law country? What does that really mean?

A: It means a country in which the law is partly comprised of judicial decisions of authority and precedential authority. We don't just have Acts of Parliament (statutes), we also have judge-made law. Every time a judge decides a case, they are making law and that carries on having a future effect. This is an excellent method of deciding cases and developing the law, I think it's extraordinarily beneficial to our society. It is responsive to change within society.

There's something about the common law which I think is its magic. The common law didn't just spontaneously come into existence, nor has it always existed. When the common law was being created, judges looked into society for the values and the customs that should be given the force of the law. Judges effectively wove into law what they saw in society, and that's part of the magic. This process of incorporating societal values and customs means that the law should connect quite well to society.

But the other part of its magic is that it has a kind of a natural correction against unpleasant majoritarian tendencies in society. There are values that run through it, and prevent anything unacceptable, for example, an abuse of power or dishonest or sharp dealing, from finding a place in the common law. While the common law method allows the law to change as society changes, it also has its own inbuilt methodology of stabilising the law. This is important because I think one of the things that the courts are meant to do is create stability in society by holding people to the law, but also by communicating and enunciating these really deep values of honesty and, fairness that run through the law and maintain its fitness for purpose.

This allows a sort of a multi-directional development of the law. Nowadays the common law does not just look to society, but also increasingly looks to statute. Statute and common law often work together. Statute law borrows from the common law; it usually codifies common law. The common law looks to statute because it's a good way of seeing where society is heading.

I should also say that although judges make law, there is another critical task of the courts. It is the task of judges to interpret and apply the legislation, that is, Acts of Parliament and secondary legislation. Statutory interpretation is in fact, a common law methodology. So, when we say it's a common law country, we don't just mean that we have judge-made law. We also mean the processes we use – the common law processes. A whole body of common law has developed around the task of statutory interpretation. Some of that is incredibly important, such as the principle of legality, which is in essence the idea that there are some principles in our law that run so deep, are so fundamental that Parliament cannot easily take them away. This means that if Parliament wishes to legislate inconsistently with one of those fundamental principles, it must speak with absolute clarity, irresistible clarity. The principle has found its way into statute. Parliament did its usual thing of picking up common law principles, putting them into the Bill of Rights. Some people see section 6 of the Bill of Rights Act as a statutory embodiment of the principle of legality. The question the courts are yet to resolve is whether it's something more than that – we shall see.

Q: Why is the independence of the judiciary an important constitutional principle?

A: The answer to this flows out of lots of the answers I've given already. Because in fact, in order to be able to hold the Executive to the law, judges must be free to do so. They should not be fearful that they will be thrown into prison because of a decision they make. That may sound extreme, but that kind of thing has happened in other jurisdictions.

Judges should also not be concerned that pay will be docked because of a decision; they shouldn't be worried that because they've been brave, they're not going to get appointed further up in the judiciary. All of these things are actually important things for us to think about. Judicial independence sounds like something that's easy to maintain, but it can be insidiously eroded in the fashion that I have described.

One of my critical roles as Chief Justice, which I should have mentioned earlier, is to support the independence of the judiciary. One of the things that we do to support the independence of the judiciary is make sure we don't get too cosy with the Executive or that we don't get co-opted into their policy and law reform processes. That last thing is a bit tricky because sometimes the judiciary has a legitimate and important contribution to make in law reform and policy, where it affects the operation of the courts or where judges have unique knowledge. The judiciary has a committee called the Legislation and Law Reform Committee. The judges who work on it are people who are very experienced and very knowledgeable about the constitutional boundaries and very experienced in the legislative process. They assist me in our engagement with the Ministry of Justice and with government in relation to legislation and law reform.

Q: The judges are assisted by the Ministry of Justice officials who carry out administrative tasks in the courts. How does this relationship work?

A: My associate is an employee of the Ministry of Justice, our judges' clerks are also, and people down in our registries most critically are also Ministry of Justice employees. But when they are fulfilling their tasks for the courts, they are operating as part of the courts, part of the third branch of government. Although they're paid by and have a contractual relationship with the Ministry of Justice, they act under judicial supervision. And that's very important because, for instance, part of judicial independence is that our records are kept separate from those of the Executive. If there was a piece of litigation involving the Ministry of Justice or other parts of the Executive, we wouldn't want officials of the Ministry of Justice coming over and looking at the judges' files. The court records, which are administered by Ministry of Justice employees are nevertheless court records.

One of the areas that I pay attention to is the management of information. There is a committee which works with the ministry to ensure that judicial and ministry information is kept separate, and the boundaries are clearly understood. Ministry of Justice access to our computers and court files is carefully circumscribed. Having said that, the Ministry of Justice has a legitimate interest in what is going on in the courts at a statistical level. It needs to understand what is required to support the courts – how many support people are needed, how the systems are operating, what funding is required. But they do not need to understand what's going on in individual files. It is really important that the demarcation is understood and observed.

Q: So, in your opinion what are the most difficult issues facing the judiciary?

A: That's the most difficult question! We are at a point in time at which New Zealand is changing very rapidly. This is driven in part by the recognition beginning in the 1970s and 1980s of the need to address the status of te Tiriti in New Zealand society and in New Zealand law. It's also driven by the rapid increase in the diversity of our society and our increased knowledge about the cohort of people who come before us in the courts, particularly our defendant cohort. We now know, for instance, that a high percentage of defendants have acquired brain injury, or other cognitive disability which hampers their ability to participate in hearings in a meaningful way. We know far more about the dynamics of family violence, information we must take into account when we're judging. The development of our processes and our law to keep pace with this increased understanding is one of the foremost challenges.

And really connected to that is a profound challenge that we now acknowledge which is the over-representation of Māori in negative statistics in our justice system, particularly in the criminal justice system and in the care and protection system. I think that is a challenge which is so profound that it goes to something we call the legitimacy of the judiciary. The legitimacy of the judiciary is something we haven't touched on, but it's important. I mentioned right at the beginning that the courts don't have access to our own money, nor do we have access to police or the army to get people to comply with our orders. Largely, judgments are complied with on a voluntary basis, and that is because judgments are respected as being made after a fair hearing, and as applying standards and values that are adequately reflective of our society.

If you have a significant part of your society that believes the law only ever comes down on them and in an unfair way, then you start to see the legitimacy of the judiciary eroded. The same is true if you have a judiciary which is seen to be unrepresentative – that it is not seen as representing the whole society. If it was a judiciary made up only of people educated at expensive private schools or only of Pākehā for example, it would not be seen as adequately reflective of our society. You do need to have a judiciary which is seen to be representative.

Diversity within the judiciary has in some ways grown rapidly in recent years. That is especially the case in the District Courts. But significant issues remain, particularly with the lack of Asian judges. I was delighted to see the formation of the NZAL Lawyers Association, as that will help us reach out to those lawyers, in the way I mentioned above.

So that's a third challenge, achieving and maintaining adequate diversity within our judiciary which is, I think, a profound challenge and one with which we will always have to engage.

Q: So how do you manage the judiciary's relationships with the government?

A: Through the Attorney-General as I discussed above. In relation to policy and law reform we manage it in quite a careful, structured way so that we don't end up being co-opted into the policy or legislative process. Judges need to be careful to retain their independence so that they can, for example, judicially review decisions made under a policy and so that they can interpret the statute at issue. It's important we can do that impartially and independently.

I think the judiciary could take more of a role in facilitating the understanding by people over the other side of Molesworth Street about what we do. For a long time, we've been content to carry out our mysterious and unknowable functions in our masonry towers. I think those days are past.

Q: To the general public, courts often seem quite inaccessible. Do you think that there are ways in which the courts can be made more user-friendly so the general public can better understand what actually goes on there?

A: I do. We really need to address this issue. The media do not do a very good job of reporting the work of the courts. And that's not a criticism, it is simply the reality we face. If you go back into the 19th century and the first half of the 20th century, the role of newspapers was not thought of as entertainment, but rather was a record of what was going on in the world and in important public institutions, including the courts. Just as they had the shipping news, they also had the news about what was going on in courts. But the funding model for media changed and the work of the courts changed too. The volume of work in the courts has increased dramatically so that the volume of cases would defeat even the most assiduous reporters.

The courts have acknowledged a responsibility to make information about their work available to the public. We have adopted a multi-pronged approach. We have a Media in Courts Committee, which works with the media to facilitate their understanding of the work of the courts.We run webinars for the media to understand the steps in litigation so that they can provide a fair account of trials and hearings when they are reported.

We have the Open Justice Committee, which I've talked about earlier – Huakina kia Tika. That committee came about during Covid-19 because I spotted a gap early, which was that when the courts had to shut down, the public couldn't come in. So how were people going to know what was going on? In order to shut down, we needed to operate remotely so we had to use technologies, some of which we were already using in a different way, and some of which we used the first time, such as Microsoft Teams. We formed the committee to see how we could use these technologies to facilitate the media having access to what was going on. So Huakina kia Tika worked on this. Then we thought, why not use this technology in a business-as-usual environment? Huakina kia Tika is now working on various projects to use remote technology to facilitate people coming into the courts who could not otherwise do so.

In the recent cases under the Marine and Coastal Area Act, we have been bringing entire hapū into hearings through the use of remote technology. We allow Law School classes to view cases. And we have a programme in the Supreme Court moving toward online, open streaming of Supreme Court hearings, and to support that with access to copies of counsel's submissions and pleadings in digital form. We are also developing an Annual Report which gives an account of how the judiciary sees the issues that the courts must address, and how they are going about addressing them.

But underlying all of this is a far bigger question, which is access to justice. In every society, you need adequate access to the courts and to information about what the law is, so that the rights of all can be upheld before the courts, and their voices heard as the law is developed.

Many societies are worried about access to justice. We have good reason to be concerned about it in New Zealand. I've spoken about this often, and there's only so much the judiciary can do. Some of the problem lies in the fact that lawyers cost too much. And that is I believe an existential threat for the profession. It is an issue to confront: lawyers are pricing themselves out of a meaningful role in society. If they are only representing large corporations and the wealthy there's a question mark over their continued relevance.

There's also legal aid. It is for the Executive as to how they fund it. But as Chief Justice, it is my role to speak about anything which bears upon access to the courts. And I think the provision of legal aid does bear upon access to courts. Legal aid is underfunded.

Another issue is the court fees that are charged for access to the courts. The fees the Executive charges people to come to court are set unacceptably high. The last time they were benchmarked they were far higher than England's court fees.

Beyond legal representation, there is the issue of how we are operating our courts. The processes we use in court can act as a barrier to people coming to court. We just talked about ensuring courts are not alien environments in form and feel, but there's also the procedural side of things. Our procedures can be seen as arcane and obscure. The Rules Committee legally has the power to make the rules, but those rules are neither short nor simple. We need to simplify our procedures. People see rules, and the Rules Committee as boring, but both are very important because of the impact they can have on access to the courts.

The Rules Committee is presently engaged in a once-in-a-generation Access to Justice Review of the rules. We have consulted with the profession, and with community groups, to understand the procedural barriers to justice before the courts. We were told that some of the problems lie in the structure of the courts – beyond the power of the Rules Committee to fix. We have drawn those issues to the attention of the Attorney-General and the Minister of Justice. On the rules side, people have supported a simplification of the presumptive procedural model to reduce the cost of coming to court.

Q: The number of litigants who represent themselves in front of the court must cause difficulties for the judges. I wonder whether there's been an increase in that because of the lack of legal aid.

A: Over the years the number of people who represent themselves before the courts has grown. Our basic model of civil and criminal justice assumes that people will be represented by lawyers, people with familiarity with the law and legal processes. That's important at many levels; quality legal argument is needed if the law is to develop. But it is also important because it is difficult for people to represent themselves effectively in an unfamiliar environment especially when they do not understand the law that applies.

When you have someone who is unrepresented with no knowledge of process and no knowledge of the law, two things can happen. One is the judge must rely on counsel on the other side to give the unrepresented person some tips on the process. The person who is paying for counsel on the other side can rightly get quite irritated. And the second thing that can happen is the judge helps the unrepresented person. This can be seen as compromising the judge's impartiality in the dispute.

Q: The judiciary is often described as being dominated by elderly white males. Why is this? And you've spoken a little bit again about the diversity programs and increasing that, but is it gradually becoming more inclusive?

A: The judiciary has become far more diverse over the last 30 years. The red robes (which I think of as Santa suits) judges used to wear helped reinforce the image of judges as being remote figures, not representative of society. And it is true that for a long time, the bench was dominated by men. When I was at law school, there wasn't anyone who wasn't an elderly white male on the Senior Courts (at least they seemed old to me, but so did anyone over the age of 30). Judicial appointment was not something I even thought about because it seemed like another species. On my mother's side my family was Croatian. I grew up in the West Auckland Dalmatian community. And so, judges did seem really alien.

Today we have a far more diverse judiciary although there is still work to do in this regard. But we also must bear in mind that representative diversity, whether it be gender diversity, ethnic diversity or socio-economic diversity can only take us so far. I think the appointment of women was important when it happened because women were, at the time, functional specialists at being at the margins – in the sense they were at the margins when the important decisions were being made. So, when women first came into the judiciary, they had experience of and could look out, in a sense, for those who are marginalised. But women will not necessarily always be functional specialists in this sense. We must also bear in mind that there are many ways identities intersect, placing people at different proximity to the 'margins' I talk about. And that probably has always been true. It's always been true that you can appoint a woman who will not be fulfilling that role of voice for the silenced.

For that reason, those we appoint as judges need to be able to look out for those issues. They must have that mindset of looking out for and seeking to understand the marginalised. That means we need judges who have empathy. We also need judges with compassion and with an interest in the society they stand in and for.

When I talk about representative diversity not being enough on its own, do you remember Don Dugdale's article about diversity? When they were talking about the importance of appointing women, he said, 'What next, a member of the Matamata South Croquet Club or the Federation of Cactus and Succulent Fanciers?'

Q: He was given to florid phrases about the Bill of Rights too.

A: Yes. We also need to look for judges who've travelled different career paths, who have had to engage with different parts of society through the work they've done. And so that's something I talk about because we also must have a vision of the judiciary which is encompassing of everybody.

Chief Justice, I just want to thank you for what has been a wonderful tour of the current New Zealand judiciary, full of insight.

References

Courts of New Zealand website: https://www.courtsofnz.govt.nzGuidelines for Judicial Conduct 2019: https://www.courtsofnz.govt.nz/assets/4-About-the-judiciary/judicialconduct/20191112gjc.pdf

Arrangement to be followed if legal practitioners have concerns about the conduct of court proceedings: https://www.lawsociety.org.nz/professional-practice/practising-well/bullying-and-harassment/

Judicial committees: https://www.courtsofnz.govt.nz/about-the-judiciary/judicial-committees/

Judicial Appointments Protocol: https://www.crownlaw.govt.nz/assets/uploads/judicial-protocol.pdf

Media in Courts Committee: https://www.courtsofnz.govt.nz/about-the-judiciary/judicial-committees/media-and-courts-committee-members

25 Inquiries

Inquiries may investigate any matter of public importance in Aotearoa New Zealand. They investigate events or controversial issues and may make recommendations on what could be improved in future. Inquiries enjoy similar coercive powers to courts, and many take on forensic qualities that make them akin to courts. They are often headed by judges, retired judges, or senior lawyers. Commissions of Inquiry, and all inquiries under the Inquiries Act 2013, are instruments of the executive government. The government appoints the members of the inquiry and sets the terms of reference.

The first inquiry appointed by the settler government in Aotearoa New Zealand was established under the royal prerogative in 1863 to determine where the capital city should be. It was conducted by politicians from states in Australia (Australia didn't have a federal government until 1901) because it was thought all our politicians would be biased. There had been big political rows about the issue in Parliament. The Commissioners recommended the capital should be Wellington Te Whanganui-a-Tara – if you do not like that you can blame the Australians!

The findings and recommendations of a Commission of Inquiry bind no one. Inquiries can, however, find fault. The Act provides:

(1) An inquiry has no power to determine the civil, criminal, or disciplinary liability of any person.
(2) Subsection (1) does not prevent an inquiry, in exercising its powers and performing its duties under this Act, from making—
    (a) findings of fault; or
    (b) recommendations that further steps be taken to determine liability.

Inquiries are reasonably popular with governments and more than 150 have been established since the first in 1863. Some big, some small. Some significant, some not so much. There are a variety of types of inquiries that can be established, under the Inquiries Act 2013. **Government**

Inquiries are established by ministers, by notice in the *Gazette*, and are reported back to the minister that established them. **Public Inquiries** are appointed by the Governor-General by Order in Council and provide a report to Parliament and to the Governor-General. **Royal Commissions** are appointed by the Governor-General on the advice of the government, in the name of the Sovereign, pursuant to the Letters Patent. They are treated as public inquiries and have the same powers as the other inquiries set up under the Act. However, Royal Commissions are usually established to inquire into matters of greater national importance than those dealt with by other commissions of inquiry.

So, when are Inquiries set up? Inquiries may be initiated when ministers are in doubt as to what to do. The policy area may be highly controversial or technical or there may be inadequate information about it, such as in the issue of genetic modification. In such cases of difficult policy areas, some systematic study with public input may be called for. Reviews are incredibly common in the machinery of government. The most common inquiries are simple policy reviews conducted by officials because of instructions from their minister. Although these can be quite elaborate, high quality, and even sometimes involve setting up interdepartmental committees of officials, policy reviews do not require the powers contained in the Inquiries Act available to the other types of inquiries detailed above.

Inquiries may also be set up when disasters have occurred. Recent instances in Aotearoa New Zealand include deaths in a coal mine, the collapse of buildings and significant loss of life due to earthquakes in Christchurch or investigating how it was that a white supremacist terrorist was able to shoot 51 people to death and injure many others at two Mosques in Christchurch in 2019. What lessons can be learned from such catastrophes? The public want to know what happened and why and whether remedial measures need to be adopted. They want reassurance. Inquiries may aid in this manner.

The inquirers must be impartial, independent, and fair. Commissioners do not decide questions put before them by litigants as a court does. They must follow the terms of reference set by the government. An inquiry decision can be subjected to judicial review by a court if it is made outside of the commission's terms of reference or defective for some other reason. Inquiries need to be used with considerable circumspection. Their findings can inflict damage upon individuals without those individuals being afforded the protection of a criminal trial. Commissions must adhere to the rules of natural justice including acting reasonably and without bias or predetermination and giving individuals the opportunity to respond to allegations prejudicial to them.

Perhaps the most famous example concerning natural justice in New Zealand was the case of the Royal Commission into the crash of an Air New Zealand plane into Mount Erebus in Antarctica on 29 November 1979. There, the Commissioner, Justice Mahon, said he had listened, during the inquiry, to '. . . *a pre-determined plan of deception . . . to conceal a series of disastrous administrative blunders . . . an orchestrated litany of lies.* The courts consequently determined that the Commissioner had not followed the rules of natural justice in arriving at his determination. These findings were never put to the Air New Zealand witnesses in the Inquiry. An award of $150,000 in costs against Air New Zealand was overturned by the Court of Appeal and the Privy Council upheld the decision.

Inquiries divide themselves into three main categories, although these can overlap. The first category is those where the prime issues revolve around behaviour or conduct and the propriety of it. Some examples include the disasters mentioned above, although those inquiries also contained policy recommendations as well. In such inquiries, there is often a need to establish with clarity what really happened to bring about the disaster or occurrence.

The second category concerns inquiries purely into policy issues, such as the Royal Commission on Social Security in 1972, the one on electoral law in 1986 that led to MMP, the Royal Commission on genetic modification that dealt with a controversial scientific subject, and the 1967 report that led to the accident compensation scheme.

The third category is a combination of the other two: both what happened may be contested and therefore needs to be ascertained and policy lessons from what happened may arise, upon which recommendations are made by the Inquiry to the government. A recent example of such an inquiry was the government Inquiry into Operation Burnham, concerning the conduct of the New Zealand soldiers in Afghanistan. The Inquiry examined what happened but made several important policy recommendations as well.

The government can also establish inquiries that are not under the

Inquiries Act. There are many different statutes that allow inquiries to be established for particular purposes. They come in many different varieties and some of them are armed with the powers of a Commission of Inquiry and others are not. For example, the Public Service Commissioner has powers to establish 'investigation and inquiries' under the Public Service Act 2020 into a variety of matters. The Prime Minister may refer, with the consent of the Chief Ombudsman, any matter the Prime Minister considers should be investigated and reported on by an Ombudsman. Under the royal prerogative, power remains to set up inquiries. The Law Commission conducts inquiries into law reform issues with an eye to making recommendations on what should be legislated by Parliament. The Waitangi Tribunal conducts inquiries into breaches of te Tiriti o Waitangi. The Auditor-General investigates and reports on instances of wrongful expenditure of public money.

Select Committees of Parliament can and do conduct inquiries. There is a long tradition of dealing with road safety issues by Select Committee Inquiry. But in recent years committees have become much bolder in deciding themselves what to inquire into. For example, in 2002 the Primary Production Select Committee decided to investigate the allocation of scampi quota where allegations of corruption against government officials were involved – even though a similar inquiry was being conducted by the Commissioner of State Services.

The choice for governments to establish or not establish inquiries is no simple matter. Inquiries are expensive. A Royal Commission was established in 2018 to inquire into abuse in care, looking at what happened to children, young people, and vulnerable adults in care. The Commission will make recommendations about how Aotearoa New Zealand can care better for children, young persons, and vulnerable adults. Although this is necessary work to be done, it will last for a long time and such inquiries are extraordinarily difficult to conduct. It will cost many millions of dollars.

Hardly a month goes by in Aotearoa New Zealand without someone calling for an independent inquiry to be established into some matter or other. Many of those calls can be better addressed by some other government action. Nonetheless, inquiries support a well-functioning democracy and are crucial in cases where high-level investigation and examination may help the country look after its people better in future.

References

Inquiries Act 2013. Inquiries are supported by the Department of Internal Affairs and its website contains links to all inquiries since 2001 allowing people to access those reports.
https://www.dia.govt.nz/Public-and-government-Inquiries
New Zealand Law Commission, NZLC R 102 *A New Inquiries Act* (2008)

26 International law, organisation and diplomacy

The key insight from this chapter is that much of the law in Aotearoa New Zealand is made elsewhere, not here. Restrictions on Aotearoa New Zealand's ability to act will depend on customary international law, our agreements with other nations, and the powers of the international organisations to which we belong. The most important organisation to which we belong is the United Nations of which Aotearoa New Zealand is a founding member. There are now 193 member states.

You may think that international law has nothing to do with your everyday life, but the truth is that the decisions that get made by organisations such as the United Nations, treaties and trade deals made between states, and international alliances can have great repercussions to people everywhere – including here. Important issues such as the Covid-19 pandemic and climate change are not just local, but global, and will require global action to combat them. However, as the Covid-19 pandemic shows, there are many limits upon international cooperation as well.

Aotearoa New Zealand's relationships with other nations, established and fostered through diplomacy, are important. The Ministry of Foreign Affairs and Trade (MFAT) conducts most of our international affairs and has more than 50 posts in overseas countries. In addition to carrying out diplomacy, the Ministry provides consular services to assist New Zealand citizens when they get into difficulties in foreign countries. International trade constitutes an essential component of our economy and Gross Domestic Product (GDP), making trading relationships a significant part of our diplomatic efforts.

Aotearoa New Zealand also belongs to a myriad of international organisations, such as the World Trade Organisation (WTO) which has an important role in regulating international trade and adjudicating disputes that arise within that context. For example, Aotearoa New Zealand was successful in efforts to contest the legality of tariffs imposed on our exports of sheep meats to the United States in 1999. As well, in 2010, the WTO ruled in favour of Aotearoa New Zealand against

Australia, overturning a 90-year export ban on the importation of our apples. Whenever you travel internationally on a plane, that flight will be governed by another international organisation, the International Civil Aviation Authority.

Aotearoa New Zealand is party to around 1,900 treaties, although that number is ever-increasing. The Ministry of Foreign Affairs and Trade maintains an online list you can search, New Zealand Treaties Online: https://wwww.treaties.mfat.govt.nz. International rules cover the relations between States in all their many forms, as well as governing many facets of contemporary everyday life such as security, postage, weather information, customs, shipping, and many others. It is frequently necessary to change our law to ensure we comply with international obligations. This country's interaction with other states has increased exponentially. We had almost no overseas diplomatic post aside from in London until 1942, at the height of the Second World War when we then sent a minister to Washington to set up a diplomatic post. Eighty years later we have become enmeshed in a web of complex relationships with other nations, all of which have an increasing impact on what happens here on our shores.

The complex web of international organisations

After the First World War, the League of Nations, an international intergovernmental organisation with the principle purpose to maintain peace, was established. It did some excellent work but failed to prevent the Second World War breaking out in 1939 and at the end of the war had, for all intents and purposes, ceased to exist. After the Second World War, 50 nations agreed to the Charter of the United Nations at the San Francisco Conference, designed to avoid such catastrophes in the future. According to the preambular paragraphs of the UN Charter, the purpose of the organisation is to:

- save succeeding generations from the scourge of war, which twice in our lifetime has brought untold sorrow to mankind, and
- to reaffirm faith in fundamental human rights, in the dignity and worth of the human person, in the equal rights of men and women and of nations large and small, and
- to establish conditions under which justice and respect for the obligations arising from treaties and other sources of international law can be maintained . . .

It was hoped that the United Nations would create a world of peace, equality and prosperity. While these goals remain, to a considerable degree, aspirational, they are worthy of effort. The Charter brought profound changes to international law and diplomacy, none more marked than the prohibition on the use of force contained in Article 2(4): *'All members shall refrain in their international relations from the threat or use of force, or political independence of any state, or in any other manner inconsistent with the Purposes of the United Nations.'*

The United Nations has six main organs, which include the Security Council and the General Assembly, as well as other bodies, committees, specialised agencies, funds and programmes all outlined below. Through these, and supported by many international civil servants, the UN aims to deal with the multitude of issues that arise around our planet: sustainable development, environmental protection, disaster relief, the consequences of conflict, equality, refugee and migrant protection, and many more. Navigating one's way around the UN system is a formidable challenge – there are so many components and their relationships so complicated. It is a world of acronyms and the *United National Handbook for 2021–22* (available free online from MFAT) contains a list of them. The list is eight pages long and that alone should demonstrate the complexity of the UN system. We publish the handbook as a service to international understanding and have done since 1961.

Security Council

The Security Council consists of 15 members: 10 elected members, including Aotearoa New Zealand, which has been elected twice, and the five permanent members who emerged as the victorious powers in the Second World War – China, France, the Russian Federation, the United Kingdom, and the United States. Under Chapter VII of the Charter, which deals with action with respect to threats to the peace, breaches of the peace, and acts of aggression, the Security Council can authorise complete or partial interruption of economic relations, means of communication and the severance of diplomatic relations. It also has the power to authorise armed intervention, that is, *'such action by air, sea or land forces as may be necessary to maintain or restore international peace.* In 2021, the Security Council had 110,000 UN peacekeepers engaged in 14 countries.

Members of the UN are also obliged to settle their disputes by peaceful means. The most significant qualifier to this is contained in Article 51: *'Nothing in the present Charter shall impair the inherent right of individual or collective self-defence if an armed attack occurs against a Member of the United Nations, until the Security Council has taken measures necessary to maintain international peace and security. . . .'*

State sovereignty is not as decisive as it once was. States that fail to protect their population from genocide, war crimes, ethnic cleansing, and other crimes against humanity are finding it harder to get away with such gross violations of human rights, due, in part, to the UN's efforts. However, conflicts and humanitarian disasters continue, as the ongoing civil war in Syria has shown. The UN is often prevented from intervening with these issues due to the capacity of the five permanent members of the Security Council to exercise a veto and stop any decision being passed or any action from being taken. This capacity often paralyses the United Nations.

General Assembly

The General Assembly of the United Nations comprises the whole membership – 193 Member States. While the General Assembly cannot be said to be a legislature, it does debate and reach decisions upon important issues. It has many important subsidiary bodies, such as the Disarmament Commission, the Human Rights Council, the International Law Commission, as well as a number of Standing Committees and ad hoc bodies.

UN programmes and funds

There are many separate UN programmes and funds, such as the United Nations Environment Programme (UNEP), the United Nations Development Programme (UNDP) (headed from 2009 to 2017 by former New Zealand Prime Minister Rt Hon Helen Clark) and the United Nations High Commissioner for Refugees (UNHCR). The Economic and Social Council of the United Nations has a loose affiliation with 19 specialised agencies such as the World Health Organisation (WHO), the World Bank group of agencies, the Food and Agriculture Organisation (FAO) and the United Nations Educational, Scientific and Cultural Organisation (UNESCO), the International Monetary Fund (IMF), the Universal Postal Union (UPU). The International Labour Organisation (ILO), one of the oldest, established in 1919, sees its role now as advancing decent social and working conditions. There are many others.

UN Secretariat

The United Nations Secretariat, headed by the Secretary-General, is an enormous organisation, located in many places around the world, but primarily in New York, Geneva, and Vienna. It has 21 departments and offices. There are also five Regional Economic Commissions. The Secretariat carries out the day-to-day work of the UN as mandated by the other main organs.

Vast as the UN system is, there are many other regional and specialised organisations to which Aotearoa New Zealand belong that are not part of the system. For example, Aotearoa New Zealand plays a significant role in the 1959 Antarctic Treaty with our station at Scott Base in McMurdo Sound. The Pacific Island Forum is important in our relations with the Pacific Island countries. We also belong to and are active in the International Whaling Commmission.

The nature and sources of international law

Diplomacy and politics are both vital ingredients of Aotearoa New Zealand's international relations – law is another. International law plays an essential role in oiling the wheels of the international system. However, international law has an entirely different character from domestic law and is easily misunderstood. It is not so much a set of rules as it is a normative system. The international community largely lacks the equivalent of a legislature – a body that can make rules that bind even those who dissent from them. However, it is in the self-interest of all nations to obey international law, nonetheless.

Aotearoa New Zealand consistently states that it will not sign up to international obligations unless it can honour them in its domestic law. Because we treat international law seriously, the obligations of international law place real restraints upon the freedom of the government. Aotearoa New Zealand consistently calls on other nations to uphold international law as well. The Ministry of Foreign Affairs and Trade also provides legal advice on a day-to-day basis to its minister and other parts of the government that require help with international law problems.

English judge and scholar Sir William Blackstone stated on customary international law: '. . . *the law of nations (wherever any question arises which is properly the object of its jurisdiction) is here adopted in its full extent by the common law, and is held to be part of the law of the land.'* While the issue is not free from difficulty, the Blackstonian view appears to be the law of Aotearoa New Zealand with some glosses. In *Zaoui No 2,* in 2005, in the Supreme Court of New Zealand, an important judgment of the Court delivered by Justice Keith found that customary international law was part of the law of Aotearoa New Zealand. Keith J later became a judge of the International Court of Justice, the first New Zealander ever to hold the office, and, while an Aotearoa New Zealand judge, wrote many of the important precedent cases dealing with international law issues.

The most authoritative statement on the sources of international law is to be found in Article 38 of the Statute of the International Court of Justice 1945, which states that the Court is to apply international law to the disputes submitted to it, and goes on to define the sources of those rules as:

1   International treaties or conventions, whether general or establishing rules expressly recognised by the contesting states.
2   International custom, as evidence of a general practice accepted as law.
3   General principles of law recognised by civilised nations.
4   Judicial decisions and teachings of the most highly qualified experts of the various nations, as subsidiary means for the determination of rules of law.
    To these should be added:
4   Declarations, statements, and other material known as 'soft' international law.

1. International treaties

Treaties are the most important source of international law and the main instruments by which international norms and rules are developed. The sheer volume of treaties is remarkable; there are more than 140 conventions concerning the environment alone! There are a variety of different names for treaties, such as convention, protocol, agreement, arrangement, statute, exchange of notes, and final act. There are also many different types of treaties. Some, multilateral treaties, have more than 100 nations as parties; many more are bilateral – they have been agreed by two nations only. One fundamental rule of international law is the principle that agreements must be kept in good faith – *pacta sunt servanda*. Therefore, a treaty has binding force and ought to be observed, whether or not there are effective enforcement mechanisms.

It is quite an undertaking for any country to keep track of all the treaties to which it is a party. The consequences of any breach can be serious and embarrassing. To keep track of its obligations our Ministry of Foreign Affairs and Trade published the New Zealand Consolidated Treaty List in 1996. By 2013, Aotearoa New Zealand was bound by the provisions of 794 multilateral treaties and 808 bilateral or plurilateral ones. Indeed, Aotearoa New Zealand is bound by more treaties than there are Acts of Parliament. The Minstry of Foreign Affairs and Trade provides a useful service on its website 'New Zealand Treaties Online'. It is also important to understand that international treaties do *not* automatically constitute Aotearoa New Zealand law. We have a 'dualist' system and can sign up to international obligations, which are binding on the government as international law, but they are not binding within domestic law unless they are specifically made part of our law.

The negotiation of treaties can be a difficult business. Multilateral conventions are usually negotiated in complicated international conferences – often, several conferences are held for a number of years. At such meetings, informal negotiations are often as important as the formal sessions in hammering out compromises and language. Particularly when there are many nations involved, there is a tendency to use ambiguous words to get the broadest agreement possible. A nation that does not agree or sign cannot be bound by the treaty, so widespread agreement is essential to ensure the aims of the agreement are upheld.

An interesting example of argument about treaty obligations involving New Zealand was the decision by the United States in the 1980s, under the ANZUS Treaty, to suspend its security obligations to New Zealand because of the latter's anti-nuclear policy. The dispute with the United States over ANZUS involved a treaty and an alliance. New Zealand took the view that the ANZUS Treaty did not oblige New Zealand to accept nuclear weapons in our ports; the Americans said they could no longer be bound by the provisions of the Treaty to come to New Zealand's aid in the event of an armed attack if we did not accept their vessels on a 'neither confirm nor deny' basis. In response, New Zealand said it was happy to have ship visits so long as the non-nuclear policy was met. The New Zealand government was prepared to make the judgment without disclosure from the Americans. The Americans said that was not acceptable and suspended their obligation under the Treaty, but they did not argue that New Zealand was in breach of the ANZUS Treaty, which is silent on nuclear matters.

Profound changes have been made to how Aotearoa New Zealand becomes bound by international treaties. The making of a treaty – its signature or ratification – is an Executive act and must be agreed by Cabinet. The standing orders of the House of Representatives now require the government to present international treaties to the House that are to be subject to ratification, accession, acceptance, or approval – or in the case that we might withdraw or denounce a treaty. This must be done even when an act has been passed on an urgent basis by the Executive. It seems now to be accepted that the government will not, except in an emergency, take binding treaty action until the minimum time for parliamentary scrutiny has expired. The Foreign Affairs, Defence and Trade Select Committee (or sometimes another Select Committee) examines treaties that are referred to the House and also brings treaties to the attention of the House if it is in the national interest, or for any other reason. If the treaty obligations require alteration of the existing domestic law, this requires legislative action by Parliament. This level of Parliamentary scrutiny appears to be working reasonably well, although the procedure does not apply on its face to most bilateral treaties, only those of 'particular significance'.

As well, a treaty may be void if *'at the time of its conclusion, it conflicts with a peremptory norm of general international law.* Not all customary international law principles are peremptory norms or *jus cogens*. Rather, peremptory norms are those *'accepted and recognised by the international community of States as a whole as a norm from which no derogation is permitted.*

2. Customary international law

Customary international law remains the bedrock of the international system. Treaty regimes are not exhaustive and there continue to be areas that are not regulated by treaties, making customary international law essential for ensuring there are no gaps. At the same time, the rules first set out in a treaty can evolve into customary international law because of a high level of adherence to them. Treaties can also codify customary international law, synthesising existing customary international law into treaty obligations – such was the case with many of the provisions of the UN Convention on the Law of the Sea (UNCLOS). However, not all custom in the international arena amounts to actual customary international law. For custom to give rise to legal obligations, a number of features must be present, the detail of which will not be gone into here.

3. Recognised general principles of law

The scope of *'general principles of law recognised by civilised nations'* is unclear, and there is considerable debate and controversy about what is meant by this source of international law. For example, some jurists argue that it affirms that pre-existing principles and norms (Natural Law) underlie international law, while others believe that it adds little to other sources of international law unless reflecting the consent of States.

4. Judicial decisions and teachings

Little needs to be said here about this source of international law as judicial decisions and the teachings of the most highly qualified publicists or experts. These are subsidiary means for determining the rules of international law.

5. 'Soft' international law

There is also an emerging species of international law known as 'soft' law. 'Soft' law comprises non-binding high-level instruments and documents, such as declarations, recommendations, guidelines, codes of practice or statements of principle that are carefully drafted and seem to rely upon the language of obligation. They usually emanate from inter-state meetings, such as high-level international conferences or meetings of international bodies. The Declaration of the United Nations Conference on the Human Environment 1972 ('Stockholm Declaration') and the Rio Declaration on Environment and Development 1992 ('Rio Declaration') are good examples.

In contrast, 'hard' law refers mainly to custom or treaties. Custom takes time and, often, a lot of state practice before it hardens into a legally enforceable rule. Treaties also take a long time to negotiate and nations tend to shy away from the specificity they often involve. Consequently, 'soft' law is a much more politically attractive approach, not least because it is frequently drafted with ambiguity. All politicians know the value of ambiguity and while such an approach may have deceptive elements and may create wrong impressions, it can also serve to secure agreement where it might not otherwise be achieved.

Methods of settling international disputes

The Charter of the United Nations outlines that all members are to settle their disputes by peaceful means in conformity with principles of international law and justice. The use of force cannot be resorted to as a means of settling disputes. Chapter VI of the Charter imposes a specific legal obligation on Member States:

The parties to any dispute, the continuance of which is likely to endanger the maintenance of international peace and security, shall, first, seek a solution by negotiation, enquiry, mediation, conciliation, arbitration, judicial settlement, resort to regional agencies or arrangements, or other peaceful means of their own choice.

The Charter provides that any Member State may bring any dispute to the attention of the Security Council or the General Assembly. The Secretary-General may also bring any matter that may threaten the maintenance of international peace and security to the attention of the Security Council. There is an extensive hierarchy of methods that can be used to arrive at a resolution – from negotiation to adjudication, and every modern method of dispute settlement in between.

At the apex of the dispute settlement pyramid sits the International Court of Justice (ICJ), another organ of the United Nations. The Court is situated in The Hague in the Netherlands and is governed by its own Statute. Do bear in mind that only 66 States that are part of the United Nations, including Aotearoa New Zealand, accept the compulsory jurisdiction of the Court under the so-called optional clause of the Statute of the International Court of Justice. Essentially, the jurisdiction of the ICJ is consensual. States are not obliged to accept the compulsory jurisdiction of the Court, and most do not, although States may accept it for a particular dispute by special agreement. This operates under a theory of reciprocity, so the ICJ has jurisdiction only to the extent that both parties have accepted a common commitment. If one nation has a condition attached to its acceptance of the Court's jurisdiction that advantages the other nation in the dispute, that other nation can take advantage of the condition. Aotearoa New Zealand has been in cases in front of the ICJ in contentious proceedings on three occasions – twice in relation to nuclear testing in the Pacific and once in relation to Japan.

The ICJ also has jurisdiction to issue advisory opinions when requested by the United Nations Security Council or the General Assembly. The General Assembly is also able to authorise other United Nations organs and agencies to seek advisory opinions, as it notably did in 1996 on the legality of the use of nuclear weapons in 1996 – where the Court held their use was illegal in most circumstances.

The forward march of international human rights law

Human rights are an incredibly important international issue that aim to ensure people's basic needs are met, to protect vulnerable or systematically disadvantaged populations, and provide for important freedoms. It is essential that there be a universal standard of human rights to hold governments all around the world accountable. The UN Charter itself contains several human rights provisions, as pointed out at the beginning of the chapter. Indeed, Article I provides that one of the purposes of the United Nations is to promote and encourage respect for human rights. In 1948, the United Nations General Assembly adopted the Universal Declaration of Human Rights (UDHR). This Declaration contains traditional civil and political rights, including the right to life, fair trial, equality before the law, non-discrimination, freedoms from torture and arbitrary arrest or detention, and freedoms of speech and expression, among others.

Two covenants were approved in 1966: The International Covenant on Civil and Political Rights (ICCPR) and the International Covenant on Economic, Social and Cultural Rights (ICESCR). The ICCPR was to become the basis for the New Zealand Bill of Rights Act 1990 and Aotearoa New Zealand has agreed to the first Optional Protocol to the ICCPR – which allows complaints by individuals to be made to the UN Human Rights Committee. Furthermore, the government of Aotearoa New Zealand must make periodic reports on the human rights situation here. There have been a number of complaints about Aotearoa New Zealand. These two covenants as well as the UDHR are often referred to as the 'International Bill of Rights'.

Apart from these Covenants, there are many other international conventions that have been negotiated over the years and have entered into force. Aotearoa New Zealand has ratified the most important ones, such as the Convention on the Rights of the Child, the Convention for the Prevention and Punishment of Genocide 1948, the Convention on the Status of Refugees 1951, the Convention on the Elimination of all Forms of Racial Discrimination 1965, the Convention on the Elimination of All Forms of Discrimination Against Women 1979, the Convention against Torture and Other Cruel, Inhuman or Degrading treatment or Punishment 1984 and the Convention on the Rights of Persons with Disabilities 2006.

The UN Human Rights Council, the successor to the Commission on Human Rights, was established in 2006 as a subsidiary organ of the General Assembly. The Council is responsible for promoting and protecting human rights. It monitors human rights in all Member States through the Universal Periodic Review mechanism. It comprises 47 Member States elected for three-year terms. The body also has a complaints procedure and makes reports and conducts investigations from time to time into specific issues. The Office of UN High Commissioner for Human Rights is also charged with the promotion and protection of human rights and is part of the UN Secretariat.

A modern and welcome development has been the creation of the International Criminal Court (ICC) in 1988. The Court was established to try individuals who allegedly commit *'the most serious crimes of concern to the international community as a whole'*, including genocide, war crimes, crimes against humanity and, more recently, the crime of aggression. The ICC is the first world court with the jurisdiction to prosecute perpetrators of international crimes. It represents the most recent development in a rapid evolution of law and institution building that began with the end of the Second World War. Unlike its predecessors that have limited geographical and temporal scope, the ICC has permanent existence and global jurisdiction. However, it is a court of 'last resort'. Nations themselves are obliged to prosecute individuals for the crimes over which the Court has jurisdiction and only if that does not occur does the Court step in.

As well as the importance of human rights law, it needs to be pointed out that international environmental law has been rapidly growing, particularly since 1972. The uncomfortable truth is that human activities seem to constitute the root cause of most of the environmental problems faced by the planet – such as climate change, depletion of the ozone layer, species extinction, air pollution, nuclear accidents, oil spills, the absence of clean drinking water in many parts of the world, hazardous waste, land-based pollution of the sea, and many others. More than a thousand international treaties and other instruments exist aimed at dealing with these problems. However, at present, they seem insufficient to meet the challenges. Much more needs to be done if we are to protect Papatūānuku and work as a global community to combat climate change.

International law and the obligations that flow from it constitute a significant check and balance on the powers of both the Executive Government and the Parliament of New Zealand. As imperfect as international law is, as a small State sometimes needing protection against bigger and more powerful states, Aotearoa New Zealand has a vital interest in robust norms of international law that are fair and reasonable.

References

James Crawford *Brownlie's Principles of Public International Law* (9th edition, Oxford University Press, Oxford, 2019); Alberto Costi (ed) *Public International Law: A New Zealand Perspective* (LexisNexis, Wellington, 2020); Malcolm Shaw *International Law* (8th ed, Cambridge University Press, Cambridge, 2021); Andrew Clapham *Brierly's Law of Nations* (7th ed., Oxford University Press, 2012); J G Merrills *International Dispute Settlement* (5th ed. Cambridge University Press, Cambridge, 2011); Henry Kissinger *Diplomacy* (Simon & Schuster, New York, 1995); Jonathan C Carlson and Geoffrey W R Palmer *International Environmental Law – A Problem-Oriented Coursebook* (4th ed., West Academic Publishing, St Paul, 2019); Geoffrey Palmer *Environment – the international Challenge* (Victoria Univesity Press, Wellington 1995).

27 The mysteries of the Crown

In Aotearoa New Zealand, we have a constitutional monarchy. Our Head of State is Queen Elizabeth II, who is also Queen of the United Kingdom. She is the longest-reigning monarch in British history. The word 'Crown' covers a wide range of matters and is often used. In literal terms the Crown is what the Queen wears on her head on ceremonial occasions, but it is a symbol for royal powers in many different contexts.

Illustration by Ursula Palmer Steeds

Over the centuries, the monarchy has evolved, and other institutions have developed. The British monarchy dates back at least to the Norman Conquest of England in 1066. In the early period, the powers of the monarch tended to be absolute. As well, the monarch personally led armies into battle and ruled personally. The King was the fount of all political power. The monarchy was and is an inherited office. By the time Aotearoa New Zealand became part of the British Empire, power was distributed quite differently from the original hierarchies of the feudal system. Nowadays, in Aotearoa New Zealand, the Queen's functions are largely ceremonial, and she has little personal power, but enormous prestige.

Reductions in royal power, however, spanned incremental changes over the centuries. The powers of absolute monarchy slowly gave way to democratic influences until Parliament at Westminster had the predominant influence. Nevertheless, the legal powers remained with the monarch, but were exercised with ministerial advice. Today, both the United Kingdom and Aotearoa New Zealand are constitutional monarchies which function in a democratic way by requiring the main decision-makers to be elected by voters in an election. Here, the Queen does not rule over this country personally. Her role is carried out, in her absence, by the Governor-General. When the Governor-General's office is vacant or the officeholder is unable to perform all or any of the functions and powers, the Administrator of the government is the Chief Justice.

HOW THE QUEEN'S POWER IS DISTRIBUTED

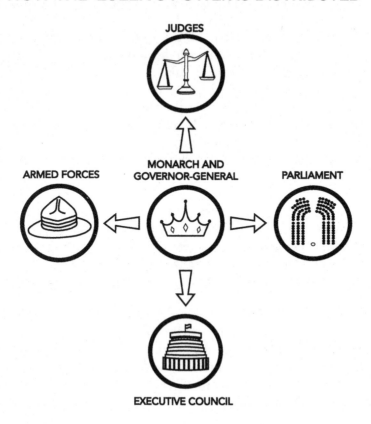

Section 2 of the Constitution Act 1986 lays down the modern law for Aotearoa New Zealand:

(1) The Sovereign in right of New Zealand is the head of State of New Zealand, and shall be known by the royal style and titles proclaimed from time to time.
(2) The Governor-General appointed by the Sovereign is the Sovereign's representative in New Zealand.

The Office of Governor-General is constituted by Letters Patent issued by the Queen in 1983. The Governor-General is appointed on the advice of the Prime Minister of Aotearoa New Zealand. The usual term is for five years. The Queen is known as Queen of the realm of New Zealand that includes the self-governing states of the Cook Islands and Niue. It also includes the Ross Dependency in Antarctica and Tokelau. The Royal Titles Act 1974 is relevant.

The Queen is also Head of the Commonwealth, a voluntary organisation of 54 states that have links to the former British Empire. Although a majority of Commonwealth member countries do not have the Queen as their Head of State, 16 of them do.

Like the Queen, the office of the Governor-General is apolitical and acts as a symbolic influence. In 2004, the Governor-General at the time, Dame Silvia Cartwright, was of the view that the office should reflect the values and identity of New Zealanders and work as a unifying mechanism. She said:

The non-political nature of the office is crucial and must not be compromised. This means refraining from doing certain things such as commenting on policies of the government of the day. The positive aspect of this is that the office is one that transcends politics. Hopefully it can represent all New Zealanders, no matter their political persuasions.

The Governor-General fulfills a constitutional role in Parliament. This includes duties such as: opening each Parliament by making a speech from the throne (which is drafted by the government), giving Royal Assent and signing Bills into law, on ministerial advice, and presiding over Executive Council meetings. The Executive Council is the mechanism by which advice on many issues is tendered to the Governor-General. No fewer than two ministers must attend these meetings. As well, constitutionally, the public service and the Executive branch of government are conducted in the name of the Queen, or the Crown.

The Governor-General also authorises diplomatic representatives of Aotearoa New Zealand to other countries and accepts the credentials of diplomats sent from other countries when they arrive here. There are about 120 such representatives and there are frequent ceremonies at Government House to mark this process.

The Queen is also the fount of the system of justice. In a way similar to how ministers are referred to as 'Ministers of the Crown', the judges are the Queen's Judges. This derives from the early developments of the system of justice in England. At first, the King was the source of all power – which included judicial power.

The Stuart Kings in Great Britain claimed to rule by divine right. Struggles to overcome that view finally resulted in the law binding the King. Parliament and the decisions of judges combined to produce this result. The Bill of Rights 1689 laid down that the King did not have authority to suspend the laws or their execution without the consent of Parliament. That law is part of the law of New Zealand. When Prime Minister Sir Robert Muldoon tried to suspend a superannuation statute that had been passed by Parliament without actually calling Parliament together after the 1975 general election and repealing it, the Chief Justice Sir Richard Wild held the action to be unlawful. Key elements of the English judicial system and law were transferred to Aotearoa New Zealand when it was annexed by Great Britain as early as 1841.

One of the difficulties in unpacking what the 'Crown' comprises is the number of different, and sometimes confusing contexts, in which the term is used. There are many governmental organisations of one sort or another that are termed, by statute, 'Crown entities'. Māori settlements under te Tiriti o Waitangi are generally talked about as being between Māori and the Crown. The deeds of settlement that precede the enactment of a statue by Parliament are negotiated directly between Māori and the Crown representatives. The term 'Crown land' is frequently used as the Crown holds a lot of land. In substance this means the public.

Listen to the *Cabinet Manual 2017* on the topic:

The expression 'the Crown' is used frequently in descriptions of New Zealand's current constitutional arrangements. The meaning of 'the Crown'

varies according to the context in which it is used. Generally, it describes
the executive government conducted by Ministers and their departments.
It does not normally include organisations having their own corporate
identities, such as state-owned enterprises.

The military also has close and formal connections to the Crown. The
Governor-General is the titular Commander-in-Chief of the New
Zealand Defence Force. This has the advantage of ensuring that the
armed forces are loyal to the State through the Governor-General, who
stands above politics. Decisions to deploy armed forces, here or overseas,
are based on the royal prerogative. These days, the powers that the
government can use from the royal prerogative fall within a relatively
narrow compass.

It is also the role of the Governor-General to appoint a Prime
Minister, usually determined by what happens after a general election
for the House of Representatives. The Governor-General can dismiss a
Prime Minister, if that person ceases to have the confidence of the House
and may also refuse to dissolve a Parliament if the Prime Minister wants
a general election but it may be a government can be formed from the
existing House without an election. Further, the Governor-General may
force a dissolution if there is evidence that the government has lost the
confidence in the House. The House is the master of the government.

Constitutional scholars have worried about the power of the
Governor-General to make decisions in a situation of crisis or emergency
that have great political consequences. One example of this is the case
when Sir John Kerr, the Australian Governor-General, dismissed Gough
Whitlam, the Prime Minister of Australia in 1975. Essentially, this
was because the Senate had not yet passed the Budget, although it also
had not yet refused to do so. The decision was extremely controversial.
Widespread expressions of outrage occurred in many quarters and later
led to Kerr resigning his office. A historian who had written a biography
of Whitlam, after years of research in the Australian National Archives,
brought a legal case to require the public release by the Archives of the
correspondence between Kerr and the Palace concerning the dismissal.

In May 2020, up to 212 letters relating to the issue were released on
the order of the High Court of Australia, despite resistance from the
Australian government and the Palace. Much of the correspondence was
between Kerr and Sir Martin Charteris, the Queen's Private Secretary.

They revealed that Kerr made his decisions alone over a long period of time and kept his views to himself, not sharing them with the Prime Minister. However, Kerr did have extensive contact with the Palace in London and with the Leader of the Opposition Malcom Fraser – who became the caretaker Prime Minister following the dismissal, and after the general election, became the Prime Minister. The Governor-General did not follow legal advice to let politics take its course.

Such situations have never arisen in Aotearoa New Zealand, although we approached a dangerous situation with Sir Robert Muldoon's refusal to devalue the dollar in July 1984, after just having lost a general election. There had been some discussion of devaluation during the election campaign and afterwards there was a run on the banks and the Reserve Bank closed the foreign exchange markets.Crisis was averted by the Deputy Prime Minister, Jim McLay, taking steps to ensure the decision was changed. The outgoing government acted on the advice of the incoming government. However, the Governor-General, Sir David Beattie, was prepared to dismiss Muldoon had the decision not been changed, it later emerged. The situation had arisen because after election night while the result was clear, special votes and overseas votes remained to be counted and the official results could not have been declared until that was done. The law was changed to avoid any recurrence of a such a situation.

Since the introduction of MMP, it has been clear that the House of Representatives is where the power lies. The Governor-General does not really have a discretion about whom to call to form a government – it is the House of Representatives that determines this. Nonetheless, it could possibly be the case in the future, under exceptional circumstances, that the Governor-General may need to act to preserve democratic propriety.

References

Philip A Joseph *Joseph on Constitutional and Administrative Law* (Thomson Reuters Wellington, 2021) Chapter 18; Alison Quentin-Baxter and Janet McLean *This Realm of New Zealand – The Sovereign the Governor-General the Crown* (Auckland University Press, 2017); Geoffrey Palmer and Matthew Palmer *Bridled Power – New Zealand's Constitution and Government* (4th edition, Oxford University Press, Melbourne, 2004), Chapter 4; Matthew S R Palmer and Dean R Knight *The Constitution of New Zealand – A contextual analysis* (Cambridge University Press, Cambridge, 2022), Chapter 31; Jenny Hocking *The Palace Letters-The Queen, the governor-general and the plot to dismiss Gough Whitlam* (Scribe Press, Australia, 2020); Janet McLean *Searching for the State in British Legal Thought* (Cambridge University Press, Cambridge, 2012).

28 Ceremony, community and constitution: A conversation with Her Excellency Dame Patsy Reddy, Governor-General of New Zealand, at Government House Wellington, August 2021

Illustration by Huriana Kopeke-Te Aho

Q: Your Excellency, we'd like to start with what you can tell us about your job, how you do it and how it works.

A: I am the representative of the Head of State in New Zealand. It has three main limbs: the ceremonial role, constitutional role, and the community role. There is also an international role, representing our country at international events.

The community role is, in practice, the role that takes up most of my time. The constitutional role is the duty of forming the government and appointing a Prime Minister, dissolving Parliament, and swearing in new ministers, following a General Election. Of course, it also embodies those theoretical, famous, reserve powers. The constitutional role also involves giving royal assent (bringing into being) to the laws of the land and also presiding over the Executive Council once a week. It's a regular part of my job, but it actually doesn't take a lot of time.

The Executive Councillors are members of the government – ministers – who come to Executive Council weekly to advise me to sign documents that require to be formalised in Executive Council. They are regulations and important appointments of public officials, proclamations where I formally acquire land on behalf of the Crown under the Public Works Act, and other similar statutory functions that must be performed by the Executive Council. I preside at those meetings. There must be a quorum of at least two ministers to advise me why I should sign the documents on the agenda. And that's my opportunity to talk with them about what's going on more generally. In Walter Bagehot speak, I'm entitled to be consulted and I can advise and warn the government, but I can't do anything beyond that. Ultimately, everything I do is on the advice of the Prime Minister and her ministers. That's the constitutional part of my role.

Another important role is at the formal opening of Parliament and reading the speech from the throne. This is actually the Prime Minister's speech which is handed to me to read, as the formal announcement of the programme for the government that has just been elected and installed in the Parliament.

The ceremonial part of my role is significant; the opening of Parliament is part of that. I also represent New Zealand on certain formal occasions, such as welcoming Heads of State to New Zealand. We have a formal ceremony to welcome them as the Head of State on the grounds of Government House. Of course, it's a while since we've done that due to the Covid pandemic.

I also receive the credentials of arriving diplomatic Heads of Mission to New Zealand and formally accept them as representatives of their government to act in New Zealand.

Similarly, investitures are an important part of my ceremonial role. In my thinking, it overlaps with my community role, because it's very much part of New Zealand. Investitures celebrate New Zealanders who've done great things: celebrating success, celebrating people who have made significant contributions in different communities around New Zealand. They are Royal Honours, so I am formally bestowing those honours on behalf of the Queen as the Monarch and Head of State.

Investitures take up a lot of my time actually, because of the way we run the ceremonies now. There are New Year's Honours and Queen's Birthday Honours announced each year. We hold investiture ceremonies at Government House in Auckland and Wellington. And we have at least one ceremony in the South Island, for those people who choose not to come north.

An innovation we developed after the Covid lockdowns in 2020 involves holding smaller ceremonies. We now have a maximum of about 14 recipients. And they are all seated at separate tables with up to seven of their whānau and friends. We have a lot of ceremonies as a result of that as I think there are about 170 recipients in each honours list. So, we now typically have 10 ceremonies in Auckland, eight to 10 ceremonies in Wellington, and then maybe two or three in the South Island. At twice a year, that's quite a lot of my time.

I represent the Head of State at important events. For example, the World War I, 100-year commemorations, as well as Anzac Day, and events leading up to Waitangi Day every year. Then there are memorial services for national tragedies, such as the Christchurch mosque massacres in 2019 and the eruption of Whakaari White Island later that year. Commemorations of important anniversaries, such as 125 years of women's suffrage, are also important. I hosted several events in 2018 representing that anniversary.

In my community role I am Patron of about 140 charitable organisations. Some are Royal patronages, which are of organisations officially recognised by the Queen where I'm directly representing her. A good example of that is St John. I'm the Prior of St John in New Zealand and I hold regular St John investitures and ceremonies recognising youth awards and the like.

I spend as much time as I can amidst all that, travelling around the country and visiting different regions and people, really to see what they're doing. It is an important aspect of my role to be able to celebrate people who are doing great work in the community.

Last week we were in New Plymouth. I had the great privilege of visiting Parihaka, which was a wonderful and emotional experience. I was told that I was the first Governor-General to go there in living memory. I think my office found out from Papers Past that there may have been visits many years ago. But in recent times, no Governor-General has been there while still in office. And it was wonderful to be there. During my term I've been to many different marae and many historically important ones. I've really enjoyed that part of my role.

In addition, I attended events celebrating 50 years of the Govett-Brewster Gallery and 30 years of the Taranaki arts festival, went up the Taranaki Maunga to meet with the DOC people who look after the national park and visited Puke Ariki, the local museum. And then I met with some young people who have set up a wonderful social enterprise charity feeding people in need. I do as many regional visits each year as I can.

Then we host events here at Government House in Wellington, functions for the different community organisations and patronages. For example, we're hosting the Royal Humane Society bravery awards here next week.

Q: There's a Government House in Auckland. Can you tell us about that?

A: Yes. There's always been a Government House in Auckland, as I understand it. Wellington did not become the capital until 1865. Last century, the Governor-General and staff would actually move up to Auckland for the summer. I'm not quite sure why as it probably would have been the worst time, weather-wise. Anyway, they used to go up there for long periods at a time.

But what we have now in Auckland is a Government House which is quite different from Government House in Wellington, which was designed and built as a working Government House. It has office accommodation for all of the staff as well as the Governor-General, who resides there.

In Auckland, the present Government House is essentially a very elegant family home dating from the 1920s. It was gifted to the nation by the Mappin family in the 1960s. They gifted it for use by the Governor-General while in Auckland. So it was a conditional gift to the Crown. It's very central, in the middle of Epsom. And it's exclusively for use by the Governor-General and for the activities of the Governor-General.

Attached to the house is a pavilion which was built in 2005 to hold larger events. It's smaller than our ballroom here at Government House in Wellington, but it can still hold events of up to a hundred people. And we use it regularly when we have events such as investitures in Auckland.

It had always been my intention to use the Auckland base at least a week a month, but it hasn't worked out quite like that. It really depends where we are needed, where our events are. And every Monday is Executive Council and it's held here in Wellington. So it's a much more fluid situation, especially in the Covid-19 environment.

Q: Would it be fair to describe your role as one of a figure of unity for the nation, that you are politically neutral and sit over the top of it all as a sort of embodiment of the State?

A: Yes, I think that's part of the magic of the role. As you can tell, I'm a supporter of the office, but then I've been in the role for five years. I believe it's important that it's apolitical and a one-term five-year appointment. So there's no sense of empire-building, there's no sense of the Governor-General trying to build their own constituency.

As Governor-General you're here to serve all New Zealanders and to represent all New Zealanders, whether it's internationally or within the country. There is the figurehead role, as the person who is present when we have great tragedies as well as great celebrations and commemorations. And at major symbolic occasions, like going to Maungapōhatu, in the Urewera, to formally apologise for the Crown's actions in 1916 in wrongfully imprisoning Rua Kēnana. That was a wonderful experience. And it meant a lot to the people of Maungapōhatu that it was the Queen's representative who gave that apology.

I think, and this is a bit controversial because people have different views on it, but in my opinion, the connection between the Governor-General and Māori – tangata whenua – is symbolic and quite special. And it's not just special for the Governor-General, I think it's special for a lot of Māori as well. As I mentioned, when I delivered the Crown pardon of Rua Kēnana, I know that was important for his descendants because I was there representing the Queen.

And similarly at Parihaka. The people of Parihaka had wanted the Crown apology to be formally delivered by the Governor-General in 2017, but I was unable to do so as I was overseas, at the World War I centenary commemorations of the Battle of Messines in Belgium at the time. So it was particularly satisfying for me to visit this year.

For Māori, there is a personal connection with the office of the

Governor-General because of te Tiriti o Waitangi. This connection has continued in the unbroken line from Governor Hobson signing the Treaty through to the Governor-General of the day. That is something I've treasured because I've seen it in practice. I've seen the reaction when I visit marae. I know it's not just for me, it's for the office that I hold. That's something that differentiates the office of Governor-General in New Zealand from the same office in the other Realm countries where the Queen is Head of State.

Q: Could you say anything about how you interact with the palace in London?

A: My interaction with the palace is fairly limited. Our head of state in New Zealand is, in practice, the Governor-General. The British Monarch is a figurehead – an historical symbol. But I think it's good to remember history and have that connection with it.

The Queen is the most remarkable woman I've ever met. She has a very clear understanding of what her role means in practice, which is that she's a symbol – an historical figurehead – as our Head of State.

Typically, she meets each Governor-General before they commence their term. David and I met with her and Prince Philip in 2016, before I took on the role, and I write to her regularly. I asked her how she wanted me to keep in touch. And she said she'd like me to write a letter, every six months. So I do that, more frequently if there's something important that I think I should touch base on. For example, I wrote to her shortly after the mosque massacres. She had sent a message of condolence immediately and I wrote to give her my view of how the country was handling that tragedy. And then last year, during lockdown, I wrote about how New Zealanders were responding. People have asked me why I don't have Zoom meetings with the Queen. But given that I don't like them much myself, I can't imagine she does either.

There is a communications triangle. The Queen needs to be informed about certain constitutional matters – formal advice goes to the Palace on royal honours and other matters. That tends to be done through the Cabinet Office, by the secretary of the Executive Council who has regular communication with the Queen's Official secretary. Of course, from time to time we've had royal visits here. We won't have another one from the Queen in her lifetime, but we did host a visit in 2019 by Prince Charles, the Prince of Wales and the Duchess of Cornwall.

Q: In 1990 the Queen and the Duke were here for nearly three weeks.

A: Well that, that would have been challenging for the Governor-General.

Q: It was pretty challenging for the Prime Minister.

A: Of course, that was in your time!

Q: Now, you must have to read a lot of documents. Do you have a big lot of paper going through here?

A: There's a lot of signing. As well as appointments and giving royal assent to bills and so forth, there's a lot of signing for the Ministry of Foreign Affairs and Trade, appointing diplomats and so on. I also sign congratulatory cards, which is a monumental task. Sending cards to everyone who turns 100, everyone who turns 105 and thereafter every year. You cannot imagine how many there are! I mean, some months there'd be 30 turning 100 and I've regularly had people over 105. We are a very long-lived nation. Extraordinary! And also 50th wedding anniversaries, 60th wedding anniversaries, 65th, 70th, 75th and more. I have even sent cards for 76th wedding anniversaries!

Every now and again, I wonder if this a good use of my time. But when you think that these people have been alive since World War I, they're worth celebrating. So, I sign them all by hand.

Q: Do you ever have to go overseas on an official business?

A: Yes. Before the pandemic I would go overseas to represent the country at certain commemorations and other celebrations. I've already mentioned the World War I Centennial commemorations. I represented New Zealand at the commemorations at Messines in Belgium, Le Quesnoy in France and the battle of Beersheba involving New Zealand soldiers in 1917 in what is now Israel. I also went to Gallipoli for Anzac Day commemorations in 2018. Those were wonderful occasions and I was very honoured to get that opportunity. I also represented New Zealand at the D-Day 75th commemorations in 2019. And at the enthronement of the Japanese Emperor later that year.

Also I did actually make a State visit to Australia in June this year. It was their first State visit for a while, and it was our first one since 2019. I went over there while the Trans-Tasman bubble was operating and managed to get to Canberra and Hobart. Hobart has a long and very interesting historical connection with New Zealand because it provided our earliest prison. We thoroughly enjoyed staying at the Governor's house there – it dates from about 1853.

Q: Have you enjoyed this office? Have you found it satisfying?

A: I have, because it's unique, in the true meaning of that word, it›s unique. And it is wonderful to meet people I would never otherwise have come across. I've met some remarkable world figures, people like Barack Obama and Dame Jane Goodall. But I've also met people from all over New Zealand and I've found them fascinating, endlessly.

Just this morning, I went over to look through the new children's hospital in Wellington which is shortly to be finished and has been largely funded by Mark Dunajtschik and his partner Dorothy Spotswood, who have donated $50 million to it. Consequently, Wellington is getting a new childrens' hospital 25 years earlier than the government would have funded it. It is the most remarkable story.

Now, those are fantastic occasions. They are small occasions, but they're the sort of thing where I think the Governor-General attending just adds a bit more kudos to being able to celebrate and congratulate the people that are working on that job: the project managers, the engineers, the builders, the hospital staff and the funders.

I've been almost everywhere in New Zealand. I went down to Whenua Hou, near Rakiura Stewart Island a couple of weeks ago. We were able to visit there because Sir Tipene O'Regan of Ngai Tahu organised it, which was very generous. He and his wife Lady Sandra came with us. I was thrilled to meet a kākāpō, who was called Ian. I said, well if there can be a kākāpō called Ian perhaps there could be a Patsy. So here's hoping.

Q: It's a strange thing about the New Zealand office of Governor-General, that it's never been controversial. Other countries have had trouble with the office, in Canada, and in Australia in 1975. We've never had these troubles.

A: Yes, I agree. But if you look more widely, at the political environment in New Zealand, it isn't a controversial environment. The closest we have come, which is a time that you and I can remember, would have been the end of Muldoon's government. I'm thinking about it from a Governor-General's perspective – the 1984 Election.

Q: I was here at Government House the night Muldoon arrived to ask Sir David Beattie for a dissolution of Parliament.

A: That could have been quite a challenge for the Governor-General. I think that probably is as close as we've got to what could have been a constitutional crisis. Not necessarily right then, but after, when Muldoon refused to leave office. So that was a time when it could have gone either way.

The Australian constitutional crisis, when Sir John Kerr sacked Prime Minister Whitlam, I still find that a puzzling situation. I have read a book about it and I listened to the recent podcast, which is fascinating. It's just how it evolved that is hard to understand.

Q: It was partly due to the fact that they designed the Australian Senate before the Lloyd George budget crisis with the House of Lords in 1909 after which the Lords lost their capacity to hold it up, and so the Australian Constitution Act doesn't reflect how the upper house now functions at Westminster.

A: There certainly was a stalemate and the Governor-General felt that he had to resolve the situation in some way. And I guess that could happen here. I mean, if you look back at our General Elections, in 2017, we had a really unusual situation. There was quite a long period when we had no idea who would be government. And we ended up with a coalition of a party who got fewer seats than the Opposition party with two other parties and that, you know, could easily have been challenging, but in New Zealand people play by the rules.

Q: Well, one of your predecessors, Sir Michael Hardie Boys, made a series of speeches, which I think settled the whole issue down quite a lot and there's been no need to revisit it really. The stability is a great important thing in any society. And I suppose the Governor-General generally has contributed to the stability of a nation. Would that be a fair statement?

A: I think the office of Governor-General, and the fact that we have had protocols and a well-established tradition helps. You mentioned Sir Michael's speeches. I think they've been built on since then. In simple terms, the Governor-General acts on the advice of the Prime Minister for everything, except appointing the Prime Minister. And there are well-established protocols for that. I gave a speech before this last election, reconfirming that I would need to see that a majority of the members of the House of Representatives supported a particular party and leader, or if there needed to be some sort of coalition of two or more parties, that there was a clear expression of majority support for a leader which was both public and binding. Even though it might not be permanent, it might not last forever, that support would need to last for at least until the first confidence vote.

And that makes it a simple job. From that point of view I haven't felt challenged constitutionally.

Q: If one looks at Australia with its Federation and the difficulties they've had with Covid, one can see that a unitary state is the easier thing to run. From a practical point of view, how often is the exceptional situation involving a Governor-General here ever going to happen? We haven't had it and we might never have it.

A: I think we need a Head of State, so I guess that's something that you might talk about in your book, but it's interesting seeing what has happened in Samoa isn't it? But it's actually to do with the people in the end, whether you're representing a monarch or not, our country is a constitutional democracy that follows the rule of law. And basically, the Governor-General is here to make sure the rule of law is complied with. And so if we had a demagogue as Prime Minister, that would be an occasion where the reserve powers might come in to play.

The fact that, theoretically, the Governor-General has the power to dismiss a Prime Minister; I think the fact that this reserve power exists in theory is somehow part of ensuring the government of the day plays by the rules of the game.

Q: Andrew Butler and I went around New Zealand with a draft written constitution. In three different towns questioners said well, of course, if Parliament passes a law that the Governor-General doesn't like, she doesn't have to sign it! I realised there are a lot of people who just don't understand how the system works.

A: There's a good example that I enjoyed talking about when we were celebrating 125 years of women's suffrage. And that is when women were given the vote. The Governor of the day, Lord Glasgow, apparently did not support women having the vote. In fact, his wife was an adamant critic – she even wrote a letter criticising the suffragettes to *The Times*. I use that as an example, as Lord Glasgow in fact signed the Bill into law, though he could have held it up so that women did not get the vote in the 1893 General Election which was a matter of weeks away. What he could have done was to say he needed to take instructions from the Colonial Office. That happened from time to time, particularly when Governors were upset about what was happening during the New Zealand wars. So he could have actually said, 'Oh, I'll have to wait and get instructions from the Colonial Office.' The Colonial office would inevitably have come back and said, 'Sign the jolly thing!' That delay would have stopped women from having the vote in 1893, but he didn't do that. He didn't agree with the law, but he signed it because he knew that was his duty.

I recall that Dame Cath Tizard once said that she if didn't like a law she was advised to sign, she signed it in red.

Q: I do remember Sir David Beattie asking questions in Executive Council about some regulations and whether they were within the scope provided in the statute to make. We had to go back and reconsider them.

A: I think there have been examples more recently of that, but not as it happens in my term, although once or twice I've questioned the need for them.

Q: And finally, what do you find to be the most and least satisfying part of your job?

A: I do enjoy investitures. I enjoy them although they can be almost gruelling, if that is the right word. They are quite emotionally draining because you're engaging with a lot of people and it's often one of the greatest days of their lives. Whether they are receiving a Queen's Service medal or being dubbed a knight, it's very important for the recipients and for their families. I've really enjoyed the opportunity to be part of giving people that joy and recognition. Whether it's for 50 years of taking swimming lessons in their community, or for doing amazing things that put New Zealand on the map internationally.

With the advice and support of my Kaumatua and Kuia we have introduced tikanga Māori into Government House investiture ceremonies. We have a karanga to call the recipients in and a karakia to commence the ceremony. This has been well received, even by people who have never experienced it before. It's been done in quite a gentle way, and it's not a long karakia or karanga. It's a bit like a fanfare.

Every now and again I have been welcomed with a fanfare of trumpets, such as at my swearing-in. That was the most remarkable day – I thoroughly enjoyed it. And there is always a fanfare at the formal opening of Parliament.

Actually, the karanga and pōwhiri with wonderful waiata and haka can be very powerful and equally as stirring. And so we have tried to bring some of that ceremony to Government House.

What don't I enjoy doing? I don't want to single anything out because if I do, it's sort of diminishing them in some way. I don't think there's anything, you know, every job has its days that aren't so much fun, with a lot of paperwork and preparation. But, is there a thing I really hate? Not really.

One of the areas I have sought to engage with in particular, is to do what I can to help improve our Treaty connections and engagement with Māori. I've tried to do that in a way where I've tried to show other people of my generation and ethnicity, as a New Zealand European, that it's not threatening, that it's possible to engage and find our connection with tangata whenua as something to be proud of.

It is, of course, different for each Governor-General. Before me, there was Sir Jerry Mataparae, who was himself Māori, and after me will be Dame Cindy Kiro, who also has Māori heritage. They each have a different perspective. But I have seen it as a part of my role to show that as a Pākehā New Zealander I can seek to engage effectively with Māori. I have found this very rewarding. I see it as worthwhile, particularly for the younger generation, to see that older generations are making an effort to improve connections and understanding between tangata whenua and tangata tiriti. Even though when we went to school, we had no such engagement or encouragement.

Finally, I want to mention the relationship of the Governor-General with the New Zealand Defence Force. I have found the connection with the military significant and worthwhile. As Governor-General I am the Commander-in-Chief of the armed forces. This is one of the constitutional functions of the Governor-General carried out with ministerial advice, as provided in the Defence Act 1990. During my term I have been supplied with two excellent aide-de camps who are Officers in the Defence Force to assist me with my duties. The NZDF carry out important duties for the defence of New Zealand, protecting our interests and supporting our neighbours in the Pacific in times of disaster. They also provide support to our allies internationally when asked to do so by the government and the United Nations. And they have been carrying out sterling public service in recent times by helping to protect us from the Covid-19 pandemic that New Zealand has faced.

Thank you very much, Your Excellency. You've been gracious and insightful about the office and we're very grateful.

29 Local government

Having now worked at two local councils, I understand that from the moment we wake up and make our morning coffee, till the time we brush our teeth at night, local government has been with us every step in our day, despite not having the public profile of central government.
– Kyle Daniel Mathijssen Whitfield, *Local government and youth voter turnout: Obstacles and solutions for Aotearoa New Zealand*, 2020

For most New Zealanders, local government is the closest part of the state involvement in our day-to-day lives. While the decisions made in Cabinet or in Parliament have significant and widespread impacts, local government decisions can be infinitely more intimate – influencing what night you put your rubbish outside, if you have to fight over parking spots on your street, and how far you have to walk to your closest bus stop. Local government is responsible for the buses that run like clockwork, and the ones that drive straight past you when you're running late for work. They are responsible for important community infrastructure, such as local roads, sewerage, water supply, libraries, and community centres. It may seem absurd to celebrate people for providing sewerage facilities, but the cliche – *you don't know what you've got till it's gone* – may be appropriate here. There are many different forms of local government including regional councils, unitary councils, district councils and city councils and all have many responsibilities. At times it can be difficult to work out who is responsible for what. However, the essence of all these institutions is simple: local decisions are made *by* local people *for* local people.

Responsibilities, functions and structure

The Local Government Act 2002 states that the purpose of local government is:

(a) to enable democratic local decision-making and action by, and on behalf of, communities; and

(b) to promote the social, economic, environmental and cultural well-being of communities in the present and for the future.

The Local Government (Community Well-being) Amendment Act 2019 provided for a number of well-being related principles that local authorities must act in accordance with. These included principles such as taking the diversity of the community into account in decision-making, having opportunities for Māori voices in decision-making, taking a sustainable development approach in considering the environmental, economic, cultural and social well-being of the community, and collaborating with other local authorities. During the second reading of the Bill, Minister Hon Nanaia Mahuta said:

community well-being is at the heart of what local authorities do. So it only makes sense for the legislation to recognise this important role. To work effectively all levels of government must listen to the needs of communities. This is the only way to ensure social cohesion, inclusion, and develop thriving and sustainable local communities.

There are several different types of institutions that make up local government, notably regional councils and territorial authorities. Regional councils are primarily concerned with environmental resource management, flood control, air and water quality, pest control, and, in some cases, public transport, regional parks and bulk water supply. Territorial authorities, such as city councils and district councils, are responsible for a wide range of local services including local roads (not state highways), water reticulation, sewerage, flood protection, refuse collection, libraries, parks, recreation services, local regulations, community and economic development and town planning.

Local government also implements central government policies on a local scale. While local government is seen as subordinate to central government, and is ultimately controlled by legislation passed by Parliament, it is nonetheless invested with substantial law-making and regulatory powers. As Local Government New Zealand Te Kahui Kaunihera ō Aotearoa (LGNZ) said some years ago: *'In a governmental system like New Zealand's, without the checks of an upper house or constitutional court, local government plays a critical democratic, as well as functional, role which we cannot take for granted.'*

Local governments also carry out a variety of health and environmental functions. These may include the registration and inspection of restaurants and cafes, providing cemeteries, liquor zoning, and functions concerning noxious plants, litter, clean air, animals, offensive trades, wildlife and civil defence. It is likely that local government will play a crucial role in climate change going forward. On the topic of climate change, Local Government New Zealand Te Kahui Kaunihera ō Aotearoa explains: *'As the sphere of government with direct responsibility for environmental planning and regulation, much of the responsibility for adaption falls to local government.'*

One of local authorities' most important powers is to levy rates. Rating is a form of tax on freehold or leasehold property set by your local and regional councils. If you are renting your home, then part of your rent will be used by your landlord to pay rates. If you are a homeowner, then you will be paying rates to the council yourself. Rates are, by far, the most important source of revenue for local government. This money will go towards services for your community, such as roadworks, cycle lanes, maintaining parks and playgrounds, and more. Local authorities may also gain revenue from petrol tax, subsidies and grants from central government, licence fees, fines, levies on developments, and fees for services such as parking.

Wellington City Youth Council member Henry Lockhart sees the role of local government as crucial to youth:

Local government is especially important for young people's futures, determining whether transport, housing, recreational, and other infrastructure will support inclusive and accessible living in vibrant towns or cities – or whether future generations will be plagued with emission-intensive sprawl and gridlock, unaffordable and poor-quality housing and a generally less vibrant community.

Case study: Te Whanganui-a-Tara Wellington student flat

Tavita rubbed his eyes wearily and stumbled out of bed. His flatmate Rosa had held her 21st birthday party at the flat last night and he was feeling a little worse for wear trying to get ready to go to his morning lectures. It had been a great night – he had smashed his friends at beer pong, mixed a drink good enough that his friend Jessie didn't immediately spit it in his face, and mustered up the courage to talk to his flatmate's cute friend Oliver. Overall, it had been epic, at least until the Noise Officer showed up . . . Apparently one of his neighbours had complained to the

Wellington City Council because having a raging party on a Monday night was excessively noisy and disruptive. They hadn't even been *that* loud. Tavita was sure he had been very responsible about the whole thing – he and his flatmates made sure that everyone got home safe and he had even remembered to put out the rubbish and glass recycling amongst all the chaos. So what if his friends were passionate about 3am karaoke?

Tavita gathered his things and left the flat to go to university. The first thing he noticed when he opened the door was the yellow bag and glass crate outside, just where he had left them the night before. Tavita sighed, this was the fourth time that the truck had skipped his street. He texted his flatmates to ask whether someone could take the rubbish back onto the property and ran down the street towards the bus stop. Thankfully, he made it with two minutes to spare.

Tavita's flatmate Tess saw Tavita's text and went out to get the rubbish. As far as she could see, there was no reason it shouldn't have been collected. It was in the right bag and it wasn't overfilled. Tess begrudgingly carried the rubbish back inside their garage. When she got back inside Tess went to wash her hands in the bathroom. To her dismay, no water came out from the tap. Annoyed, she checked the tap in the kitchen. Nothing! Tess made do with some hand sanitiser and contacted her landlord. The landlord called the council and found out that they had turned off the water while doing some road works at the top of their street. Some notice might have been appreciated!

Tavita's day had not improved. His lecturer glared at him when he tried to sneak in through the back door late. The bus he had meant to catch never came. He had waited 10 minutes after it was scheduled to arrive just in case it was running late but, at that stage, he knew that if he didn't leave he would miss his lecture entirely. Law school stops for no one. This had been happening a lot recently. Buses were frequently running late or not coming at all. Even the schedule up at the bus stop hadn't been right for months. Tavita had had enough! First the rubbish, then the bus. What else could go wrong? At this point, something the lecturer said piqued Tavita's interest . . .

The public law professor was rambling on about the ways the public can hold the government accountable. What grabbed Tavita's attention was when the professor reminded the class that local government was still government. If that was true, then they could be held accountable for the problems with the buses, the rubbish, and the water. All Tavita had to do was pay attention for the remainder of the lecture and then hopefully he would have a way to fix all of his and his flatmate's problems.

That afternoon, Tavita called an emergency flat meeting with Tess and Rosa. He had worked out that the Wellington City Council was in charge of rubbish, water, and noise control. They were also in charge of the bus stops, but not the buses themselves. That was managed by the Greater Wellington Regional Council. The flatmates first went onto the Wellington City Council website. They scrolled to the bottom of the home page to the 'Report a problem' section and filled in the online form. They saw that there was a specific 'rubbish and recycling' box that they could check and made a report about the rubbish under that. Next, they addressed the water situation. There was a 'water' box, however the students thought that the more important issue was the lack of communication from the council before the water was shut off. They decided to made a 'general complaint' instead and explained their frustration in the description.

Tavita also filled in the online contact form on the Greater Wellington Regional Council website to explain that the bus system had not been up to scratch lately. He noticed that he could also email the Chair of the regional council's Transport Committee directly and decided to draft an email later after he had handed in his latest law essay that night. While Rosa was also annoyed about the Noise Officers showing up uninvited to her 21st birthday party last night, the flatmates checked the information about noise complaints on the WCC website and figured that their neighbours were within their rights to make a complaint. They'd just have to keep it down next time.

Reforms

The system of governance in Aotearoa New Zealand is not stagnant and local government is an excellent example of this. There have been significant reforms of local government in the past, and it is currently going through a significant period of review and reform.

The Auckland 2009 reforms

In the ever-widening diversity that characterises modern Aotearoa New Zealand there is a great deal of difference between various regions and their attitudes to local government. Local government arrangements across the country need to recognise disparities between regions and allow for different approaches depending of the needs of each community. The cliché *one size does not fit all* is true – even of local government. In 2009, a new structure was introduced for our largest city, Auckland Tāmaki Makaurau.

In Auckland Tāmaki Makaurau, it had been clear for many years that the governance problems in the larger metropolitan area were holding the city back. There were serious clashes and disagreements between the seven units of local government in Auckland Tāmaki Makaurau. The Auckland Region Mayoral Forum explained: *'Rapid growth in the region is placing considerable pressure on the physical and social infrastructure, the economy, and the environment, while creating enormously complex urban challenges very different to those anywhere else in New Zealand.'* These pressures caused the uniform pattern of local government to be radically changed. In 2008, a Royal Commission recommended that the Auckland Regional Council and all seven territorial authorities be dissolved and replaced by a new single unitary authority – the Auckland Council. After a long, and sometimes fraught, process the recommendation was implemented, but with significant changes compared with the Royal Commission's blueprint.

The organisation and powers of the Auckland Council are different from other councils in the country. The Mayor has an explicit leadership role and an enhanced office. As well as the Council, there are 21 elected local boards and an Independent Māori Statutory Board who share in the decision-making. This evolution has had implications for the whole pattern of local government in Aotearoa New Zealand. The creation of the Auckland Council has broken the model. The precedent of a more powerful form of local government has caused some regions to think they may need similar changes to keep up.

Three waters reform

In 2016–2017 a government inquiry investigated the widespread outbreak of gastroenteritis in Havelock North in 2016 during which more than 5000 people were estimated to have fallen ill, with up to four deaths associated with the outbreak. The inquiry found that the situation needed to be urgently addressed. The government response was to undertake further work that may result in fundamental reform. Then, in 2020 the government launched the Three Waters Reform Programme. This programme aims to reform the delivery arrangements of drinking water, stormwater, and wastewater services. In the words of Minister for Local Government Hon Nanaia Mahuta:

All New Zealanders need safe, reliable drinking water, wastewater and stormwater services. We depend on these for health and wellbeing of our communities and our environment. For the last two decades, central and local government have discussed the issues facing councils in continuing to deliver these services. Without action, the situation is only going to get worse.

The reform project proposes to pass legislation to establish four publicly owned multi-regional water services that will have the scale, expertise, operational efficiency, and financial flexibility to provide safe services for everyone in Aotearoa New Zealand. If it goes through it will have profound effects and the role of local government will be significantly transformed. However, the proposal has met strong resistance and it is not clear at the time of writing what will go ahead. The proposed timeline would see these water service entities operational by mid 2024.

Ministerial review into the future for local government

At the time of writing there is also a ministerial review into the future for local government as a whole. The final report will be available in April 2023. According to the interim report, *Ārewa ake te Kaupapa: Raising the platform* the review is:

an opportunity to look beyond fixed structures and roles, to design a system of local governance that is built on relationships; is agile, flexible and sustainable enough to meet future challenges, even those that are large and unpredictable.

It is an opportunity to create a system in which the many organisations that contribute to local wellbeing can work together to more effectively address challenges and deliver shared goals and aspirations, now and into future generations. It is an opportunity to consider how roles and responsibilities can best align with inherent strengths and capabilities, and to build a system that is agile and flexible, reflects local voices, embodies partnership under Te Tiriti o Waitangi, and delivers better lives for all of this country's diverse communities.

The issue of authentic partnership in how local government upholds te Tiriti o Waitangi will be a significant issue in the review. In March 2021, the Local Electoral Act was amended to ease the provisions allowing for the creation of Māori wards in local body elections. It repealed the provisions in the Local Electoral Act that provided for polls of electors on the establishment of Māori wards and Māori constituencies. It prohibits the binding council-initiated polls on whether to establish Māori wards and provides for a transition period. As a result, many councils have moved to establish Māori wards for the 2022 local elections.

There is a need for greater collaboration between local government and central government, iwi, businesses, community groups and residents. Both fashioning and enacting the reforms will be a formidable task. This is a new and exciting time for governance in Aotearoa New Zealand and an opportunity to create a structure based on community and wellbeing. Think about the type of local government that you would want to see – this is the time to express your views.

Have your say

Community is at the heart of local government. Your views on how the community should be run, what you'd like to see, your ideas for how things could be made safer, and your complaints all carry weight. There are many ways that you can engage with local government.

Local government elections are held every three years. However, in 2019, the average voter turnout across the country was just over 40 per cent. In a local election, your vote is one of thousands, not millions. Therefore, every vote is much more valuable. For example, the 2019 Wellington City Council mayoral election was decided by just 62 votes! Elections are an incredible way to engage with your local authorities – turn out and vote, engage in debates about issues affecting your community, and bring your own issues to the table.

Transparency is key for keeping local government accountable. The law requires local authorities to conduct their business in an open, transparent and democratically accountable manner. The Local Government Official Information and Meetings Act 1987 (LGOIMA) provides that anyone can make a request for any information held by local government. You can make a request using any form of communication – over the phone, in writing, in an email, even over Twitter! However, a lot of information about what your local council is doing may already be available on their website or social media. Check those out and stay up to date if you want to find out more about upcoming plans in your community.

Councils are obliged to consult on big policies and projects. You can make a submission, attend or speak at local meetings, or get in contact with a councillor about any of these issues or consultations. If you can see an issue that your local council isn't doing anything about, you can create a petition, make a formal complaint, or contact your local MP who can raise the issue on your behalf. If you believe that there is wasteful expenditure from your local council you can complain to the Auditor-General. Many councils also have youth council branches that rangatahi can engage with and become members of. Take an interest in the current reform process and think about the type of local government that you would like to see.

Help take care of your community – have your say.

References
Kenneth A Palmer *Local Authorities Law in New Zealand* (Thomson Reuters, Wellington, 2012); Jean Drage and Christine Cheyne *Local Government in New Zealand: Challenges and Choices* (Dunmore Publishing, Palmerston North, 2016).
Local Government New Zealand (LGNZ) represents the Councils in New Zealand and information is available on its website: https://www.lgnz.co.nz
Three Waters Reform https://www.dia.govt.nz/Three-Waters-Reform-Programme
Resource Management Act reforms will have a profound effect on local government: https://environment.govt.nz/what-government-is-doing/key-initiatives/resource-management-system-reform/overview/
Ministerial review into the Future for Local Government: https://www.futureforlocalgovernment.govt.nz/

Thank you to Henry Lockhart for supplying a quote for this chapter. We also acknowledge the excellent work done on this chapter by Leilani Taula, when she was Geoffrey Palmer's research assistant.

Part Three

Public Engagement

30 Political communication

According to scholar Brian McNair, political communication is any 'purposeful communication about politics'. This may include communication *by* political actors themselves, communication *to* political actors from members of the public or organisations, and communication *about* political actors, primarily in the media. Political communication can be anything. It is the way we joke about a politician's latest blunder with our friends, the #BLM hashtag trending on Twitter, the photos that appear on the Ministry of Youth Development Te Manatū Whakahiato Taiohi website, and when Jacinda Ardern called us 'the team of five million'. Political communication is the depiction of gender roles in boy band music, Merata Mita's film *Patu!* depicting public protests to the Springbok tour in 1981, and Madonna singing 'freedom of speech is as good as sex' in a Rock the Vote 'PSA' encouraging young people to vote aired on Music Television in 1990.

One fundamental concept in the field of political communication is the idea of the public sphere. The theory of the public sphere was first conceptualised by philosopher Jürgen Habermas and refers to any 'space' where the public is able to come together to meet, mix, and mingle and discuss and debate political issues, matters, and solutions. Habermas originally modelled this idea on European coffee houses in the 17th century, although a public sphere can be any forum, such as town halls, newspapers, Twitter threads, associations, and more. The public sphere is the arena of citizen opinion. The second half of the 17th century in Europe saw massive advances in material and technological conditions. The press became more accessible and so more people began to read the news and learn about a range of issues that were affecting people from across the nation, rather than simply their own community issues. Coffee houses and club culture began to rise and so people had a place to discuss issues and ideas. Consequently, the general citizen body developed a voice, when historically it had just been the aristocracy and nobility who had this power. However, although Habermas's ideal of the public sphere was open to all, the coffee house culture of the late 17th century was not inclusive and was more of a male bourgeois sphere.

We are currently experiencing similar massive developments in political communication and communication technologies. How does the invention of social media affect political campaigns? How does TikTok work as a global public sphere? Are there people who are still left out of these conversations? Are newspapers still a relevant way to keep people informed? What will come next?

Political actors and the people

There are many reasons why political actors, such as politicians, political parties, public organisations, governments etc, need to communicate with the public. Political campaigns during democratic elections are an extraordinary example of this. Politicians and wannabe-politicians canvass the country talking to people, star in political advertisements, and make long speeches all in the name of trying to secure your vote. Political party volunteers may call you up on the telephone, knock on your door, or hand you a free sticker or information at a fair or event. However, campaign season isn't the only time political actors communicate with the public – informing people as to what is going on and what they are doing about it is also a crucial task. Public agencies, organisations, departments, and ministries frequently publish project reports, MPs may make updates on social media as to what they're working on, and political party websites hold copious amounts of information on their party policies and initiatives. Another reason why political actors may reach out to you is to get your opinion, consult on matters that are important to you, and simply, to try to help you.

In a democracy, the relationship between political actors and the people is a two-way street. Members of Parliament are *your* representatives, and you have the right to contact any of them to raise an issue, complain, or simply have a chat about your community's concerns. In Aotearoa New Zealand, our politicians are some of the most accessible in the world. If there is an issue that is incredibly important to you, you can create a petition and bring it to Parliament. You can organise a peaceful protest and stand on Parliament lawn or outside your local council to have your voice heard. You can attend and listen to many of our local councils' meetings and watch Parliament meet live or online and on television. You can make submissions on local council projects or make a submission to a Select Committee at Parliament. Your voice matters in a democracy, and you have the right to have it heard.

Political actors and the media

Journalists and politicians have an intertwined and dependent relationship with one another. Journalists are dependent on politicians as news sources and politicians are dependent on the media so they may gain public attention. Part of this relationship is balancing the opposing interests that journalists and politicians may have. Politicians and their public relations teams want to 'manage' the media and get their policy ideas across to the public, to make them look good and attract new voters. In contrast, one of the most important roles of the media in a democracy is to act as the State's 'watchdog' – to hold political actors accountable and expose their wrong doings. So, there is a sort of tug-of-war at play here.

Politicians are increasingly devoting their time to media and communication-related activities, such as undertaking media training, preparing for interviews and other media opportunities and events, and running their own social media pages. In democracies all over the

Journalist and Politicians' tug-of-war
Illustration by Tayla Mereana Hartemink

world, politicians now often have full teams dedicated to managing their image and messages – public relations staff, social media staff, speech writers, and more. Public sector communications spending has increased from $57 million in the 2016/17 financial year to $88.7 million in the 2020/2021 year. The number of communications staff has also increased by almost 50 per cent in the same time: there were 547 communications staff employed in the public service in 2021. At the same time, the number of journalists in Aotearoa New Zealand is only decreasing. Political actors also have some control over how much access a journalist has in the political world – from managing press gallery access, denying interviews or comments, or cooperating and making a reporter's job much easier.

However, journalists hold an important trump card in this game. The media have an important role in providing information and educating the public and act as 'gatekeepers' to the public sphere by determining what, and who, ends up on the news and what does not (although, whether or not there are still gatekeepers in a social media world is up for debate). This means politicians *have* to interact with the media and adapt their behaviour so that they are deemed 'newsworthy' enough to capture media and public attention. Journalists get the final word in news stories and can easily damage a politican's career.

It's a journalist's job to cut through the spin and find what is in the public interest and then present it in a variety of ways that are easy to consume for people using different mediums. The internet has revolutionised our way of consuming news and information, with some advantages and disadvantages. There is now much 'clickbait' and 'soundbite' coverage where reporters use only short clips of politicians speaking while they narrate and paraphrase instead of including lengthy speeches or policy debates. However, Parliament is now televised and so are some press conferences. There is more raw information and a much wider range of views presented on the internet and those interested can easily find a range of longer-form written or podcast content to expand their knowledge.

So, who wins the tug-of-war? Well, it might not be as clear cut as that. The relationships between politicians and journalists may actually be less like a power struggle, and more like a symbiotic, mutually beneficial arrangement. Members of Parliament and members of the Press Gallery work in very close quarters and often form friendships as well as their professional relationships. One News political editor Jessica Mutch McKay explains that in a day-in-the-life: *'I could do a negative story on somebody and then be standing next to them in the queue buying a cup of coffee at the Parliament café the next day.'* As well, in the Press Gallery offices in Parliament, you have reporters from a whole range of media outlets across the country working in one place – going to the same press conferences, waiting on the same bridge between the Beehive and Parliament trying to catch politicians walking past to get the latest scoop, and sitting in on the same public select committee hearings. At the end of the day, politicians from across the political spectrum and journalists from across the media landscape might get together to have a drink. The world of politics we see on TV news may seem dramatic, adversarial, and full of conflict, but behind closed doors, they're just people.

The media and the people

There has been a great debate in media scholarship over what effects media can have on its audience. There have been eras when scholars believed that media have a very minimal ability to influence people, and periods when some scholars have thought that media can have strong effects, impacting on what we believe and how we understand the world. Most members of the public do not directly experience the inner workings of the political arena – even though we have access to watch Parliament sitting, either online or in person, most of us get our political news through watching the 6pm news or scrolling through news apps on our phone over our morning coffee. So the media has a crucial role in influencing and developing our understanding of politics. However, research has now come to the conclusion that media effects are moderate at best and are usually highly conditional, so they do not affect everyone in the same way and are highly dependent on a number of factors.

One way the media may affect public opinion is through 'agenda-setting'. Put simply, agenda-setting is the media's ability to influence what both the public and political actors see as important or salient issues. Media scholar Bernhard Cohen famously said that the press *'may not be successful much of the time in telling people what to think, but it is stunningly successful in telling its readers what to think about.* Framing is *how* something is presented in the media – what aspects are made more prominent, what is left out of the story, who is quoted as the main source. It is the lens that the story is presented through. Framing can influence how the audience responds to a particular issue or whether they see it as positive or negative.

Access to information and the media is an essential component of our democratic public sphere. As well as the news informing us about political matters, political actors can get an idea of public opinion through the media. This may include such things as opinion polls, letters to the editor, blogs, citizen journalism, and more. Although the news media often focuses on the world of the elite – politicians, big businesses, celebrities – it also reports on the people. Such events as local protests, the effects of the Covid-19 pandemic on small business owners, and the success of a local community fundraiser are all newsworthy stories. As part of their jobs, MPs naturally become news junkies and generally well-informed about what is going on around the country – not just what is happening in the Beehive.

The evolution of political communication and social media

The digital world, the internet, and social media mark a new era of political communication. The world is not the same – political actors can bypass the media gatekeepers and communicate directly with the public; people increasingly get their news through their Facebook feeds rather than from the paper dropped on their doorsteps in the morning; political movements like #MeToo and #BLM turn into international phenomena overnight on social media; young people may recognise politicians more for the memes they're in than the policies they've pushed forward; and political campaigns are increasingly professionalised as politicians and policies are sold to us in shiny packages. The repercussions are endless.

One of the buzzwords of this new era of political communication is the term 'fake news'. Social media creates an environment where fake news is easily produced and spread, often generating more engagement than actual news stories. In part, this is because people are less likely to question information if they consume it in private or if it is shared by a peer. Misinformation refers to misleading or unintentionally inaccurate content, whereas disinformation is deliberately false content, often created to advance a particular agenda. Of course, these distinctions are never clear-cut. Social media feeds can also easily turn into echo-chambers, where people are only exposed to content that reaffirms their pre-existing beliefs. Because people can choose who they like or follow, they can screen out people and views that they don't agree with. Social media algorithms pick up on this and reinforce it, showing a user content that aligns with what they've already interacted with and liked. This creates feeds that do not represent diversity of opinion or challenge people's perspectives, which can be dangerous.

However, there are also positives to the changing media landscape. Access to the internet means people have a variety of news sources from around the world at their fingertips. In many ways it is also easier to interact with politics than ever. It only takes a few clicks to start and share a petition online at change.org, staying up to date with the news is as simple as a scroll through your phone, and you can share your own opinions and connect with likeminded people easily. Politicians seem closer than ever when you can see their selfies on Instagram, read their responses to news stories that they share on Twitter, and share photos from their days on Facebook. It is difficult to see what the future of political communication will look like. In a world of 'post-truth' permanence and the popularity of populism it is easy to fear for democracy. But while the digital era can bring division, it has also brought us community.

References
Hannah Arendt *The Human Condition*(University of Chicago Press, Chicago, 1958)
Jürgen Habermas, Thomas Burger (trans) *The Structural Transformation of the Public Sphere* (MIT Press, Cambridge, 1991); Brian McNair *An Introduction to Political Communication* 6th ed (Routledge, London, 2017); Aeron Davis *Journalist-Source Relations, Mediated Reflexivity and the Politics of Politics* (Journalism Studies 10:2, 204–219, London, 2009); Aeron Davis, Natalie Fenton, Des Freedman, and Gholam Khiabany *Media, Democracy and Social Change: Re-imaging Political Communications* (Sage Publications Ltd, London, 2020); Michael Neilson *Government communications spending increases 50 per cent in four years* (NZ Herald, 5 August 2021) Retrieved from: https://www.nzherald.co.nz/nz/government-communications-spending-increases-50-per-cent-in-four-years/2C3ZMNP6A7TBIVORCAHOBMTU5M/; Irra Lee *Life in the press gallery* (RNZ, 6 April 2020) Retrieved from: https://www.rnz.co.nz/national/programmes/the-house/audio/2018741373/life-in-the-press-gallery

31 Media, news and politics

The importance of effective news media in a democratic society is unquestionable. The news media fulfils many roles from informing both the public and decision-makers on current events and political matters, holding politicians to account, providing us with entertainment and catchy news stories about politicians embarrassing themselves that we can make memes about, and potentially influencing the way people look at and understand the society around them. The changing arena of media worldwide due to the digital revolution and social media has impacted traditional media dramatically. This chapter will focus primarily on traditional media forms, such as newspapers, free-to-air television, and radio broadcasting; social media will be covered in the next chapter. The accurate distribution of facts relating to government activity is vital in a functioning democracy.

The media landscape in Aotearoa New Zealand

The nature of political reporting has changed over time. Many people now get their daily news from their Facebook feeds rather than newspapers rolled up and dropped off at their doorsteps in the morning. Newspapers flourished here, and globally, in the 19th century. They carried lengthy accounts of what was said in Parliament, something that continued up to the 1970s. While there may be less of that, all proceedings in the Chamber of the House of Representatives are now transmitted live on the internet, radio, as well as free-to-air and pay television. It is also possible to look at previous proceedings 'on demand' on the internet.

For the last 150 years there has been a Parliamentary Press Gallery in Aotearoa New Zealand. The Press Gallery is made up of journalists who provide parliamentary news and are provided facilities at Parliament including a gallery above the Speaker where they can watch the proceedings in the House. Members and the rules governing the Gallery must be approved by the Speaker.

Television has had a significant impact on political reporting – leading politicians seemed more human than when their opinions were only available in the written word or on the radio. Suddenly politics was three-dimensional and alive in the corner of most people's living rooms. In the famous words of media scholar Marshall McLuhan, 'the medium is the message', and the television method certainly reinvented the world of politics. Image, charisma, and star factor became important factors for parties choosing a political leader. Radio and television began to compete with newspapers. Advertising revenue for papers fell, first from broadcasting and then, catastrophically, from the internet.

As a result of the many technological and communication developments we have seen, there have been massive changes in the pattern of news media ownership in Aotearoa New Zealand in the past 30 years. In 2020 alone, our media landscape transformed when the *Stuff* website was sold in May to its then New Zealand Chief Executive Sinead Boucher for $1 from its Australian owner Nine Entertainment. Consequently, *Stuff* went from corporate ownership to independent private ownership and is also now proudly New Zealand-owned. Stuff Ltd, formerly called Fairfax, owns dozens of newspaper and magazine titles, including the Sunday Star-Times, the Press, and the Dominion Post. They say they employ more journalists than any other media outlet in this country. In contrast, MediaWorks owns about half the commercial radio stations broadcasting here and sold its television operations, including Newshub on Channel 3, to Discovery, an American corporation. Due to the impacts of Covid-19, Bauer Media closed its magazines in the Aotearoa New Zealand market, which included publications such as *Woman's Day, New Zealand Woman's Weekly, The Listener,* and *Your Home & Garden.* The company was later sold to Mercury Capital, which now owns some of those former publications.

There are a variety of media organisations and broadcasters that operate here. We have three Crown-owned entities: Māori Television Service, Radio New Zealand Te Reo Irirangi o Aotearoa (RNZ) and Television New Zealand Te Reo Tātaki o Aotearoa (TVNZ). Both the Māori Television Service and RNZ are funded through the public purse – Māori Television receives funding from the government and RNZ is funded by the Ministry for Culture and Heritage and NZ on Air. Although these organisations are owned and funded by the government, this does not at all mean that they are mouthpieces for the government of the day. They remain entirely independent in all of their functions. State-owned public broadcasters are normally tasked with certain roles and are funded because the government deems these roles to be necessary for the country. The Māori Television Service must promote te reo and tikanga Māori and RNZ performs several public interest functions and must act as a 'lifeline utility' in emergency situations. Although TVNZ is Crown-owned it is funded commercially, through advertisements, but it must pay a dividend to the government if sought.

Some of our privately owned media companies include Allied Press and Mediaworks. There have also been not-for-profit ventures such as Scoop, e-Tangata, and The Spinoff. Both NZME and SkyTV are listed on the New Zealand Stock Exchange (NZX) with public shareholding. NZME has a stable of newspapers and radio stations, including the *New Zealand Herald* and a number of regional newspapers. Its radio networks include Newstalk ZB, The Hits, ZM, Radio Hauraki and more. Sky Television operates a subscriber satellite television service with many channels mostly sourced from overseas, including sport, movies, television shows and some news channels.

Media ownership matters. The way a news platform is funded has significant impacts on the content it creates. American political commentator Michael Tracey puts it quite simply: '*In a public system, television producers acquire money to make programmes. In a commercial system, they make programmes to acquire money.*' What this means is that Crown-owned public broadcasters like the Māori Television Service and RNZ who already have their funding secured can produce high-quality content that may only attract a small audience, aiming to represent particular communities and minorities. In contrast, the rest of the media outlets in Aotearoa New Zealand are funded on a commercial basis and must focus on content that will attract a mass audience which can then be sold to advertisers. Consequently, commercially incentivised norms drive news to clickbait, sensationalist headlines, and entertainment. In politics, the main emphasis is not debate, but, the much more sinister, conflict. The focus of coverage has shifted away from what happens in the House of Representatives to scandal and 'infotainment'.

How the news media will develop in the future is difficult to know, but the changes are likely to continue for some years. Many journalists in Aotearoa New Zealand are concerned about the trends, but no clear consensus has emerged about the future of journalism. The media here has become highly fragmented, with a proliferation of platforms offering news. Meanwhile, Facebook and Google, the digital giants controlled by massive multi-national companies, are eating into the revenues of media companies worldwide. Efforts have been made to recoup money for the news they use, and some are bearing fruit.

The decline of traditional news sources, the demise of the cooperative news agency the New Zealand Press Association (NZPA), the arrival of blogging, and the numerous alternative sources of news on the internet have all had an impact. Political reporting, long-form journalism on policy, and detailed reporting of public documents and legislation have all noticeably declined. In the last three or four years, however, it appears that traditional long-form journalism may be making a come-back, with some concentration on hard news and more in-depth investigations, including through podcasts. How financially secure and sustainable our present media landscape is is hard to assess. More change seems inevitable.

Much internet material is sourced from overseas and it can be difficult to correct inaccuracies beyond the reach of New Zealand law. Nevertheless, there are significant protections contained in the Harmful Digital Communications Act 2015 where remedies are available against material harmful to particular individuals posted on the internet here. There is also a New Zealand organisation, Netsafe, that gives free advice on what to do if you object to something on the internet:

https://www.netsafe.org.nz/what-is-the-hdca/

Our media landscape is regulated by domestic law. Media is subject to such laws as defamation, contempt of court, and a number of other statutory controls. The New Zealand Media Council acts as an independent forum for resolving complaints about:

- Content of newspapers, magazines and periodicals in circulation in New Zealand including their websites.
- Online content of the following broadcasters – TVNZ, Mediaworks, Māori Television, Sky Network Television, NZME Radio and Radio New Zealand.
- Digital sites with news content, including blogs characterised by news commentary, that have been accepted as members of the Media Council.
- Classification of Video-on-Demand content of the following providers – TVNZ, RNZ, Mediaworks, Māori Television, Lightbox, Netflix, Stuff, NZME and Amazon.com.

Radio and television broadcasts are subject to a different regime, the Broadcasting Standards Authority, a Crown entity that acts as an independent complaints service for TV and radio programmes. Complaints specific to advertising are dealt with by a voluntary industry body called the Advertising Standards Authority.

Māori media and journalism, Māori television and decolonisation

The repercussions of British colonisation in Aotearoa New Zealand influence almost every aspect of our society, including the way we tell our stories in the media. According to Georgina Lockie: *'While explicit Colonial violence is rightfully perceived as shameful, the dismissal and suppression of Māori spirituality, ontology, and philosophy as well as Māori political and legal theory is barely perceived.'* The media have great power here with the choice to actively represent te ao Māori rather than continuing the historical pattern of marginalising Māori perspectives. Although there is still much mahi to be done, there have been a number of efforts to recognise Māori culture in our media. There are 21 iwi radio stations that make up Te Whakaruruhau o Ngā Irirangi Māori, the Māori Radio Network, which are important public broadcast networks and, according to Rawiri Waru, these stations act as *'depositories of whakapapa, mātauranga Māori, hītori and trusted sources of information.'* There are also many television programmes that promote te ao Māori. Some notable examples made for a rangatahi audience include *This is Piki, Ahikāroa,* and *Aroha Bridge.*

One of the most notable examples of Māori media in Aotearoa New Zealand is Māori Television, launched in 2004, and joined by its connected channel Te Reo in 2008, which broadcasts exclusively in te reo Māori. These have been an essential addition to our media environment, which was otherwise primarily monolingual and privileged Pākehā perspectives and Western storytelling conventions over Māori representation. The broadcaster was established to honour the agreement between the Crown and Māori after a court case that claimed that the lack of Māori representation and usage of te reo Māori was a breach of Article II of te Tiriti. Preceding this, in 1986, the Waitangi Tribunal concluded: *'it is consistent with the principles of the Treaty that the language and matters of Māori interest should have a secure place in broadcasting.'* The Tribunal noted that the dominance of English in our broadcasting had negative effects on the preservation of te reo and therefore breached te Tiriti since te reo is protected as a taonga. Despite this, there are criticisms that the way Māori Television is run still follows Western media models and is therefore not entirely successful at centering the Māori worldview. The historic suppression of te reo and tikanga, continued effects of colonisation, and otherwise Pākehā-centric media landscape are no easy obstacles to overcome.

Māori representation in our mainstream news media has often left much to be desired. In 2020 *Stuff* issued a public apology for its historic and current racist coverage and introduced a new company charter honouring te Tiriti o Waitangi. Leonie Hayden called out the lack of te ao Māori issues in the first leader's debate during the 2020 general election in a *Spinoff* article, saying: *'Meanwhile, over on TVNZ, you'd be forgiven for thinking Jacinda Ardern, Judith Collins and John Campbell's ancestors sailed to these shores and settled on pristine, empty lands. All three spent the entire debate in a blissful, alternate, Māori-free universe.'* Nonetheless, Māori stories are represented far more than they were historically. Press Gallery reporter Rukuwai Tipene-Allen, who works at Te Ao Māori News, speaks of the importance of writing stories about mainstream politics from a Māori perspective, following the advice from a mentor who told her to *'ask the questions your aunty would be asking if she was sitting on the couch watching'*.

The role of the news

The news is tasked with a vital role in a democracy. In 1841, British historian Thomas Carlyle wrote: *'Burke said there were Three Estates in Parliament; but, in the Reporters' Gallery yonder, there sat a Fourth Estate more important far than they all.'* The term 'Fourth Estate' refers to the media and how it is seen as an integral cog in the machine of democracy, alongside the other three estates – a historical British term referring to the House of Commons, the House of Lords, and the Church of England. The media's function here is often seen as being a check and balance on the exercise of public power. The media acts as a 'watchdog' by digging out information on policies, blunders, and abuse that the elected officials and public servants would rather not see the light of day.

There is a standard voluntary set of codes of practice that help journalists do their jobs and deliver meaningful and accurate content to the masses. These are not legally enforceable, however, there may be consequences for journalists not following this standard. News values may determine what makes something 'newsworthy' such as ensuring a story's relevance or timeliness. Media is also traditionally expected to remain neutral and objective. Despite these aims, journalistic practices and societal norms inevitably distort the way the news media presents reality. For example, news values are often criticised for being overly masculine which may perpetuate sexism in the media. As well, in the context of Aotearoa New Zealand, using Western news values over tikanga Māori reinforces the inequalities already present in our news.

The new world of media and its political consequences

Some understanding of the implications of the internet and the digital revolution on politics, political communication, and policy work has become essential to understanding how systems of government operate in democracies nowadays. Digital developments appear to have weakened the traditional media of newspapers, radio and television. 'Mediatisation' refers to the influence of media on other societal institutions, such as how political and parliamentary practices have become increasingly shaped by media practices. Politicians must learn how to manage media, speak in soundbites, look good on television, and even be able to make TikToks. There are so many more platforms available now.

How digital media will influence politics in the long term cannot yet be fully known and will not be known for some years. But there can be little doubt that political decision-makers and the institutions of government are profoundly affected by these changes, especially in terms of how they can interact with the public – and how we can interact back. New means are available for promoting ideological goals, influencing decision-makers, and expressing public opinion. Truth does not always prevail in these engagements and there is difficulty in knowing what information to believe and what to discount. During the Covid-19 emergencies in the last two years, conspiracy theories and the peddling of wrong and unverified information has been common.

Fake news is a problem even here in Aotearoa New Zealand. The traditional protections provided by the Electoral Act 1993 are largely impotent when it comes to the spread of disinformation online. People make up their own minds about what to believe and the facts may be discounted.

How all of this influences the psychology of voters in making their choices is also largely unknown so far. For example, how much real influence does the Twitter-sphere have? Tweets provide new ways of conducting political campaigns, reticulating information, and securing public support, as we have seen with former US President Donald Trump. This new era of political communication seems to be democratic, in the sense that there are few barriers to communication. Whether we have lost or gained from the developments remains to be seen.

An analysis in 2017 by Dr Gavin Ellis argued that the civic and democratic function of the media in Aotearoa New Zealand remains the provision of information on which to base opinions and collective political decisions. However, he concludes, somewhat dismally: *'What has changed is the media ecology, which has been destabilised by disruptive technologies and rapacious financial interests.'*

Politicians strive for political oxygen to secure the attention of the media. They go to great pains to polish their image and cultivate the art of impression management. The rest of us watch these decision-makers as if they are on some kind of reality TV show. More and more voter decisions seem to be determined by whether they would like to have a beer with the party leader they follow on Instagram. Nonetheless, trust in politicians has never been particularly high in Aotearoa New Zealand, nor worldwide, with many democracies reporting low levels of confidence in their representatives. In 2020, New Zealanders' trust and confidence in politicians was reported to be only 22 per cent. Does the media's tendency to focus reporting on political conflict and drama over stability and cooperation contribute to this? Journalists themselves were also found to not be well trusted, with the same poll showing that New Zealanders' trust and confidence in the media was only 23 per cent.

Governments in Aotearoa New Zealand know that the media matters. Virtually every MP watches the nightly television news. The media have an important role in agenda-setting in this way. What is covered on the news, what the media is asking questions about and demanding responses on and critiquing can all have an influence political decision-making. Almost all ministers have a media adviser. Government departments have many of them. There are now far more spin doctors in the Beehive and working for government departments than there are members of the press. These people are employed to frame and write media releases on government announcements and advise ministers what to say in interviews and speeches.

Where to from now? Will newspapers still exist in 10 years or will they be entirely digital? Does it matter? Will television channels survive or will streaming services, such as Netflix, take over completely? Will news diminish entirely into entertainment and scandal? Will journalism transform and lead to a more involved and informed population than ever seen before? Who knows? We'll just have to find out.

References

Gavin Ellis 'The Media we want by 2020' in 'The Media' (unpublished 2017 paper supplied to Geoffrey Palmer); Gavin Ellis and Peter A Thompson 'Restoring Civic Values to the News Media Ecology' (2016) 12(2) Policy Quarterly 37 at 40; Emma Johnson and others (eds) *Don't Dream It's Over: Reimagining Journalism in Aotearoa New Zealand* (Freerange Press, Christchurch, 2016); Mel Bunce *The Broken Estate-Journalism and Democracy in a Post-Truth World* (Bridget Williams Books, Wellington, 2019); Jack Vowles and Jennifer Curtin *A Populist Exception – The 2017 New Zealand General Election* (Australian National University, Canberra, 2020); Georgina Lockie *Towards decolonising constitutionalism: An introduction* (Counterfutures, Wellington, Issue 5, 2018); Waitangi Tribunal *Report of the Waitangi Tribunal on the te reo Maori claim* (Wai 11)(Brookers, Wellington, 1986); Michael Tracey *The Decline and Fall of Public Broadcasting* (Oxford Scholarship Online, 2011); Shaun Bamber *Walking the talk with Rukuwai Tipene-Allen from Te Ao Māori News* (Stuff, Oct 14 2021)Retrieved from: https://www.stuff.co.nz/entertainment/tv-radio/126665313/walking-the-talk-with-rukuwai-tipeneallen-from-te-ao-mori-news; Leonie Hayden *Māori don't exist, according to our political leaders so . . . talofa* (The Spinoff, 23 Sept 2020), Retrieved from: https://thespinoff.co.nz/atea/23-09-2020/maori-dont-exist-according-to-our-political-leaders-so-talofa/; Sunday Morning *Politicians, journalists rated NZ's least trusted figures* (RNZ, 2 August 2020) Retrieved from: https://www.rnz.co.nz/national/programmes/sunday/audio/2018757587/politicians-journalists-rated-nz-s-least-trusted-figures

32 Social media

Back then [in college], I was building an early version of Facebook for my community, and I got to see my beliefs play out at a smaller scale. When students got to express who they were and what mattered to them, they organised more social events, started more businesses, and even challenged some established ways of doing things on campus. It taught me that while the world's attention focuses on major events and insitutions, the bigger story is that most progress in our lives comes from regular people having more of a voice.
—Mark Zuckerberg, Facebook CEO

Social media is a double-dealing, two-faced con. It has the potential to reinvigorate political engagement and enliven the discussions by giving access and information to everyone. At the same time, it also poses grave danger for democratic debate. The development of social media platforms such as Facebook, YouTube, Twitter, Instagram, Reddit, Snapchat, TikTok and many others has allowed friends across the world to keep in contact, the sharing of adorable pet photos, and viral videos that bring laughter to millions. However, they have also provided the opportunity to express extreme views and conspiracy theories with no accountability for the consequences. Many scholars have dubbed this a 'post-truth world' – where opinions trump facts and anything goes. In a Te Herenga Waka Victoria University of Wellington podcast, political science Professor Jack Vowles explains this new environment:

As we all know, the advent of social media has created a revolution in how people communicate with one another, no more so than in politics. [. . .] But, of course, the big difference between contemporary social media and established mainstream media is the relative absence of 'gatekeepers', or in the terms of journalism, 'editorial oversight'. Newspapers, radio, and television have limited space and time and so they curate what they publish and in New Zealand are usually, although not always, subject to norms of balance and accuracy. By contrast, social media is, if you like, the wild West. While objectionable content is removed – we don't see porn or extreme violence on Facebook – the threshold for removal has been very low and as a result, social media is rife with what's become known as 'fake news'.

Digital democracy or disinformation and distraction?

Like any technology, social media is neither inherently good nor evil. It is an ever-growing complicated web of digital expressions of human nature. Its potentials must be explored and its dangers must be regulated if it is to remain an effective tool for political communication. Whether the advantages outweigh the disadvantages is up for debate. How digital media will influence politics in the long term cannot yet fully be known. But there can be little doubt that political decision-makers and the institutions of government are profoundly affected by these changes. New means are available for promoting ideological goals, campaigning for votes, and to influence political decision-makers.

Illustration by Ursula Palmer Steeds

One of the fundamental advantages of social media, especially in terms of politics, is the interaction and access that it offers. Instead of just reading about a new policy announcement or a politician's view on an issue, citizens can express back how they feel about things – by liking a post, commenting on it, or through emojis 'angry' or 'sad' reacting to something. The comments section of any social media post is a war zone. As deluded and off the wall as some views may be, everyone is entitled to freedom of speech and their own opinions. As well, politicians may post content that isn't explicitly related to politics – giving the public a behind-the-scenes look into their everyday life. This kind of interactive and laid-back communication is refreshing in comparison to the top-down talk often offered by people in power. However, it may be that social media doesn't actually offer the participatory engagement with politicians that it promises us – but simply the illusion of this. It is doubtful that MPs have the time to read through all the comments or see all the posts they've been tagged in. As well, social media often gives the impression of speed and direct action, but does it actually make politicians more effective at responding to immediate political issues?

Although the internet offers us an abundance of content and choice, the existence of digital giants like Facebook and Google mean that only a handful of corporations have a monopoly over the online sphere. For example, the company Meta owns three of social media's main players: Instagram, Facebook, and Whatsapp. These corporations have huge influence over our means of communication, the way content is created, algorithms that determine what we see and what we don't, and how we interact socially and politically. Social media companies' revenue relies on what has been dubbed an 'attention economy'. These platforms want us to spend our time trapped in endless scrolling because that's the way they make money – they literally sell our attention to advertisers and the more time we spend clicking and scrolling the more data they generate, making it easier for them to successfully target advertisements. Is the content we're provided with always worth what we're paying for it?

Social media can be a wonderful way to share and connect with your fellow citizens. Although it may not be the perfect 'public sphere,' in many ways social media opens up important channels for debate and deliberation. It has never been so easy to find out information about a politician, you can mobilise people to join a protest with a few clicks of a button, and connect with people with the same interests or ideology all around the globe. On the other hand, the sheer amount of information available is overwhelming. If your main source of current affairs and news is Facebook, you are likely to learn about your friend's new kitten before a human rights disaster. Important issues can get lost in the sea of information.

The digital public sphere is also under threat from online hate and harassment. Often this discrimination targets already marginalised or systematically disadvantaged groups, such as disabled people, LGBTQIA+ people, and people of colour. Sexism and racism scream loud on the internet. At the same time, however, everyone may have a voice on the internet. Social media also improves equal access for such marginalised groups and helps them bring awareness to political issues that have been out of the limelight for far too long.

The design behind social media platforms is not entirely congruent with democratic debate. Social media algorithms are designed to use mass amounts of data to predict what a user wants to see based primarily on a user's own history as well as similar activity from other users on the platform. These tailor-made cherry-picked social media feeds do not often tell us the whole story – rather, they simply reinforce what we want to hear. Instead of being exposed to a wide array of diverse perspectives, social media instead often provides 'echo-chambers' where we are only exposed to content that reaffirms our pre-existing beliefs. In terms of politics, this can have dangerous consequences and may lead to mass polarisation on the basis of ideology. Big data and algorithm opacity also open up social media to misuse, such as seen with the Cambridge Analytica/Facebook data breach and the scandal that ensued with its influence in the Brexit referendum in the United Kingdom and the Presidential Election in the United States in 2016.

Scholars Joanne Waitoa, Regina Scheyvens, and Te Rina Warren discuss the effects social media could have in terms of Māori political empowerment in Aotearoa New Zealand:

Digital technology can provide a platform to develop Māori political consciousness. User-generated social media has influenced awareness and mobilisation of disenfranchised groups overseas including the 'Twitter revolutions' in the Middle East and the #IdleNoMore campaign in Canada [. . .]. Similarly, social networking sites provide alternative spaces where

Māori can engage with politicians, political discussions and political
perspectives alternative to those in mainstream media.

However, there are significant concerns for Māori, and other indigenous communities, surrounding social media. These include the potential for misrepresentation online, particularly of images that are tapu; excluding kaumātua, who may not use social media, in conversations; the Western frameworks and bias of social media platforms and; censorship. Nonetheless, social media may offer Māori a space to build upon networks and connections and engage politically.

The Christchurch Call

Aotearoa New Zealand learned of the horrors of social media from the terrorist attack by a lone gunman on Christchurch masjidain on 15 March 2019. The attack killed 51 Muslim people worshipping in mosques at Christchurch and injured many more people. We wish to acknowledge and send love to the affected survivors, witnesses, and whānau.

Horrifically, the terrorist attack was livestreamed for 17 minutes and went viral. Two months later our Prime Minister Jacinda Ardern and the French President Emmanuel Macron gathered with international tech providers and Heads of State and government representatives to create the Christchurch Call. The Call acts as a pledge from these leaders to take action to eliminate terrorist and violent extremist online content. It sets out commitments that governments' online service providers must work to meet including through improving education, awareness, and media literacy, effective legal action and enforcement for the creation and dissemination of such content, transparent terms of service from online providers that refer to policies regarding terrorist and violent extremist content, supporting research into solutions in this area, and much more. It also includes similar pledges to support oversight and regulation of social media, by the companies which run those platforms.

The Royal Commission of Inquiry report into the terrorist attack *Ko tō tātou kāinga tēnei* explains:

The terrorist attack was driven by an extreme right-wing Islamophobic
ideology. Its purpose was to promote chaos and disharmony in New
Zealand. This purpose failed. In the days, weeks and months that followed,
New Zealanders united around those affected and spoke out against racism,

extremism and extremist violence. There was a period of national reflection about our shared values, our collective lives and what it means to live in New Zealand.

Social media campaigning

With the digital world, political campaigners can now add social media to their toolbox. Using social media in political campaigns offers a lot of new technological opportunities – candidates can easily link to further information, use captivating images and even memes, and pay to promote posts to easily reach certain targeted demographics. Campaign strategies must take into account things such as a candidate's personality and social media skills, the demographics of the audience they're trying to reach, and the infrastructure of the social media platform itself. Social media campaigning has been found to be more successful at mobilising partisan followers than reaching and persuading new voters. So the messages shared on these platforms are often designed to reach an audience that already favours a candidate or party's political views. In Aotearoa New Zealand, many of our current MPs run their own social media accounts, however, they may be assisted or advised by professionals.

During the lead up to the 2020 General Election in Aotearoa New Zealand, Dr Mona Krewel and Professor Jack Vowles conducted the New Zealand Social Media Study (NZSMS) which examined candidate and party social media usage. The project was part of an international comparative project called Digiworld that 13 countries are currently participating in, which analyses social media campaigns for various national elections as well as the European Parliamentary Elections. The NZSMS examined the Facebook posts from political parties including Labour, National, the Greens, ACT, New Zealand First, the Māori Party, the Opportunities Party (TOP), New Conservatives, and Advance NZ/ New Zealand Public Party, as well as from the leaders of each of these parties in the four weeks leading up to the election. The study posted interim reports on a weekly basis to report findings and keep the public informed during the election period.

The study came back with a number of interesting findings. The amount that political candidates were using social media was not insignificant. Over the four-week period, the Labour Party and Jacinda Ardern combined made 465 posts, closely followed by the Māori Party and John Tamihere with 427 posts, and the National Party and Judith

Collins who made a total of 399 Facebook posts. Of the more than 3000 Facebook posts the NZSMS analysed, more than 2500 referenced content about policies or issues. The economy was the most important issue mentioned across the board, followed by social and environmental issues. Dr Mona Krewel explains the significance of this:

It means today's campaigns are wrongly accused of being unpolitical. Modern campaign tools such as social media are not necessarily superficial and about only personalities rather than issues. However, that there is a certain number of non-political posts also shows social media is a medium that requires political leaders to be more informal and personal.

Despite the high degree of issue-focused content, the NZSMS also found that during the first week of their study, 36 per cent of Labour Party leader Jacinda Ardern's posts and 22 per cent of National Party Leader Judith Collins's posts were non-political.

For the most part, it seems as though Aotearoa New Zealand avoided the negative attack-style campaigning that is becoming increasingly common overseas. Based on data from the first 1800 posts analysed, the NZSMS found that 74 per cent of National's posts and 70 per cent of Labour's posts were positive. Comparatively, 22 per cent of National's posts and only 6 per cent of Labour's posts at this stage were overtly negative. Strikingly, 50 per cent of ACT's Facebook posts were negative. Later data from the study shows that the National party became increasingly negative as the campaign went on. Dr Mona Krewel explains that there is a point to these negative campaign strategies '*as negative posts psychologically stick with our brains. And once negative information is planted, it is hard to forget. It is more "sticky" than positive information and we unfortunately remember it much better than positive information and give it more weight.*'

Fake news

Although there is nothing new about politicians exaggerating and making misleading claims, the internet has proliferated the spread of fake news. Disinformation and rumours are spread frequently on social media and with deliberate political purpose. Although we may think of fake news as outlandish claims, obviously edited photos, and outrageous stories, it can be incredibly easy to fall for fake news – especially if you perceive it as coming from a trusted source, like if it's shared by your peers. Netsafe reports that a third of New Zealanders have accidentally shared fake news online and almost half of us are worried about unwittingly spreading it.

If you are concerned that something you are seeing on the internet is fake news, avoid sharing it. Commenting on a post may help let other people know the information is false, but at the same time, the more interactions (likes, comments, shares, etc) a post gets, the more traction social media algorithms will give it, potentially spreading the fake news further. You could either leave a comment or contact the person that has shared it directly and let them know you are concerned the information is incorrect. You can share accurate information from a reputable source if you think this will be helpful. Most of the time, people spread fake news unwittingly, so do not assume that they had ill intent.

The New Zealand Social Media Study found the amount of fake news shared by political parties and their leaders in the lead up to the 2020 General Election was actually quite minimal. Nonetheless, the fact there was any evidence of false information being shared is cause for concern. The study classified some content as 'half-truths' – that was not completely false but information presented in a misleading way. The National party posted nine half-truths and their leader Judith Collins posted one, New Zealand First leader Winston Peters posted one half-truth, and the ACT party posted two half-truths with their leader David Seymour posting one. The biggest culprits here however were the New Conservatives and Advance NZ/New Zealand Public Party. The New Conservatives posted 15 half-truths and leader Leighton Baker posted eight while Advance NZ/NZPP posted 29 half-truths, with Billy Te Kahika contributing seven half-truths throughout the campaign. Fake news was found in nine Advance NZ posts and four of Billy Te Kahika's, two New Conservative posts and one Leighton Baker post, one Judith Collins post and two National Party posts.

Because the NZSMS posted interim reports about their findings every week in the lead-up to the election it was able to call out parties and candidates for spreading fake news. Dr Mona Krewel explains that *'seeing a measurable decrease in misinformation [. . .] over the course of the campaign was a success, as far as we were concerned'* as parties adjusted their behaviour knowing they were being watched. These findings contributed to exposing information the Advance NZ's party had posted regarding Covid-19 and vaccinations which led to Facebook removing the party's page for violating its misinformation policy, just days before the election. The dangers of disinformation lurk on social media. Adequate policy and regulation, faster fact-checking, and complaints services have far to go to catch up. Luckily, in Aotearoa New Zealand we are not seeing the same decay of democracy or divides of digital spheres that other countries are experiencing. However, if we wish not to go down the same path we must adapt to the reality of political communication in the modern world and do more to ensure there are effective safeguards that protect us from these risks.

References
Ko Tō Tātou Kāinga Tēnei: Royal Commission of Inquiry into the Terrorist Attack on Christchurch Masjidain on 15 March 2019 (Department of Internal Affairs, December 2020) Volume 1; Joanne Waitoa, Regina Scheyvens and Te Rina Warren *E-Whanaungatanga: The role of social media in Māori political empowerment* (AlterNative 11(1), 45–58, March 1 2015); The Workshop *Digital Threats to Democracy* (The Workshop, May 2019); Wellington Faculty of Humanities and Social Sciences *How fact-checking can positively impact online political campaigning* (Te Herenga Waka Victoria University of Wellington, 16 November 2021); https://www.wgtn.ac.nz/fhss/about/news/how-fact-checking-can-positively-impact-online-political-campaigning
New Zealand Election 2020: Key Social Media Trends (Victoria University of Wellington – Podcast, September 2020) https://open.spotify.com/episode/2sabw3ldhrPLLLnza8uzkK

Additional resources
The Christchurch Call: https://www.christchurchcall.com/
New Zealand Social Media Study results: www.wgtn.ac.nz/election

33 How to complain

There are many avenues through which you can lodge a complaint if you believe the institutions of government have 'done you wrong'. There are many independent agencies that have been established by Parliament to monitor the conduct of various state agencies that exercise coercive powers over people (although sometimes the powers of these organisations extend to private conduct as well). Often these institutions give people a right to complain – from this, an investigation can be conducted and the wrong put right. These remedies do not require expensive court cases and usually involve no cost at all on the part of the complainant. There are many of these 'watchdog' agencies, and it may be difficult to figure out which one you need to speak to if you have a complaint. The growing number of such agencies may give the impression of an increasing number of shrubs in a bureaucratic thicket.

Illustration by Tayla Mereana Hartemink

All of our complaint agencies are organised as Crown Entities except for two, the Ombudsman Tari o te Kaitiaki Mana Tangata and the Parliamentary Commissioner for the Environment Te Kaitiaki Taiao a Te Whare Pāremata who are Officers of Parliament. None of these agencies are controlled directly by the Executive or subject to the doctrine of ministerial responsibility, although they are funded by Parliament. The total appropriations Parliament made in the 2021–22 Budget for these agencies was more than $90 million, led by the Ombudsman Tari o te Kaitiaki Mana Tangata at almost $50 million. Three of the agencies have powers to provide remedies to people injured, even damages adjudicated on by the Human Rights Tribunal – this protection applies to human rights, privacy, and breaches of health consumer rights.

The independence and impartiality of these agencies is essential as they increase the accountability of the officials (and sometimes private citizens) whose actions they examine. The conduct of the Police, public servants, local government, and many other public authorities, as well as private organisations, are all subject to scrutiny by these watch dogs. They must be seen as part of the framework of democratic control and accountability for breaching standards, promoting important democratic values and a sense of fairness.

Parliament

Those who feel that something needs putting right, whether it be policy or administration, should never neglect the oldest avenue of redress – Parliament. You can easily visit or write to your local Member of Parliament, or, indeed, to any MP. From this, your MP can write to the relevant minister on your behalf. Then the whole machinery of the public service swings into action to examine the gripe, respond to it, and provide an answer for the minister's consideration. The minister will write back to the MP saying what the position is and whether, in the government's view, anything is wrong. Although ministerial correspondence is usually drafted by public servants, it enjoys a high priority in the system and matters can quite often be corrected in this way.

MPs can also put down questions in Parliament, written or oral, that can elicit official answers from ministers, upon which they can be further questioned. Furthermore, Select Committees can investigate any matters of policy, administration, and expenditure that they choose through Select Committee inquiries. Some grievances can be so serious that they warrant attention of this sort.

Another time-honoured method to force parliamentary consideration of a grievance is the petition to Parliament. The right to petition Parliament for redress of grievances is acknowledged as a fundamental principle of our constitution, going as far back as Parliament itself. Petitions may call for an alteration in the general law; others ask for some reconsideration of an administrative decision. Petitions are dealt with by a special Select Committee, the Petitions Committee. It either publishes a report to Parliament about every petition it considers, asks another specialist subject committee to consider the petition, or requests a minister to reply.

Petitions have frequently borne fruit in Aotearoa New Zealand. They are an important safety valve in the political process, a last resort where there is little other hope of action. The most dramatic example remains the main suffrage petition in July 1893, signed by about 24,000 women, that led to a law being passed giving women the vote.

How to complain

Everyone has the right to present a petition, and it is Parliament's function to consider the petition and make recommendations to government about what, if anything, should be done. Petitions must comply with the standing orders of the House. Petitions must: be addressed to the House of Representatives; ask that the House do something about a policy, law, or problem; be in English or in Māori; use respectful language; be serious in intent; be succinct; and not include statements that cannot be authenticated.

You can submit a paper, electronic, or hybrid petition. To submit a paper petition you must include a cover letter which includes information such as your contact details. You must then collect signatures – people will need to write their full name and sign the document. Then you must find a current MP to present your petition to the House; your local MP may be a good start. To submit an electronic submission, go to this website and follow the steps: https://www.parliament.nz/en/petitions/create

To create a hybrid petition simply follow the instructions above to create both a paper and an electronic petition. You can find further information here: https://www.parliament.nz/en/get-involved/have-your-say/guide-for-petitions/

If you are wanting to contact an MP, you will be able to find their contact details on this page: https://www.parliament.nz/en/get-involved/have-your-say/contact-an-mp/

The Ombudsman
Tari o Te Kaitiaki Mana Tangata

The Ombudsman Tari o te Kaitiaki Mana Tangata, established in 1962, is charged with handling complaints about public sector agencies, investigating administrative decisions, and making recommendations around possible defects. The Ombudsmen are officers of Parliament because their function is to redress grievances of citizens, which is historically a job that belongs to MPs. Although there has usually been more than one Ombudsman Kaitiaki Mana Tangata, for some years now there has been only one, as well as a staff of more than 100 people to help. The responsibilities of the office have been added to over the years. Currently they are to:

- form opinions about complaints made by citizens about central, regional, and local government
- review decisions to decline to release information under the Official Information Act and the Local Government Official Information and Meetings Act
- provide guidance and information to employees using the 'whistleblowing' procedures of the Protected Disclosures Act 2000 that involves serious wrongdoing at work and protecting whistleblowers
- visit places of official detention and check upon the treatment of those detained
- monitor people detained at health and disability facilities including aged care facilities
- monitor the rights of disabled people and investigate complaints about government agencies
- support tamariki/children in care
- monitor Covid-19 managed isolation facilities.

The Ombudsman Kaitiaki Mana Tangata can investigate complaints made by members of the public, or can, on their own initiative, investigate any administrative decision, recommendation, act or omission of government departments, related organisations, and local authorities affecting a person individually. The Ombudsmen have no power to alter decisions; they simply investigate and report on them. Nonetheless, the process of investigation itself, the power of the office, the capacity to report to Parliament, and the publicity given to the reports exert a considerable influence in righting administrative injustices and changing the way in which officials approach some tasks.

New Zealand has ratified the *United Nations Optional Protocol to the Convention against Torture and Other Cruel, Inhuman or Degrading Treatment or Punishment.* The Ombudsman Tari o te Kaitiaki Mana Tangata carries out inspection of our prisons and other facilities to ensure we are meeting our obligations. The UN subcommittee can also conduct inspections as well from time to time. Many complaints under the Ombudsmen Act come from prison inmates. Apart from prisons, the government agencies most frequently complained of, and not unexpectedly, are those with most contact with the public: ACC Te Kaporeihana Āwhina Hunga Whara, Inland Revenue Te Tari Taake, Ministry of Social Development Te Manatū Whakahiato Ora, and Immigration New Zealand.

How to complain

To complain to the Chief Ombudsman, you can write a letter or an email or do it online. It is free. In this complaint you should describe what you think is unfair about the situation you are complaining about, be concise, and outline your desired outcome. You should first try to sort out your issue directly with the agency whose actions you wish to complain about. For more information see: https://www.ombudsman. parliament.nz/what-ombudsman-can-help

Independent Police Conduct Authority Mana Whanonga Pirihimana Motuhake

The 1981 Springbok tour and its aftermath, together with police shootings, led to the passage of the Police Complaints Authority Act, now the Independent Police Conduct Authority Act 1988. For many years the Ombudsman Tari o te Kaitiaki Mana Tangata had jurisdiction to examine complaints against the Police, but an internal investigation had to be done by the Police first. Another important feature of the law is that where a Police employee *'acting in the execution of his or her duty causes, or appears to have caused, death or serious bodily injury to any person'* the Commissioner of Police *'shall as soon as practicable give the authority a written notice setting out the particulars of the incident.'*

The Independent Police Conduct Authority Mana Whanonga Pirihimana Motuhake (IPCA) has trained investigators and can access the Police and the information they hold so that complaints are fairly and impartially investigated. The Authority also has a Memorandum of Understanding with the Commissioner of Police where the Commissioner refers matters of serious misconduct to the Authority. The law makes clear that the Authority must act independently in the exercise of its functions.

It is important to understand that the IPCA does not have any power to prosecute, require disciplinary proceedings or otherwise direct the Commissioner of Police to do anything. The agency can only make findings and recommendations. If there is not a satisfactory answer from the Commissioner to a recommendation, the agency is required to notify the Attorney-General and can table a report in Parliament. This ensures a high level of compliance with recommendations if they are made. The Authority was busy with 3882 complaints in 2020. It can oversee investigations conducted by Police, not the agency, and in 2020 this resulted in 1242 agreed resolutions. The Authority's annual reports contain fascinating accounts of high profile cases dealt with.

How to complain

Complaints can be made online, by email, post or fax. There is a complaint form. The Authority asks for as much detail as possible so the complaint can be properly considered. You must include your name and full contact details, relevant dates, times and places, details of any Police staff involved including names, badge numbers or other details, information about the incident, and anything else that is relevant evidence. You can find more information about making a complaint here: https://www.ipca.govt.nz/Site/complaints/

Human Rights Commission
Te Kāhui Tika Tangata

The Human Rights Commission Te Kāhui Tika Tangata advocates for the protection of human rights in Aotearoa New Zealand. It provides a human rights information and support service and a dispute resolution service to the public. If you believe that you have faced unlawful discrimination you can contact the Commission. The Commission makes proactive efforts through various mediation procedures to resolve complaints, and then a route exists to secure a remedy. There is an office of Human Rights Proceedings whose independent Director can consider applications from complainants who have not had satisfaction.

Aotearoa New Zealand has had a Human Rights Commission since 1977 but the Human Rights Act 1993 legislation extended the range of protections and methods of dealing with complaints where the standards have been breached. In December 2001, there was a further far-reaching reform of the legislation that determined how the Human Rights Act applies to the Crown and changed the structure and operation of the Commission. The Human Rights Act 1993 provides a framework to protect and promote human rights in Aotearoa New Zealand. Essentially, the Human Rights Act itself was in the beginning an anti-discrimination law – prohibiting discrimination by public and private organisations on specified grounds in specified areas of life with specified exceptions. However, the Commission now has become of wider significance and focuses on broader human rights issues. The Human Rights Act provides informal practical methods of dealing with complaints when unlawful discrimination prohibited by the Act occurs.

The Bill of Rights Act also protects citizens from the State regarding a broader range of rights and freedoms subject to a general balancing justification. The Bill of Rights Act covers discrimination on the same grounds as the Human Rights Act but also covers other fundamental rights, such as the right not to be deprived of life and not to be tortured, and freedoms such as freedom of speech and religion and rights in criminal procedure. The main interpreter of what the Bill of Rights means in various situations is determined by the courts, but the Human Rights Review Tribunal Te Taraipiunara Mana Tangata also has a significant role.

How to complain

If you make a complaint to the Human Right Commission Te Kāhui Tika Tangata, a mediator from the Dispute Resolution team will contact you and attempt to start a dispute resolution process. If this does not resolve the issue you can take your case to the Human Rights Review Tribunal Te Taraipiunara Mana Tangata. You can apply to the Office of Human Rights Proceedings to get free legal representation if you decide to take this step. The Tribunal is presided over by a senior lawyer and a panel. It has adjudicative powers and can give various forms of relief for breaches of human rights. It also has jurisdiction in respect of Privacy Act breaches, and the Code of Health and Disability Consumers' Rights.

Complaints are easy to make online and you can do so here: https://www.hrc.co.nz/complaint-form/

The Privacy Commissioner
Te Mana Mātāpono Matatapu

The Privacy Act 2020 is a far-reaching piece of legislation that extends and refines the Privacy Act 1993. The Privacy Act 2020 applies to virtually every person, business, and organisation in Aotearoa New Zealand. It imposes some onerous obligations and serious penalties can be imposed for breaches. More than 7,700 inquiries into breaches were received by the Privacy Commissioner Te Mana Mātāpono Matatapu in the 2020–21 year. The basic right that the Act protects is the right to access your personal information and to ask for it to be corrected if you think it is wrong.

The principal interpreter of the act is the Privacy Commissioner Te Mana Mātāpono Matatapu, who has many tasks under the Act. The wide-ranging functions of the Commissioner include:

- to promote an understanding and acceptance of the privacy principles through education and publicity
- when requested to do so, conducting audits of personal information
- monitoring the use of unique identifiers and reporting to the Prime Minister on the results
- maintaining directories of personal information
- advising ministers, although the Commissioner must act independently.

Further, the Commissioner has wide-ranging powers to issue a Codes of Practice in relation to the Information Privacy Principles (IPP) that can change the law as enacted by setting more or less stringent standards and exempting any action from an IPP and also setting out how IPPs are to be applied. There is a procedure to be followed before Codes of Practice are issued. The protection against wrongful use of such a wide-ranging power lies in the fact that they may be disallowed by Parliament, usually after a hearing in front of the Regulations Review Select Committee.

Certainly, the Privacy Commissioner Te Mana Mātāpono Matatapu in Aotearoa New Zealand is armed with powers necessary to defeat the Orwellian scenario of a 'Big Brother' watching over you – an important value in a democracy. The generality of the privacy principles, however, mean that much of their public credibility lies in the way in which they are applied – making the skills and experience of the Privacy Commissioner Te Mana Mātāpono Matatapu important to the effective functioning of Aotearoa New Zealand's privacy law.

How to complain

The resolution of complaints has been a primary function of the Privacy Commissioner Te Mana Mātāpono Matatapu. A complaint may be made alleging that an action of an agency is, or appears to be, an interference with the privacy of an individual. You may make a complaint to the Commissioner either orally or in writing. Assistance is provided by the Commissioner's office where that is needed. You can find the online complaints form here: https://www.privacy.org.nz/your-rights/making-a-complaint/complaint-self-assessment/

The Commissioner investigates complaints and may also investigate on their own initiative without waiting for a complaint. The Commissioner must advise the complainant, and the person to whom the complaint relates, of the procedure to be adopted. The Commissioner can decide to take no action on a complaint. Where no settlement can be reached, the Commissioner may refer the matter to the Director of Human Rights Proceedings who may decide to bring civil proceedings before the Human Rights Review Tribunal. Otherwise, an aggrieved individual may bring proceedings before the tribunal if they wish to do so.

The Parliamentary Commissioner for the Environment Te Kaitiaki Taiao a Te Whare Pāremata

The Parliamentary Commissioner for the Environment Te Kaitiaki Taiao a Te Whare Pāremata is an Officer of Parliament appointed under Section 4 of the Environment Act 1986. The mission of the Commissioner is to provide *an independent check on the capability of the Aotearoa New Zealand system of environmental management and the performance of public authorities in maintaining and improving the quality of the environment*. This also entails looking at what the private sector has done. The office is concerned with policy implementation and the policy itself, as well as individual instances of environmental mismanagement. The Commissioner gives advice to Parliament, central and local government.

How to complain

The Commissioner is not an agency to produce justice for individual cases, but rather has a policy emphasis. However, you can bring an environmental issue to the Parliamentary Commissioner for the Environment in writing, or by email or telephone. You can find out how to contact the Commissioner here: https://www.pce.parliament.nz/about-us/contact

Health and Disability Commissioner Te Toihau Hauora Hauātanga

The Health and Disability Commissioner Te Toihau Hauora Hauātanga was established by the Health and Disability Commissioner Act 1994. The purpose of the Act is to promote and protect the rights of consumers of health and disability services and to facilitate the fair, simple, speedy, and efficient resolution of complaints relating to the infringement of those rights. The Act applies to all health care providers and disability service providers.

The Code of Health and Disability Services Consumers' Rights details the rights of consumers and duties of providers, summarised as the:
- right to be treated with respect;
- right to freedom from discrimination, coercion, harassment, and sexual or financial exploitation;
- right to dignity and independence;
- right to services of an appropriate standard;
- right to effective communication;
- right to be fully informed;
- right to make an informed choice and give informed consent;
- right to support;
- rights in respect of teaching or research;
- right to complain.

The Act also creates a Director of Advocacy in relation to health and disability services and a Director of Proceedings, who takes proceedings on behalf of complainants. The Commissioner acts independently from these officers. The Director of Advocacy's role is to administer, promote, and monitor advocates for health and disability services consumers, including receiving complaints. The Director of Proceedings' function is to decide whether to institute or participate in complaint proceedings, either proceedings before the Human Rights Review Tribunal, or disciplinary hearings, or both.

How to complain

There are generally more than 2,000 complaints made to the Commissioner each year and may include matters such as inadequate/inappropriate clinical treatment, missed/incorrect/delayed diagnosis, lack of access to services, and more. If you wish to complain directly to the service, you can contact a health and disability advocate to help with this process by calling 0800 555 050. The advocacy service can also help you understand your options and what your rights are.

If you would like to complain to the Health and Disability Commissioner Te Toihau Hauora Hauātanga you can do so by post, fax, email, telephone, or by using the online complaint form available here: https://www.hdc.org.nz/making-a-complaint/complain-about-care-you-received/

You can find more information about the complaint process here: https://www.hdc.org.nz/making-a-complaint/complaint-process/

The Mental Health and Wellbeing Commission

In 2020, a Mental Health and Wellbeing Commission Act was enacted, and the Commission established. This short law sets up a mechanism to contribute to better and equitable mental health and wellbeing outcomes for people. It contains a strong emphasis on the mental health of Māori with a strong emphasis on te Tiriti in that respect. It is not an agency that determines individual complaints concerning treatment – that will still be the task of the Health and Disability Commissioner – although there is likely to be some overlap on some issues. In 2019, it was reported that one in five New Zealanders suffered mental distress or an addiction in any given year. For Māori the figure was one in three and for tagata Pasifika, one in four. LGBTQIA+ people are also more likely to have a mental illness.

The functions of the Commission are to:

- assess and report publicly on the mental health and wellbeing of people in New Zealand
- assess and report publicly on factors that affect people's mental health and wellbeing
- assess and report publicly on the effectiveness, efficiency, and adequacy of approaches to mental health and wellbeing
- make recommendations to improve the effectiveness, efficiency, and adequacy of approaches to mental health and wellbeing
- monitor mental health services and addiction services and to advocate improvements to those services
- promote alignment, collaboration, and communication between entities involved in mental health and wellbeing
- advocate for the collective interests of people who experience mental distress or addiction (or both), and the persons (including family and whānau) who support them.

How to complain

The Mental Health and Wellbeing Commission does not handle complaints about mental health or addiction services. If you encountered a problem while using these services, you can complain to the Health and Disability Commissioner using the steps explained above.

If you need support you can find an extensive list of helplines on the Mental Health and Wellbeing Commission here: https://www.mhwc. govt.nz/contact-us/where-to-get-support/
Anyone can free call or text 1737 any time for support from a trained counsellor.

Children's Commissioner
Manaakitia a Tātou Tamariki

In 2003 an Act was passed that reconstructed and strengthened the role of the Children's Commissioner Manaakitia a Tātou Tamariki. The Commissioner's primary role is as an advocate for children and to enable the Commissioner to give better effect in Aotearoa New Zealand to the UN Convention on the Rights of the Child which Aotearoa New Zealand has ratified and is therefore bound by. Some of the general functions of the Commissioner include raising awareness of and advocating for the rights and interests of children, promoting research on children's welfare, presenting to courts and tribunals on proceedings that relate to children's interests or welfare, and more. For more details, see the Oranga Tamariki Act 1989.

How to complain

If you would like support or advice about matters concerning children's rights, there are a number of organisations that may be able to help you here: https://www.occ.org.nz/childrens-rights-and-advice/who-to-contact/

If you would like to complain about Oranga Tamariki Ministry for Children you can call 0508 FAMILY (0508 325 459), email feedback@ot.govt.nz, or fill out the feedback form available here: https://www.orangatamariki.govt.nz/children-in-our-care/information-for-children/feedback-form/

The Criminal Cases Review Commission Te Kāhui Tātari Ture

The Criminal Cases Review Commission Act 2019 aims to provide a means of investigation and review of convictions and sentence and to decide whether to refer them to the appeal court. The Commission is an independent Crown Entity governed by a Board of appointed Commissioners. It employs specialist staff with the mandate to investigate possible miscarriages of justice. This function replaces the referral function currently performed by the Governor-General, part of the royal prerogative of mercy.

How to complain

Anyone can apply to have their conviction or sentence referred to an appeal court if they believe a miscarriage of justice has occurred. Be warned, this will not happen easily. The initial step depends upon filling out an application that is available online from the Commission's website. Information on how to do this is available here: https://www.ccrc.nz/make-an-application/

Grounds for referring conviction or sentence to the appeal court:
- The Commission may refer a conviction or sentence to the appeal court if the Commission, after reviewing the conviction or sentence, considers that it is in the interests of justice to do so.
- In deciding whether to refer a conviction or sentence, the

Commission must have regard to—a) whether the eligible person has exercised their rights of appeal against the conviction or sentence; b) the extent to which the application relates to argument, evidence, information, or a question of law raised or dealt with in proceedings relating to the conviction or sentence; c) the prospects of the court allowing the appeal; and d) any other matter that the Commission considers relevant.

The Inspector-General of Intelligence and Security

The Inspector-General of Intelligence and Security independently oversees two of Aotearoa New Zealand's main intelligence and security agencies, the New Zealand Security Intelligence Service Te Pā Whakamarumaru (NZSIS) and the government Communications Security Bureau Te Tira Tiaki (GCSB). The Inspector-General's work may involve investigating complaints about these two agencies, conducting inquiries into their conduct, and reviewing the agencies' warrants, authorisations, and compliance procedures.

The Inspector-General can start inquiries on their own initiative, or at the request of the minister responsible for the intelligence and security agencies, the Prime Minister, or the Intelligence and Security Committee of Parliament. An inquiry can address the lawfulness or propriety of anything done by the NZSIS or the GCSB.

How to complain

You can complain to the Inspector-General of Intelligence and Security if you believe you have been 'adversely affected' by the NZSIS or GCSB. Current or former employees of either intelligence and security agency can also complain and the Protected Disclosures Act 2000 protects people during the process when making a 'protected disclosure' or 'whistleblowing'. You can learn how to make a complaint here: https://igis.govt.nz/complaints/making-a-complaint/

References
The best sources are the statutes mentioned and the annual report to Parliament of the various agencies, all available online.

34 How to campaign

No voice is too soft when that voice speaks for others —Janna Cachola

It is a cheesy cliché, but everyone has a voice, and everyone has a story. Campaigning, advocacy, and lobbying are tools that can help this voice be heard and this story be told. Change is something that starts with each and every one of us. The world we live in has been influenced by the ideas, inspirations, and inventions of the past and we continue to be spun forward into the future by each other's dreams. In the popular Disney children's movie *Moana,* the protagonist Moana Waialiki goes on an adventure to save her island Motunui and her people, going against the rules set by her father, the chief of Motunui. At the beginning of the film, Moana sings: *'And when I think of tomorrow / There we are / I'll lead the way / I'll have my people to guide me / We'll build our future together.'* Campaigning, advocacy, and lobbying can be tough, gruelling, and burdening work but in the end, we are all stronger for it. We build better communities when we are all heard. So, let's learn how.

How to campaign

Petitions

In the previous chapter we explained how to submit a petition to Parliament. Paper, electronic, or hybrid petitions can be submitted to Parliament, asking the House of Representatives to do something about a policy, law or problem. There are also many ways to easily create and share a petition online. Aotearoa New Zealand community campaigning organisation ActionStation hosts a website where you can start your own petition-based campaign. It's as easy as pressing a large yellow button! You can address your petition to anyone including a specific politician, a CEO of a company, the House of Representatives, or even your school board. In your petition, outline exactly what you would like to see happen. It may also be good to explain the significance and the potential impacts of your call to action and why people should care. Through platforms like these you can easily collect signatures, share your petition on social media, and email people who have supported your campaign. You can find ActionStation's website and create your own petition here: https://our.actionstation.org.nz/

Petitions are an easy way to attract attention to an issue. The ease of signing and sharing a petition online allows causes to gain traction and offer a concrete way to prove that there is widespread support or agreement for a call to action. You can create a petition on anything. At the time of writing, there are petitions on ActionStation on: calling for nationwide free public transport for community service card holders, under 25s, and all tertiary students; asking the Kirikiriroa Hamilton City Council to update the Hamilton City Emblem to an emblem which reflects a commitment to te Tiriti o Waitangi; requesting that the SPCA prosecute a man who shared a video on the social media platform TikTok of him punching a possum in the face; and one advocating for the film 'Music' made by musician Sia to be banned in Aotearoa New Zealand cinemas for its discriminatory and harmful depiction of an autistic character.

Open letter

Open letters are letters directed at an open audience or addressed to a specific person or organisation(s) but also designed to be read by a wider audience. Open letters are great opportunities to go into detail about a specific view or issue and potentially persuade or gather wider support from members of the public while holding an individual or organisation accountable. They can also be delivered in conjunction with or attached to petitions where you may ask people to sign in support if they agree with your letter. Open letters can also easily be shared online. One example was the open letter signed by 42 organisations addressed to the Prime Minister, Minister of Foreign Affairs, and Trade Minister on supporting a People's Vaccine, asking them to support a proposal made by India and South Africa to temporarily suspend intellectual property rules outlined in the WTO Agreement on Trade Related Aspect of Intellectual Property Rights.

Select Committee submissions

If there is a Bill currently being considered by Parliament that you are concerned about or would like to reflect your views on, you can make a submission to a Select Committee. Input and views from public submissions will be used by select committees to inform the legislative decision-making process. You can see what is currently open for submission on the website below. Simply click on the name of the item you wish to submit to for further information: https://www.parliament.nz/en/pb/sc/make-a-submission/

You can make a written digital submission on this website. First, you must declare whether you are making the submission as an individual or on behalf of an organisation as well as selecting whether you wish to also make an oral submission to the select committee. Then you can enter your contact details. Finally, you make your submission either by uploading a file or writing into a text box on the website outlining your comments and recommendations. You can write this in te reo Māori or English. Alternatively, you can email or post a written letter to Parliament to make a submission. You are also able to submit by providing a video in NZSL either by uploading it online and providing a link or by mailing a physical recording to Parliament.

If you elect to make an oral submission to the select committee you will either go into Parliament to talk to the committee in person or remotely through video conference. Under the current Covid-19 Traffic Light Protection Framework, vaccinated people can attend select committee meetings in person and unvaccinated people can submit to a select committee through video conference or in person but under certain restrictions. If you are going to Parliament House to submit to a select committee you will have to first go through security and then find your way to the committee rooms. There will be a screen outside saying whether the committee is currently open to the public or not; if it is not, simply wait outside, otherwise you can go in. When the chairperson invites you forward you can begin your submission.

Talking to representatives, officials, and organisations

Talking to representatives can be a great way to get them to start a conversation in decision-making rooms. You can contact any MP by mail, email, telephone, or by going into their electorate office if they are your local MP. You can find information on what roles MPs hold and how to contact them here: https://www.parliament.nz/en/mps-and-electorates/members-of-parliament/

However, Members of Parliament may not be the only people that you want to talk to. It pays to investigate the world of advocacy and see if there are any established groups that are already campaigning on the issue you're interested in, or a similar issue. Forming relationships may help you gain useful connections and resources. Being able to tag team tasks and support each other is beneficial for everyone. As well, established groups may have connections on the inside. Public service officials and policy analysts are critically important in running the country and therefore are critically important to talk to. Making connections like these may help you get support and advice.

Protests

There are many different types of protests – such as marches, occupations and sit-ins, walk-outs, boycotts, strikes, art, online activism, hīkoi, demonstrations, speeches, music and concerts, and fashion. In 1977 Bastion Point was occupied by hundreds of people protesting the government's decision to permit a housing development on Ngāti Whātua land. In 1981 more than 150,000 people took part in demonstrations protesting the Springbok tour in Aotearoa New Zealand as they were against allowing the All Blacks to play the South African rugby team due to the South African system of apartheid. In 2005 a cover of the Mutton Birds song 'Anchor Me' featuring many famous Aotearoa New Zealand artists such as Anika Moa, Hinewehi Mohi, Kirsten Morrell and others was released along with a music video featuring doves, Greenpeace vessels, and nuclear explosions to mark the 20th anniversary of the Rainbow Warrior sinking.

There are many ways to hold a protest and no two protests are ever the same so it is difficult to explain, in much detail, how to protest – that part is up to you. You may wish to think about what type of protest will be most effective for your cause. Do you wish to bring public awareness to something? Perhaps art or online activism could work. Do you want to mobilise a large group of people? Think about a march or occupation. The most important thing to consider when planning a protest is how you are going to keep yourself and the other people involved safe. This may be more important for some forms of protest than others. Nonetheless, any form of advocacy can be tough and stressful work and it is good to be mindful of your safety, mental health, and well-being while engaging in mahi like this.

While Aotearoa New Zealand law recognises the right to protest, you need to be careful to remain within the law or you may be arrested and brought before the courts. The Community Law Centre has some helpful guidance: https://communitylaw.org.nz/community-law-manual/chapter-4-activism/organising-a-protest-some-rules-you-might-need-to-comply-with/

The Summary Offences Act 1981 contains criminal offences such as disorderly behaviour, use of offensive language and wilful damage to property. There are more serious offences in the Crimes Act 1961. Riots are unlawful and can be suppressed by force. An assembly can become unlawful under the Crimes Act where it causes persons in the neighborhood to fear on reasonable grounds that violence against a person or property is going to be used. The law does not favour breaches of the peace. You cannot use force against people as part of your protest.

A good example of a protest that got out of control was the occupation in Parliament Grounds and its surrounds in February 2022, during which many people were arrested. Covid-19 was spread among the protestors. Disruption to the public was considerable. Remember, the State enjoys a near monopoly on the use of force. Breaking the law can have serious consequences. The Police began to use force to disperse the protestors seriously on 2 March 2022.

If you would like to hold a peaceful protest or demonstration on Parliament Grounds in Whanganui-a-Tara Wellington it is advised that you get in contact with the Speaker's Office first. You can book Parliament Lawn and find out if there are any other events or protests scheduled for that day. You can email or mail the Speaker's Office to provide details for your protest or demonstration. Further information and standard conditions for protesting on Parliament Grounds can be found here: https://www.parliament.nz/en/visit-and-learn/how-parliament-works/office-of-the-speaker/protests-demonstrations/

Raising awareness

There are many different roads you can go down if you want to raise public awareness for an issue. You can design a leaflet with information to give out or drop into people's letterboxes. If you don't trust your design skills there are many easy-to-navigate websites with templates, such as canva.com. You can also go door knocking to talk kanohi ki te kanohi, face to face, with your neighbours to discuss a community issue or even to ask for donations. You can also set up stalls outside supermarkets or malls (ask permission first!) or at community events and fairs to talk to people and hand out leaflets and resources. Social media works wonders for getting the word out. You could create a TikTok, a thread on Twitter venting about an issue, or informative images on Instagram. You never know when something is going to go viral. You can also create event pages on Facebook to let more people know about a protest, benefit, or event you are planning. You may also wish to get mainstream media attention. A good way to do this is to write your own media release explaining what you are doing and why it matters to send to journalists and media outlets. Creating artwork and putting up posters around your community may also be an effective way to call attention to an issue. This can be particularly effective if you are trying to call out a physical space for being inaccessible or unsafe. Be creative with how you spread the word. What always gets the most attention is passion.

Top tips

Know what you're talking about. Even if research sounds boring to you, it is a critical step for getting your campaign off the ground. If you wish to educate the public about an issue you must first know the ins and outs of it yourself. This involves knowing the relevant law and the policies each political party has relating to the topic. Remember you can easily view policies and positions on political parties' websites and all of Aotearoa New Zealand's legislation can be easily accessed at this database: https://www.legislation.govt.nz/

Have a clear goal. There is no point in asking for change if you do not know exactly what you are asking for. Brainstorm potential solutions and the steps needed to achieve them. Be pragmatic about this – what are the barriers and why hasn't a solution happened already? Coming up with clear demands or possible solutions makes it easier for decision-makers to know what you're asking for and what they can do to help. You need to discipline yourself to write down what you want and the reasons why the change should be supported. And is your choice the best option available? Why is your idea better than the present situation? Remember the much-repeated English saying against change: *'Reform, Reform – Aren't things bad enough already?'* Producing change is hard and requires a very persuasive case to succeed.

Figure out who is involved. Who is affected by this issue? Who has the power to make change on the issue? Who is likely to care about it? Are there other groups or individuals who are doing work in this area? Who may be against you? Who might become your ally? What perspectives might you not yet be considering?

Political neutrality. Think about whether you would like to align yourself with a political party or be publicly politically neutral and non-partisan. If you are trying to get a specific law or policy change, there may be advantages to political party alliances as they might be able to argue for the changes in Parliament on your behalf. Otherwise, there are many advantages to being non-partisan as it may be easier to make connections and have conversations with people from across the political sphere – potentially gaining unexpected alliances and greater overall support.

Prepare rebuttal. Think about why people may not agree with you. Thinking of counterarguments to help persuade them of your case may be useful. However, even more so, *really* consider their perspective – is there something in there that you have overlooked? Could tweaks to your solutions help get more people on board without compromising your original vision?

Review public perception. What do people already know and think about your issue? If it is something that not a lot of people are aware of, you may have to have a greater focus on education. If it is already a popular issue, you're going to have to think about what perspective you bring to the table that is not already there. If it is a divisive issue your focus may be on persuasion.

Words matter. Choosing the right words and constructing the right narrative is essential for a successful campaign. You want to communicate what you see as the problem, what you see as the solution, and what you see as the importance or significance of this. Having a catchy name or slogan associated with your campaign or work may sound cheesy but it helps stick in people's minds. You want to offer hope, not just doom and gloom.

Make friends. The more people you can get on board the better. Kōrero with organisations, whānau, strangers, political actors, officials on all sides of your argument and see if you can make friends with them – or at least healthy connections and relationships – despite your different opinions. Even when negotiating with people you disagree with it's important to remember that they are people. Offer them kai, check in with how they are doing, and really listen to them.

Use everything available in your toolbox. Don't just focus your strategy on one thing. If you are holding an occupation, you may also want to contact the media, make informative resources to tell the public why you are occupying a site, and run a social media event or page. If you wish to focus your efforts primarily online you may wish to think of complementary in-person actions people can take. Different messages and styles resonate with and reach different people. But be careful to obey the law, you do not want to get arrested. Remember, occupations of land or premises are usually illegal and can attract the provisions of the Trespass Act 1980. If you are warned to leave and do not, you commit an offence and you may be arrested.

Show people how they can get involved. If you get the word out successfully people are going to want to know how they can help. Have ideas of tasks people can do – from joining your team or volunteering to simply sharing something on social media or talking to their friends and whānau.

Case studies

Native forest preservation, collaboration, and the Maruia Declaration

Environmental activism in Aotearoa New Zealand in the 1970s and 1980s saw the creation of the Department of Conservation, and a new wave of environmental petitions and demonstrations, even involving people sitting in trees while chainsaws were roaring underneath them. Environmentalist and co-founder of the Native Forest Action Council Guy Salmon was part of the movement wanting to protect native forests in Aotearoa. He talks about the steps he took that helped result in the 1986 West Coast Forest Accord:

So, we came up with a phrase for what we would nowadays call a just transition. We put in a submission to the Forest Service, which was the agency in charge of all these forests in those days and the idea was that in the North Island areas, where there was already pine forest available nearby, the sawmills would be helped to change over into pine so they wouldn't lose employment. However, in the West Coast it was a much more difficult thing because while there were some pine plantations already

*established, and much of them in the ashes of native forest, there was a
15-year delay before there would be any harvesting from them. So right at
the start we devised this document that we all agreed on called the Maruia
Declaration, which had six points to it, and we later made it into a
petition. It became the largest ever petition in New Zealand's history.*

The Maruia Declaration asked Parliament to: consider recognising and
protecting native forests in law; ban the burning of indigenous forests
and wildlife; phase out the logging of virgin forests (with exceptions);
create an organisation who holds the responsibility for native forests and
protection; reduce commercial pressures on native forests; and be mindful
of conservation in the consumption of forest products. The petition was
first signed in 1975 and was circulated publicly and submitted to the
government in 1977 with more than 340,000 signatures. It was a catalyst
for the creation of the Department of Conservation and now almost all
of the Maruia Declaration's demands have been met.

Alongside the Maruia Declaration, Guy Salmon explains that they
followed two main strategies. The first was setting deadlines for phasing
out native forest milling in the North Island as well as the West Coast.
The second was accounting for some sustainable production for special
purpose timbers, both for the production of some native timber furniture
and so Māori were able to use totara and other wood to build maraes and
other buildings and items. The Native Forest Action Council also went
to the Commerce Commission and persuaded them that the controls on
the price of native timber should be lifted. This made it a more premium
product so that less had to be cut to maintain the same revenue and levels
of employment.

Guy Salmon continues:

*We went through several elections sort of saving one bit of forest at a
time as a result of our publicity campaigns, but we didn't really get a big
breakthrough until the Labour Government came into power in 1984.
They had quite a good policy on phasing out logging in the North Island
forests very rapidly but in the South Island and the West Coast, you know,
the West Coast is the birthplace of the Labour Party, so they really felt
like they couldn't do anything down there without the agreement of West
Coasters. So, Andy Kirkland, who was the Director General of the Forest
Services, suggested to Roger Blakely, who was the new Chief Executive*

for the Ministry for the Environment, that we should try a kind of
collaborative process.

We had a big meeting in Wellington of all the people who had an
interest in West Coast forests and agreed on a process we would follow
culminating at the end of the year negotiating a settlement. That meeting
also elected a working party, which had all the main players represented.
The newly created Department of Conservation had a seat, the joint
campaign on native forest which I was in charge of had a seat, the saw
miller's association had a seat, and the West Coast local authorities – there
were six of us all together [. . .]. And we agreed! It was quite an important
milestone really. Essentially, we carved up all those forests into a whole set
of reserves, an area that was called stewardship land which we were going
to set aside in the meantime because we didn't have enough information
to make decisions on, and a third category which was going to be used for
some timber production. That last category was also divided in two, part of
it getting us through those 15 years, until the pine plantations could take up
jobs and the other part beyond that 15-year period that would be used for
specialty timber production.

This agreement, the 1986 West Coast Forest Accord, was signed and
legally binding. It was signed by environmental organisations such as
Forest and Bird, Federated Mountain Clubs, and the Native Forest
Action Council as well as the West Coast Timber Association and the
West Coast Regional Council. This resulted in the preservation of more
than 180,000 hectares of native forest. Guy Salmon explains what he
learnt from this experience:

I guess the lessons I was thinking might be of interest from that little story is
really the importance of being willing to recognise sources of opposition and
mitigate those. Throughout that period, I was kind of constantly having a
bit of a battle with other environmentalists who thought that we shouldn't
make any compromises – we should sort of go for the whole hog, you know,
close everything down. It was quite a challenge to prevail on that, but the
fact that we kept on getting these successes made it easier and, in the end,
I think the outcome was good. So, it was really a question of having a
strategy, not just having a single-minded campaign.

Covid-19 and student rent strikes

The first Alert Level 4 lockdown during the Covid-19 pandemic in Aotearoa New Zealand was a massive adjustment for us all. For students, it was a time of online tutorials in pyjamas, watching lecturers struggle to learn how to use Zoom, and trying to find the motivation to do assignments amid the chaos. For students who were residents at Te Herenga Waka Victoria University halls the lockdown also came with the unwelcome surprise that they would have to pay a $150 holding fee each week to keep their rooms, despite not being able to live there over lockdown. Azaria Howell, who was living in Capital Hall prior to the lockdown, was one of the students who started the VUW Rent Strike movement, protesting the university's decision to implement this placeholder fee. She explains:

It wasn't really like one day we all just decided to protest. It was more of an ongoing thing. Some of us had sent emails to the university saying we weren't supporting the placeholder fee and got responses back that weren't very supportive to us, they basically almost doubled down. Then, through social media, essentially through a Facebook group, we were able to get a lot of students who were really willing to stand up and really willing to speak their minds about the things that they had faced with university accommodation. Then, due to the work of myself and my peers we helped launch the inquiry into student accommodation, which was a government inquiry. It has now finished and made a lot of solid recommendations in terms of how to make university accommodation and rentals and halls of residence a lot fairer and safer for students. So, I think that is really positive.

The 'VUW Halls of Residence Rent Strike' Facebook group got about 1500 members against the placeholder fee. There were about 3,000 students living in Te Herenga Waka Victoria University of Wellington halls at the time. The group allowed students to connect and created a collective voice for them. Media attention also helped. Azaria says one thing that helped get that attention was getting a lot of people and organisations involved:

Chloe Swarbrick endorsed the rent strike, Nicola Willis wrote an open letter to the university supporting the movement, every political youth wing for the parties that were in Parliament at the time supported us in one way or another, we had people on the Wellington City Council, the mayor of Lower Hutt, a lot of university staff, the Tertiary Education Union, and VUWSA, the student association, supporting it as well. So, we had a lot of big groups with their names out there backing us which made it seem more credible I suppose. I found it really useful to have, not necessarily 'celebrity' endorsements, but definitely, you know, people with political influence endorsing it. That was really helpful.

Eventually, the Rent Strike was successful, and the university did not end up charging the placeholder fee. Azaria Howell says that the main piece of advice she would give to other people advocating for a cause is:

It really helps to be passionate about it, obviously. I was really, really serious about this topic and I took it as far as I could – I was willing to get evicted from my hall because of this injustice, because that's how much it meant to me. I think it's really important to remind yourself why you're doing it. It can kind of be hard to take a step back and really take a bigger look at why you're campaigning or protesting but it's essential to keep that passion and that purpose.

Mau Whenua, parihakatanga, and saving Shelly Bay

In 2009 the Port Nicholson Block (Taranaki Whānui ki Te Upoko o Te Ika) Claims Settlement Act 2019 came into force, after the Deed of Settlement was first signed on on 19 August/Ākuhata 2008. The Settlement included transfer of land and commercial redress. The Port Nicholson Block Settlement Trust (PNBST) later bought land at Marukaikuru Shelly Bay on behalf of Taranaki Whānui. This land was later sold to the Wellington Company. However, according to Mau Whenua, who are occupying land at Marukaikuru Shelly Bay, this sale was neither just nor legal under Māori law or the formal Aotearoa New Zealand legal system.

Because the sale was for a substantial amount of land, under the PNBST constitution, they needed to put the sale to a vote and reach 75 per cent agreement. This vote failed. Further to that, around 12,000 iwi members missed out on this vote. Iwi never consented to the sale. To get around this lack of consent, the land was broken up into multiple smaller sales so that a vote was not needed for the separate transactions. Resident artist for Mau Whenua, Tayla Mereana Hartemink explains:

A lot of what we talk about is that this is not just a one iwi issue. It's actually revealing a lot of issues with the system itself. For example, one of the biggest issues with Māori trusts have is that is no mechanism to hold the trustees accountable, so you have this problem where trusteees have a lot of systemic power. So that's kinda the problems we have, you know. We lose our voice as iwi members. We lose our vote on our whenua, we lose our ability to even contest what decisions are being made, who is making these decisions, why and what for.

In 2020, Mau Whenua started occupying Marukaikuru Shelly Bay. Tayla says this:

It's historically the way that Māori have been able to fight for their land – just to stay on it. Just to sit on it and hold the space. So we're occupying for that, we're occupying for the justice of the iwi members, and for the land itself. The development is also quite bad for the environment, it's a big housing development on the last untouched bit of the harbour and there's a population of endangered kororā there. As well, I think my auntie Karen was telling me about how the levels of iron are quite bad in the area. Also, the community doesn't even really want it. It's a huge housing development right next to the airport on this one little road. What people love about Shelly Bay – and this isn't even about anything Māori – is that it's a place to ride your bike, take a visit to the Chocolate Fish café, and it's just an area that's a slice of nature right in the middle of the city. It's pretty awesome.

Central to the core of the Mau Whenua occupation is parihakatanga and peaceful protest. Tayla explains that: 'Parihaka was a settlement, it was the first indigenous peaceful protest, and it was pretty much an occupation. They were occupying their own land that had been stolen and they were just peacefully staying there. So it's the same mindset – to peacefully hold your own whenua in the face of injustice.' In 1881 Parihaka was invaded and one of the first actions of the British troops was to trample the gardens. Because of this, one of the first things Mau Whenua did when they started the occupation was to plant a garden. Tayla says: *'We put our hand up, look at us – we're not doing anything, we're being peaceful. We are the victims of this system.'*

Tayla describes the importance of inspiration and finding beauty even amongst the challenges:

For a lot of people in marginalised communities, you have to come back to your pride and festivities. You know, just having fun and maintaining that aroha. You need that pride to lift you up and have a little bit of fun and take a break from politics. 'Cause it can get you down a lot when you start to really think about it. 'Cause it seems so corrupt on paper and then you're like how did this even happen? You have to have hope and you have to be in that aroha and maintain that ihi, wehi, and mana.

The Save Shelly Bay movement had impact in Wellington Te Whanganui-a-Tara and eventually a new deal for the sale was proposed which involved Taranaki Whānui having a greater stake in the development, further financial compensation, ownership of some of the land, and proposed the building of a wharenui, Te Whare Marukaikuru, in the area. The PNBST trust accepted this deal, but Mau Whenua did not. Tayla declares:

We cannot let our whenua go. Because piece by piece we lose it. We are tangata whenua. This is our tūrangawaewae. This is who we are, so we can't lose it.

Are you a hero?

Near the end of the Disney movie *Moana*, the spirit of Moana's grandmother Tala sings to her:

'Sometimes the world seems against you / The journey may leave a scar / But scars can heal and reveal just / Where you are / The people you love will change you / The things you learn will guide you / And nothing on earth can silence / The quiet voice still inside you / And when that voice starts to whisper / Moana, you've come so far / Moana, listen / Do you know who you are?'

Heroes fight not only for what they believe in but for who they are. Democracy only really works when everyone's voices are represented. If you have a cause you believe in, a change you'd like to see, or simply something that's been bugging you, go out there and campaign. Politics is nothing without people standing up for what they believe is right.

References
An immense thank you to Guy Salmon, Azaria Howell and Tayla Mereana Hartemink for agreeing to be interviewed for this chapter and for your profound contributions.

Thank you to Bryce Johnson for the excellent kōrero about campaigns and resources you provided that helped inform this chapter.

35 How to obtain information and stay in the know

It's easy to feel like politics is a mystery: 65-page proposed Bills are difficult to decode unless you are familiar with policy jargon; MPs and councillors are so busy it's hard to keep track of what they're doing and what they've been saying; and secret documents land on minister's desks frequently. One of the first steps in engaging with politics is simply having the knowledge to do so. But how do you stay up to date and find information? What do you do if the information you want isn't freely available? How do you find out more? How do you stay in the know?

The value of open government and transparency is an increasing trend in democracies. Public opinion is an essential check of power, but it only works if the people know what is going on. In the digital age, much more information is available but securing what you want is sometimes not easy. As famous American Judge Louis Brandeis once said: *'Publicity is justly commended as a remedy for social and industrial diseases. Sunlight is said to be the best of disinfectants; electric light the most efficient policeman.'* People having access to official information is an important part of our democratic arrangements – and you knowing how to find and request information is a part of that.

The Official Information Act

Both the Official Information Act 1982 (OIA), and its companion, the Local Government Official Information and Meetings Act 1987 (LGOIMA), create a legal presumption of openness. They afford that official information is to be made available unless there is a good reason not to do so. A report by the Danks Committee in 1980, which led to the passing of this legislation, details the purposes of removing the old automatic cloak of secrecy over government information:

- A better-informed public can better participate in the democratic process.
- Secrecy is an important impediment to accountability when Parliament, press, and public cannot properly follow and scrutinise the actions of government.

- Public servants make many important decisions that affect people, and the permanent administration should also be accountable through greater flows of information about what they are doing.
- Better information flows will produce more effective government and help towards the more flexible development of policy. With more information available, it is easier to prepare for change.
- If more information is available, public cooperation with government will be enhanced.

These laws also provide for people to be able to ask for official information held by ministers and central or local government agencies. In order to make a request under the OIA you must either be a New Zealand citizen or permanent resident, a person currently in New Zealand, or a corporate entity which has a place of business in New Zealand or is incorporated here. Official information can be any information that is held by one of these agencies. What you request will depend upon what you want to know and how much you already know about the topic you are inquiring into. If you want to find clarity about where to begin and what information you should be asking for you can consult the *Directory of Official Information*, available here: https://www.justice.govt.nz/about/official-information-act-requests/directory-of-official-information/ The OIA requires that this be published every two years by the Ministry of Justice. The Directory also sets out the structure of central government organisations so you are able to find out exactly where you should direct your requests for information.

All you need to do to make an official information request is contact the agency that holds the information you are requesting and ask for it. You can communicate your request in any format, including online or over the telephone as well as in writing, and you do not need to refer to the OIA or LGOIMA or use any legal language. However, if you make an oral request and written clarification is necessary you may be asked for it. It is useful to be specific about the information you are asking for so that the agency is able to identify what you mean and find it for you. If officials are put to a great deal of work to collate information, charges for the time collating it can be levied. It is best to be precise about the information you want and not engage on a widespread fishing expedition in which every document on every topic of interest to you is requested. The agency or organisation you are making a request to is required to provide reasonable assistance to you. Requests should be answered within 20 working days, although a notice of extension may be delivered in some circumstances.

You can also make an official information request online on social media or using FYI, a website set up specifically for making OIA or LGOIMA requests. When making a request through social media it might be useful to specify what Act your request is under so it is not overlooked in the hundreds of posts ministers are tagged in every day. You might like to also specify how you want their response to be conveyed – do you want them to just Tweet back to you, an electronic response, for the information to be posted to you, or something else? If making an OIA request, you may also be asked for further personal details to establish your eligibility to make the request. One issue with making requests on social media is that they may be overlooked and it may be difficult to establish when the request was received as there may be a delay between you making a social media page and the agency/organisation seeing it. If you are making a request through FYI you need to be aware that responses will be published publicly online automatically. To make a request, simply go to this website and follow the steps: https://fyi.org.nz/

However, do not run away with the idea that you will get everything you want by requesting information under the OIA or LGOIMA. The government has large swathes of intelligence and other classified information that is unlikely to be given out, especially in matters that would compromise the security of the country if made public. Spies and other countries would benefit from seeing some information held by government agencies, and this might not be in our best interests. The expectation on the government to manage personal, physical, and information security are outlined in the *Protective Security Requirements* which can be found here: https://protectivesecurity.govt.nz/

The Ombudsman Tari o te Kaitiaki Mana Tangata guards the gates to official information and can investigate complaints about non-disclosure. They will examine the situation and if their investigation shows that the information should have been released, it usually is. If necessary the Ombudsman Tari o te Kaitiaki Mana Tangata can make formal recommendaions to release. It used to be the case that Cabinet could veto the release of information but now it appears that power is in the hands of the Prime Minister or Attorney-General. In any event no veto has ever occurred. Grounds for refusal of information requests are detailed in the OIA. Your request may be refused on the basis of administrative reasons, conclusive reasons, good reasons, or refusing to confirm or deny the existence or non-existence of information. You can consult the Official Information Act 1982 for further detail about reasons to decline.

There is some disquiet about the administration of the Official Information Act within the journalistic community, who are big users of the Act. In 2015, the Chief Ombudsman carried out an investigation on the OIA and made 48 recommendations for change. However, these were strictly connected to administrative processes and how the Act was put into practice instead of recommending legislative improvement. The report was not well received by journalists who generally maintained that the report did not go far enough to address the right issues, and neither was it likely to be effective if implemented. Successive governments have also resisted efforts to improve the Act. A strengthened Act would increase protection against corruption and questionable decision-making in government, and yet somehow it is never a political priority. Progress in making more information available has not been as extensive as it should have been and there are State agencies untouched by the OIA and therefore excluded from it. For example, the Ombudsman Tari o te Kaitiaki Mana Tangata, the Auditor-General, Parliamentary Counsel Office Te Tari Tohutohu Pāremata, the Office of the Clerk of the House of Representatives, and the Speaker.

One important provision of the Official Information Act that can be of assistance to people is Section 23. It gives people the right to seek reasons for the decisions that have been made about them in their personal capacity by State agencies. It includes being told of material findings of fact. A written statement must be supplied.

Information, communication, and the media

The media plays a significant role in communicating information to the public and keeping us up to date with what is happening in the world of politicians. However, there are also many ways that political and public actors communicate information directly with the public.

Each public organisation or agency, from ministries to district health boards and educational institutions, will have its own official website designed to help inform the public and address common queries. The government holds vast amounts of information on every conceivable subject. Government information today is a far cry from the old paper files the public service used to work with 30 years ago. Modern digital technology has made the gathering of information much easier, and that means that there is much, much more of it. Much of this information is available on the web – however, the trick is knowing where to find it. These websites will also often contain the latest media releases they have put out. Media releases are a way of providing information to the media and are the sources for many news stories. For example, one easy way to keep up to date with the latest information and statistics during the current Covid-19 pandemic is to look at the media releases available on the Ministry of Health Manatū Hauora: https://www.health.govt.nz/news-media/media-releases

Social media is increasingly becoming a tool used for political communication. Whether it's MPs tagging their fellow politicians and expressing criticism, or an MP retweeting memes, following political actors is an easy – and sometimes hilarious – way to stay engaged with political matters. Current Prime Minister Jacinda Ardern champions this communication channel and frequently uses Facebook Live to communicate updates and quick summaries of government decision-making and policies. One of these Facebook Lives held on 8 November 2021, even has her turn to her daughter who has just entered the room and say *'It's bedtime darling, pop back to bed I'll come and see you in a second'*, interrupting her rundown on Cabinet's recent decisions about Covid-19 restrictions. Social media therefore offers a powerful, interactive, direct, and accessible form of communication between governors and the governed and following these accounts is an easy way to stay informed about current affairs.

During the Covid-19 pandemic, another method of communication arose in the form of the 1pm daily update media conferences. These live streams contained up-to-the-minute Covid-19 related updates and decisions, and were created to ensure that all media outlets were informed on health matters accurately and promptly as well as to help public awareness and understanding. Luke Malpass explained in a Stuff article: *'The government and Ministry of Health decided that instead of confirming cases on the fly, they would pull it all together once a day to give a clear picture and stop reporters going around and knocking on the doors of people they thought might be sick.'* All around Aotearoa New Zealand, people stopped what they were doing to tune in and the briefings became a quintessential part of the lockdown experience here. Even a satirical IMDb page for the '1pm Daily Update' was set up, explaining the synopsis of the show as:

Set in a dystopian world where autocratic and populist leaders are in charge of the USA, China, UK, Brazil and many other nations. 1pm Daily Update takes place in the imaginary island nation of New Zealand, a utopian society where science, facts, strong leadership and a genuine care for its people and environment take precedence over money and big business.

Reviews piled in on IMDb, declaring the show a success, with comments like: *'Is Ashley Bloomfield the next McDreamy', 'Better than Shortland Street'* and *'Stellar cast but depressing plot'.*

The Prime Minister also holds post-Cabinet press conferences most weeks, usually on a Monday, detailing recent Cabinet decisions and announcements. They are normally streamed live on the Prime Minister's Facebook page as well as by major news outlets such as One News and RNZ. You can also find the transcripts of recent post-Cabinet press conferences here: https://www.beehive.govt.nz/feature/post-cabinet-press-conference

Covid-19 1pm press conference
Illustration by Tayla Mereana Hartemink

Aotearoa New Zealand has one of the best organised and most easily accessible legislative databases in the world. Every Act, Bill, and piece of secondary legislation is freely available to read and download at: https://www.legislation.govt.nz/ You can browse legislation by year or by name or simply by searching for what you are looking for. This means if you want to find out exactly what is in our law you can do so, easily. The database aims to be as accessible as possible and is not just reserved for politicians or lawyers, but offers an avenue to make understanding our law accessible to all.

You can also access judgments made by the Courts in Aotearoa New Zealand. Judgments from each case are like reports outlining the judge's findings and conclusions from the case. You can access these by going to this website: https://www.courtsofnz.govt.nz/the-courts/ Simply press on the relevant Court and then 'Judgments' to access a list of recent judgments.

References

Paul Roth and Graham Taylor *Access to Official Information* (2nd ed., LexisNexis, Wellington, 2016); Louis D Brandeis *Other Peoples' Money and how Banks use it* (R Adams AM Kelly, New York, 1971); Ombudsman *Making official information requests: A guide for requesters:* https://www.ombudsman.parliament.nz/resources/making-official-information-requests-guide-requesters; Luke Malpass *Covid 19: Is it time to ditch the 1pm livestreamed updates?* (Stuff, Oct 14 2021); 1pm Daily Update IMDb page https://www.imdb.com/title/tt12511606/?ref_=tt_urv

36 Interest groups and lobbying

The realm of lobbyists, interest groups or pressure groups, social movements, and single-issue groups is ever influential in the political world in Aotearoa New Zealand. Unfortunately, it is also a realm too often shrouded by some ambiguity and secrecy. Transparency is lacking. Organised attempts to influence policy, law, and decision-making occur on many levels. Interest groups may grow out of grassroots movements and volunteer efforts, or they may be well-established and well-funded organisations that employ a number of professional staff. Interest groups and lobbyists can demonstrate the incredible strength of citizen engagement in politics and can have considerable effects on the way the State is run. Members of Parliament are charged with representing public interest and therefore citizen lobby groups expressing their interests, ideas, and concerns often help turn the cogs of the decision-making process. Bear in mind that under Section 14 of the New Zealand Bill of Rights Act 1990: *'Everyone has the right to freedom of expression, including the freedom to seek, receive and impart information and opinions of any kind in any form.'* A vital element of democracy, clearly.

Defining interest groups and lobbying

Most legislatures have lobbies located on the way to the chamber where lobbyists would wait to speak to political representatives. This is where the term 'lobbyist' originated both in England and the United States. Broadly speaking, lobbying can be any attempt to influence or persuade a decision-maker on an issue. Such a definition would encompass many everyday acts of citizen political participation, including bringing up an issue with an MP, making a submission to a Bill, and even signing a petition. However, this is very different from the professional industry we normally associate with the term lobbying nowadays. Professional lobbyists are charged with influencing decision-makers on behalf of those who retain them. Or they may be hired as in-house employees that work solely on behalf of one organisation, or as consultants who can be hired or contracted by third-party organisations. Consultant lobbyists may be employed by specialist lobbying or communications organisations that take clients.

Interest groups are organised groups of people that aim to lobby or influence decision-makers and represent the interests of their members or a particular cause. Interest groups may focus on economic or business interests, the preferences of a particular group of people or workers, or a cause, such as the environment. For example, some of the interest groups in Aotearoa New Zealand include Federated Farmers, which represents the interests of farmers and does rural advocacy work, BusinessNZ which aims to represent Aotearoa New Zealand businesses, and the New Zealand Nurses Organisation Tōpūtanga Tapuhi Kaitiaki o Aotearoa which gives a voice to nurses. Iwi or hapū may also be active in advocating. There has been some debate over the blurry line between social movements, activist networks, and interest groups. In contrast to the former, interest groups will normally have a defined membership base (sometimes with membership fees), an established leadership structure, and a corporate legal existence.

Lobbyists and interest groups may engage in activities such as providing feedback to decision-makers and political officials on policy decisions, making submissions to select committees, meeting with MPs and establishing relationships, and donating to political parties and offering gifts to MPs. They may also attempt to influence public opinion and gain more widespread support through educational campaigns or raising awareness. Former Minister Richard Prebble once joked, after a man had sat in the Air New Zealand Koru lounge for a week on the likelihood Prebble would at some point enter, that *in New Zealand instead of being known as lobbyists they should be called korus'.

Positive and negative influences

Lobbying provides many benefits to democracy in Aotearoa New Zealand. Representation, participation, and public engagement with the government is the most important part of democracy. Many interest groups and lobbyists are experts in their fields or on a particular issue which means that they can provide many effective recommendations and advice to MPs. However, it is important for MPs to consult a wide variety of advice and not just rely on one side of the argument. Former MP Sue Kedgley explained that she was once contacted by a lobbyist who had written a Private Member's Bill and proposed that she put it forward: '*Let's face it, a lot of MPs are very short-staffed, don't have their own researchers and so they like it if they can get someone who will draft them legislation and write their questions for them. I can see the temptation to take up those offers,*' she said. While this makes life easier for many of our decision-makers, it may also cross a line. MPs must represent all people, not just those with the resources to make their voices loud.

The danger with lobbying, especially with professional corporate lobbying, is that some interests are overrepresented while others continue to be marginalised. Professional lobbyists can be especially effective at pushing a cause due to their experience, knowledge, and connections. However, these services come at a cost and in so doing can privilege the representation of elite and business interests. The professionalisation of lobbying and interest groups may be an effective method for change, but we must consider if it is always the most beneficial avenue. There are concerns about the lack of transparency surrounding lobbying in Aotearoa New Zealand. One common phenomenon is the 'revolving door' in politics in which former MPs, Parliamentary staff, or political officials leave their government jobs and go to work as lobbyists or otherwise influence the government from the outside.

In many countries, there is a 'cool off' period where former politicians cannot work as lobbyists until a certain amount of time has passed since their time in office. There is no such convention here. As well, much of the activity of interest groups and lobbyists is unknown to the public – which is worrying considering the prominent role they play in politics. One study found that lobby groups were only identified as 'lobby groups' in 3 per cent of news stories. This means that people may not be aware of what interest groups are operating in our country or not be aware of the motives or goals of such groups.

Regulation

There is some legislation in place to regulate the activity of lobbyists or interest groups. Bribery and corruption in respect of both Ministers of the Crown and Members of Parliament are serious criminal offences under the Crimes Act 1961. Trading in influence is also an offence.

There are also extensive provisions in the Cabinet Manual about conflict of interest and some rigorous rules set out that bind ministers. These conflicts of interest sometimes come under scrutiny, for example, as exposed by Nicky Hager's book *Dirty Politics: How Attack Politics is*

Poisoning New Zealand's Political Environment.

The *Cabinet Manual 2017* has a long section on the acceptance of gifts and hospitality received by both ministers and MPs. Here are the first three sections of it paragraphs 2.84–2.86:

The Standing Orders require members of Parliament to disclose to the Registrar of Pecuniary and Other Specified Interests of Members of Parliament any gift received with an estimated market value of more than a prescribed amount (or more than one gift from the same donor in the period with a total value of more than the prescribed amount), and the name of the donor. This declaration includes hospitality and donations in cash or kind.

Ministers who receive gifts worth more than the prescribed value must not only disclose them in their annual (or initial) return to the Registrar, but must also relinquish them, unless they obtain the express permission of the Prime Minister to retain them. Any gift received by ministers may be relinquished to the Parliamentary Service to arrange appropriate display or storage. Gifts that ministers receive from close family members need not be relinquished.

If a minister is sent an unsolicited gift that is returned to the donor before the minister takes possession of it, the gift does not need to be declared. However, once the minister takes possession of the gift, it must be declared in a return. If the gift is subsequently returned to the donor or donated to another person or organisation, this information can be noted in the minister's return to the Registrar.

The prescribed amount mentioned is an estimated market value of more than $500 as set out in clause 8(1)(b)(i) of Appendix B, 'Pecuniary and other interests' to the Standing Orders of the House of Representatives.

There is, however, little legislation in place to ensure transparency of lobbying. This can mean that the impacts, activities, and role of lobbying are swept under the rug. Many countries have compulsory registers of lobbyists but Aotearoa New Zealand's lack of such a register makes it very difficult to discern the number of active lobbyists and who they are.

In 2012, Green Party MP Holly Walker introduced the Lobbying Disclosure Bill, first drafted by former MP Sue Kedgley, into Parliament. It would have established a compulsory register of lobbyists and given the power to the Auditor-General to develop a lobbying code of ethics. During the first reading of the Bill, Holly Walker explained:

Sue launched this Bill out of a concern about the growing influence of lobbying in New Zealand. After 12 years in Parliament, she thought that lobbying was becoming increasingly entrenched in our political system, and she was concerned that it was unregulated and often happening behind closed doors, outside the public sphere.

However, there was concern that the Bill was too wide-ranging and would potentially inhibit citizens' political participation. The difficulty of defining the term 'lobbyist' meant that it was possible for everyday citizens engaging in activities such as contacting an MP about an issue, or making a submission, could be seen as lobbyists and would therefore have to register and adhere to the code of ethics, potentially discouraging people away from political participation. The grey area was difficult to navigate. The Bill never passed. Although there was validity in these concerns and the Bill required alteration, some form of regulation or requirement for transparency may be beneficial.

Your engagement

It is easy to become a member of an interest or pressure group. If there is a particular issue you are passionate about but the thought of campaigning for change by yourself is too daunting, an interest group might be a good way to start. Paying membership fees or volunteering are fantastic ways to support a cause and participate politically. For example, in the 2020–2021 financial year, 62,761 people donated to the SPCA and 5000 people volunteered assistance. The SPCA also does lobbying and advocacy work. Over 31,000 registered nurses and 1500 enrolled nurses were members of the New Zealand Nurses Organisation in 2020. Forest & Bird has around 80,000 members and supporters. Trends show us that in many established democracies, political party membership is declining while interest group or single-issue group membership rises. Is there a group you would like to be a part of?

It is good to realise that lobbyists and interest groups are active in the political scene in Aotearoa New Zealand, even if we can't always see them clearly. In 2003 the Rt Hon Trevor Mallard said that, as a minister, he had people contact his office every week seeking his views or wanting to meet with him. *'I might hear from people who want me to stop the school review process; sports organisations might lobby me over proposed legislation that might impact them – like the Health and Safety in Employment bill; and I might be contacted on the hot issue of the day.'*

Even if you don't consider yourself a policy wonk, a political science nerd, or even that interested in politics in the first place, you probably *do* care about the decisions that get made in Parliament and how they affect you. Wanting to influence those decisions – to stop something from happening or be a catalyst for some long overdue change – is only natural.

References

Catherine Strong and Fran Tyler 'New Zealand media camouflage political lobbying' (*Pacific Journalism Review* 23(2), 2017); Thomas Anderon and Simon Chapple 'Grease or Sand in the Wheels of Democracy? The market for lobbying in New Zealand' (*Policy Quarterly* 14(2), 2018); Janine Hayward, Lara Greaves and Claire Timperley *Government and Politics in Aotearoa New Zealand* (Oxford University Press Australia & New Zealand, 2021); Francine Tyler *Lifting the lid on lobbying in New Zealand: An investigation into how these political players avoid being labelled lobbyists* (Massey University, Master's Thesis, 2015); Nicky Hager *Dirty Politics: How Attack Politics is Poisoning New Zealand's Political Environment* (Potton & Burton, Nelson, 2014); Geoffrey Palmer 'Lawyer as lobbyist: The Role of lawyers in influencing and managing change' [1993] New Zealand Law Journal 93; Trevor Mallard *Lobbying and the Government* (Beehive, 2003) https://www.beehive.govt.nz/speech/lobbying-and-government; *Lobbying Disclosure Bill – First Reading* (New Zealand Parliament, 2012) https://www.parliament.nz/en/pb/hansard-debates/rhr/document/50HansD_20120725_00000036/lobbying-disclosure-bill-first-reading

37 Climate change

Is this how our society is due to end? A tale of the smartest species doomed by that all-too-human characteristic of failing to see the bigger picture in pursuit of short-term goals.
—Sir David Attenborough, address to world leaders at COP26

According to the International Panel on Climate Change (IPCC) sixth assessment report *Climate Change 2021: The Physical Science Basis*: *'It is unequivocal that human influence has warmed the atmosphere, ocean and land. Widespread and rapid changes in the atmosphere, ocean, cryosphere and biosphere have occurred.'* It is not that climate change is some far off threat, our climate *is* changing, our climate *is* warming, and it will continue to warm, causing catastrophic harm to the environment if we do not act. The threat of climate change is one of the few things that every species on this planet and all of humankind has in common. The fight for our planet offers us an incredible opportunity to all stand up and stand together, united by this one issue. However, it may also be the thing that tears our world apart.

The science

Human impacts and greenhouse gas emissions have contributed to environmental degradation and global warming at a rate that has not been seen in the last 2000 years. The IPCC's sixth assessment report outlines a series of findings that are cause for concern including: the last four decades have been warmer than any decade since before 1850; the rise in global mean sea level has been faster since 1900 than in any previous century in the last 3000 years, between 1901–2018 the global mean sea level has increased by 0.15–0.25m; in 2019, the atmospheric carbon dioxide concentrations were the highest they've been in the last two million years and the concentrations of methane and nitrous oxide were higher than they've been in at least 800,000 years. Things are not looking pretty. The IPCC explains that:

*Human-induced climate change is already affecting many weather and
climate extremes in every region across the globe. Evidence of observed
changes in extremes such as heatwaves, heavy precipitation, droughts, and
tropical cyclones, and, in particular, their attribution to human influence,
has strengthened since [the previous assessment report 2013/2014].*

The report includes predictions of possible climate futures, including
some of what would occur if we reached 1.5 degrees celsius of warming,
rather than 2 degrees celsius warming, compared to pre-industrial levels:

*At 1.5°C global warming, heavy precipitation and associated flooding
are projected to intensify and be more frequent in most regions in Africa
and Asia (high confidence), North America (medium to high confidence),
and Europe (medium confidence). Also, more frequent and/or severe
agricultural and ecological droughts are projected in a few regions in
all inhabited continents except Asia compared to 1850–1900 (medium
confidence); increases in meteorological droughts are also projected in a
few regions (medium confidence). A small number of regions are projected
to experience increases or decreases in mean precipitation (medium
confidence).*

*At 2°C global warming and above, the level of confidence in and the
magnitude of the change in droughts and heavy and mean precipitation
increase compared to those at 1.5°C. Heavy precipitation and associated
flooding events are projected to become more intense and frequent in the
Pacific Islands and across many regions of North America and Europe
(medium to high confidence). These changes are also seen in some regions
in Australasia and Central and South America (medium confidence).
Several regions in Africa, South America and Europe are projected
to experience an increase in frequency and/or severity of agricultural
and ecological droughts with medium to high confidence; increases are
also projected in Australasia, Central and North America, and the
Caribbean with medium confidence. A small number of regions in Africa,
Australasia, Europe, and North America are also projected to be affected
by increases in hydrological droughts, and several regions are projected to
be affected by increases or decreases in meteorological droughts, with more
regions displaying an increase (medium confidence). Mean precipitation is
projected to increase in all polar, northern European and northern North*

American regions, most Asian regions and two regions of South America (high confidence).

Future Earth, The Earth League, and the World Climate Research Programme's report *10 New Insights in Climate Science 2021* outlines some key findings that we all must bear in mind:

- **'Stabilising at 1.5°C warming is still possible, but immediate and drastic global action is required.'** This requires at least an average reduction of 2 gigatonnes of CO_2 emissions each year until we reach net zero emissions. We would need to see incredible transformation across all areas of society and in all sectors of the economy.
- **'Rapid growth in methane and nitrous oxide emissions put us on track for 2.7°C warming.'** Although they are often overlooked, around 21% of current global warming is caused by non-CO_2 factors, such as the emissions of methane and nitrous oxide. There would also need to be a reduction of these emissions, such as by limiting the use of nitrogen fertilisers and using more sustainable livestock management practices.
- **'Megafires – Climate change forces fire extremes to reach new dimensions with extreme impacts.'** Changes in the climate are already leading to more frequent and intense wildfires and fire seasons and it is likely that there will be an increasing number of megafires (an intense fire that spreads over a large area). There is medium confidence that human influences contribute to this.
- **'Climate tipping elements incur high-impact risks.'** Tipping elements, such as the melting of ice sheets, changes to ocean currents, and deforestation of rainforests, would likely lead to irrevocable damage to our planet. Some tipping elements may also impact or trigger one another. We must be aware of these risks and work to combat them, such as with preservation efforts of the Amazon rainforest.
- **'Global climate action must be just.'** Climate change will exacerbate existing inequalities. Between 1990–2015 the richest 1% were responsible for over 15% of global carbon emissions. The report explains that: *'A just distribution of the carbon budget would require the richest 1% of the global population to reduce their current emissions by at least a factor of 30, while per capita emissions of the poorest 50%*

of the global population could increase by around three times their current levels on average.'

- **'Supporting household behaviour changes is a crucial but often overlooked opportunity for climate action.'** We must all adapt to '1.5°C lifestyles' and reduce our individual emissions, such as by consuming sustainably, reducing car use, and following a low-meat or plant-based diet. Many of these changes have also been found to support positive well-being. Individual and household behaviour and consumer changes must be supported by policies and businesses.

- **'Political challenges impede effectiveness of carbon pricing.'** Carbon pricing is the setting of price for emitting or storing carbon and other greenhouse gases. Carbon prices need to increase and be applied to a larger share of global emissions. Equity must be considered in these policies.

- **'Nature-based solutions are critical for the pathway to Paris – but look at the fine print.'** Nature-based solutions, such as natural habitat restoration, are critical for conservation and combating climate change. However, there is potential that a focus on nature-based solutions could put an undue and inequitable burden of decarbonisation onto less industrialised countries and vulnerable communities.

- **'Building resilience of marine ecosystems is achievable by climate-adapted conservation and management, and global stewardship.'** Protecting the ocean and marine ecosystems and biodiversity is an essential part of our climate solutions. Coastal and marine ecosystems capture and store large amounts of carbon. Increasing seaweed farming could offer climate-friendly solutions to sustainable food production and seaweed-based plastic alternatives are already starting to appear.

- **'Costs of climate change mitigation can be justified by the multiple immediate benefits to the health of humans and nature.'** Although efforts to combat climate change may, in some cases, be costly, the benefits of saving lives, maintaining healthy ecosystems, and reducing health risks due to climate change and pollution outweigh the costs. We must adapt to a net-zero economy.

The policy

The Intergovernmental Panel on Climate Change was established in 1988 to gather and report on the most up to date scientific information on climate change so that governments around the world are able to access and use this when developing climate policies. Following this, the United Nations Conference on Environment and Development in Rio de Janeiro in 1992, also known as the Rio Earth Summit, brought together 179 countries focusing on environmental and development issues. Many important agreements came out of this conference, including the **United Nations Framework Convention on Climate Change** (UNFCCC). This agreement was first signed in 1992 and came into force in March 1994. Today, 197 parties (196 States and the European Union) have ratified the agreement. The ultimate objective of the UNFCCC is to achieve *'stabilisation of greenhouse gas concentrations in the atmosphere at a level that would prevent dangerous anthropogenic interference with the climate system'*.

The UNFCCC considered *'the specific needs and special circumstances of developing country Parties, especially those that are particularly vulnerable to the adverse effects of climate change'*. There are some commitments that all parties who signed are bound by in the agreement, and some that only industrialised countries (Annex 1) are bound by. This was because these Annex 1 Parties were responsible for a bigger share of greenhouse gas emissions and had more financial and technological resources available to combat climate change. Overall, the UNFCCC was a crucial first step in acknowledging that there was a problem, promoting efforts to reduce carbon emissions, and establishing channels to keep track of country's emissions and climate action.

Each year there is a Conference of the Parties who have ratified the UNFCCC called COP. The first COP was held in 1995 in Berlin. At COP3 in 1997 parties signed the first extension to the Convention – the **Kyoto Protocol**. The Protocol came into effect in February 2005 and is currently ratified by 192 Parties. It required 37 industrialised countries and the European Union (Annex B) to reduce their greenhouse gas emissions by 5 per cent compared to their level of emissions in 1990, during the first commitment period from 2008 to 2012. The Protocol also set up an improved monitoring, review and verification system and introduced a compliance system as well as introducing market mechanisms so that Parties were able to trade emissions permits. There were significant drawbacks to the effectiveness of the Kyoto Protocol due to the fact that the United States of America did not sign it and big emitters like China and India were not classified as Annex B Parties and therefore were not bound to reduce their emissions.

In 2012 the Parties to the Kyoto Protocol adopted the **Doha Amendment** which set up a second commitment period from 2013 to 2020. The Amendment required Parties to reduce their emissions by 18 per cent compared to 1990 levels over the commitment period. It also revised the list of greenhouse gases Parties had to report their emissions of and made small amendments to multiple articles of the Kyoto Protocol that needed to be brought up to date. For the Amendment to come into effect, at least 75 per cent of the Parties to the Kyoto Protocol needed to deliver an instrument of acceptance and agree to the Amendment. Because of this, the Amendment did not enter into force until December 2020. The Doha Amendment is now ratified by 147 Parties and binds 30 industrialised countries and the European Union to reduce their emissions.

In 2015, at the 21st Conference of the Parties (COP21) the **Paris Agreement** was signed. The agreement is a partially legally binding international treaty that commits parties to *'Holding the increase in the global average temperature to well below 2°C above pre-industrial levels and pursuing efforts to limit the temperature increase to 1.5°C above pre-industrial levels, recognising that this would significantly reduce the risks and impacts of climate change.'* The Paris Agreement was ratified by 190 Parties; however, the United States of America withdrew from the treaty in 2017. Parties must make significant efforts both to reduce their greenhouse gas emissions but also make adaptations to strengthen resilience to the potential threats and consequences of climate change. In contrast to the Kyoto Protocol and UNFCCC, *all* Parties to the Paris Agreement are bound to reduce their emissions and make efforts to combat climate change, however, the level of commitment may vary for each country. Parties determine their own plans and targets, consistent with their own resourcing and technological capacities, known as Nationally Determined Contributions (NDCs), and communicate the actions they will take to strengthen climate resilience and reduce emissions. The Paris Rulebook provides guidelines for these NDCs. The Agreement also establishes a financial, technical, and capacity building support framework where industrialised countries are obliged to provide support to other countries. However, there are plenty of weasel words in the agreement and the means of enforcement are lacking.

The Paris Agreement has a five-year cycle so that plans and progress have to be reviewed every five years, and increasingly ambitious plans can be developed for the next cycle. Countries were required to submit their NDCs by 2020, although some countries submitted their NDCs in 2021 due to delays because of the Covid-19 pandemic. COP26 in 2021 in Glasgow marked the first review at the Conference of the Parties since the Paris Agreement was signed in 2015 (this was meant to occur in 2020 but was delayed due to the Covid-19 pandemic). Out of this summit came the **Glasgow Climate Pact** which sets out the agreements made at COP26 to continue to aim to keep global warming to 1.5°C. The *COP26 The Glasgow Climate Pact* report sets out the conference's primary achievements as:

- **Mitigation** – reducing emissions
- **Adaptation** – helping those already impacted by climate change
- **Finance** – enabling countries to deliver on their climate goals
- **Collaboration** – working together to deliver even greater action.

These COPs truly are monumental events in addressing climate change. You have world leaders, youth activists, big business, and world leading science experts all gathered together to focus on one sole cause – our planet. The immense significance of the decisions made at these events isn't lost on attendees. At COP26 15-year-old environmentalist Vinisha Umashankar addressed world leaders, saying:

Me and my generation will live to see the consequences of our action today. Yet none of what we discussed today seems practical to me. You are deciding whether or not we will have a chance to live in a habitable world. You are deciding whether or not we are worth fighting for, worth supporting, and worth caring. Many of my generation are angry and frustrated at leaders who have made empty promises and failed to deliver, and we have every reason to be angry. But I have no time for anger. I want to act.

Whether the clunky machinery of the COPs can produce the necessary transformative changes is in doubt. Glasgow was the 26th Conference of the Parties and yet we are *still* not on track to meet targets or head towards any truly meaningful international political action. In fact, the situation is just getting worse. Over 50 per cent of all our carbon emissions have occurred since 1990. Bold new initiatives are necessary if we are to stand a chance of survival. The state of international law on climate change is not fit for purpose and it cannot be made fit for purpose unless a new approach is adopted. Climate change activist Greta Thunberg explained in her speech at the Fridays for Future rally in Glasgow that:

The COP has turned into a PR event where leaders are giving beautiful speeches and announcing fancy commitments and targets while behind the curtains the governments of the Global North countries are still refusing to take any drastic climate action.

This is not a conference, this is now [. . .] a two weeklong celebration of business as usual and blah blah blah. The most affected people in the most affected areas remain unheard and the voices of future generations are drowning in their green wash and empty words and promises. But the facts do not lie, and we know that our emperors are naked.

If a bird is to fly it needs two wings. For climate action, one wing consists of domestic policies in each state, reducing the emission of greenhouse gases. The emissions profile of each country will be different and so the measures adopted need to be different. The other wing consists of international commitments to reach climate change targets set for various categories of emissions. International cooperation is vital since no nation alone can save the climate.

We are far from securing the level of international agreements that are necessary. Furthermore, Aotearoa New Zealand has been a laggard in adopting domestic measures to stop climate change. This is due, in part, to a range of pressure group activities from farmers and businesses whose activities will be curtailed by reducing emissions. Export industries are involved, such as dairying and the meat industry, which makes the issues politically sensitive. Aotearoa New Zealand has put in place machinery to address these problems, but it has not activated that machinery at the time we are writing. Our emissions far exceed what they were in 1990. Transformative measures will have to be adopted and there is not much time. The measures so far in place are plainly insufficient. A Climate Change Commission has been established and it has provided a comprehensive report. But by the end of 2021 no significant new reduction measures have been adopted, although machinery has been put in place. See the Climate Tracker: https://climateactiontracker.org/countries/new-zealand/

The people

Although climate change may seem like an impossibly enormous issue, there is hope in the fact that each and every one of us can take action on the ground, in our own ways. Where there is a great threat there is also a great opportunity to come together in our communities, and also as a global community, and give back to our earth, to Papatūānuku, and take care of her. Climate action can look like a million different things – from making more sustainable changes in your own everyday life to taking to the streets to protest or suing the government. The case studies below outline incredible stories from Aotearoa New Zealand and the many ways in which rangatahi have made an impact right here. Perhaps you can too?

Generation Zero and the creation of the Zero Carbon Act

Generation Zero is a youth climate action group that began after a group of rangatahi attended COP16 in Cancún in 2010. One of the group's most powerful achievements so far was the Zero Carbon Act Campaign, which began in 2016. The group drafted a law that holds Aotearoa New Zealand to account to reduce our greenhouse gas emissions (excluding biogenic methane) to net zero by 2050 and sets targets for us to contribute to keeping global warming to 1.5°C. The Climate Change Response (Zero Carbon) Amendment Bill was passed by Parliament in 2019. Incredibly, some of our most important legislation on climate change came about because of a grassroots campaign and the fact that a group of young people were brave enough to dream it up.

Activist and academic Lisa McLaren was the national convenor for the Zero Carbon Campaign Act for four years. She talks about the process:

So, it was incredibly hard to make climate law sexy – or even just something that people want to get involved with. We designed a law with a policy reference group which was made up of a lot of different experts but, at the same time, we were going out and getting public support. We just started talking to people and went out and did a bunch of presentations around why we thought climate law was a good idea. We met with MPs from all across the political spectrum, saying why they should be backing this once we designed it and got it into their hands. And we really targeted the youth political party wings because we thought if anyone could convince their political party, it was them. That was probably one of the key turning points for the campaign and was when people started to take notice, when the Young Nats publicly backed the idea for a Zero Carbon Act.

Hundreds of volunteers helped out to campaign for the Zero Carbon Act and over 10,000 signatures were collected to be presented to Members of Parliament before the second reading of the Bill. Lisa explained some of the strategies Generation Zero used to get people on board:

There were a few tactics that we used to get people engaged. One of those was 'Adopt an MP'. So, we got our volunteers, or anyone that was interested, to sign up to adopt their local MP and to politely harass them as much as possible – go and meet with them, go and give them cookies, go and have a chat with them and ask them to support the Zero Carbon Act, and go and have a conversation with them around why that's a good idea. So, that was alongside our lobbying by Gen Zero members and that was more community based. We also did the 'Elbow your Elders' collaboration with School Strike, so, getting young people to have conversations with elders in their lives around why they should care.

The success of the Zero Carbon Act is monumental for youth political participation in Aotearoa New Zealand. Lisa explains:

I think that says a lot about how our civics is designed – it's not designed to let young people in, it's not designed to take them seriously, and it's not welcoming to young people in any way. It's very technical, it's very 'old boys' club' and very Pākehā-centric. But I think the power of the Zero Carbon Act has shown that young people do know their stuff and can play a major role in shaping how society functions and how we respond to the climate crisis.

Te Ara Whatu and international indigenous sovereignty

Te Ara Whatu are a group of indigenous rangatahi from Aotearoa New Zealand and across the Pacific that works in the field of climate justice and indigenous sovereignty. The group does incredible work both on our shores and internationally, especially in terms of international indigenous solidarity. Tiana Jakicevich from Te Ara Whatu explains:

What you see in the international arena is that you have indigenous peoples from quite literally all corners of the earth, from the Ecuadorian Amazon to the Arctic, to Africa, to Aotearoa, to the Pacific, from anywhere and everywhere that you can imagine, we all work in tandem, and we all work in solidarity. Unlike a lot of people we're not interest holders in solving the climate crisis, we're rights holders and we, for starters, have the solutions to the climate crisis, and second have been already protecting so much of the biodiversity that the world needs to survive.

Some of the mahi Te Ara Whatu does domestically involves holding wānanga for indigenous rangatahi across Aotearoa New Zealand to learn more about te taiao, connect and kōrero with other young people, and learn from other climate advocates. Tiana talks about the impact of these wānanga:

It's heartwarming because there's so many Māori and indigenous rangatahi that know that they're indigenous, that know that they're Māori but aren't connected to their whenua, aren't connected to their marae, hapū, iwi, and so often join or try and come into kaupapa like this and it might be their first taste of te ao Māori. So, what's really heartwarming is being able to help build the connections and give them the tools to be able to connect back home to where they come from [and] be able to stand on their tūrangawaewae.

Tiana also explains the paramount importance of decolonisation and re-indigenisation to solving the climate crisis. Worldwide, indigenous peoples make up about five per cent of the global population, hold roughly 20 per cent of their territories, and yet protect more than 80 per cent of the world's biodiversity. Indigenous peoples hold many of the solutions to us surviving this climate crisis and in many cases are already working with nature, with te taiao, to protect our earth. However, all too often indigenous peoples are kept out of conversations and decisions or consulted briefly on issues rather than being treated like meaningful partners. Tiana elaborates on this:

Our systems of science won't work at a table that's not ours. Our solutions aren't chocolate chips to be added to an already baked pie. Our ways of being are never going to be able to create the change that is fundamentally required to solve this climate crisis unless we start talking about the relinquishment of power from states, or even states utilising their responsibility to hold institutions accountable for the destruction and damage that they're causing the environment. Will that happen in my lifetime? Honestly, I'm not sure.

Climate change is an issue that affects and connects us all. Tiana talks about the intersectionality of climate justice:

People think that the climate crisis is like siloed into reducing emissions and I'm like it's not! Climate justice is social justice, it's disabilities justice, it's queer justice, it's all these things all wrapped into being able to enable people, ngā tangata o Aotearoa, all the people of Aotearoa, to live as their truest self in right relationship with the land in a way that is mana enhancing for all people, for plants, for animals, for humans.

School Strike 4 Climate and the fight for our lives

After leaving high school, Kāpiti coast teenager (current Kāpiti Coast District Councillor) Sophie Handford started the School Strike 4 Climate (SS4C) movement that took Aotearoa New Zealand's streets by storm. She retells the beginning of her story:

At the end of 2018, I decided not to go to uni and then that kinda lead me down a path of having a gap year and during that year having seen what was happening overseas with the strike movement I was like – wow, I wonder if we've got anything like that happening in New Zealand? So, my first step for trying to get something off the ground – 'cause I've been passionate about the environment since way [back] – but the first thing I did was to get in touch with other organisations in the climate space, like Generation Zero, 350 Aotearoa, Pacific Climate Warriors, and Te Ara

Whatu. So, I got in touch with them and was like – okay, has any one thought of doing this? Is it on your radar? And is it something that you've kinda had groups with other organisations about this or started to put together some demands? And they were all like, 'no, not really'. So, I was like okay, this is a new space then. This is an untapped space and there's an opportunity for young people.

So, Sophie engaged a team of five young people to set up the movement, which quickly grew to a national team of more than 60 people involved in organising. SS4C held their first strike on 15 March 2019, inviting students to skip class for the day and join protests all around the country, including outside Parliament in Te Whanganui-a-Tara Wellington. Young people called for extensive climate action from politicians and decision-makers. In response, at that first strike in March in Wellington, Finance Minister and Deputy Prime Minister Grant Robertson said: *'There's an old saying that the best time to plant a tree is 30 years ago, and the second-best time is today. You have planted that tree today and we are listening.'*

Examples of signs at a SS4C protest
Illustration by Ursula Palmer Steeds

The School Strike 4 Climate movement continued to flourish, holding more national strikes on 24 May 2019, 27 September 2019 and 9 April 2021. There was also an Online Strike 4 Climate held on 15 May 2020. During the 27 September strike the movement delivered 'An Open Letter from the Youth of Aotearoa' with over 12,200 signatures to the House of Representatives. The organisers report that over 170,000 people from all around Aotearoa New Zealand joined the strike that day. Sophie explains what it felt like to be part of mobilising a crowd of that size:

Even though we're a small group of young people from across the country with next to no money and literally we have like eight-year-olds in our organising group – and people would look at that and be like nope, there's no way that they could be a part of mobilising that many people. But it just comes down to the passion and determination of everyone involved in the climate movement. And especially in what I've seen from being involved in School Strike 4 Climate – the amount of passion that every single young person involved in that has, led to that many people being able to find out the strike was on and then actually feel empowered to come and march with us. [. . .] People who are business owners or workers or young people, parents, grandparents, scientists – all of those people walking alongside each other is really important because it shows climate change is an issue which doesn't have boundaries. Everyone needs to have their voice heard and be a part of the conversation.

Students for Climate Solutions and taking the government to court

A group of students have launched a judicial review case in the Wellington High Court challenging Energy Minister Hon Dr Megan Woods's decision to grant two new onshore oil and gas exploration permits for the Taranaki region. In 2018, all offshore oil and gas exploration was banned in Aotearoa New Zealand, however, it was signalled that applications for new onshore oil and gas exploration permits would continue for at least the following three years. Students for Climate Solutions argue that this decision was inconsistent with the Zero Carbon Act and the Paris Agreement. Rilke (Ri) Comer, Co-Founder of Students for Climate Solutions and 2022 Co-President of Te Herenga Waka Victoria University's Climate Clinic group, explains how this began:

Climate Clinic exploded in July when we had a meeting with Generation Zero, almost accidentally. They had a bunch of projects coming up, and we did too, especially with the RMA reforms. So, we asked if we could tag team anything – what can we help you with, what can you help us with? And at this meeting Alison Anitawaru Cole and her dog Kurī showed up. So, we met her, and she told us all these amazing things about herself, and we were like oh my god – you know in cartoons when characters go bug-eyed? Kinda like that. So, she's like, are you guys mainly law and geography students? And we're like, yeah that's our whole shtick. She goes: where have you been all my life? I've just qualified for the bar here, I'm going into climate litigation, I have like eight cases launching, and I need research assistants and associates and potentially claimants, can you do that? And we're like, can we do that? We're made for that!

The group spent four months researching, consulting with people, and making their own incorporated society so that they could take the government to court. It was a steep learning curve for the group of (predominantly) law students – *'Like, sifting through IPCC reports is not what I want to do with my weekend, especially for no money whatsoever,'* says Ri. In their judicial review case, a legal process meaning that the Judge will review the decisions made by the government and whether they were legal or if they, as the students argue, breached our legal obligations to the Zero Carbon Act and the Paris Agreement. The students also argue that the granting of permits was unreasonable. Ri says:

Legal unreasonableness is a really high threshold to prove; almost nothing qualifies for it. We're hoping to set a precedent that ignoring the foremost unequivocal science in the world which states that we cannot keep extracting and burning fossil fuels, meets that threshold of ridiculously unreasonable.

Ri speaks of the harsh reality of being a climate activist and growing up as a young person today with the threat of global warming influencing how you see and what you hope for your future – *'I think I'm in a pretty constant state of climate burnout.'* However, they also have hope:

I think when I am motivated by fear I probably get less done because I'm so scared that what I'm doing isn't of a quality that it needs to be, or isn't good enough, or isn't happening at the right time. But when I'm motivated by whatever hope I see glimmering through I think I do get more done because I think there's a better world out there, so to speak, and I think other people are working just as hard, if not harder, to make that happen.

We must be kaitiaki to our planet. We must be kind. We must make sustainable change. The effects of climate change threaten to be catastrophic to humanity. We have the chance to act now – the solutions are at our fingertips while the world burns at our feet. In many ways our current political and legal systems are not equipped to deal with the challenge: three-year democratic election cycles do not seem to incentivise long-term solutions and actions and the current machinery of international climate law does not seem efficient or adequate. Our planet has faced many changes in climate before, but current anthropogenic climate change is the most significant threat that humankind has faced so far.

Are we up to the challenge?

References
Future Earth, The Earth League, WCRP *10 New Insights in Climate Science 2021* (Stockholm, 2021); Intergovernmental Panel on Climate Change *Climate Change 2021 The Physical Science Basis: Working Group I Contribution to the Sixth Assessment Report of the Intergovernmental Panel on Climate Change – Summary for Policymakers* (IPCC, Switzerland, 2021); Dave Lowe *The Alarmist-Fifty Years measuring Climate change* (Victoria University Press, Wellington, 2021).

Additional resources
Extensive information about the UNFCCC, COPs, Kyoto Protocol, Doha Amendment, Paris Agreement, and Glasgow Climate Pact is available at: https://unfccc.int/
Sir David Attenborough's Address to World Leaders at COP26 is available at: https://www.youtube.com/watch?v=qjq4VWdZhq8
Vinisha Umashankar's Address to World Leaders at COP26 is available at: https://www.youtube.com/watch?v=zvLD6waVlkk
Greta Thunberg's speech at the Fridays for Future rally in Glasgow, November 2021 is available at: https://www.youtube.com/watch?v=BNDVJgL_ECg

A profound thank you to Lisa McLaren, Tiana Jakicevich, Sophie Handford, and Rilke Comer for the interviews featured in this chapter as well as their incredible climate justice mahi, wisdom, and for taking the time to kōrero.

38 Rangatahi

Politics is when people, by virtue of wanting to be in power and make important decisions, are allowed to be in power and make important decisions. It's good because they're always arguing about how we can be doing things better, but it's bad because they're always too busy arguing to actually action anything. —Kate Morris, 20

Politics is what determines every aspect of our lives. —Monica Lim, 20

Politics to me is a responsibility to fight for my tupuna who weren't recognised by these political systems, and for my mokopuna so that they can be protected within te ao Māori and te ao Pākehā.
—Ella Rigby-Crayford, 17

Politics is the act of making decisions that affect wider groups, environments, or contexts beyond your own. —Hannah Pym, 22

Politics is representative parties and elected officials coming together to express their communities' ideas on how to improve our way of life in society. —Anya Khalid, 20

Politics is an argument that we've normalised as a society.
—William Hall, 19

Politics is the fight for rights, the pain of not being heard, the strain of yelling for years and for falling on deaf ears. —Ivan Cantwell, 18

To me, politics is underpinned by involvement in and awareness of our social climate. It's interesting to see how different groups can have varying effects on politics based on their own interests and what mobilises them.
—Rhea Dias, 21

Politics is the philosophy of governance and its consequences.
—Fraser McConnell, 20

Politics is a relatively complicated game that is significantly more important than Monopoly but possibly less important than UNO. —Holly Kennedy, 23

Politics is, unfortunately, one of the few ways to make real change in Aotearoa. In order to genuinely improve the future of Aotearoa for my generation and those generations to come, I keep finding myself coming back to politics. —George Hobson, 18

To me, politics is the nonsensical mess that governs all our futures.
—Amos Duthie, 19

Young people have a reputation for being disengaged from politics. They don't care, they can't be bothered, they're too dumb to understand, and they'd rather waste time on their phones. However, a quick look into the history of student protests, the amount of young people furious and fearing for their lives because of climate change, and constant complaints about the student loan process and cost-of-living dispels this myth. It is true that rangatahi are less likely to engage in the traditional political structures such as by joining a political party or voting. However, this does not mean that they don't care – nor does it mean that young people aren't finding their own unique ways to engage with politics. Sylvia Nissen's study into student political action in Aotearoa New Zealand reports that young people *feel "ignored", "powerless" and "alienated" by a professional political elite perceived to be pursuing a narrow, self-serving agenda'*.

Why would you engage with a system if you don't feel like your voice will be heard?

Apathy? Engagement? Cynicism? Protest?

Youth voter turnout has always been low in Aotearoa New Zealand. In the 2020 General Election, 78 per cent of 18–24 year olds and 74 per cent of 25–29 year olds who were enrolled voted. This compares to 89 per cent of those aged 65–69 and 87 per cent of people aged 70 or older. And this is only the data for people who were enrolled to vote. It is estimated that by June 2020 only 68.9 per cent of those between 18–24 were enrolled. We see similar trends worldwide. Whereas older generations have grown up experiencing a higher level of trust in democratic institutions and politicians, youth are being born into a climate of distrust and critique. Young people in Aotearoa New Zealand are not being brought up with the attitude that politicians will take care of them, but instead with the consequences of a warming planet, fear they won't ever be able to afford a house, and the prominence of critical movements such as #MeToo and #BLM pointing out long-existing inequalities.

Nonetheless, many young people are extremely passionate about different political issues. The Zero Carbon Act 2019, some of our most important climate change legislation, was first brainstormed and drafted by Generation Zero, a group of mostly 20-somethings; Te Herenga Waka Victoria University of Wellington students held a rent strike after being asked to pay for rooms they couldn't stay in during the Covid-19 pandemic; in 2021, 22-year-old Alice Mander set up the National Disabled Students' Association to dismantle barriers for disabled tauira; 14-year-old Leah Bell and 16-year-old Waimarama Anderson set up a petition to commemorate the Land Wars and have its history taught in schools in 2016; there are currently 30 local councillors under 30 years old, some elected while still in their teens.

There are many valid reasons for young people's growing disillusionment with the current political systems. Most youth see traditional party politics as something separate from them, as part of the elite political sphere, rather than something they can personally become involved in. Rangatahi may not feel like they have the necessary skills to engage in the political process. It's not like submitting in local government consultations, figuring out who to vote for, or even understanding how the system works is made easy for 16-year-olds. And where is the civics education in schools to help young people with this? Many young people simply do not know that they can become part of a political party or what a select committee is. This is not their fault. Most political institutions tend to be inaccessible. Rangatahi may also be facing a large amount of pressure at this stage in their lives, all of which act as barriers to political participation. Scholar Sylvia Nissen explains:

There is a double standard here that needs to be acknowledged. Students are expected to be politically 'engaged' with processes that are not necessarily responsive to their views. They are told to 'make a difference', while taking on high levels of debt to pay for their education, working long hours to meet week-to-week expenses and worrying about the future implications of their actions. And they are encouraged to 'be the change', while finding it challenging to make friends at university and experiencing worry that they are not 'enough'.

One of the most significant obstacles to youth political participation is the lack of civics education in Aotearoa New Zealand. Before even considering political action, people need to have the knowledge to be able to do this, and to believe that participation is worthwhile. Because of the historical low turnout rates among youth, campaigning wannabe-politicians don't often focus their efforts towards reaching young people, and, in a vicious circle, that means that young people often don't feel like they know enough about the candidates running to make an informed vote. Topics such as citizenship education and political science can be incorporated as part of social science courses in schools, however, there is currently no requirement that these be taught.

Formal participation

Youth Parliament

Every three years, a Youth Parliament is held. About 140 rangatahi from all around the country participate as Youth MPs, Youth Press Gallery members, and one Youth Clerk in a replication of the Parliamentary process. The programme currently includes a two-day event at Parliament as well as a six-month long tenure, which may include activities such as completing their own community project or attending an event with their MP. During the two-day event, Youth MPs will act as real MPs do, engaging in issues that are important to them through mock replications of debates, select committees, and question time. The Youth Press Gallery members will report on these activities and learn from political journalists in the process. The Youth Clerk role was first introduced for 2022 and will support the running of the Youth Parliament with the opportunity to learn more about how Parliament works from the Clerk of the House of Representatives.

Azaria Howell is currently studying political communication at university and wants to become a press gallery journalist. She speaks about how her experiences with Youth Parliament were part of what sparked this passion:

Youth Parliament was a life-changing experience. As a Youth MP, I had a fascinating time in Wellington learning about New Zealand's political system first hand by speaking on legislation, sitting in general debate, and working with my colleagues in my chosen select committee. I was able to experience the inner workings of Parliament and gain real experience and insight as well as meet other politically-interested young people. I also worked to 'shadow' my selected Member of Parliament, seeing what politicians do on a day-to-day basis. It greatly enhanced my passion for politics and my community.

Youth wings of political parties

In Aotearoa New Zealand, many of our major political parties have their own youth wings, such as Young Labour, Young Nationals, Young ACT, Young Greens, and Young New Zealand First. These youth wings often host events, run campaigns, and develop policies of their own, independent of their associated political party. They often also make up dedicated volunteer bases for their political party and rally support for the party from young people, particularly at university events and O-weeks, or through supporting election campaigns. Any young person can become a member of a youth wing and there are many levels of engagement – from running for leadership positions within the wing to attending a couple of events or volunteering to go door knocking one time.

Youth councils

Most local councils around Aotearoa New Zealand run youth council programmes to engage rangatahi in the inner workings of local government. These forums provide important representation for young people to share their opinions, concerns, and issues with councillors and work towards making a difference. Youth councils will run regular meetings, make submissions on local government policy, work on projects that impact rangatahi in their communities, create petitions, and more. If you have a youth council in your area you can go along to any of their open meetings or think about becoming a member yourself. Unfortunately, there are still areas of Aotearoa New Zealand that do not have youth councils set up – you can always contact your local council about the possibility of setting one up.

Current Wellington City Youth Council member Henry Lockhart describes his experience:

I love being part of a Youth Council. Being passionate about politics, it is great to have an avenue to bring a much needed youth perspective to the Council table and learn more about local government myself. Youth Councils can ensure that a youth perspective is always brought to the Council's attention at some stage of the process. This is especially valuable given the highly inequitable voting rates by age and dominance of residents' associations (who largely represent older home-owning residents) in submission hearings.

Rito o te Pāremata – Parliament's youth reference group

Rito is a recent innovation of Parliament's. Rito is a youth reference group that was created in 2020 to change how Parliament connects and works with rangatahi. The group attends workshops at Parliament and members have the opportunity to work on a project aimed at increasing youth engagement with parliamentary politics. The 2020 Rito group created a short film series called 'Rarapa: Shining a light on our democracy' which are short clips educating people on ways they can participate politically and telling stories of young people that have made a difference.

Alternative participation

Young people are engaging in politics in new ways, such as through social media. The digital world allows rangatahi to access information and news about politics, and social media offers a platform that is profoundly interactive. When the first step in joining a political movement is as easy as sharing a post with a certain hashtag or becoming a member of a Facebook group, political participation can easily find its way into many peoples' lives. Petitions can spread like wildfire online and offer an easy route to action for youth. Rangatahi can create digital networks of like-minded peers from around the globe and connect on issues that affect us all. Although the term 'slacktivism' has been coined to dismiss political action through social media, online petitions, or similar as lazy, there is a role for this type of engagement. Online activism offers an avenue that is much more accessible for disabled people and is an easy and simple way for people to engage with what matters to them. You don't have to spend hours researching and start a campaign or protest in the streets for your voice to matter.

One potential development in political participation that may appeal to young people is the idea of eVoting. This would enable people to vote in elections simply by using a device connected to the internet. In 2004, the Electoral Commission Te Kaitiaki Take Kōwhiri investigated the possibility and developed a long-term strategy for eVoting. The Minister of Justice at the time, Hon Annette King planned to trial telephone and eVoting for blind or disabled people from 2014. However, the trial did not go ahead due to security and privacy concerns from the government Cyber Security Bureau Te Tira Tiaki and the Electoral Commission Te Kaitiaki Take Kōwhiri. However, if the technology is developed to make eVoting a secure option we may see it in elections in the future.

In her research, Sylvia Nissen explains: *'In our conversations students spoke with enthusiasm about the political issues that mattered to them, even if they might not necessarily describe themselves as 'political'.'* Instead of engaging with the political system as a whole, rangatahi may prefer to simply focus on the issues that hit home the most for them, whether it be inequality, transport, LGBTQIA+ issues, environmental issues, social connection, racism, or poverty. Young people may not see activities like beach clean ups or calling out their friend's racist comments as inherently political – but politics isn't just what happens in the marble buildings in Pipitea. Instead of joining formal political groups, such as Youth Wings, rangatahi now might be more aligned with joining issue-focused community groups or politically focused university and student clubs.

Passionate environmentalist and Chief Policy Lead at Forest & Bird Youth, George Hobson, explains what he sees as the role of such groups and organisations:

The youth voice in politics is so crucially important, and yet so often overlooked. We are the only ones who are able to truly view issues from an intergenerational perspective, and therefore our opinions must be heard. Organisations like Forest & Bird Youth are so important, because they give a voice to rangatahi who otherwise wouldn't be heard by decision makers. And they provide an incredible sense of community; it can be pretty reassuring to know that there are other people who think and feel the same way you do.

Lowering the voting age

There is increasing public debate about whether or not the voting age should be lowered to 16. The legal voting age is a reserved provision of the Electoral Act 1993 and so it would need a majority vote of 75 per cent of the House of Representatives or a referendum carried by a majority for it to change. Widespread support across political parties does not currently seem likely. The Make it 16 campaign was launched in 2019 by a group of young people who met while attending the Youth Parliament and now works to advocate for a change in voting age. In an article she wrote for the *Spinoff*, Co-Director of the project Gina Dao-McLay asks:

Young people will be impacted the most by decisions made on how Aotearoa will recover and rebuild from Covid-19. The statistics show newly unemployed people are mainly rangatahi, so why don't we have a say at this election on who our representatives are that will be making these important decisions on our future?

In Aotearoa New Zealand, 16 year-olds can drive, buy a chainsaw, own a gun, and consent to sex. They can also pay taxes – and yet do not get a say as to where their tax money goes. They can leave school and go to work. If unemployed, their interest in government decisions would be quickened. Some consistency with other rights and responsiblities seems fair. Opponents say young people lack the political maturity, however, allowing young people to vote at 16 would encourage them to be more interested in civics education at school and to think about the choices available. Stimulating interest early may prevent the decline of particpation in voting by adults. The history of the vote in liberal democracies historically has been that it was restricted. Women could not vote in Aotearoa New Zealand until 1893 and could not stand as candidates until 1919. Early in our history there were property qualifications to be satisfied before a person was eligible to vote. The most powerful argument, however, lies in the fact that decisions made now or not made on such vital issues as climate change will affect the lives of the young to a much greater degree than those of older people. There are issues of generational fairness here. Another question to consider is if it should be compulsory to vote at general elections, as it is in Australia?

The stereotype of youth apathy does not hold up against the reality of young people's immense passions for their futures. It is up to our political system to adapt rather than expecting youth to adapt to outdated and inaccessible platforms. It's time for rangatahi to shape their own paths.

So, in the wise words of Sophie Handford, the School Strike 4 Climate National Coordinator:

Sorry adults! You're more than welcome to participate, but we're leading this one!

In December 2021 the Court of Appeal announced its decision on the case brought before the courts by the Make it 16 group. They sought a declaration of inconsistency from the court that the restriction to 18 was inconsistent with the Bill of Rights Act provision that prohibited discrimination on the ground of age. The court held while the provision was a limitation on the right, it was not inconsistent because it could be justified as being reasonable in a free and democratic society. But that burden had not been met by the Crown. The Court's decision rests not on a positive finding that discrimination on grounds of age cannot be justified but rather on a failure to attempt to justify it. The matter is intensely and quintessentially political involving the democratic process itself. Further, the matter is much in the public arena already, including being part of a recently announced review of electoral law. Given the context, the Court chose to exercise restraint. No declaration was issued. Thus, the issue remains open.

References

Sylvia Nissen *Student Political Action in New Zealand* (Bridget Williams Books, Wellington, 2019); Veronica Tawhai 'Youth Engagement' in Janine Hayward (ed) *New Zealand Government and Politics* 6th edition (Oxford University Press, 2015); Kyle Daniel Mathijssen Whitfield *Local Government and youth voter turnout: Obstacles and solutions for Aotearoa New Zealand* (thesis, Otago University, 2020); Gina Dao-McLay *I'm 17 and I'm ready to vote. Here's why I should count in this year's election* (The Spinoff, June 18 2020) https://thespinoff.co.nz/politics/18-06-2020/im-17-and-im-ready-to-vote-heres-why-i-should-count-in-this-years-election
Electoral Commission *Jump in youth voting* (2020): https://elections.nz/media-and-news/2020/jump-in-youth-voting/
Make it 16 Incorporated v Attorney-General [NZCA] 681(14 December 2021) https://www.courtsofnz.govt.nz/assets/cases/2021/2021-NZCA-681.pdf

Additional information
Youth Parliament: https://www.parliament.nz/en/get-involved/youth-parliament-2022/
Youth wings: https://thespinoff.co.nz/authors/youth-wings
Youth councils:https://www.myd.govt.nz/young-people/youth-councils-local-government.html
Rito: https://www.parliament.nz/en/get-involved/features/attention-young-kiwis-of-aotearoa/
Make it 16: https://makeit16.org.nz/

A profound thank you to the many young people who provided quotes for this chapter: Kate Morris, Monica Lim, Ella Rigby-Crayford, Hannah Pym, Anya Khalid, William Hall, Ivan Cantwell, Rhea Dias, Fraser McConnell, Holly Kennedy, George Hobson, Amos Duthie, Azaria Howell, Henry Lockhart and Sophie Handford.

39 Equality, inclusion and decolonisation

In this chapter we briefly outline some of the social issues that may need attention through the democratic process in Aotearoa New Zealand in the future. What do you see when you look to the future? What do you want to see happen on the shores of Te Ika-a-Māui and Te Waipounamu? What is the Aotearoa New Zealand you'd like to see?

That hapū and iwi are strong collectives with revitalised and vibrant systems relating to atua, whenua, moana, te reo, tikanga, tapu, mahi toi, mātauranga, hauora and social organisation – anchored in the exercise of tino rangatiratanga. —Safari Hynes, tauira

I'd love to see an Aotearoa where we fully embrace and celebrate diversity in all aspects of life. —Molly Doyle, filmmaker

The Good Bitches Baking mission is to make Aotearoa the kindest place on earth. Our view of this future is one where kindness is commonplace, people are thoughtful and noticing of others' needs, and equitable inclusion and access is the default rather than the aspiration.
—Katy Rowden, General Manager, Good Bitches Baking

E manako ana au, a tōnā wā, ka arero Māori katoa a Aotearoa. Ma reira e mana ai ngā hekenga tōtā a kui, a koro mā. Ka mutu, ka whai wāhi mai ngā uri whakaheke, ā, haere ake nei, ki ngā hua nui katoa o te ao Māori. —Watene Campbell, tauira

The Aotearoa we see today is one where young people can usually look and find someone like them who is accomplishing great things. One day te whāriki o Aotearoa will be so richly woven with diversity that young people won't even have to look for it anymore. —Rosie van Beusekom, stripper

An Aotearoa where Te Tiriti is upheld, where all can afford to live peacefully, and where our history is openly and honestly reflected upon,

accepted, and – where appropriate – celebrated. Āe, that is the Aotearoa I would like to see.
—Michael Turnbull, 2020 President of Te Herenga Waka Victoria University of Wellington Students' Association (VUWSA)

I hope to one day see an Aotearoa New Zealand that is so accepting of diversity, the success, cultures, and presence of ALL peoples becomes banal.
—Edwina Harris, Pasifika student

As an Australian in New Zealand I would love to see Aotearoa New Zealand act as a signpost for Australia, leading the way in becoming more socially and economically sustainable (e.g. with renewable energy and housing). —Tim Dench, Zoo educator

The National Disabled Students Association wants to see a future where everyone is supported to get equal opportunities in life. Importantly, our future Aotearoa is one in which disabled students are seen and treated as meaningful contributors to the development of a more equitable society.
—Alice Mandler, founder and President of the National Disabled Students Association

What you have been reading is a survival guide to democracy in Aotearoa New Zealand. This book has aimed to unravel the mysteries of our political system and explain how you, as a member of this democracy, can navigate the political world and influence the decisions made by government. Now it's your turn to take what you've learnt and do something about it. What is the Aotearoa New Zealand that you'd like to *build* and how can you achieve this? Do you think more should be done to make things fair, equal, and inclusive? Do you think tangata whenua are getting a fair go? Do you think Aotearoa New Zealand is a free, independent state? What are your dreams for the future and how can we get there?

In/Equality

Despite our carefully curated image of a clean and green country which promises everyone a fair go, inequity lurks on our shores. Structural discrimination as defined by the Public Service Commission Te Kawa Mataaho, occurs *'when an entire network of rules and practices*

Connection and aroha
Illustration by Tayla Mereana Hartemink

disadvantages less empowered groups while serving at the same time to advantage the dominant group, and this is cemented in the way our State is organised and run. Our political system is based on the British Westminster system. Can it be changed? Should it be changed?

Aotearoa New Zealand has a fantastically diverse population of a little over five million people. According to the 2018 census, 70.2 per cent of our population is Pākehā/European, 16.5 per cent is Māori, 15.1 per cent is Asian, and 8.1 per cent is Pasifika. Around 27 per cent of the people who live here were born overseas. In June 2020, Statistics New Zealand Tatauranga Aotearoa reported that 4.2 per cent of adults in Aotearoa New Zealand are part of the LGBTQIA+ community and 0.8 per cent of adults are transgender or non-binary. The 2013 Disability Survey found that 24 per cent of people in Aotearoa New Zealand are disabled. In 2018, 2,264,601 people responded to the census reporting that they had no religion, while 314,913 people responded Anglican, 57, 276 reported Islam (not further defined), 40,908 people responded Sikhism, 43,821 identified with Rātana, 12,336 with Ringatū, and 3,348 responded Judaism (not further defined). As well, there are, apparently, 20,409 Jedis in Aotearoa New Zealand, a philosophy popularised by the sci-fi film series Star Wars.

Māori are tangata whenua of Aotearoa New Zealand. The continual repercussions of colonisation in this country have caused significant harms and have led to many inequities for Māori to this day. For example, Māori have the worst health outcomes of any ethnic group in Aotearoa New Zealand and the life expectancy for Māori is about eight or nine years less than non-Māori, and Māori have a higher disability rate. It is also widely known that Māori are overrepresented in our justice system: 52.5 per cent of prisoners are Māori as of September 2021. Māori children are also more likely to live in low-income houses than Pākehā children. These statistics tell an unsettling tale of institutional racism in Aotearoa New Zealand.

Aotearoa New Zealand has a relationship with the Pacific islands that stretches back hundreds of years. Tagata o le Pasifika from the islands of Niue, Tokelau and the Cook Islands are New Zealand citizens by birth. Tokelau is an Aotearoa New Zealand territory while the Cook Islands and Niue are self-governing territories in free association with Aotearoa New Zealand. Samoa was once a German territory but was administered by Aotearoa New Zealand from 1919 until 1961, first under the League

of Nations Mandate after the First World War and later as a United
Nations Trusteeship. Unlike the other islands governed by Aotearoa
New Zealand, Samoa chose to become fully independent in 1962.

Like Māori, tagata o le Pasifika often face institutionalised racism
in Aotearoa New Zealand. Pacific peoples are overrepresented in our
prison populations, have disproportionately poor health outcomes, and
Pasifika children are more likely to live in low-income households. In
2002, Aotearoa New Zealand gave a formal apology to Samoa on the
fortieth anniversary of Samoan interdependence. During this apology
then-Prime Minister Helen Clark said:

*But before coming today I have also been troubled by some unfinished
business. There are events in our past which have been little known in New
Zealand, although they are well known in Samoa.*

*Those events relate to the inept and incompetent early administration
of Samoa by New Zealand. In recent weeks as we have been preparing
to come to Samoa, there has been a focus on those historic events, and the
news has been a revelation to many New Zealanders.*

*That focus has come about because my government believes that
reconciliation is important in building strong relationships. It is important
to us to acknowledge tragic events which caused great pain and sorrow in
Samoa.*

Clark apologised for specific actions of the Aotearoa New Zealand
colonial administration such as allowing a ship with passengers who
had influenza to dock in Apia in 1918 which caused an outbreak of
influenza in Samoa where over 20 per cent of the population died. She
also apologised for shootings by the New Zealand Police arising from
the Mau movement in 1929 in which one New Zealand policeman and
11 Samoans were killed. In 2021 Aotearoa New Zealand apologised
for the Dawn Raids in which New Zealand Police Ngā Pirihimana O
Aotearoa entered homes and stopped people on the street to ask for visas
and passports – these were racially targeted. There is still more to be
done to recognise Aotearoa New Zealand's colonial injustices against
the Pacific Islands.

Asian people make up the third largest ethnic group in Aotearoa New
Zealand. The majority of our Asian immigrants come from India and
China. In 2020, Chinese and Japanese were the most popular foreign

language subjects at NCEA Level 3. By 2038, Statistics New Zealand Tatauranga Aotearoa predicts that there will be more people of Asian descent than Māori in this country. However, multiple studies have found that Asian people report experiencing discrimination more than any other ethnic group in Aotearoa New Zealand.

LGBTQIA+, people from the 'rainbow' communities, also face significant discrimination and unsafeness in Aotearoa New Zealand. However, there have been some significant legal successes for the community – the Homosexual Law Reform Act decriminalised consensual sex between men aged 16 and over in 1986, and The Marriage (Definition of Marriage) Amendment Act passed in 2013, allowing same-sex couples to get married. At the date this is being written, conversion therapy (any attempts to change someone's sexuality or gender identity) is currently legal in Aotearoa New Zealand, although the Conversion Practices Prohibition Legislation Bill, which would ban conversion therapy, is going through the legislative process. More than 100,000 people made select committee submissions to this Bill, which is more than any piece of legislation has ever received in history. In 2021, Lonely Planet rated Aotearoa New Zealand second on its list of 'The most gay-friendly places on the planet'. Despite this, LGBTQIA+ people are significantly more likely to experience bullying or social exclusion and face mental health issues.

Disabled people also suffer from these issues. Aotearoa New Zealand commonly uses the United Nations definition of disability: *'Persons with disabilities include those who have long-term physical, mental, intellectual or sensory impairments which in interaction with various barriers may hinder their full and effective participation in society on an equal basis with others.'* The social model of disability holds that people are disadvantaged or impaired by societal barriers and inaccessibility, rather than their disability itself. About a quarter of the people in Aotearoa New Zealand have one or more disabilities – or 11 per cent of children (14 per cent of Māori children), 21 per cent of young and working aged people (32 per cent of Māori young and working age), and 59 per cent of seniors (62 per cent of Māori seniors) according to the New Zealand Health and Disability System Review Hauora Manaaki ki Aotearoa Whānui.

Another cause for inequality is economic. Journalist and researcher Max Rashbrooke explains in *Inequality: a New Zealand Crisis:*

And this is what the numbers show:
- *New Zealand now has the widest income gaps since detailed records began in the 1980s*
- *From the mid-1980s to the mid-2000s, the gap between the rich and the rest widened faster in New Zealand than in any other developed country*
- *The average household in the top 10 per cent of New Zealand has eight times the income of one in the bottom 10 per cent*
- *The top 1 per cent of adults own 22 per cent of the country's total wealth, while the bottom half put together just over 2 per cent.*

Māori and Pasifika households are also disproportionately affected, with one in five Māori or Pasifika households living below the poverty line. A fair and inclusive Aotearoa New Zealand means that people should not have to live without access to essential goods and services.

One significant cause for inequality is our current housing crisis. According to the June 2021 Housing Affordability Report produced by CoreLogic, property values rose up to 15 per cent from January-June 2021 while household incomes only rose an average of 1 per cent in the same time period. It is now taking an average of 10 years for first-home buyers to save for a deposit. More than a third of households in Aotearoa New Zealand rent, up from only a quarter of households in 1991. Statistics New Zealand Tatauranga Aotearoa found that renting households were more likely to find their housing unaffordable and generally had lower standards of living for their accommodation: 40.5 per cent of renters said that their homes were sometimes damp in comparison to 25.3 per cent of homeowners and 47.4 per cent of renters and 29.7 per cent of homeowners said their home had mould. In December 2021 a garage was listed as a room for rent in Auckland Tāmaki Makaurau, featuring a photograph with a single bed next to a silver car.

Clearly, inequality persists in Aotearoa New Zealand. This trend does not appear to be currently reversing. Structural oppression, systemic discrimination, and poverty are significant problems and working towards solutions looks like an ambitious but necessary task. What action should be taken?

Inclusion and political participation

Aotearoa New Zealand is a democracy. That means that the people are in charge – that you are in charge. However, for this to function well, *all* voices must feel free to speak and know that they'll be heard. Inclusion and active participation are essential ingredients in our political system. However, as with all aspects of our society, political participation is often inaccessible and exclusionary.

Although it has historically looked more like an old boys' club, our House of Representatives is the most representative it has ever been. As of the 2020 General Election, 58 of our MPs are women, 24 are Māori, and nine are Pasifika, out of the total 120 seats. Aotearoa New Zealand also proudly sports the largest proportion of openly LGBTQIA+ members in Parliament in global history, with 11 MPs who are part of the rainbow community. Diverse representation in politics is certainly increasing, although we still have a long way to go to ensure that our Parliament accurately reflects our community. There is a notable under-representation for the Asian community, with the number of MPs being about half what the proportion of the population would warrant. The disabled community is also under-represented.

There are barriers that people might face in political participation. Lengthy documents with policy and legal jargon are enough to confuse even skilled professionals, let alone the average citizen. Disabled New Zealanders may be limited due to inaccessible voting methods and political events being held in physical inaccessible environments. Even alternative participation such as protesting is often planned without considering the needs of disabled people – protests and marches may be held in physically inaccessible locations and are often difficult for people with sensory disabilities, deaf people, and neurodiverse people. The Chamber itself, where Members of Parliament debate, is incredibly inaccessible to people with a physical disability and difficult to navigate with a mobility aid. LGBTQIA+ people may also experience systemic difficulties in terms of civic engagement.

One innovation in terms of political participation in Aotearoa New Zealand is the programme iSpeak developed and run by the Pacific Youth Leadership and Transformation (PYLAT) Trust. The iSpeak programme involves regular discussion seminars on political topics that Pacific young people can engage with. Over a short 24 minutes they cover two polarising views on the topic, give time for Pacific young people to talanoa in small groups, and then they collectively write a submission. These young people have the opportunity to consider different persspectives, ask questions, mull over the topic together, and participate as a collective. PYLAT co-founder Josiah Tualamali'i explains that:

The thing that our communities ask for constantly is for us to be together, face-to-face, and for people to not pull the punch of the information from us, 'cause so many people do that already and expect us to not have a view or have discriminatory attitudes and think we're stupid. We can be well-informed and we can influence decisions when given the right support. When we do this, Pacific young people, who typically don't participate at all, end up being the only young people who have submitted on some bills.

While there have been Māori Members of Parliament since 1867 and there are now Pasifica MPs, there is a substantial body of opinion that regards the system as still inherently colonial and exclusive. To honour te Tiriti o Waitangi our political system should reflect true partnership between tangata whenua and tangata Tiriti. Tikanga, kaupapa Māori politics, and Māori tino rangatiratanga must be acknowledged in the foundation of our State. How do you think this can be brought about?

Decolonisation

Our colonial history has done much to shape our political institutions. Are there policies we can adopt to rectify the injustices that still linger? There are many different perspectives on what decolonisation might mean in the context of Aotearoa New Zealand, and even what colonisation is in the first place. Decolonisation is about the restoration and repatriation of what was lost or stolen. But first, what is colonisation? This is a complicated subject with an enormous literature that we cannot do justice to here. In short, colonisation is: *'The act of sending people to live in and govern another country'* – Cambridge Dictionary. But there is much more to it. For us, two passages from the Māori scholar Dr Moana Jackson sums up the essence of the issue contained in the book *Imagining Decolonisation*:

Colonisation had no time for the niceties of tikanga. It fractured the hoped-for interdependence and denied the possibility of continuing Māori interdependence. The colonisers' need to impose their laws and institutions on people who already had their own allowed no room for an honourable relationship with iwi and hapū. Instead, colonisation fomented injustice: a systemic privileging of the Crown and a relationship in which it assumed it would be the sole and supreme authority.'

And then:

'Decolonisation' may not be the most appropriate word for that kind of remedy because, like colonisation, it came from somewhere else. Perhaps it could be replaced with the ethic of restoration. The use of this term would seek to replace colonisation not by merely deconstructing or culturally sensitising the attitudes and power structures that it has established, but by restoring a kawa that allows for balanced relationships based on the need for iwi and hapū independence upon which any meaningful interdependence must rest.

Our first step may simply be whakawhanaungatanga – to listen to each other and build or rebuild a sustainable Treaty relationship. What the ethic of restoration may look like depends on all of us, but a discussion is always a good place to start. We need nationwide kōrero and engagement on the Aotearoa New Zealand that we'd all like to see.

So, what do you want to see?

References
Bianca Elkington, Rebecca Kiddle, Moana Jackson, Ocean Mercier, Mike Ross, Jennie Smeaton and Amanda Thomas *Imagining Decolonisation* (Bridget Williams Books Ltd, Wellington, 2020); State Services Commission (now called the Public Service Commission Te Kawa Mataaho) *EEO Policy to 2010: Future Directions of EEO in the New Zealand Public Service* (1997); Max Rashbrooke (eds) *Inequality: A New Zealand Crisis* (Bridget Williams Books Ltd, Wellington, 2018); Max Rashbrooke *Too much money-How wealth disparities are unbalancing Aotearoa New* Zealand (Bridget Williams Books, Wellington, 2021); CoreLogic *Housing Affordability Report New Zealand| Quarter 2, 2021* (CoreLogic, Wellington/Auckland, 2021); Gloria Fraser *The Rainbow Mental Health Support Experiences Study: Summary of Findings* (Te Herenga Waka Victoria University of Wellington, Wellington, 2019); The Health and Disability System Review Hauora Manaaki ki Aotearoa ki Aotearoa Whānui *Health and Disability System Review Interim Report Pūrongo Mō Tēnei Wā* (August 2019); Dr Rogena Sterling and Kyle K.H. Tan *Diversity, Belonging and Inclusion in Aotearoa New Zealand: a review of consultation and community engagement* (The Inclusive Aotearoa

Collective Tāhono project, 2020); The Human Rights Commission Te Kāhui Tika Tangata *A fair go for all? Rite tahi tātou katoa? Addressing Structural Discrimination in Public Services* (July 2012); S. Gordon, S. Davey, A. Waa, R. Tiatia, and T. Waaka *Social Inclusion and Exclusion, Stigma and Discrimination, and the Experience of Mental Distress* (Mental Health Foundation, 2017); The Human Rights Commission Te Kāhui Tika Tangata *COVID-19 fueling discrimination against Tangata Whenua and Chinese communities* (2021); The Human Rights Commission Te Kāhui Tika Tangata *Confident, equal and proud? A discussion paper on the barriers Asians face to equality in New Zealand* (2010); Jo Smith *Aotearoa/New Zealand: An Unsettled State in a Sea of Islands* (Settler Colonial Studies, 1:1, 111–131); Statistics New Zealand Tatauranga Aotearoa *Renting vs owning in NZ* (June 2019) https://www.stats.govt.nz/infographics/renting-vs-owning-in-nz

A profound thank you to the people who provided quotes for this chapter: Safari Hynes, Molly Doyle, Rosie van Beusekom, Edwina Harris, Tim Dench, Alice Mandler, Michael Turnbull, and Katy Rowden. Thank you to Josiah Tualamali'i for incredible kōrero and for providing a quote for this chapter – your conversation helped greatly. We also acknowledge the excellent work done on content surrounding tangata o le Pasifika by Leilani Taula when she was Geoffrey Palmer's research assistant.

40. And now?

We end at the place we began. Living in a democratic society means that everyone should get a say; the governed should play a part in how they are governed. We quoted a Māori proverb or whakataukī in the first chapter. Now we quote another that speaks to the future:

Ka Pou Ruha – Ka Hao te Rangatahi
When the old net is cast aside, the new net goes fishing

Although the world of politics can sometimes seem shrouded in mystery, we hope this survival guide gives you a way to navigate it. There are many benefits to a thriving democracy in Aotearoa New Zealand. We need to be vigilant and alert to preserve and strengthen it. In a world full of uncertainty and unprecedented challenges, overseas trends show that rot and decline of democratic institutions can easily set in. The most potent force in stopping that trend is the public. As a small country we are fortunate to enjoy generous amounts of social capital, strong institutions, and a widely accepted value system. We need to nourish civic participation to keep it that way.

Our views, our engagement and our representation can help contribute to good government and sound decisions that will enhance and improve life here. A strong civil society can help to ensure that decisions are made in the public interest, not those of vested interests. These steps can assist in that aim:

- The development of a compulsory curriculum that is taught to every child in school that includes: a) the history of Aotearoa New Zealand, who we are, where we came from, and how that relates to the present, b) the political system, because in order to take part and make change people need to understand how the system already functions.
- A commitment to the rule of law, an impartial and independent judiciary and an understanding of the law and the role of the courts.
- Improvement in understanding of what goes on in Parliament and the other branches of government, and in keeping the institutions of

government in good order.
- Designing and implementing an improved system of local government.
- Development of protections against the spreading of false claims and conspiracy theories that mislead people.
- An understanding of competing political philosophies and the role of the State.
- A commitment to openness and transparency.
- The promotion of human dignity, tolerance, and respect for people from diverse cultures.
- Upholding fundamental freedoms and human rights including cultural, economic, and social rights.
- Honouring the agreements made in te Tiriti o Waitangi and o He Whakaputanga te Rangatiratanga o Nu Tireni.
- A commitment to fairness, tikanga Māori, equality, utu, environmental sustainability, and kaitiakitanga.
- Addressing the harms of colonialism and moving towards decolonisation.

The late Sir Michael Cullen, in his final 2021 book, best summed up the situation we are in:

We make it easy to vote and we have a system in which all political parties have to compete on a reasonably level playing field for public support. The more people actively engage in political life, in one way or another, the better the decisions made for our future are likely to be. An absence of participation is the biggest threat to democracy and our freedoms.

And there is a little more required.

We need to sort out a framework for our public philosophy that people can relate to and identify with. We need to be clear of the values this country stands for and delivers on. We need to avoid fanning divisions on the grounds of race, religion, ethnicity, or social background.

Our social values need to encourage human dignity and respect for others. While New Zealand is inhabited by people of many different cultural identities, it is necessary that a sense of community and whanaungatanga bind the whole country together. If the experience with Covid-19 has taught us anything, it is that all communities in Aotearoa

New Zealand are mutually interdependent. Hopefully the pandemic has increased belief in the values of the collective and reduced the feeling that every individual is an island.

We need to be proud of who we are and confident of our sense of national identity, but not consumed by some sort of blind nationalism that goes in extreme directions. Aotearoa New Zealand will always need to be outgoing and connected with the wider world. We need to be comfortable with our own diversity and alert to the dangers of racism and demagogues. Too many democracies in recent times have gone down the authoritarian road. Above all, the inhabitants of these islands need to believe that the government is serving the interests of the many, not the few.

Living in Aotearoa New Zealand means we inhabit a set of islands surrounded by vast oceans, with a landscape of mountains, rivers and lakes of stunning beauty. It is an environment and climate that engenders a spiritual quality and love of the outdoors. The unique flora and fauna add to the special feeling – we are known as kiwis.

Our remoteness has helped to protect us from many threats. Yet we must keep a sharp eye on international trends and engage in international diplomacy and nourish international trade.

Our size of five million people is an advantage. We can change more easily and adjust to challenges that are more difficult for more populous nations with a lesser sense of community and social cohesion. We have a similar sized population to Ireland, Denmark, the island of Sicily in Italy, the state of Colorado in the United States or the state of Queensland in Australia. There is no point in wishing we can be a super-power.

We must learn to celebrate our unique culture and deepen and extend it. The mechanisms of government can help the plight OF many people and use the power of the State to improve things within a strong democratic framework. We need for this purpose a strong economy, with innovation, entrepreneurial flair and resilience.

But, most of all, we need you. We need to put the people back in politics, the *demos* back in *demo*cracy. To build a system that represents and works for us all.

So, get involved – it's your future.

References

Felipe Fernández-Armesto *Out of Our Minds – What We Think and How We Came to Think It* (Oneworld Publications, London, 2020)

Tips and tricky words

Politics is not always accessible. In order to help you to better understand the contents of the book – and the system of government you live under – this section outlines some helpful and easy-to-navigate resources you can go to as well as providing definitions for potentially unfamiliar terms.

Tips

Legislature

Massive amounts of information on how things work can be found on Parliament's website. However, the trick is knowing where to find it. A good place to start may be here: https://www.parliament.nz/en/visit-and-learn/how-parliament-works/

The Parliament website contains a list of all current MPs. If you click on an MP's name you will be taken to a separate page containing further information on them including their photo, where they sit in the House of Representatives, current roles and responsibilities and their contact details. You can find this here: https://www.parliament.nz/en/mps-and-electorates/members-of-parliament/

Throughout this book, we mention the names of many Acts of Parliament. All Acts and secondary legislation can be found online here: https://www.legislation.govt.nz
You can browse legislation by year or by name or simply by searching for what you are looking for.

Executive

The Department of the Prime Minister and Cabinet contains a great deal of information about how the Executive branch works. You can also nominate someone for a New Zealand honour on their website. The website is: https://dpmc.govt.nz/

The key to unlocking information about Cabinet is the Cabinet Manual. The Cabinet Manual 2017 can be found here: https://dpmc.govt.nz/sites/default/files/2017-06/cabinet-manual-2017.pdf

Judiciary

The Courts website provides information on the courts system, jury service, or even the judicial ceremonial robes. You can learn more here: https://www.courtsofnz.govt.nz/learn-about-our-courts/

You can also access judgments made by the Courts in Aotearoa New Zealand. You can access these by going to this website: https://www.courtsofnz.govt.nz/the-courts/ Simply press on the relevant Court and then 'Judgments' to access a list of recent judgments.

Tricky words

Act of Parliament: laws passed by Parliament.
Attorney-General: a minister who is the Chief Law Officer of the Crown with special responsibilities for the rule of law and the appointment of judges.
Backbencher: an MP who sits on the backbenches in the House of Representatives and is not a Minister of the Crown.
Bill: draft of a new law that will be known as a statute or Act of Parliament when it is passed by Parliament.
Beehive: the colloquial name given to the Executive wing of the parliamentary complex because of its beehive-like appearance. Ministers have their offices in the Beehive with their staff. Both the Cabinet Room and the Cabinet Committee Room are in the Beehive.
Beehive Theatrette: the theatrette room in the Executive wing of the parliamentary complex which is often used for government press conferences.
The Budget: the annual financial statement made by the Minister of Finance to the House of Representatives setting out the fiscal strategy of the government, with appropriation proposals for spending money. The statement is accompanied by a mountain of information and economic data. The Budget must be debated, examined, and passed by the House. See chapter 19.

By-election: a by-election is held when an electorate seat in the House of Representatives becomes vacant due to death or resignation. Where a list member dies or resigns that MP is replaced from the relevant party list at the time of the last general election.

Cabinet: a key-decision making group made up of the Prime Minister, the Deputy Prime Minister and other senior ministers. Not all ministers are members of Cabinet.

Cabinet committees: groups created to provide more detailed deliberation and consideration on matters relevant to Cabinet. The structure, chair, and membership of each Cabinet committee is decided by the Prime Minister.

Cabinet Manual: the guide which sets out the constitutional arrangements for Executive decision-making.

Cabinet Legislation Committee: a Cabinet committee that is responsible for considering the legislative programme, of the government, approving Bills and regulations, and more.

Cadre party: political party dominated by highly qualified or trained individuals or elites.

Caucus: The members of a party elected by Parliament. They usually meet each week in a closed meeting to decide what their parliamentary actions and tactics will be.

Coalition: an alliance or agreement between political parties.

Common law: the common law of New Zealand is the law contained in judicial decisions made by judges who follow judicial precedents in their decisions. It is not law made by Parliament. There is a substantial quantity of it. See chapter 22.

Conscience vote: votes held in Parliament where MPs vote according to their individual preferences, not in accordance with a party policy established by caucus decision.

Confidence and supply: a Cabinet must enjoy the 'confidence' of the House of Representatives, meaning in a confidence vote the majority of the House of Representatives must vote that they have confidence in the Cabinet. The government must secure 'supply' from the House to carry out the tasks of government, so it must pass budgets or appropriations. See chapter 19.

Constitution: establishes the main institutions of governance, their structures, and power. In Aotearoa New Zealand the place to start is the Constitution Act 1986, but our constitution is not codified so it is not contained in a single document and trying to find our constitution is a bit like hunting the snark.

Constitutional conventions: customary practices of political obligation generally followed but which are not usually legally binding.

Constitutional monarchy: is a state where the Head of State is a hereditary monarch (King or Queen), but the main decisions are made by elected Members of Parliament. See chapter 8.

Electorate: a geographical area from which an MP is elected to represent the people of that area in the House of Representatives. In Aotearoa New Zealand, there are electorate MPs, and list MPs – who are elected because of their position on the party's list. See chapter 13.

Entrenchment: a statute passed by Parliament that requires more than a 50 per cent majority plus one to pass it – the best example being 75 per cent, as is the case with the entrenched provisions of the Electoral Act 1993.

Executive: The branch of government that applies and actions the law. In Aotearoa New Zealand, this is the ministers, the Cabinet, and the Public Service.

Executive Council: A meeting of ministers presided over by the Governor-General that advises the Governor-General to sign various legal instruments, many of which are known as Orders in Council. See chapter 27.

Federation: a nation state with a central government that also has within it several smaller areas that have defined rights of self-government. For example, the Commonwealth of Australia and its six states and three territories that also have elected legislatures and governments.

FPP: First-Past-the-Post. Our previous electoral system in which the candidate with the most votes wins, although may not attain a majority of the total votes cast. See chapter 13.

The Gazette: the *New Zealand Gazette* is the weekly publication of the Aotearoa New Zealand Government that contains important announcements and decisions, often quite technical.

General election: an election where Members of Parliament are voted for and chosen. There is a general election every three years in Aotearoa New Zealand. See chapter 13.

Gerrymander: A process named after an early Governor of the State of Massachusetts, in which the drawing of electoral boundaries are manipulated for party political advantage by incumbent politicians. It is still common in the United States. This is not possible under electoral law in Aotearoa New Zealand because boundaries are set by the independent Boundaries Commission.

Government: governs the country. The government of the day refers to the party or group of parties (such as in a coalition or confidence and supply arrangement) that enjoy the confidence of the House of Representatives.

Governor-General: the Sovereign's representative in Aotearoa New Zealand.

Hansard: a published written record of what is said in the House of Representatives. Also known as NZPD, New Zealand Parliamentary Debates.

Head of State: The Sovereign. In the case of Aotearoa New Zealand, the Queen is our Head of State.

House of Representatives: is where elected MPs meet to debate. Parliament is the House of Representatives AND the Governor-General.

Judgment: the announcement by a judge setting out the decision and the reasons for it.

Judiciary: the branch of government authorised to make decisions on disputes sitting in courts: Judges.

Leader of the House: a minister who is responsible for the conduct of government business in the House of Representatives.

Leader of the Opposition: the leader of the largest group of MPs in the House of Representatives who are not part of the government.

Legislature: a governing body that makes laws and can amend or repeal them. In Aotearoa New Zealand this refers to Parliament.

Letters Patent: a legal proclamation by the Crown. The Office of the Governor-General of New Zealand is set up under Letters Patent.

Ministers of the Crown: the most important actors in the Executive government. Ministers are appointed by the Governor-General upon the nomination of the Prime Minister. See chapter 15.

Missionary: a person sent on a religious mission. Often refers to people sent to promote Christianity.

MMP: Mixed-Member Proportional. The electoral system in Aotearoa New Zealand, based on the system in Germany and recommended by a New Zealand Royal Commission in 1986. It replaced an electoral system known as FPP. See chapter 13.

Orders-in-Council: type of secondary legislation made by the Executive Council.

Parliament: the House of Representatives *and* the Governor-General. Parliament is the supreme law-making body. See chapter 19.

Parliamentary Counsel: the people that drafts and publishes legislation.

Parliamentary Privilege: a complicated branch of law that provides special privileges and immunities to Parliament so it can carry out its duties. Freedom of speech for MPs is one of the most important of the privileges.

Parliamentary Under-Secretaries: members of the government who have specific responsibilities similar to but less than associate ministers.

Party list: a ranked list of candidates nominated by the political party. In Aotearoa New Zealand, there are list MPs – who are elected because of their position on the party's list – and electorate MPs – who are elected by their electorate. See chapter 13.

Portfolio: a minister's area of responsibility. Ministers can hold several portfolios.

Prime Minister: the highest political post and the leader of the government.

QUANGO: Quasi-Autonomous Non-governmental Organisation. An organisation or body which is not part of the Public Service but receives financial support from the government.

Question Time: the daily procedure in the House of Representatives where MPs put specific questions to Ministers. Parliamentary questions can be either written or oral.

Regulations Review Select Committee: a select committee which is responsible for making sure the authority to make secondary legislation has been properly exercised.

Royal Assent: The Governor-General as the Head of State's representative must sign all Acts of Parliament passed by the House of Representatives in order to become law. Signing is done in accordance with ministerial advice.

Royal Commission: a type of inquiry. See chapter 25.

Secondary legislation and legal instruments: law made by entities or people other than Parliament through power delegated to them by Parliament under an Act. Secondary legislation comprises regulations, Orders-in-Council, or orders of individual ministers that have legal effect.

Secretary of Cabinet: a senior official who provides services to the Office.

Select committee: committees established by the House of Representatives to carry out tasks assigned to them by the House.

Sitting day: a day when the House of Representatives meets.

Sovereign: a supreme ruler or monarch.

Sovereignty: Sovereignty has many meanings. It can mean 'supreme power'. States have sovereign power to make law. It can also refer to the power of Parliament to make any law, sometimes known as parliamentary sovereignty.

Standing Orders of the House of Representatives: The Rules of parliamentary procedure made by the House to govern its proceeedings.

Statute law: laws passed by Parliament.

Unicameral: a legislature with only one House.

Ultra vires: a decision that was beyond the decision-maker's power

Upper house: the higher house in a bicameral legislature. Aotearoa New Zealand has a unicameral legislature without an Upper House.

Urgency: allows the legislative process to be speeded up so that a Bill can be enacted more quickly.

Westminster system: a system of government based on the English system of government.

Whips: members of a party caucus entrusted with a coordinating role, especially in relation to activities in the House of Representatives ensuring members are where they need to be at particular times. They also have a role in setting speaking order for debates, granting leave to members to be absent, and generally keeping an eye on the welfare of members who are under stress. The term comes from the 18th-century English hunting term 'whipper-in' which referred to a huntsman's assistant who drove straying hounds back to the main pack using a whip. While Whips do not use physical force in the House they do have some authority. The Green Party refers to this role within their caucus as a 'musterer'.

Māori words

Aroha: love
Hapū: kinship group, clan, tribe, subtribe
Hākari: feast
Hīkoi: march
Hui: meeting
Kaitiaki: guardian, trustee, custodian, caregiver
Kaumātua: elders in Māori society who may provide guidance to others
Kōrero: speech, narrative, discussion, conversation
Ihi: essential force, excitement, thrill, power, charm
Iwi: extended kinship group, tribe, nation, people
Mahi: work
Mana: authority, prestige, control, power, influence, status
Muru: wipe, rub off, smear, plunder
Papatūānuku: Earth, Earth mother, wife of Rangi-nui
Parihakatanga: the way of Parihaka, philosophy or symbol of peace and passive resistance
Rangatahi: youth
Rangatira: chief
Rangatiratanga: chieftanship, right to exercise authority, chiefly autonomy, self-determination
Rohe: a boundary, region, district, or territory
Taiao: world, Earth, environment
Tangata whenua: people of the land, indigenous people, people born of the whenua
Taonga: precious treasures, property goods, possession
Tapu: status of being sacred, prohibited, restricted or forbidden
Tauira: student, pupil
Tikanga: the correct or right way of doing things, law, rule or custom, customary system of values and practices
Utu: reciprocity, maintaining balance in society, including retaliation for wrongs
Wehi: to be awesome, afraid, fear, amazement and surprise

Whakama: shame, embarrassment
Whakapapa: genealogy, lineage, descent
Whakataukī: proverb or significant saying
Whānau: an extended family or family group, sometimes used also to address a wider range of people
Whanaungatanga: relationship, kinship, familial connection
Whenua: land

We acknowledge assistance from *Te Aka Māori Dictionary, Te Murumara Foundation, maoridictionary.co.nz*

Acknowledgments

Many people have been very generous with their time and expertise to help us with this project. We would like to express gratitude to them all.

Our biggest debt is to those who were interviewed for the book: Rt Hon Jacinda Ardern the Prime Minister, Rt Hon Trevor Mallard the Speaker of the House of Representatives, Hon Judith Collins the Leader of the Opposition when she was interviewed, Rt Hon Dame Patsy Reddy the Governor-General who was interviewed shortly before she left office, and the Chief Justice Rt Hon Helen Winkelmann. Thank you very much for your time, expertise, and immense contribution to this book. We have benefitted from discussions with Hon Justice Matthew Palmer, to whom both authors are related, and for a proof copy of his book with Associate Professor Dean Knight, *The Constitution of New Zealand – a contextual analysis* (Cambridge University Press, Cambridge, 2022).

Fergus Barrowman and his team at Te Herenga Waka University Press have been excellent as always.

We owe a special debt to Sir Kenneth Keith, who read the whole manuscript in draft and made many helpful comments. He has been reading and commenting on Geoffrey's work since 1968. We have also had the benefit from many discussions with him until the protestors evicted us in February 2022 from Vic Books café. The Faculty of Law at Te Herenga Waka Victoria University have been good enough to read drafts and comment. In particular, Professor Mark Hickford, Associate Professor Dean Knight, and Paul Scott. Thank you also to Professor Aeron Davis from the School of History, Philosophy, Political Science and International Relations at Te Herenga Waka Victoria University for useful discussions and help with Part Three.

Rachel Hayward and Charlotte Doyle of the Cabinet Office have saved us from errors, and we are most grateful. Dame Marie Shroff, Chair of the Electoral Commission, provided helpful comments on drafts.

Ross Carter, Counsel to the Parliamentary Counsel Office Te Tari Tohutohu Pāremata has provided us with important information. Chris Penk MP, the chair of the Regulations Review Select Committee and the Clerk of the Committee, Tara Elmes, helped us untangle the secondary legislation on Covid-19. Dr Warren Young provided help. Josiah Tualamali'i provided helpful kōrero and advice.

The Deputy Secretary of Education, Ellen MacGregor-Reid enlightened us on matters concerning civics in the education system. Hugh Rennie QC lent us his expertise on the media. Tom Broadmore, a retired District Court Te Kōti Matua Judge, provided helpful comments on legal matters. Dr Peter Beatson was helpful. Several Treasury officials, led by Jolyon Swinburn and Peter Lorimer, were helpful and did a lot of work to explain the system of public finance. Joanna George Research Associate, Faculty of Law, Cambridge University also provided insightful comments on some chapters.

We are extraordinarily grateful for the illustrations and diagrams in this book. We would like to thank Huriana Kopeke-Te Aho, Ursula Palmer Steeds, and Tayla Mereana Hartemink for the illustrations and Helena Palmer for the diagrams, as well as many helpful comments.

Bernard Steeds has shared with us his expertise and provided many helpful edits. Rebekah Palmer has provided superlative editing skills. Both Bernard and Rebekah have forever been incredibly supportive and are infinitely appreciated. Gwen would also like to thank many friends for constant reminders to take a break, laughter, and kindness. Margaret Palmer has been helpful in so many ways and without her this project, and many others, could never come to fruition.